NATIONAL INDEX OF PARISH REGISTERS

The volumes of the National Index are provisionally scheduled below. The compilers reserve the right to alter the number or composition of the volumes. Those already published or in advanced preparation are asterisked.

NATIONAL INDEX

OF

PARISH REGISTERS

A Guide to Anglican, Roman Catholic and Nonconformist Registers
before 1837, together with information on Marriage Licences,
Bishop's Transcripts and Modern Copies.

VOLUME V

South Midlands and Welsh Border
comprising the Counties of Gloucestershire, Herefordshire,
Oxfordshire, Shropshire, Warwickshire and Worcestershire.

Compiled by

D. J. STEEL M.A., F.S.G.

Assisted by

Mrs. A. E. F. STEEL

and

C. W. FIELD

Published for the
SOCIETY OF GENEALOGISTS

PHILLIMORE
London and Chichester

Published by
PHILLIMORE & CO. LTD.
Shopwyke Hall, Chichester, Sussex
for the
Society of Genealogists

SBN 900592 45 1

Printed by photo-lithography and made in Great Britain at the Pitman Press, Bath

VOLUME 5

Contents

GENERAL INTRODUCTION TO THE SERIES

The National Index of Parish Registers evolved from the plan of
Mr. J.S.W. Gibson to prepare a new edition of the pre-War Index of
Parish Register Copies. His idea was to produce the work, not as previously with the parishes arranged alphabetically throughout the
volume, but under counties and with each parish listed whether or not
copies of the registers had been made.

The starting date of the original registers was also to be included. This in itself was an ambitious project and without his
initiative this Index would have never come into being.

Assisted by the Hon. G.R. Strutt, Mr. Gibson started making a slip
index for all parishes and on the slips was entered available information on the starting dates of registers and details of known copies.
In 1959 Mr. Gibson appealed for volunteers to assist in checking at
the Society of Genealogist's Library, the British Museum Library and
elsewhere. By July 1960 drafts had been prepared for Bedfordshire,
Berkshire, Buckinghamshire, Cambridgeshire, Cheshire, Dorset and
Durham, and slips had been made for all parishes in England and known
copies entered. At this point Mr. Gibson found that with his extensive
work on Oxfordshire registers it was impossible for him to cope with
the Index as well, and passed over the work to Mr. C.W. Field. At
approximately the same time I was elected Chairman of the Parish
Register Sub-Committee, and agreed to act as Editor of the work.

Work now proceeded rapidly. Mr. Field circularized every library
in the country, and entered all printed, typescript and manuscript
copies he.could locate on to the slips. When work on each county was
completed he typed out a provisional list. As almost all my spare
time was engaged in the organization of Parish Register transcription,
my part was limited to organizing the checks of Mr. Field's lists at
the Society of Genealogist's Library and the British Museum Library.

By 1962 work on the list of copies was nearing completion, except
for a few counties where particular difficulties had arisen. However,
the work done, particularly on starting dates of registers had made
it increasingly obvious that except for a few counties there was
little reliable information in print on the dates of original
registers and less still on the Bishop's Transcripts and I decided to
broaden the scope of the project to include this extra material. In
July 1962 therefore, I handed over the organization of transcription
work to Mr. M.A. Pinhorn in order to concentrate on the National Index.

An excellent team of volunteers was built up and work on all counties progressed simultaneously. Whilst it might have been better to concentrate on one group of counties at a time, I decided against this as so much surveying and depositing of parish registers and sorting and listing of Bishop's Transcripts was going on all over the country that I felt it was better to accumulate all easily accessible existing material, after which it was quite likely that much more would be available on both original parish registers and Bishop's Transcripts, and that the information given would not in the main become out of date so quickly. This indeed proved to be the case. In Warwickshire for example the bulk of the deposits at the diocesan record offices have been made in the last few years. In Kent and Worcestershire the Bishop's Transcripts have only recently been fully listed. The drafts of some counties, such as Hampshire or Dorset were more or less completed two years or more ago but publication was delayed because other counties in the projected volumes were not yet ready. For many counties, such as Norfolk and Gloucestershire the sorting and listing of the Bishops Transcripts is still in progress.

The response of the county Archivists to the project has been superb. List after list of queries has been sent as checks have revealed discrepancies of all kinds and these queries have invariably been dealt with promptly and extremely thoroughly.

So many people have helped with listing and checking that it is almost invidious to single out any for special mention. However, a few have done an enormous volume of work over a prolonged period. Mr. F.M. Barrell over a period of four years has done a large part of the checking at the Society of Genealogists and has continually helped with tricky queries. Miss D.I. Lloyd, Mrs. D. Perry, Mr. F.L. Leeson, Mr. A.D. Francis, and many others have done extensive work on listing and checking for many counties at the Society of Genealogists, the Public Record Office, the British Museum and the National Register of Archives. In addition, almost every county has had its dedicated helper or helpers who have assisted in the listing of registers or Bishop's Transcripts. Mr. A.J. Willis circularized Hampshire incumbents at his own expense, a generous contribution to the work, and many others have put in an enormous amount of time and effort. Thus Mr. P.C. Withers personally examined page by page the eighty per cent of Berkshire registers deposited at the County Record Office and circularized the incumbents holding the remainder, Mr. C.P. Neat has forwarded list after list of Northumberland and Durham registers and Mr. C.M. Turner listed in detail all Warwickshire deposited registers. Lack of space precludes the mention of more names here, but all are mentioned in the acknowledgements at the front of each county section, regrettably a quite inadequate recognition of their services.

Mr. Field in the meantime made slips for all Welsh parishes, and completed the work of preparing the original county drafts, and since 1962 my mother Mrs. A.E.F. Steel has been working full-time on this project, sorting co-ordinating and listing information from all sources, typing correspondence and, since 1964, preparing rough drafts for all counties.

In 1965 the work moved into its penultimate phase. This involved the circularization of all Anglican clergy on whose registers reliable information had not been obtained from elsewhere, of Church Secretaries of every Nonconformist Church founded before 1837 for which registers could not be traced, of 600 Methodist Circuits Superintendents and of nearly all Parish Priests of Catholic Churches founded before 1837. The dates and parishes included in Boyd's Marriage Index were added and Mr. J.R. Cunningham of the Church of Jesus Christ of Latter Day Saints very kindly put at my disposal the records of the extensive microfilming on which the church has been engaged. With the assistance of Edward Milligan Archivist of Friends' House, Euston, an attempt was made to identify Quaker surrendered registers, the catalogue of surrendered registers being totally unreliable. Furthermore, from the excellent records at Friends House information was abstracted on the composition of the Monthly Meetings at various times and the administrative history of every Quaker Meeting House. This item took over a year of irregular visits to Friends' House, Euston, to complete.

By January 1966, the preparation of the County lists was almost complete, and work was commenced on the General Articles for volumes I and II, and on the General Information sections of those counties it was considered most convenient to publish first. Here again I received more help than I could possibly have anticipated, and I should like to express my gratitude to those who have contributed articles to the first two volumes, to those authors and publishers who have allowed published material to be used, and to the very large number of people who assisted with the General Articles in volumes I and II or the County prefaces, and in the Scottish volume (XII).

It is intended that the General Volumes should serve not only as an introduction to the Series, but also as a standard work of reference on sources of births, marriages and deaths.

* * * * * * * * *

General Information Section of each County

These county prefaces include information on Record Repositories, Original Registers, Bishop's Transcripts, Modern Copies,

Marriage Indexes, Marriage Licences, Nonconformist and Catholic
Registers, Regimental Registers, pre-1837 Newspapers, Publishing
Societies, other local Societies and a bibliography. The only item
which may cause any mild surprise is the newspapers, which have been
included as the information is often not readily accessible and these
may be a useful source for Births, Marriages and Deaths. Only
newspapers of which a fairly consecutive series for a few years or
more exists have been included. Every effort has been made to ensure
that the information on local Societies is as up to date as possible.
The county bibliographies do not claim to be comprehensive, and list
only some of the more important printed works of genealogical
interest. For reasons of space, local histories have normally been included only when these contain specifically genealogical material,
though of course any local history may prove invaluable to the
genealogist. Information on Wills has not been included as this is more
than adequately covered by Mr. A.J. Camp's book "Wills and their
Whereabouts".

One point which may surprise users of the index is the repetition
of material in two or more county prefaces even if they appear in the
same volume. This particularly applies to Bishop's Transcripts and
Marriage Licences where one diocese, such as Lichfield, may extend
over several counties. However, this has been done so that each county
section is an entirely self contained unit, thus leaving the way clear
for the publication of individual counties should this be decided upon
at any future date. Occasionally where the information given is fairly
detailed and lengthy, only a summary has been given in the preface to
another county which has only a few parishes in that diocese.

Parish Registers

The basic aim has been to cover only registers dating before 1837.
Parishes founded after 1837 have therefore not normally been entered,
unless they were previously chapelries of another parish and kept
separate registers. However, where the registers of pre-1837 parishes
have been deposited at a County Record Office or elsewhere, the
terminal dates are given even if these are long after 1837, but of
course deposited registers of parishes formed after 1837 have not been
included, an illogical but unavoidable distinction. In the case of
Original Registers still with the incumbent, the starting dates are
normally given with a + sign meaning "onwards". In practice this
invariably means "beyond 1837". In the case of Original Registers,
but not Bishop's Transcripts it normally indicates that entries continue from the date listed up to the present.

It is important to remember that the index gives only a summary of
the registers. Duplicate and overlapping registers have therefore

normally been ignored. An effort has been made to include registers of Banns, but returns made for the National Register of Archives or completed circulars returned to me have often been deficient in that respect and no guarantee can be made that where no Banns register is listed, one does not exist. The dates given for Banns include all Banns whether they are in a separate register or in a combined register with the marriages.

Bishop's Transcripts

The amount of information it has been possible to include with regard to the Bishop's Transcripts varies considerably from county to county. This is partly because many records have not been fully sorted and listed and partly because the degree of completeness of the Transcripts themselves varies. In some counties it has been possible to show every missing year, in others only four year gaps have been noted and in others only ten year gaps. In the case of one or two counties, such as Gloucestershire, the only information given is the date of the first transcript. It is most important that users of this index should read the section on Bishop's Transcripts in the relevant County preface to familiarise themselves with the degree of detail recorded for that particular county.

When the + sign is used after Bishop's Transcript dates, it indicates that the transcripts continue beyond 1837, but unlike Parish Registers, it must be borne in mind that they do not normally continue beyond the 19th Century.

Modern Copies

An attempt has been made to include all known copies whether Printed, Typescript, Manuscript, Photostat or Microfilm in libraries and record repositories in England and Wales. Repositories outside England and Wales have not normally been included with the solitary exception of the Genealogical Society of the Church of Latter Day Saints, Salt Lake City, Utah, U.S.A. whose collection is so vast that American users of this book may find it handy to have some indication that there is a copy there. However, a word of warning is necessary. The Church is microfilming registers and Bishop's Transcripts at such a rate that if no copy at Salt Lake City is listed it does not necessarily mean that one does not exist. Any list including Mormon material is bound to be out of date before it is printed.

In the case of a printed volume it may be assumed that there is a copy in the British Museum Library and, unless otherwise stated, in the Society of Genealogists' Library. There is normally also a copy at Salt Lake City. Except in the case of very rare books it may safely be assumed that the County Library has a copy and more often than not, the County Record Office.

Every attempt has been made to keep the list of typescript and manuscript copies up to date and as regards copies in the Society of Genealogists' Library, each county list is up to date at the time of going to press. In the case of other libraries and repositories however, it has not been possible to recircularize them all, so it is quite possible that copies deposited recently may not have been included.

In using modern copies the attention of readers is drawn to the general article on the subject which points out some of the many pitfalls. In compiling the index every effort has been made to overcome one of these – the possibility that the "copy" may consist of extracts only. Every parish register copy in the Society of Genealogists' library has been examined to check on this, and this point was emphasized in the questionnaires sent out to libraries. Normally extracts have been excluded except in cases where they are substantial or else the original register from which they were taken has since disappeared. In these cases the word *Extracts* or the abbreviation *Extr.* has been used. In spite of all precautions, however, it is more than likely that many extracts have slipped through disguised as complete copies. Difficulty has sometimes arisen in that a copy has in the past sometimes been described as "Extracts" when in fact it gives an accurate *summary* of every entry as with most copies, or when it contains a complete copy of a restricted number of years. These have been included in the index as ordinary copies.

Nonconformist Chapels and Catholic Churches

Urban chapels and churches have been included at the end of the list of Anglican parishes for each town – Catholic churches first and then Nonconformist chapels. In the case of London and Middlesex this has involved several separate sections.

Rural chapels and churches have normally been listed under the Anglican Parish. In many cases however, the place in which they were situated is better known than the Anglican parish, or they drew their Congregations from several Anglican parishes and the entry has been made under the place name with a suitable cross reference under the relevant Anglican Parish. In the case of Nonconformist or Catholic churches which were founded before 1837 but which did not surrender registers, the starting date of registers in church hands is noted even if these are after 1837. Copies made at the time of the surrender of the original registers have been listed under OR rather than Cop as frequently fresh entries were added to these after 1837.

Whenever the information has been easily accessible an attempt has been made to include every known Nonconformist chapel and Catholic Mission or Church in existence before 1837 whether registers are known or not. In the case of existing Nonconformist Churches, many Church Secretaries failed to return completed questionnaires, and the name and foundation church have been entered with the cryptic phrase "No information". When a "nil return" has been made, the phrase "No registers known" has been used. In the case of pre-1837 Nonconformist chapels now no longer in existence, as with most other information, the thoroughness of the listing varies to some degree from county to county, and whilst it is true that further research would bring to light many unlisted defunct chapels, the time has simply not been available to explore this subject thoroughly. However, all denominational Unions and Associations were approached in an effort to locate any registers.

Roman Catholics

In the case of many Catholic Missions and Churches covering a wide area cross references have been put in for the principal Anglican parishes mentioned in the registers. All Dioceson Archivists and Bishops' Secretaries have been asked if they held any registers.

Independents

This designation has been used throughout except when an existing church is referred to for the location of registers when the more familiar "Congregationalist" (or the abbreviation 'Cong') has been used, e.g. Minister, X Cong. Ch.

Baptists

It is important to bear in mind that the abbreviation 'C' is used here for adult Baptisms. Except in a few counties it has not been possible in the time available to distinguish between General Baptist and Particular Baptist churches, although these were of course entirely separate denominations.

Methodists

An entry has normally been made under the Circuit heading listing known churches within the Circuit in 1837 and any circuit registers and referring readers to any individual church which kept registers. Under the name of the Church, the circuit to which it belonged in 1837 is listed. Sometimes more detail on the administrative history is given.

An entry has been made for each Monthly Meeting, listing meeting houses within it at various periods and any Monthly Meeting registers. It is then necessary to consult the entries for individual meeting houses to discover if there were additional registers, though when only one or two isolated meeting houses within the Monthly Meeting kept registers these have been indicated. Under the name of each meeting house is the Monthly Meeting to which it belonged at various times, to which reference should be made to discover whether registers exist.

Composition of Volumes

In December 1966 publication began with volume V which covers the South Midlands and Welsh Border. An overall picture of the series will be included in all volumes, but it must be emphasized that unforeseen circumstances may affect their number and composition, and the compilers reserve the right to make alterations without notice. This has, in fact, already occurred since the first provisional list was printed, for though originally only one general volume was planned, as work progressed it became apparent that two volumes would be necessary, with an additional one (XII) devoted to Scottish sources.

* * * * * * * * *

The National Index does not make any claims to be regarded as a definitive work. It aims only to provide Genealogists with a reference work of a practical nature which gives some indication of the records available. New deposits of registers are continually being made at Record offices and new copies – especially the microfilm copies of the Church of Jesus Christ of Latter Day Saints – are being made at a considerable rate. Moreover although much checking and rechecking has been done to try and eliminate errors, many of the figures for original registers may be incorrect, being often based on inadequate or out-of-date returns. I should be grateful if readers will point these out so that some at least of the more blatant may be corrected.

Members who have awaited this Index for years may feel that a very long time has elapsed since work commenced. There have been two reasons for this. Firstly the volume of work has been far greater than I ever anticipated or than the average user of the index would imagine. Secondly, the work on copies and original registers has proceeded in series rather than in parallel which would of course have cut down the time of preparation by at least two years. However, with the organization of transcription work occupying the whole of my spare time from 1960 to 1962, I was unable to commence my part of the work until Mr. Field's work on copies was well advanced. Theoretically

it would, of course have been possible to publish an Index of copies
alone in advance of the main series, but the bulk even of this
limited work would have been formidable and in practice it is unlikely
that the funds would have been available for the publication of a work
that would be superseded within a few years, or alternatively if it
was published it seems probable that the information on original
registers, Bishop's Transcripts, Nonconformist and Catholic registers
would not have been published for many years if at all.

That the Society of Genealogists has in fact been able to publish
an index of this size is largely due to the generosity of the trustees
of the Pilgrim Trust who have made an interest-free loan to cover
the cost of publication.

In conveying my thanks to them and to all others who have made
this work possible I should also like particularly to mention the
printers, Sir Isaac Pitman and Sons Ltd., Bath for their unfail-
ing courtesy and their kindness in dealing with many small problems
which became apparent only at the printing stage, the staff of the
Society of Genealogists for their co-operation, and my two principal
assistants Mr. C.W. Field and my mother Mrs. A.E.F. Steel for whose
unflagging efforts in coping with what has often been very tedious
work, no praise can be excessive.

D.J. Steel

PREFACE TO VOLUME 5

Any division of a multi-volumed work into County groups must be
arbitrary, and the choice of the counties included in this volume is
open to criticism. Oxfordshire, for example has longer common boundaries with Berkshire and Buckinghamshire than with Warwickshire or
Gloucestershire, and the inclusion of Staffordshire would have made a
more compact block of counties. However, an effort has been made to
keep all volumes approximately equal in size, and as Staffordshire is
included in Volume 6, the whole of the Midlands will in fact be contained in two volumes.

Since this volume is the first to be published, the information
may well prove more incomplete than that included in other volumes.
The most noticeable omission is, of course, any detail with regard to
the Gloucester Bishop's Transcripts, the sorting and listing of these
although well advanced, having not yet been completed. However, it is
likely that this deficiency will be remedied before long by the publication under the auspices of the Marc Fitch Fund of a comprehensive
catalogue of Diocesan Records in the Gloucester City Library. Similarly
the information given on Bishop's Transcripts for the Diocese of
Hereford is complete for the majority of Herefordshire parishes but
not for most of those in Shropshire. Much listing and sorting of the
Lichfield Transcripts has still to be done. For the dioceses of
Worcester and Oxford the information given is complete within the
limits mentioned in the relevant county prefaces.

With regard to original registers, whilst the information on
Gloucestershire, Oxfordshire, Shropshire and Warwickshire is, it is
hoped, fairly reliable, complete and up to date, the information on
some Worcestershire and many Herefordshire parishes is not as complete
as one would wish, and although a large number of circulars were sent
to incumbents, some whose holdings were doubtful failed to reply.

So far Comprehensive guides to Parish Records have been published
for only two of the Counties − Shropshire and Gloucestershire, but
the latter, recently published by the Bristol and Gloucestershire
Archaeological Society, is a model of its kind and will, one hopes,
encourage other local societies to produce a similar work.

Although some of the work on Modern copies of Parish Registers
and Bishop's Transcripts was completed up to two years ago every effort
has been made to keep the information up to date and recent acquisi-
tions by the Society of Genealogists Library, some County Record Offices,

Shrewsbury Borough Library, Gloucester City Library and the Bodleian Library Oxford have been included, as has also the extensive microfilming by the Church of Jesus Christ of Latter Day Saints. However, it is possible that other libraries may have recently acquired copies which are not listed, but the number is likely to be small.

The overall picture with regard to Parish Register copies in this region is quite good. In addition to numerous parish registers in all six counties the Church of Jesus Christ of Latter Day Saints has microfilmed the Bishop's Transcripts of the diocese of Worcester and at the time of going to press, half those of the diocese of Oxford. The microfilming of those of Lichfield Diocese is also in progress, but no details are as yet available. The Shropshire Parish Register Society printed a large number of registers and the Shropshire Archaeological Society has copied many more in manuscript or typescript and has had almost all the remainder microfilmed. A manuscript index to these is with the transcripts in Shrewsbury Borough Library. In Gloucestershire, in addition to the publication of a Phillimore Marriage series, Mr. E.A. Roe has been extremely active in copying the Bishop's Transcripts and many Parish Registers, besides compiling his invaluable Marriage Index which supplements the incredible work of the late Mr. Percival Boyd. In North Oxfordshire there has been the extensive work of Mr. J.S.W. Gibson in conjunction with the Banbury Historical Society, as well as the Oxfordshire Marriage Index planned by Mr. Gibson and compiled by Mr. R.C. Couzens which has now reached the typing stage and should before long be available for consultation. In Warwickshire, although fewer registers have been copied, the original registers have largely been centralised thanks to the work of Revd. G. Holbeche and the County Archivist Mr. A. Wood and the co-operation of the Bishops of Birmingham and Coventry. The least work on transcription has been done in Herefordshire, which until recent years lacked even a County Record Office. Miss Paul and the staff of the Record Office are now vigorously attacking the task of surveying Parish Registers. Nevertheless, genealogists working on Herefordshire families must surely yearn for another Roe or Gibson.

The position is similar with regard to Catholic Registers. Father J.D. McEvilly, Archivist of the Archdiocese of Birmingham, which includes Warwickshire, Worcestershire, Oxfordshire and Staffordshire has encouraged the depositing of registers at Archbishop's House, Birmingham; the Worcestershire Recusant Society has been active and the Warwickshire Record Office has surveyed all Warwickshire Catholic Registers. Many registers have been published by the Catholic Record Society and most of the Shropshire ones by the Shropshire Parish Register Society.

As with the rest of the country, very few Nonconformist registers have been copied, although those of Dudley, Worcestershire were printed

in a special volume and many Shropshire registers were copied by the
Shropshire Parish Register Society. The centralisation of Nonconformist
registers in London makes, however, the lack of copies less of a
handicap than in the case of Parish Registers.

In general little work has been done on Marriage Licences. Indeed
they seem comparatively rarely used by genealogists; thus the Diocesan
Registrar of the Diocese of Lichfield states that in the past ten
years he has had no enquiries regarding the Marriage Bonds, Licences
and Affidavits for Lichfield Peculiars kept in the Cathedral Library.
However, in recent years much more publicity has been given to the
value of Marriage Licences, and in the area covered by this volume it
is to be hoped that the publication by the Bristol and Gloucester
Archaeological Society of the early Gloucester Bonds and Allegations,
edited by Mr. B. Frith, marks a break-through.

Oxfordshire is the only county in this volume to have produced a
recent comprehensive bibliography − that of Cordeaux and Merry −
though the bulky catalogues of the Gloucester City Library's local
collection perform a similar function and are invaluable sources of
reference for the Gloucestershire genealogist. The list of Shropshire
books prepared by the late Mr. J.L. Hobbs, Librarian of Shrewsbury
Borough Library is also useful. An important new publication which
should be of great value to Midland genealogists is "West Midland
Genealogy", the publication of which, under the auspices of the West
Midland Branch of the Library Association, should have shortly preceded that of this volume. It is a survey of local genealogical
material which is available in the public libraries of Herefordshire,
Shropshire, Staffordshire, Warwickshire and Worcestershire.

May I once again take this opportunity of thanking all those who
have helped with the preparation of this volume, and of asking users
of the book to point out any errors or supply information on any
points, however trivial.

D. J. Steel.

NATIONAL RECORD REPOSITORIES AND LIBRARIES

See also the lists at the beginning of the "General Information" section of each county.

P.R.O. – The **Public** Record Office, Chancery Lane, London W.C.2. (Hours 9.30 - 5, Sat 9.30 - 1) holds the bulk of the Nonconformist registers of the whole country and a certain number of Catholic Registers, mainly from the North of England.

S.G. – Society of Genealogists, 37 Harrington Gardens, London S.W.7 (Hours: Tues, Fri 10 - 6; Wed, Thurs 10 - 9; Sat 11 - 5; Mon closed) holds the largest single collection in this country of **Printed**, Typescript and Manuscript copies as well as a vast amount of other genealogical material. The library is open to non-members at a fee of 17/6 for a whole day, 10/6 for a half day.

B.M. or Brit. Mus. – Department of Western Manuscripts, British Museum Library, London, W.C.1. (Hours 10 - 4.45). A reader's ticket is necessary.

G.L. – Guildhall Library, Basinghall Street, London, E.C.1. (Hours Mon-Sat 9.30 - 5) holds many London Original Parish Registers and a large number of copies of registers of many counties, especially those made by the late W.H. Challen.

Somerset House, London, W.C.2. (Hours 10 - 4 Sat 10 - 1) As well as Civil Registration and Probate Records, holds all Regimental Registers. The Nonconformist and other Non-Parochial Registers were transferred to the Public Record Office in 1960.

Phil. Ms. – Manuscript copies of Parish Registers in the possession of Phillimore & Co. Ltd., Shopwyke Hall, Chichester, Sussex. A fee is normally charged.

N.R.A. – National Register of Archives, Quality House, Quality Court, Chancery Lane, London, W.C.2. has detailed information on Parish Registers and all other archives which have been inspected.

H.L. – House of Lords Record Office, Houses of Parliament, London, S.W.1. (Hours Mon-Fri 10 - 5).

Bod. – Bodleian Library, Oxford (Hours: 9 - 7 (10 pm in full term), Sat 9 - 1).

B. I. – Borthwick Institute of Historical Research, St. Anthony's Hall, Peaseholm Green, York. (Hours Mon-Fri 9.30 - 1, 2 - 5).

C of A – College of Arms, Queen Victoria Street, London. (The Library is not open to the public) holds many copies of Parish Registers.

Religious Denominations

Church of England – Lambeth Palace Library, London, S.E. 1. (Hours 10 - 5).

Roman Catholics – Archbishop's House, Westminster, London, S.W. 1.

Nonconformists – Dr. Williams' Library, 14, Gordon Square, London, W.C. 1. (Hours Mon-Fri 10 - 5).

Baptists – Baptist Union Library, Baptist Church House, 4, Southampton Row, London, W.C. 1. (Hours 9.30 - 5).

Congregationalists – Congregational Union of England and Wales, Memorial Hall, Farringdon Street, London, E.C. 4. (Mon-Fri 10-5).

Methodists – Methodist Archives and Research Centre, 25-35, City Road, London, E.C. 1. (Mon-Fri 10 - 5).

Society of Friends (Quakers) – Friends' House, Euston Road, London, N.W. 1. (Mon-Fri 9.50 - 5.30) holds consolidated digests of all surrendered Quaker registers.

Presbyterians – Presbyterian Historical Society of England, 86, Tavistock Place, London, W.C. 1. (Mon-Fri 10 - 4 by appointment).

Unitarians – Unitarian Church Headquarters, Essex Hall, Essex St., London, W.C. 2

Huguenots – Huguenot Library, University College, Gower Street, London, W. 1. (not open to non-members).

Jews – Jewish Museum, Woburn House, Upper Woburn Place, London, W. 1. (Mon-Thurs 2.30 - 5, Fri, Sun 10.30 - 12.45).

WALES

N. L. W. – National Library of Wales, Aberystwyth, Wales. (Hours 9.30 - 6, Sat 9.5).

SCOTLAND

Scottish Record Office, Her Majesty's General Register House, Edinburgh. (Hours 9.30 - 4.45, Sat 9.30 - 1.0).

National Library of Scotland, Department of Manuscripts, George IV Bridge, Edinburgh. (Hours Mon-Fri 9.30 - 8.30, Sat 9.30 - 5.0).

The Mitchell Library, North Street, Glasgow, C3. (Hours 9.30 - 9. Sundays Oct - Mar 2 - 8).

FOREIGN RECORD REPOSITORIES

In general these are beyond the scope of this index, but one has been included, viz:-

S.L.C. – Genealogical Society of the Church of Jesus Christ of Latter Day Saints, Salt Lake City, Utah, U.S.A.

This holds the largest collection of genealogical material in the World.

A list of Secretaries and addresses of National Societies and denominational Historical Societies will be found in Vol. 1.

OTHER ABBREVIATIONS USED THROUGHOUT THE SERIES

See also the supplementary abbreviations in the 'General Information' section of each county.

Add. Ms.	–	Additional Manuscript (British Museum).
Arch. Soc.	–	Archaeological Society.
B.	–	Burials.
Bapt.	–	Baptist (never Baptisms).
bef.	–	before.
Boyd.	–	Marriage Index compiled by the late Mr. Percival Boyd (Copies at S.G. and S.L.C.).
Boyd Misc.	–	In Boyd's Miscellaneous volumes (See General Article on Boyd's Marriage Index).
B.T.	–	Bishop's Transcripts. For convenience this abbreviation has been used for any annual Parish Register copies sent in to an ecclesiastical superior.
c.	–	circa.
C.	–	Baptisms (Also used for Adult Baptisms of Baptists).
Calv. Meth.	–	Calvinistic Methodist (Presbyterian Church of Wales).
Cath. Ch.	–	Roman Catholic Church.
Ch. Sec.	–	Church Secretary (For name & address consult current yearbook of the relevant denomination).
C.I.	–	Society of Genealogists' Great Card Index.
Circ. Sperint. or Circ. Supt.	–	Circuit Superintendent (For name & address consult current edition of 'Minutes of the Methodist Conference')
cl.	–	closed.
Cong.	–	Congregationalist (used only when referring to present name of church. Otherwise *Ind* is used).
Constit. Meetings	–	Constituent Meetings.
Cop.	–	Modern Copies.
C.R.S. or Cath. R.S.	–	Catholic Historical Society publications.
D.	–	Deaths.
Dio.	–	Diocese.
disc.	–	discontinued.

D. Mss.	–	In boxes of Deeds and Manuscripts at the Society of Genealogists.
Extr.	–	Extracts.
f.	–	founded.
Gen. Bapt.	–	General Baptist.
I.	–	Indexed.
Inc.	–	Incumbent. For convenience this has also been used for Catholic Parish Priests.
Ind.	–	Independent (Congregationalist).
Lady Hunt Conn.	–	Countess of Huntingdon's Connexion.
M.	–	Marriages.
Meth. New Conn.	–	Methodist New Connexion.
Mf.	–	microfilm.
M. Lic.	–	Marriage Licences.
Mo. Mg.	–	Monthly Meeting.
Ms.	–	Manuscript.
N & Q	–	Notes and Queries.
Nonc.	–	Nonconformist.
OR	–	Original Registers
p/s	–	photostat.
Part Bapt.	–	Particular Baptist.
Phil.	–	Phillimore's Printed Marriages (Number refers to volume number in the appropriate county series).
Phil. Ms.	–	See National Record Repositories above.
P.R.	–	Parish Register.
Pres.	–	Presbyterian.
Prim. Meth.	–	Primitive Methodist.
Ptd.	–	Printed.
regs.	–	registers.
R.C.	–	Roman Catholics.
S of F	–	Society of Friends (Quakers).
Unit.	–	Unitarian.
Vol.	–	volume.
Wes.	–	Wesleyan Methodist.
Z.	–	Births.
+	–	Onwards. Invariably means "until after 1837", and in the case of original registers normally indicates that the registers continue from the date listed up to the present.

GLOUCESTERSHIRE

ACKNOWLEDGMENTS

The Editor gratefully acknowledges the assistance of the following persons in compiling this section:-

Miss F. Ralph, City Archivist, Bristol Archives Office: Mr. I.E. Gray, Records Office, Shire Hall Gloucester and Mr. A.J. Parrott, Librarian, Gloucester City Library and his Staff for supplying information, dealing with various queries and for reading the County Preface and offering numerous comments and suggestions: Mr. B. Frith for considerable assistance in writing the County Preface: Major A.C.R. Welsh for compressing information on original registers into the required form: Mr. F.M. Barrell for checking the holdings of the Society of Genealogists and starting dates of original registers and for dealing with various queries: Mr. F. Leeson for listing surrendered Nonconformist registers: Mr. Levi Fox, Director of the Shakespeare Birthplace Trust for supplying information on their holdings: Mr. E. Roe for supplying information on his Marriage Index and his copies of registers and Bishop's Transcripts, and for reading through the Preface and offering many useful comments and suggestions: Miss P.A. Powley, Secretary Gloucestershire Community Council, for supplying details of Local Societies: Mr. J.R. Cunningham of the Church of Jesus Christ of Latter Day Saints and Edward Milligan, Archivist of Friends' House, Euston Road, London, for granting access to their records: The Bishop's Secretary, Catholic Diocese of Clifton: The Secretaries of Baptist and Congregationalist Unions and Associations: and numerous Librarians, Catholic Parish Priests, Methodist Circuit Superintendents, Baptist and Congregationalist Ministers and Secretaries for supplying information.

GENERAL INFORMATION

Record Repositories *(see also list on page xx)*.

GRO – *Gloucestershire Record Office, Shire Hall, Gloucester.*
(Hours 9.15 - 12.45, 1.45 - 5 – Sat 9.15 - 11.15)
This holds the bulk of the records of the county including some
Original Parish Registers. A catalogue of the deposited col-
lection of Gloucestershire books collected by Sir Francis Hyett
of Painswick has been published (1949).

BAO – *The Bristol Archives Office, The Council House, Bristol 1.*
(Hours 9 - 5 – Sat 9 - 12)
This holds the records of parishes in the Bristol Diocese
except for those in the Swindon Archdeaconry. They include many
Parish Registers, the bulk of the Bishop's Transcripts and
many copies, including a digest of the registers of the Quaker
Bristol and Somersetshire Quarterly Meeting. Amongst much other
genealogical material are the *"Notes and Extracts relating to
Bristol"* made by Edward S. Byam. These include extracts from
14 Bristol Churches, notes on various families and genealogies
of dignitaries of Bristol Cathedral.

CLG – *Gloucester City Library, Brunswick Road. (Hours 9 - 8.30, Sat 9 - 7)*
This holds the Bishop's Transcripts and Marriage Bonds and
Allegations for the Diocese of Gloucester, a copy of the Roe
Marriage Index and many copies of Registers. The Library of the
Bristol and Gloucestershire Archaeological Society is housed in
the City Library, and whilst only members may borrow books, it
is open to the public for reference purposes. In addition to
much other material such as wills, particularly useful to
genealogists are the *Hockaday Abstracts*. This series of bound
volumes forms an extensive calendar containing material from
the 13th to 19th century, taken from a wide selection of sources.
Entries have been made on separate sheets, and the collection is
arranged chronologically. The work is named after its compiler,
a well-known local antiquary who was active c. 1920-1930. There
is also a microfilm of the 1851 Census for the City of Gloucester
The Library has published a catalogue of its Gloucestershire
collection (1928). A supplementary catalogue 1928-1955 is
available in the original typescript in the City Library as well
as being for sale on microfilm. Marriage Allegations and

2

Marriage Licence Bonds are listed and appear in the Catalogue. The City Library's Local History pamphlet No. 3 gives a useful parish by parish indication of records.

WRO — *Worcestershire Record Office, St Helen's, Fish Street, Worcester (letters to Shire Hall) (Hours 9 - 12.45, 2 - 5 — Sat closed).* This holds the Bishop's Transcripts for a few parishes in the Diocese of Worcester.

Bristol Public Library. This holds some records relating to the City of Bristol, including newspapers, but no Parish Register material.

Bishop's House, St. Ambrose, Leigh Woods, Bristol 8. This holds the diocesan archives of the Catholic Diocese of Clifton but no registers.

SOA — *Shakespeare's Birthplace Trust Library, Henley St, Stratford-upon-Avon. (Hours 10 - 1, 2 - 5 — Sat 10 - 12.30)* See *modern copies* below.

Other Abbreviations used in this Section *(see also list on page xxiii).*

Roe — Copies of Bishop's Transcripts by Eric Roe — See *Modern Copies* below.

ER — Typescript copies in the possession of Mr. E. Roe — See *Modern Copies* below.

RMI — Roe's Gloucester Marriage Index. q.v.

Parishes

Ancient Parishes, 347 (including 9 in Gloucester and 19 in Bristol).

Changes in County Boundaries

These have been fairly numerous, the principal changes taking place in 1931. The boundaries with Worcestershire and Warwickshire have been especially affected. Cross references have been included in all cases.

Original Parish Registers

Most Gloucestershire Registers are still in the hands of the incumbents and though some have been deposited at the County Record Office, or the Bristol Archives Office, there is no strong policy of centralisation. Where deposits have been made, they tend to be mainly of the pre-1813 registers only. The Gloucester City Library holds the registers of one parish, Matson. Gloucestershire, including the City has 28 registers commencing in 1538 or 1539, whilst 6 have their original paper copies. Bristol has 4 registers commencing in 1538 whilst St Nicholas is the only Bristol Church where both the original register and the parchment copy survive. Many registers have been lost or damaged since the 1831 Abstract, among them the entire pre 1812 registers of Woolstone and Harescombe.

This list gives only the starting dates of Baptisms, Marriages and Burials and any major gaps before 1837. Duplicate and overlapping registers have therefore been ignored but full details together with much other useful information will be found in "Bristol and Gloucester Parish Records".[1]

The searcher for a missing marriage in Gloucestershire, having exhausted obvious parishes, may well find that the marriage took place either in Gloucester Cathedral or in one of the City parishes. This frequently applies to marriages by Licence, where the couple would come into the City to apply for the Licence at the Registrar's adjacent to the Cathedral, and then almost immediately went along to the Cathedral for the marriage to take place, or to such church where the incumbent may have been available.

Sometimes a very large number of marriages took place in the main parish in particular Deaneries, whilst some incumbents seemed to specialise in Marriages and have been referred to as "Marriage-mongers". Two of the most notable parishes were Hampnett (where the Reverend Simon Hughes, a Surrogate, performed 346 such marriages in the period 1737-1754, some of them no doubt being clandestine), and Newington Bagpath.

Bishop's Transcripts

Diocese of Gloucester (indicated by "G" in the text).

Formed 1541 from dioceses of Worcester and Hereford. It is divided into two Archdeaconries, Gloucester and Cheltenham. The Bishop's Transcripts are at the City Library, Gloucester. Pre-1813 transcripts are in Parish order. 1813-c.1868 in bound volumes year by year.

Pre-1813 Transcripts

The bundles of transcripts, mostly on vellum are assembled in parishes, and some of them, on paper, are dated as early as 1569. The general pattern, however, is that a few early pre-1600 documents are followed by c.1607 then a few in the mid 1610's, a fair number in the 1620's and very few in the 1630's. There is invariably a gap for the period 1640-1660 or so. From then the transcripts continue, often with only a few, if any, years missing.

See *General Works of Reference* at end of this preface.

For the most part the transcripts at Gloucester are in good condition and more complete than the Bristol transcripts. The storage of
the Gloucester transcripts in an unsuitable place in Gloucester
Cathedral during the 1939-1945 War has, however, affected some, which
are being repaired. Formerly in paper bundles, the transcripts have
now been put into boxes. One or two parishes, thought to have been
missing, were discovered during the transfer from the Diocesan
Registry.

At some date, unknown, a number of boxes marked "Gloucester
Diocesan Registry" were transferred to the City Library, long before
the main bulk of the Bishop's Transcripts were received. These were
found to contain a very large number of loose, undated, unidentified
or illegible transcripts which at some time had become separated from
the main series, and represented many of the gaps in the runs of the
transcripts. Work on identifying these is in progress and the gaps
are slowly being filled. It is unlikely that all of these loose
transcripts can be identified since some have neither date, nor
parish, nor identifiable names on them, whilst others are too faded
to be of help.

Certain gaps in the Bishop's Transcripts can obviously never be
filled. Many of the Forest of Dean parishes have the same two or three
years missing in the late 1730's (usually 1736, 1738 and 1739) which
almost certainly no longer exist.

There are a number of very early transcripts for some of the
Gloucester City parishes whose churches were destroyed or taken down
at the time of the Siege in 1643. Invariably no parish registers
remain. Unfortunately there are no Bishop's Transcripts for the
Cathedral, except after 1812. This is to be regretted as the
registers themselves only commence in 1661.

Peculiar jurisdictions in the Diocese of Gloucester

    Bibury: (Bibury, Barnsley and Chapels of Aldsworth and Winson[1].)
Only a few pre 1812 transcripts are known to survive.

    Bishops Cleeve:[2] (Bishops Cleeve and Chapel of Stoke Orchard.)
More transcripts than for Bibury Peculiar, but fewer than for
normal parishes.

    Withington: (Withington and Chapel of Dowdeswell, Deerhurst,
Child's Wickham) — as Bishops Cleeve.

Post-1813 Transcripts

From 1813, when the transcripts were entered on proper forms and
bound up in yearly volumes, all parishes seem to have sent in their

---

[1]   Not Winstone as erroneously printed in "Wills and their Whereabouts".

[2]   The Officials of Bishops Cleeve were especially jealous of their Peculiar
rights. See General Article on Bishop's Transcripts in Vol. 1.

transcripts, including the Peculiar parishes. These volumes also include many transcripts for the Bristol Diocese which cannot be removed without seriously affecting the books. The Transcripts continue in these volumes up to about the year 1868, and then in bundles.

Considerable work has been carried out on the re-binding of these volumes from 1813. Having suffered from damp and rough handling they are now in excellent condition and much easier to handle, though very bulky. Most years have about four volumes to cover all parishes. The repair work is proceeding.

Dates listed in the Index

It has not been possible to include in this index any information other than starting dates, as the work of sorting and listing is still in progress. Even some of these may not be reliable. However, a catalogue of all Diocesan Records in the Gloucester City Library is in preparation and will probably be published in 1967 under the auspices of the Marc Fitch Fund. This will be an invaluable guide to much genealogical information at present little used. The definitive list of Bishop's Transcripts will appear as an appendix, and offprints of this will be available. In these circumstances there has seemed little to be gained by printing in this index a provisional list which would not only be inaccurate but would soon be superseded.

Diocese of Bristol (indicated by "B" in the text).

Formed 1542, re-united with Gloucester 1836. Re-formed 1897. Pre-1812 transcripts at Bristol Archives Office. Post 1812 – the majority are at the Bristol Archives Office, though some are in bound volumes with those of the Diocese of Gloucester at Gloucester City Library.

On the whole, fewer transcripts have survived than for the Diocese of Gloucester. However, the transcripts have been fully sorted and listed and it has been possible to include in this Index a note of all missing years.

Modern Copies of Parish Registers and Bishop's Transcripts.

Printed

Phillimore's Gloucestershire Marriages (indicated in text as Phil with volume number). These 17 volumes cover a large number of parishes. The copies vary in reliability and seem to be mainly taken from the Parish Registers, only without correlation with the Bishop's Transcripts. Thus, in some cases, gaps are shown which can be made good from the Bishop's Transcripts. Missing marriages of Thornbury are printed in the Genealogists Magazine Vol 13 No 8 Dec 1960. All entries in Phillimore Marriages are included in Roe's Marriage Index (*see below*).

Copies printed by Sir Thomas Phillipps. These are often scrappy and
the exact dates often omitted.

A few other registers have been printed including those of
Bristol Cathedral and Dymock.

Typescript and Manuscript

Copies of Bishop's Transcripts by Eric Roe. These are an invaluable supplement to the Phillimore series.

At present Mr. Roe's work amounts to 15 volumes, viz.

(i)   Bishop's Transcripts in the Diocese of Bristol. Copies of
       BT's of 4 parishes to 1837, with Index to Surnames and
       Index to Stray registrations.

(ii)   Gloucestershire Bishop's Transcripts Vol 1. Copies of BT's
       of 15 parishes to 1812.

(iii) Gloucestershire Bishop's Transcripts Vol 2. Copies of BT's
       of 3 parishes to 1812, with index to Stray registrations
       in these parishes arranged under Parishes of Origin.

(iv)   Gloucestershire Bishop's Transcripts Vol 3. Copies of BT's
       of 18 parishes in (ii) and (iii) above continued from 1813
       to 1837.

(v)   Index to (ii), (iii) and (iv) above (Gloucester BT's
       Vols 1-3).

(vi)   Gloucestershire Bishop's Transcripts Vol 4. Copies of BT's
       to 1812 of 3 parishes printed by Phillimore, including
       amendments and entries missing from the printed volumes.
       Indexed.

(vii) Gloucestershire Bishop's Transcripts Vol 5. Copies of BT's
       of 40 parishes printed by Phillimore continued from 1813
       to 1837.

(viii) Index to (vii) above (Gloucester BT's Vol 5).

Copies of the following parishes with the P.R. and B.T's correlated:
(ix) Berkeley; (x) Yate and Little Sodbury; (xi) North Nibley; (xii)
Wotton-under-Edge; (xiii) Iron Acton and Westerleigh; (xiv)
St Nicholas, Gloucester. Full details in text. All indexed.

All volumes are in the Society of Genealogists' Library with the
exception of (xiii). (i) and (xiii) are also at the Bristol Archives
Office and (ii)-(xiv) are at the Gloucester City Library. Copies of
(ix)-(xiv) went to the incumbents of the parishes concerned. In the
text, the volumes of Gloucestershire Transcripts are indicated by
"Roe" and the volume number, and the others are written in full.

In addition to these, Mr. Eric Roe holds copies of BT marriages
from 13 North Gloucestershire parishes, and all the parishes in the
Bristol Diocese where the BT's are still held at Gloucester, mostly

from 1813 to 1837. These are typed but not yet fully indexed. They are indicated in the text by the abbreviation 'ER'.

Apart from the 15 completed volumes and those in progress there is the Roe "Index to Gloucester Marriages" which continues the work of Boyd. It is important to remember that the above indexes (i), (v), (viii) and (ix)-(xiv) are NOT also included in the main series of the Marriage Index volumes (see Gloucestershire Marriage Index below).

Society of Genealogists' Collection (SG). In addition to the Phillimore Printed Volumes and the copies by Mr. E. Roe, the Society has many typescript and manuscript copies.

Gloucester City Library (CLG). Some manuscript copies are to be found in the Hockaday Abstracts. There are also a number of other copies including the Phillimore and Roe Volumes.

The Shakespeare Birthplace Trust Library, Stratford-on-Avon (SOA) holds a large collection of typescript and manuscript copies which include a number of Gloucestershire parishes, though many of these extend only to dates in the 18th Century and very few go beyond 1812. Apart from those listed there are also a great number of partial copies or extracts made for various purposes such as notes relating to particular families or when a single series contains a full transcript down to a particular date and notes thereafter. All these are excluded from the list. Also excluded are a few cases where the intention, or performance, of the transcriber is uncertain. With one or two exceptions, therefore, the list contains only substantial portions of registers or transcripts copied as far as is known in full; though they have not been checked with the originals. These copies are all included in the Roe Marriage Index.

Cheltenham Library. This holds a few transcripts for Cheltenham and District.

Phillimore Manuscripts. These are manuscript copies of marriages in the possession of Phillimore & Co. Ltd., Shopwyke Hall, Chichester, Sussex. These marriages are included in the Roe Marriage Index. Searches will be made in these on payment of a fee.

Bristol Archives Office holds a number of typescript copies.

The College of Arms has a few copies, from which the marriages were included in Boyd's Miscellaneous Volumes. They are not included in the Roe Index (see below).

Microfilms

Gloucester County Record Office.

During the 1939-45 War, many Parish Registers were microfilmed for safety's sake, and then stored until the end of hostilities, but many of the original films seem to have disappeared. A list of those which have gone is in existence, and included important parishes such as Cheltenham. Those that remain, numbering about 135 parishes are stored in the County Record Office. Newington Bagpath registers having been damaged by flooding since being filmed, the parish now holds enlarged prints of the microfilm. These microfilms have not been listed in the Index.

Roe's Gloucestershire Marriage Index (RMI)

Index to Gloucestershire Marriages by Eric Roe. This is the Gloucestershire continuation of Boyd's Marriage Index. Copies of this Index, based on Marriages in copies of Parish Registers or Bishop's Transcripts whether printed, typescript or manuscript are to be found at the Society of Genealogists, Gloucester City Library and the Genealogical Society, Salt Lake City. The arrangement is similar to that of the rest of Boyd's Marriage Index.[1] The dates covered are added under each parish after the copies, with the abbreviation RMI.

This index is invaluable if used correctly. It is important to note however that the main series (on shelves with Boyd at the Society of Genealogists' Library) *does not include marriages from Mr. Roe's own copies of Bishop's Transcripts, and must be supplemented by the following indexes.*

(i)   Index to Bishop's Transcripts in the Diocese of Bristol.

(ii) Separate Index to Roe's Gloucestershire Transcripts Vols 1, 2 and 3.

(iii) Index at the back of Roe's Gloucestershire Transcripts Vol 4.

(iv) Separate Index to Roe's Gloucestershire Transcripts Vol. 5.

(v)   Individual Indexes to the six volumes of Parish Register Copies (Nos ix to xiv on list under 'Modern Copies' above).

At the time of going to press none of these volumes is with the main series at the Society of Genealogists' Library but they are all with the copies on the Gloucestershire shelves.

Although there is a typescript list of dates and parishes covered by the Index, the Society of Genealogists' Publication *A Key to Boyd's Marriage Index* and the typescript catalogue prepared by the Church of Jesus Christ of Latter Day Saints, a copy of which is in the Society of Genealogists' Library are both very misleading here, and the matter, which has come to light only during the preparation of the index will be clarified in future editions of the former publication.

Searchers may have noted that the dates given for parishes differ between the two volumes, particularly with regard to whether parishes

---

[1]   See General Article on Boyd's Marriage Index in Vol 1.

are included in Roe's Index up to 1812 or to 1837, though often the complete series for individual parishes is affected. Neither work is accurate for the volumes at present on the shelves of the Society of Genealogists' Library with the remainder of Boyd's Index. The Church of Jesus Christ of Latter-Day Saints Key lists all parishes included in the main series of volumes *plus* parishes in separate volumes (i) and (ii) listed above.

The Society of Genealogists' *Key to Boyd's Marriage Index*, in addition to the main series, lists also all parishes in volumes (i) to (iv) listed above.

Some Gloucestershire Parishes are included in the miscellaneous volumes of the main Boyd series. The marriages in these, however, are mostly duplicated in Roe's main series and have not been listed except where this has not been done (in all cases marriages abstracted by Boyd from copies at the College of Arms).

In addition to Roe's main series and the four volumes listed above, there is a further volume entitled *An Index of Gloucestershire Parishes and Marriages* extracted from Phillimore's Gloucestershire Parish Registers. The title as abbreviated on the spine of the bound copy in the Society of Genealogists' Library (*Index-Gloucestershire Parishes Phillimore's Marriages*) is misleading. The work actually lists stray registrations in Gloucestershire registers (i.e. marriages where one or both parties came from another parish). All these marriages are duplicated in the main series, but this volume lists them under their places of origin which do not appear at all in the entries as given in the main series. Stray registrations are also included in the index to Roe Vol 2. Although marriages from the Bishop's Transcripts are included in the Indexes (i) to (iv) above, additional marriages contained in the six volumes of copies of Parish Registers are not included and will be found in the index to each volume.

Marriage Licences

Diocese of Gloucester.

Originals – *City Library, Gloucester.*

A list of Marriage Bonds and Allegations appears in the City Library's Supplementary Catalogue 1928-1955.

Allegations. Marriage Licence Allegations in single sheets survive for the period 1747-1837 with very few gaps. There are also 94 volumes of Allegations 1637-1823 which relate to affidavits sworn at Gloucester.

Bonds. Varying numbers have survived for the period 1730-1823 except for years 1731, 1733, 1735, 1745, 1791. The numbers of documents per year range from 1 to 508.

Licences. The only considerable number of marriage licences surviving
is for 1822 (84 items).

There are marriage licence indexes for the period 1830-54 and
1876-1906.

Copies. Gloucestershire Marriage Allegations 1637-1680, Surrogate
Allegations 1637-1694 have been printed by the Bristol and Gloucestershire Archaeological Society (Records Section No 2). The Allegations
up to 1705 have been copied in manuscript by Mr. B. Frith for future
publication.

Gloucester Marriage Allegations and Grants of Marriage
Licences, 1637, 1638, 1660-1733. Copied and indexed by C.V. Appleton
Ms (SG).

<u>Diocese of Bristol.</u> Originals - *Bristol Archives Office.*

Registers 1750-1752, 1762-1871 (14 Volumes).

Bonds. 1 bundle containing 6 Bonds 1632-1643, 1660-72, 1675-1709,
1713-33, 1737-44, 1746, 1748-1816 in annual bundles. 1817-1823 containing both Bonds and Affidavits.

Allegations. Before 1746 some allegations are to be found in the
bundles of Bonds. 1746, 1749-52, 1757, 1759-92 in annual bundles.
1793-98 in one bundle.

Affidavits. 1817-23 see Bonds above. 1824-1962 in annual bundles.

Copies. Bonds 1637-1700 excluding Archdeaconry of Dorset (B and G
Arch Soc. Records Section Vol. 1, 1952). Bonds 1700-1800 Ms unbound,
Phillimore, property of Bristol Record Society (BAO). Bristol Marriage
Bonds and Allegations 1660-1686 and 1637-1693 Ed. by W.E.A. Fry
(issued as supplements to Gloucestershire Notes and Queries).

Roman Catholics

The whole of Gloucestershire is included in the Diocese of
Clifton and before 1837 there were only three Catholic Churches — at
Bristol, Cheltenham and Gloucester, although a fourth was founded at
Chipping Sodbury in 1838.

The parish priests of Cheltenham and St. Mary on the Quay, Bristol
(formerly St. Joseph's Chapel) hold pre-1837 registers, those of the
former having been printed by the Catholic Record Society. The
registers of Gloucester do not survive before 1853. Bishop's House,
St. Ambrose, Leigh Woods, Bristol 8 holds no Gloucestershire
registers.

Baptists

43 pre 1837 Churches have been listed. The detailed breakdown is as follows.

7 17th Century foundations. 2 (Broad Mead, Bristol and Cirencester) surrendered registers beginning in the 17th Century; 1 (Bourton-on-the-Water) has deposited registers but not before 1801; 1 (Tewkesbury) has registers with the Church Secretary but not before 1787. No registers are known for Meysey Hampton and no information has been received from the Church Secretaries of the remaining three (Old King St Bristol, Chipping Sodbury, Kings Stanley).

14 18th Century foundations. 4 surrendered registers: (Chipping Campden, Eastcombe, Hawkesbury, Wotton-under-Edge).1 (Coleford) has registers with the Church Secretary. For 1 (Hillesley) no registers are known, but the Church Secretary holds lists of members from 1768. For 1 (Shortwood Nailsworth) there are registers both at the PRO and held by the Church Secretary.[1] No registers are known for four others, though at Hanham there is a disused burial ground with M.I's dating back to 1725. No information has been received from the remaining three Church Secretaries.

21 Churches founded between 1800 and 1837. 2 surrendered registers; 1 (Lechlade) has registers with the Church Secretary. No registers are known for 5 others, and no information has been received from the remaining 13 Church Secretaries.

No registers are held by the Gloucestershire and Herefordshire Association or the Bristol and District Association.

Independents (Congregationalists)

54 pre-1837 Churches have been listed.

9 17th Century foundations. 6 surrendered registers, though none of them start until the 18th Century or even early 19th Century. 1 (Cam) has registers with the Church Secretary beginning in 1702, the earliest Independent Gloucestershire register known, and Kingswood (founded 1662) has registers with the Church Secretary beginning in 1806. No information has been received about Clifton Down (founded 1662).

16 18th Century foundations. All these surrendered registers with the exception of Hope Chapel Bristol and Long Ashton about which no information has been received.

---

[1]   There is a history of Shortwood Church 1715-1765 by R.M. Newman. (Copies from Rev. R. Jones, Brentmoor, Nailsworth.)

29 *19th Century foundations.* 10 of these surrendered registers;
1 (North Nibley) has registers with the Church Secretary; for 5 more
no registers are known to exist and no information has been received
about the remaining 10.

No registers are held by Page and Co, Solicitors, Bristol Chambers,
St Nicholas Street, Bristol 1, custodians of the documents of the
Congregational Union of Gloucestershire and Herefordshire or by the
Secretaries of the Bristol and the Cheltenham and Gloucester districts.

Presbyterians and Unitarians

The Barton St Chapel, Gloucester is described in the catalogue of
surrendered registers as " United Presbyterian and Unitarian. " There
were two other Churches in Gloucestershire (Wotton-under-Edge and
Frenchay) and one in Bristol. All four of these churches surrendered
registers.

Methodists

Wesleyans

The whole of Bristol and Gloucestershire was covered by 9 circuits
of the Bristol District: Bristol North, Bristol South, Kingswood,
Stroud, Dursley, Downend, Gloucester, Cheltenham, and Ledbury and the
Forest of Dean. All of the circuit churches, with the exception of
Ledbury surrendered registers, and it seems possible that the register
catalogued as "Newent" is in fact the Circuit register for the
Ledbury and Forest of Dean Circuit. In Bristol and Gloucestershire a
greater number of churches than elsewhere appear to have kept separate
registers. Thus, in addition to the circuit churches, pre-1837
registers were surrendered from the following: - Alkerton and
Eastington, Clifton, Cirencester, Littleworth, Redfield and
Westbury-on-Trym and post 1837 registers from Coleford. A duplicate
register for Portland St Chapel, Westbury-on-Trym is at the Bristol
Archives Office. No further registers are known, and it seems that
the surrender of registers was more complete than in most counties.

Primitive Methodists

There was a Primitive Methodist Circuit of Bristol, but no
circuit in Gloucestershire. No registers are known for the Bristol
circuit.

Methodist New Connexion

There were no circuits or churches in either Bristol or
Gloucestershire.

Bible Christian

There was a circuit of Drybrook. No registers are known.

Modern Methodist Circuits

Bristol (North)
Bristol (Clifton and Redland)
Bristol Mission
Bristol (South)
Bristol (East)
Bristol (Kingswood) — No registers held
Bristol (Staple Hill and Fishponds) — No churches founded before 1837
Bristol (South Gloucestershire)

Gloucester
Forest of Dean — No pre-1837 registers held
Cheltenham — No pre-1837 registers held
Stroud and Cirencester
Dursley and Stonehouse — Registers held from 1838 only
Tewkesbury — No pre-1837 registers held

Lady Huntingdon's Connexion

There were three churches in Gloucestershire and one in Bristol. All surrendered registers.

Calvinistic Methodists

There were two churches in Bristol, for one of which (Broadmead) there are registers at both the PRO and the National Library of Wales, the latter being presumably a contemporary copy made at the time of surrender. Two other churches (Rodborough and Wotton-under-Edge) also surrendered registers.

Society of Friends (Quakers)

The Gloucestershire Quarterly Meeting was founded in 1668 with the following Monthly Meetings:-

Nailsworth — (1668-1854)
Gloucester — (1668-1854)
Stoke Orchard — (1668-1755)
Westbury or Forest — (1668-c1750)
Stow and Campden — (1668-1790)

Westbury Monthly Meeting was dissolved before 1750 and Stoke Orchard in 1755, the Constituent Meetings of the latter being joined to Gloucester Monthly Meeting. Stow and Campden Monthly Meetings were dissolved in 1790 and its constituent meetings joined to Warwickshire South Monthly Meeting. (*See Warwickshire — Birmingham Monthly Meeting*)

In 1788 the *Gloucestershire* Quarterly Meeting was joined to the *Wiltshire* Quarterly Meeting to form the *Gloucester and Wilts Quarterly Meeting.*

The *Bristol and Somerset Quarterly Meeting* included the Monthly Meetings of Bristol (2 weeks meeting 1668-1784, Monthly meeting 1784-1870) and Frenchay (1668-1870).

Registers

All pre-1837 registers known seem to have been surrendered, but the catalogue of surrendered registers is completely inaccurate, and no reliance should be placed on its descriptions of registers.

Gloucestershire Quarterly Meeting. Z 1647-1683, M 1656-1693, B 1657-1680 (PRO 575). No other register for the Gloucestershire Quarterly Meeting is known.

Gloucester and Wilts Quarterly Meeting. Z 1786-1837, M 1785-1835, B 1785-1837 (PRO 578, 579, 581-584).

Bristol and Somerset Quarterly Meeting. ZMB 1776-1837 (PRO 101-115).

The Monthly Meeting registers will be found listed under the Monthly Meetings.

Birth and Burial Notes for the Gloucestershire and Wiltshire Quarterly Meeting 1776-1794 and Marriage Licences 1775-1794 are also at the PRO (Nos. 1469-71).

"Digests" (i.e. abstracts of all entries arranged alphabetical-ly)[1] of all surrendered registers for both the Gloucestershire Quarterly Meeting and the Bristol and Somerset Quarterly Meeting are held by Friends' House, Euston Road, London N.W.1. A copy of the Digest for Bristol and Somerset Quarterly Meeting is at Bristol Archives Office, and a copy of that of the Gloucestershire Quarterly Meeting is at the Gloucestershire Record Office. These digests also have separate supplements with details from registers surrendered later.

The Gloucestershire Record Office also holds copy registers for the Gloucestershire Quarterly Meeting of Births 1838-1864 and Burials 1829-1864.

Huguenots

There was a French Church in Bristol, that of St Mark the Gaunt whose registers have been printed by the Huguenot Society.

---

[1]   For a description of these Digests, see General Article on Quaker Registers in Vol. 1.

Moravians

There were three Moravian Churches, one in the City of Bristol, one at Kingswood, both of which surrendered registers, and one at Apperley (later purchased by Methodists) of which no registers are known.

Jews

A congregation was established in Bristol in 1753 and in Gloucester shortly afterwards. No registers are known, though the MI's of the latter have been copied by H.Y.J. Taylor and there is an article in Gloucestershire Notes and Queries.

Regimental Registers

These cover Births, Baptisms, Marriages and Deaths for the period 1790-1924 and are at Somerset House, London. They are the original registers kept by various regiments. They are indexed, and to search this index, one does not need to know the regiment. For Marriages, Deaths and Burials it is preferable, though not essential, to know the regiment. The most likely regiments for infantrymen were the 28th Regiment of Foot (North Gloucestershire) and the 61st Regiment of Foot (South Gloucestershire).

Search should also be made of the Guards' Regiments, the Royal Artillery, the Royal Engineers and the Royal Marines.

Monumental Inscriptions

Bigland (see *Useful General Works of References* below) lists many monumental inscriptions arranged by parishes alphabetically, including a large number now illegible. Others are included in Fosbrooke' *History of Gloucester*, I.M. Roper's *Monumental Effigies of Gloucester and Bristol* (1931), and C.T. Davis' *The Monumental Brasses of Gloucestershire* (1899) is also useful.

About 1965 the Local History Committee of the Gloucestershire Community Council started a tombstone survey of Gloucestershire. This has been conducted by Mr. Jones, who has to date (1966) visited 155 churchyards including 12 Gloucester churchyards or cemeteries, 9 at Cheltenham, 3 at Cirencester and 4 at Stroud. He recorded only those stones which were of particular historical and architectural interest, giving their situations in the churchyard, the names of people commemorated and the dates, and giving a description of the shapes and styles. Masons' signatures where they existed were also noted, as

were unusual or interesting epitaphs. In some cases Mr. Jones also
took photographs of the stones. The results of the survey are housed
in the Gloucester Collection in the Gloucester City Library. The
survey is continuing.

Newspapers

Only pre-1837 newspapers for which there is a reasonably connected
series available have been included. Others, for which only a few
stray issues exists, will be found in G.A. Cranfield's *"A Handlist
of English Provincial Newspapers and Periodicals 1700-1760"*,
(pub. Bowes & Bowes, Cambridge 1952). It may be assumed that the
British Museum Newspaper Library has a reasonably complete series of
most papers listed after 1760.

Bristol

The Bristol Journal (1713-1807). Bristol Reference Library (Incomplete
    series).
Bristol Weekly Intelligence (1741-59). Bristol Reference Library
    1748-52. Bodleian Library — most of 1750.
Oracle or Bristol Weekly Miscellany (1742-1749). Almost complete
    series at Bristol Reference Library. Only two 1742 copies at
    British Museum Newspaper Library, Colindale.
Felix Farley's Bristol Journal (1752-1853 (— incorporated with
    Bristol Times). Bristol Reference Library 1752 onwards.
Bristol Gazette and Public Advertiser (1700-1872).
Sarah Farley's Bristol Journal (1782-85).
Bristol Mercury (1806-1901). Continued as Bristol Daily Mercury 1901-9.
Bristol Mirror (1819-1864).
Bristol Observer (1819-1823).

Gloucester

Gloucester Journal — 1722 onwards (from the late 18th Century).
    Extremely useful for Marriages and Obituaries). Gloucester Library.
    A complete series from No. 1, April 9th 1722 to date. British
    Museum Newspaper Library, Colindale — odd numbers 1725-36; 1749,
    1750, 51-2 almost complete, 1756-57. The complete series has been
    microfilmed and is available from Micro-Methods Ltd of Wakefield.
Gloucester Mercury (1828-9).

Cirencester

Cirencester Flying Post (1740-9). Gloucester City Library from 1740:
    Bingham Public Library, Cirencester 1741-44).

Cheltenham

Cheltenham Chronicle (1809-date).
Bath and Cheltenham Gazette (1825-1897).
Cheltenham Free Press (1834-1908).

Publishing Societies

Bristol and Gloucestershire Archaeological Society, Council House, Bristol 1. (Library at City Library, Gloucester). Publications include: *"Transactions"* (1876 onwards); *"Bristol and Glos. Parish Records"* (1963); and *"Marriage Bonds and Allegations"* (1954).
Bristol Record Society, University of Bristol.

Other Local Societies

Gloucestershire Community Council's Local History Committee, Community House, College Green, Gloucester acts as the co-ordinating committee for all local Societies and keeps an up to date list with the names and addresses of their Secretaries.
Historical Association — Cheltenham and Gloucester Branch (Secretary, c/o St Paul's College, Cheltenham).
Forest of Dean Local History Society, The Vicarage, Newnham.
Cotteswold Naturalists' Field Club, Secretary F.W.A. Morris, Esq., 35 Shepherd Way, Minchinhampton, Glos. This Society was formed in the early 1840's. Its Library is housed at the City Library, Gloucester.

Useful General Works of Reference

Bristol and Gloucester Parish Records (published Bristol and Gloucester Arch. Soc. 1963). This contains comprehensive information on all parish records, whether still in the parish churches or deposited elsewhere.
Gloucestershire Notes and Queries (Nos. 1-91). Vols. 1-10 part. 7. (1879-1914).
Hyett and Bazeley — *"Manual of Gloucestershire Literature"* (1895).
Catalogue of Gloucestershire Collection at Gloucester City Library (1928).
Catalogue of Gloucestershire Books collected by Sir Francis Hyett of Painswick (now deposited at GRO).
R. Bigland and others — *"Historical Monumental and Genealogical Collections of Gloucester"* (3 volumes) printed 1791, 1792. continuations 1838-1889. This contains much useful information of a general nature and especially monumental inscriptions. (q.v.)
Rev. T.D. Fosbrooke — *"History of Gloucester"* (1819).
W. Hobart Bird — *"Old Gloucestershire Churches"* (1928).

J. Smith — *"Men and Armour for Gloucestershire in 1608"*. (A full list of names of men fit for war service (1902)).

J. Stratford, *Gloucestershire Biographical Notes* (1887).

J. Stratford — *Bristol Worthies and Notable Residents* (2 vols 1907-8).

W.R. Williams — *"The Parliamentary History of the County of Gloucestershire 1213-1898"*. (includes biographical and genealogical notes) (1898).

"Inquisitiones post mortem" in the Index Library Vols 9, 13, 21, 30, 40, 47.

Gloucester Wills 1541-1800 — Index Library 2 Vols (1895, 1907).

In addition to the above, the *Victoria County History of Gloucestershire* is in progress, and the *Guide to the Diocesan Records* will probably be published in 1967.

ABENHALL (or ABINGHALL). **OR** CMB 1597 + *(gaps CB 1750-1762, M 1750-1754 and 1790)* (Inc). **BT** 1621 + (G). **Cop** (PR) C 1596-1860, M 1596-1856, B 1596-1812 Mf (SLC).

ABSON. **OR** CMB 1687-1812 (Inc Wick) *(gap CMB 1813 – formation of Wick parish in 1880)*. **BT** 1600-1812 *(gap 1640-1661)* (B). **Cop** CMB 1687-1812 (City Hall, Gloucester). *See also Wick.*

ACTON TURVILLE. **OR** CB 1665 + *(gaps CB 1730-1, M 1730-1812)* (Inc). **BT** 1599 + (G). **Cop** M 1671-1723 (Phil 13), M (BT) 1813-37 Ts (Roe 5 SG and CLG). *M 1671-1723 in RMI. M 1812-37 not in RMI but in Index to Roe Vol. 5.*

ADLESTROP. **OR** CMB 1538 + *(gap 1674-7)* (Inc). **BT** 1580 + (G). **Cop** CMB 1538-1603 (CLG) Mf of PR (GRO).

ALDERLEY. **OR** C 1557 + *(gaps 1663, 1665-1671, 1738-1747, 1750-1751)*, M 1559 + *(gaps 1654-59, 1663, 1664, 1737-51, 1797)*, B 1560 + *(gaps 1606-8, 1657, 1663, 1664, 1738-51)* (Inc). **BT** 1570 + (G). **Cop** M 1559-1812 (Phil 10), CMB 1557-1749 (CLG), M (BT) 1813-37 Ts (Roe 5 – SG and CLG). *M 1559-1812 in RMI. 1813-37 not in RMI but in Index to Roe Vol. 5.*

ALDESTROP. *– see Adlestrop.*

ALDERTON. **OR** CB 1596-1812, M 1596-1753 (GRO), CMB 1813 + (Inc). **BT** 1625 + (G).

ALDSWORTH. **Peculiar** *of Rector of Bibury.* **OR** CMB 1683 + *(gap M 1746-1753)* (Inc). **BT** 1612 + (G).

ALKERTON. *Parish of Eastington, near Stonehouse.* **OR** CMB 1558 + *(gap M 1659, 1660)* (Inc). **BT** on Eastington returns (G). **Cop** M 1558-1812 (Phil 13). *See also Eastington.*

ALKERTON and EASTINGTON. (Wes). *f 1809.* **Dursley Circuit.** **OR** ZC 1802-1837 (PRO), C 1839-1881 (Minister, Dursley).

ALMONDSBURY. **OR** CMB 1653 + (Inc). **BT** 1672, 85, 87, 1733, 35-36, 38-40, 1748, 50, 54, 56-63, 73-98, 1800-04, 06-59, 68-70, 99 (B). **Cop** M (BT) 1813-37 Ts I (ER).

ALSTONE. *– see Worcs.*

ALVESTON. **OR** CMB 1742 + (Inc). **BT** 1674, 82-83, 87, 89, 99, 1701, 1762-63, 67-69, 1799-1800, 1802-06, 08-59 (B). **Cop** M (BT) 1814-37 Ts I (ER). *Extracts in RMI.*

ALVINGTON. **OR** CB 1688 +, M 1698 + *(gaps C 1781-1800, M 1752-56)* (Inc). **BT** 1629 + (G). **Cop** M 1698-1836 (Phil 14). *M 1698-1836 in RMI. See also Woolaston.*

AMBERLEY. **OR** C 1838 +, M 1841 +, B 1837 + (Inc). *No BT's.*

AMPNEY CRUCIS. **OR** C 1566 + *(gaps 1684, 1708-1718)*, M 1561 + *(gap 1744-53)*, B 1559 + (Inc). **BT** 1607 + (G). **Cop** M 1561-1837 (Phil 15). *M 1561-1837 in RMI.*

AMPNEY, DOWN. **OR** CMB 1603 + *(gaps M 1695-1712, 1753, 1754, B 1693-1713)* (Inc). **BT** 1572 + (G).

AMPNEY. St **Mary. OR** CB 1602-1812, M 1602-1807 (Inc). **BT** 1608 + (G).

AMPNEY. St **Peter. OR** CB 1599-1812 *(gap 1733-1742)*, M 1599-1811 *(gap 1733-53)* (Inc). **BT** 1613 + (G).

APPERLEY. (Moravian). *Chapel purchased by Methodists and used until 1904. No registers known. Not at PRO or Tewkesbury Circuit Supt.*

ARLINGHAM. **OR** C 1539 + *(gaps 1552-90, 1613-49, 1661-4)*, M 1566 + *(gap 1645-1649)*, B 1540 + *(gaps 1547-1573, 1647, 1648, 1662-1663, 1685, 1752-56)* (Inc). **BT** 1573 (G). **Cop** M (BT) 1661-1812 Sep I Ts Roe 1 (SG and CLG), M (BT) 1813-1837 Ts Sep I (SG – Roe 3), M (BT) 1661-1837, except 1663, 6, 9, 73, 95, 1731, 55, 58, 64, Ts (CLG). *M (BT) 1661-1837 not in main RMI but in Index to Roe Vols. 1-3.*

ASHCHURCH. **OR** CMB 1558 + (Inc). **BT** 1606 + (G). **Cop** M 1555-1837 (Phil 14). *M 1555-1837 in RMI.*

ASHLEWORTH. **OR** CMB 1566 + (Inc). **BT** 1599 + (G). **Cop** CMB 1566-1576 Ms (CLG), M (BT) 1660-1837 Ts (ER). *M 1660-1812 in RMI.*

ASHLEY. – *see Wilts.*

ASHTON, COLD. – *see Cold Ashton.*

ASHTON, LONG. (Ind). *f 1792. Not at PRO. No information.*

ASHTON-UNDER-HILL. *Transferred to Worcs 1931. See Worcs. (M 1586-1778 are in RMI.)*

ASTON BLANK (or COLD ASTON). **OR** CB 1727 +, M 1728 + (Inc). **BT** 1599 + (G) **Cop** M 1728-1812 (Phil 17). *M 1728-1812 in RMI.*

ASTON SOMERVILLE. *Transferred to Worcs. 1931.* **OR** CMB 1668 + *(gap M 1753-9)* (Inc Childswickham). **BT** 1617 + (G). **Cop** M 1661-1812 (Phil 4). *M 1661-1812 in RMI.*

ASTON-SUB-EDGE. **OR** C 1537 + *(gap 1758-1760)*, M 1537 +, B 1539 + (Inc). **BT** 1612 + (G). **Cop** M 1539-1812 (Phil 3), Extracts C 1539-1586, M 1539-1718 (Ptd), CM 1539-1812, B 1539-1810 (SOA), CMB 1813-1820 (C of A), CM 1539-1812, B 1539-1810 (CLG). *M 1539-1812 in RMI.*

AUST. **OR** CMB 1538 + *(gaps C 1659-1708, M 1659-1712, 1753-1756, B 1673-1708)* (Inc Henbury). **BT** 1813-59, 65, 69-77, 81 (B). *Earlier BT's on Henbury returns.* **Cop** Extract (SG).

AVENING. **OR** CB 1557-1812, M 1557-1813, Banns 1754-1776 (Inc). **BT** 1620 + (G). **Cop** M 1557-1812 (Phil 10), M (BT) 1813-37 Ts (Roe 5 – SG and CLG). *M 1557-1812 in RMI. 1813-37 not in RMI but in Index to Roe Vol. 5. See also Nailsworth.*

AVENING. Forest Green Ch, Nailsworth. (Ind). – see *Nailsworth.*

AVENING, Upper Forest Green (Ind). *f 1822.* OR ZC 1822-1837 (PRO).

AVENING, Tetbury Hill. (Bapt). *f 1819. Not at PRO. No information.*

AWRE. OR CMB 1538 + *(gap 1706-1707)* (Inc). BT 1566 + (G).
Cop (PR) CM 1538-1856, B 1538-1865 Mf (SLC), M (BT) 1661-1837
Ts (ER).

BADGEWORTH. OR C 1559 +, M 1553 +, B 1586 + *(gaps C 1580-85, M 1573-85, CMB 1754)* (Inc), Mar. Lic. 1785-1806 (GRO). *C 1606-1624 inserted after 1637 in register of Shurdington. Badgeworth registers also contain CMB for Shurdington 1723-1789.* BT 1570 + (G).

BADGINGTON. – see *Bagendon.*

BADMINTON, GREAT. OR CMB 1538 + (Inc). BT 1596 + (G). Cop M 1538-1812
(Phil 13), M (BT) 1813-1837 Ts (Roe 5 – SG and CLG). *M 1539-1812
in RMI. M 1813-37 not in RMI but in Ind to Roe Vol. 5.*

BADMINTON (S of F). Frenchay Monthly Meeting. OR Z 1666-1680, M 1680-
1746, B 1673-1778 (PRO 590).

BAGENDON (or BADGINGTON). OR CB 1630-1812, M 1630-1808 *(gap CMB 1740-
1742)* (Inc). BT 1577 + (G). Cop CMB 1577-1579, 1607-1608 (CLG).

BARNWOOD. OR C 1651 +, M 1652 +, B 1670 + (Inc). BT 1569 + (G).
Cop CMB (BT) 1569-1651 (CLG).

BARNSLEY. Peculiar *of Rector of Bibury.* OR C 1574-1897, Z 1653-1659,
M 1574-1839 *(gaps 1640-44, 1646, 1648-52, 1661, 1662, 1704-7,
1756-57),* B 1574-1812 *(gaps 1642, 1643, 1652, 1653, 1659)* (GRO).
BT *A few BT's only.*

BARRINGTON, GREAT. OR CMB 1547 +, Mar. Lic. 1767-1867 (7), Non
residence Lic. 1812 and 1814 (2), Banns 1757, 1764 (Inc).
BT 1600 + (G).

BARRINGTON, LITTLE. OR CB 1682 +, No M (Inc). BT 1605 + (G).

BATSFORD. OR CB 1562-1754, M 1562-1811 (Inc). BT 1599 + (G).
Cop M 1565-1812 (Phil 6). *M 1565-1812 in RMI.*

BAUNTON. OR CB 1625-1754, M 1625-1808, CMB 1813 + (Inc). BT 1629 + (G).

BEACHLEY. OR CMB 1833 + (Inc). *No BT's.*

BECKFORD. *Transferred to Worcs. 1931. See Worcs. (M (BT) 1607-1700
in Boyd Misc.)*

BEDMINSTER. – see *Somerset.*

BERKELEY. OR CB 1562 + *(gaps 1651, 1652),* M 1598 + *(gaps 1635-1652,
1791-1801)* (Inc). BT 1571 + (G). Cop Extracts CMB (BT) 1571-1599
(CLG), C 1562-1563, M 1619-1634 (incomplete), B 1619-1650 Ts (CLG),
CMB 1653-1677 I (Ptd Ed. F.A. Crisp 1897), M (BT) 1624-1812
Ts Sep I (Roe 2 – SG and CLG), M (BT) 1813-37 Ts Sep I (Roe 3 –
SG and CLG), M (BT and PR) 1624-1837 Ts I (Roe – Sep Volume).
*M 1571-78, 1596-98, 1653-1677 in RMI. M (BT) 1624-1837 not in main
RMI but in Index to Berkeley Marriages Volume. See also Stone.*

BERKELEY. Newport Meeting (Ind). *f 1712.* **OR** ZC 1822-1836 (PRO).

BEVERSTONE. **OR** CMB 1563 + *(gaps C B 1809-12, M 1782, 1783, 1805, 1806)* (Inc). **BT** 1599 + (G). **Cop** M 1563-1836 (Phil 6), M (BT) 1813-1837 Ts (Roe 5 – SG and CLG). *M 1563-1812 in RMI. 1813-37 not in RMI but in Index to Roe Vol. 5.*

BIBURY. **Peculiar** *of the Rector of Bibury.* **OR** CMB 1551 + *(gaps C 1649-1653, M 1665, B 1589-1601, 1648, 1649, 1651-1653)* (Inc). **BT** 1740 + (G).

BISHOP'S CLEEVE. **Peculiar** *of Rector of Bishop's Cleeve.* **OR** CMB 1563 + (Inc). **BT** 1599 + (G). **Cop** M 1563-1812 (Phil 3). *M 1563-1812 in RMI.*

BISHOPSWORTH. – *see Somerset.*

BISLEY-WITH-LYPIATT. **OR** CB 1547-1808, M 1547-1812 (Inc). **BT** 1608 + (G). *Extracts in RMI. See also Stroud.*

BISLEY. France Meeting, Chalford Hill. (Ind). – *see Chalford.*

BITTON. **OR** CB 1572 +, M 1571 + *(gaps CM 1674-1677, B 1669-1677)* (Inc). **BT** 1571-1574, 1593, 96, 98, 1608, 12, 16-17, 20-23, 25-26, 28-32, 1637-40, 60-65, 69-70, 72, 76, 78-80, 82-93, 95-97, 1705-06, 08-10, 1712-1813 (B), 1813-37 (G). **Cop** C 1572-1674, M 1571-1674, B 1572-1668 I (PRS 32), M (BT) 1813-37 Ts I (ER). *M 1571-1674 in RMI. See also Hanham, Oldland and Kingswood (near Bristol).*

BLAISDON. **OR** CMB 1635 + *(gaps CB 1695-1753, 1811-13, M 1695-1767, 1802-13)* (Inc). **BT** 1583 + (G). **Cop** (PR) C 1635-1860 *(gap 1694-1755)*, M 1635-1860, B 1635-1863 *(gap 1798-1813)* Mf (SLC).

BLAKENEY. **OR** C 1813 +, M 1853 + (Inc Awre). *Previously in parish of Awre. BT on Awre returns.* **Cop** C 1813-1860, M 1853-1856 Mf (SLC). *See also Awre.*

BLAKENEY. High St (Bapt). *f 1833.* **OR** B 1834-1837 (PRO). *Z regd at Dr Williams Library, London.* (PRO non authent.).

BLAKENEY. (Ind). – *see Newnham.*

BLEDINGTON. **OR** C 1703 +, M 1712 + *(gap 1760)*, B 1710 + *(gap 1759)* (Inc) **BT** 1605 + (G). **Cop** Mf of PR (GRO).

BLOCKLEY. – *see Worcs.*

BODDINGTON. **OR** C 1652 +, M 1656 +, B 1654 + *(gaps C 1728-83, M 1691-1783, B 1783)* (Inc). **BT** 1612 + (G). **Cop** CMB 1612-1784 Ms (CLG), M (BT) 1676-1837 Ts (ER). *M 1676-1813 in RMI. See also Staverton.*

BODDINGTON (S of F). **Stoke Orchard Monthly Meeting.** *f 1666.* **OR** ZC 1666-1680, M 1680-1746, B 1673-1778 (PRO).

BOURTON-ON-THE-HILL. **OR** CMB 1568 + *(gaps M 1754, 1811-12)* (Inc). **BT** 1598 + (G). **Cop** CMB 1568-1620 Ms (CLG).

BOURTON-ON-THE-WATER. – *including Clapton and Lower Slaughter until 1814.* **OR** CMB 1654 +, *(gap M 1804-12)* (Inc). **BT** 1605 + (G). **Cop** M 1654-1837 (Phil 17). *M 1655-1837 in RMI. See also Slaughter, Lower.*

BOURTON-ON-THE-WATER. (Bapt). *f 1650*. OR ZB 1801-1836 (PRO).

BOUTHROP. - *see Eastleach Martin.*

BOXWELL WITH LEIGHTERTON. OR Boxwell and Leighterton CB 1548 +,
Leighterton M 1572 + *(gap 1746-1753)*, Boxwell M 1597 + (Inc).
BT 1606 + (G). Cop M 1572-1812 (Phil 13), M (BT) 1813-1837
Ts (Roe 5 - SG and CLG). *M 1572-1810 in RMI. M 1813-37 not in RMI
but in Index to Roe Vol. 5.*

BREAM. *(Chapelry of Newland)*. OR C 1752 +, M 1855 +, B 1827 + (Inc).
BT *only a few of late date. Earlier BT's on Newland returns.*

BRIMPSFIELD. OR CMB 1587 + *(gaps C 1611-15, 1679-83, M 1611-16, 1639-
65, B 1611-54, 1786-1812)* (Inc). BT 1616 + (G).

BRISLINGTON. - *see Somerset.*

BRISTOL CATHEDRAL. (Abbey Church of St Augustine). OR CMB 1669 +
(Dean and Chapter). *No BT's traced.* Cop CMB 1669-1837 I (Ptd 1933).
M 1669-1837 in RMI.

BRISTOL, All Saints. OR C 1560 +, M 1560 +, B 1561 + (Inc).
BT 1663, 71, 75-76, 78-80, 83-84, 87, 89-96, 99, 1716, 27, 35-37,
1740-44, 46-50, 53, 59-63, 68-70, 76, 78, 81-82, 1785-1800,
1802-39, 41-53, 64, 67, 68-72, (B). Cop *Extracts in RMI.*

BRISTOL, Christchurch. *United with St Ewen 1788.* OR CMB 1538 + (Inc),
Banns 1754-1902, Mar. Lic. 1822-1903 (BAO). BT 1670-73, 75-77,
1679-1707, 1709-14, 16-18, 21, 23, 26-39, 45, 48, 50-52, 58-80,
1785, 87-88, 1790-1805, 09-59, 64, 66, 67 (B). Cop I to Regs 1538-
1800 (2 Vols) (Inc). *Extracts in RMI.*

BRISTOL, Holy Trinity. OR 1831 + (Inc). BT 1834-60, 63, 69-71 (for
1833, *see St Philip and Jacob*) (BAO). Cop *Extracts in RMI.*

BRISTOL, St Augustine the Less. OR C 1577-1853, M 1577-1848, B 1577-
1826 (Inc). BT 1664, 66, 72, 76, 79, 84, 87-9, 1696, 98, 1704,
1734-37, 62, 64-66, 1774-1802, 06-48, 50-60, 66 (B). Cop CMB 1577-
1700 (Ptd. Ed by Arthur Sabin 1956). *Extracts in RMI.*

BRISTOL, St Ewen. *United with Christchurch 1788.* OR CB 1538-1791,
M 1538-1792. *Index 1542-1775.* (Inc Christchurch). BT 1673, 74, 76,
1680, 85, 87-92, 94, 96, 1700, 07, 10-11, 13-14, 23, 32, 41-42,
1744-45, 58-62, 64-65, 67-69, 72-79, 82, 85-91 (B). Cop *Extracts
in RMI.*

BRISTOL, St George. OR CMB 1759 + (Inc). BT 1756-1805, 1807-1858 (B).
Cop *Extracts in RMI.*

BRISTOL, St George. Brandon Hill. OR C 1832 +, M 1833 +, B 1833 + (Inc).
BT 1832-1860, 1866, 1869 (B).

BRISTOL, St James. OR CMB 1559 + *(gap M 1777-91)* (Inc). BT 1676-78,
1683-84, 1701-2, 16, 1720-1850 (B). Cop *Extracts in RMI.*

BRISTOL, St John the Baptist. (City). **OR** CMB 1558 + (Inc), Banns 1855-1935 (BAO). **BT** 1675, 78, 80, 83-87, 89, 93, 96, 1740-42, 44-54, 1756-59, 62-65, 67, 70-75, 1784-1867, 1869-1897 (B). **Cop** *Extracts in RMI.*

BRISTOL, St Leonard. *United with St Nicholas 1768.* **OR** CMB 1689-1768 (BAO). **BT** 1674-75, 78-79, 82-84, 86, 91, 94-96 (for 1697 *see St Nicholas*), 1698-1705, 1707-18, 20, 22, 31-40, 47, 51-52, 56-67 (B). **Cop** *Extracts in RMI.*

BRISTOL, St Mary. Fishponds. *Formed 1830.* **OR** CM 1836 +. **BT** 1870-1885 (B).

BRISTOL, St Mary le Port. *All records destroyed by enemy action 1941.* **BT** 1669-72, 76-79, 81, 83-87, 95-97, 99, 1701-07, 09-20, 22-24, 1726-34, 36-46, 48-76, 78-79, 82-83, 86-89, 1791-1858 (B). **Cop** CMB 1560-1654 (CLG). *Extracts in RMI.*

BRISTOL, St Mary Redcliffe. **OR** CMB 1559 +, Banns 1790-1814 (Inc). **BT** 1665, 72, 75-79, 81-87, 92, 1699-1711, 15-16, 18-25, 27-69, 1771-75, 84-85 (*very badly worn*), 1787-1808, 12-29, 31-55, 56, 1865-1906 (B). **Cop** *Extracts in RMI.*

BRISTOL, St Michael the Archangel. (City). **OR** CMB 1653 + (Register 1637-1650 lost), Banns in B register 1763-1773 (Inc). **BT** 1610, 1665, 72, 75-79, 81-84, 86-88, 90-91, 1693-1705, 07-09, 11-14, 1716-45, 1749-1850, 54-61, 68-70 (B). **Cop** *Extracts in RMI.*

BRISTOL, St Nicholas. *United with St Leonard 1768.* **OR** CMB 1538 + (*gap M 1647-1652*) (Inc). **BT** 1670-79, 83-87, 90, 92-94, 99, 1701, 04, 1706-11, 14, 18-20, 23, 26-29, 31-44, 46-52, 55-57, 73-75, 1784-1906 (B). **Cop** *Extracts in RMI.*

BRISTOL, St Paul. Portland Sq. *Formed 1794.* **OR** CMB 1794 + (Inc). **BT** 1794-1859 (BAO). **Cop** *Extracts in RMI.*

BRISTOL, St Peter. *All records destroyed by enemy action 1941.* **BT** 1611, 67, 76-78, 80, 83-86, 96-97, 1700-06, 09-12, 14-25, 1727-34, 36-48, 50, 52-55, 59-69, 1771-1859, 69-72 (B). **Cop** *Extract in RMI.*

BRISTOL, St Philip and Jacob. **OR** CMB 1576 +, Banns 1750-64 (Inc). **BT** 1679, 81, 85, 87, 1774-78, 80, 81, 84-95, 1797-1848, 50-52 (BAO). **Cop** CMB 1576-1840 (Inc). *Extracts in RMI.*

BRISTOL, St Stephen. (City). **OR** CMB 1559 + (Inc). **BT** 1671-72, 74-95, 1699-1700, 1702-33, 36-82, 1784-1860 (B). **Cop** *Extracts in RMI.*

BRISTOL, St Thomas the Martyr. **OR** C 1552 +, M 1558 +, B 1554 +, Banns 1777-1820 (Inc). **BT** 1610, 35, 70, 75-77, 79-87, 1699-1710, 1714-15, 18-25, 27-52, 54-81, 85, 1787-1802, 1813-59, 69-1893 (B). **Cop** *Extracts in RMI.*

BRISTOL, St Werburgh. **QR** CMB 1558 + (Inc). **BT** 1677, 80, 83-85, 88, 1692-96, 1700-01, 03-05, 07, 09, 10-14, 16, 20, 24, 29-37, 39-51, 1754, 1756-1813, 14-40, 42-52, 54 (B). **Cop** *Extracts in RMI.*

BRISTOL, Temple or Holy Cross. **OR** CMB 1558 $^+$, (Inc St Mary Redcliffe), Banns 1813-1873 (BAO). **BT** 1671-72, 74-88, 93-95, 97, 1699-1769, 1771-80, 85, 87-88, 1790-1857, 1867-1868 (B). **Cop** *Extracts in RMI.*

BRISTOL, St Mark the Gaunt. (French Ch.). **OR** CMB 1687-1807 (PRO − *cat. under foreign churches section*). **Cop** CMB 1687-1807 (Hug. Soc. 20). *M 1688-1744 in RMI.*

BRISTOL, Stonehouse French Church. − *see Stonehouse.*

BRISTOL, St Joseph's Chapel. Trenchard Lane.(RC). *Now Church of St Mary on the Quay.* **OR** ZC 1777 $^+$, M 1787 $^+$ (Inc). **Cop** ZC 1777-1808, M 1787-1808 (Cath R.S. 3). *M 1787-1809 in RMI.*

BRISTOL MONTHLY MEETING (S of F). *Two weeks meeting until 1784. United with* **Frenchay Monthly Meeting** *1870. One Constituent Meeting only. Friars, Bristol.* **OR** Z 1654-1685, 1757-1768, M 1659-1691, B 1675-6, 1745-69 (PRO 1507-1511), Z 1654-1837, M 1659-1837, B 1655-1837 (PRO 116-126). Z notes 1677-1784, B notes 1703-1784 (PRO 1512-1525). Z notes 1822-1837, certs. 1826-36, M certs. (3) 1673-1759, M 1838-1949, B (Friars Burial Ground) 1794-1810, 1808-1946, B (Redcliffe Pit) 1796-1843. B notes 1834-1891, 1901-1937 (BAO).

BRISTOL, Friars.(S of F). − *see* **Bristol Monthly Meeting** *above.*

BRISTOL, Broadmead. (Bapt). *f 1679.* **OR** Z 1726-1784, 1787-1837, B 1679-1837 (PRO *cat. under Somerset*).

BRISTOL, Old King st. (Cairns Rd). (Bapt). *f 1650. Perhaps identical with above.*

BRISTOL, City Rd. (Bapt). *f 1835. Not at PRO. No information.*

BRISTOL, Wells Rd, Counterslip. (Bapt). *f 1804. Not at PRO. All records with Ch Sec. destroyed in 1940.*

BRISTOL, Stapleton Rd, Kennington. (Bapt). *f 1832. No early registers known. Not at PRO or Ch Sec.*

BRISTOL, Maudlin St Welsh Chapel. (Bapt). *f 1820. No registers known. Not at PRO. Chapel now closed.*

BRISTOL, The Tabernacle, Penn St. (Calv Meth). *f 1755.* **OR** ZC 1775-1837 (PRO *cat. under Somerset*).

BRISTOL, Broadmead, Welsh Chapel. (Calv Meth). *f 1798.* **OR** ZC 1808-1837 (PRO *cat. under Somerset*), C 1808-1883 (NLW).

BRISTOL, Bridge St (Ind). *f 1671.* **OR** C 1714-1837 (PRO *cat. under Somerset*).

BRISTOL, Brunswick Chapel. (Ind). *f 1834.* **OR** ZC 1834-1856, B 1837-1856 (PRO *cat. under Somerset*).

BRISTOL, Bishopsworth. (Ind). − *see Somerset.*

BRISTOL, Brislington. (Ind). − *see Somerset.*

BRISTOL, Castle Green Meeting. *Now Green Bank Rd, Easton.* (Ind). *f 1670.* **OR** ZC 1784-1837 (PRO *cat. under Somerset*).

BRISTOL, Hope Chapel. (Ind). *f 1784. Not at PRO. No information.*

BRISTOL, Lower Castle St. (Ind). *f 1822. Not at PRO. No information.*

BRISTOL, Zion, Bedminster Bridge. (Ind). *– see Somerset.*

BRISTOL, Trenchard St. (Lady Hunt's C.). *f 1773.* OR ZC 1820-1837, B 1830-1837 (PRO *cat. under Somerset*). Cop B 1830-1837 (BAO).

BRISTOL, Upper Maudlin St. (Moravian). *f 1755.* OR ZCB 1755-1837 (PRO *cat. under Somerset*).

BRISTOL, Lewins Mead. (Pres). *f 1718.* OR C 1718-1840, B 1768-1837 (PRO *cat. under Somerset*).

BRISTOL Ebenezer Ch, King St. (Wes). *f 1745.* OR ZC 1796-1837 (PRO *cat. under Somerset*). *(Probably a Circuit register of the* **Bristol North Circuit.**)

BRISTOL, Langton St. (Wes). *Circuit Church for* **Bristol South Circuit.** *No regs known, but see below.*

BRISTOL, Old Market St, St Philip's Chapel. (Wes). *f 1816.* OR ZC 1817-1837, B 1818-1837 (PRO *cat. under Somerset*). *Possibly a Circuit register for the* **Bristol South Circuit.**

BRISTOL, Portland St Chapel. (Wes). *– See Westbury-on-Trym.*

BRISTOL, Redfield. (Wes). *f 1815.* OR ZC 1820-1837 (PRO *cat. under Redfield*).

BRISTOL, PRIM METH CIRCUIT. *Not at PRO. No information.*

BRISTOL, Newfoundland St. (Gideon Chapel). *f 1822.* (Ind). OR ZC 1822-1837 (PRO *cat. under Somerset*).

BRISTOL, Gt George St. (Bethesda Chapel). *f 1832.* OR ZC 1832-7 (PRO *in register of above*).

BRISTOL. (Jewish Synagogue). *f 1753. Present congregation has no historical continuity with earlier one. No registers known.*

BRISTOL, Bedminster. *– see Somerset.*

BRISTOL, Bishopsworth. *– see Somerset.*

BRISTOL, Brislington. *– see Somerset.*

BROAD RISSINGTON. *– see Rissington, Great.*

BROADWELL. OR CMB 1539-1812 *(gaps CMB 1642-59, 1673-1696, M 1753 and 1754)* (GRO). *M 1605-1812 in RMI.* BT 1605 + (G). Cop M 1605-1812 (Phil 14).

BROCKTHROP. *– see Brookthorpe.*

BROCKWORTH. OR CB 1559-1780, M 1559-1811, CMB 1813 + (Inc). BT 1600 + (G).

BROMSBERROW. OR CMB 1558 + (Inc). BT *many transcripts but in poor condition. Cannot be used until repaired.* Cop CMB 1558-1812 Ms,(SG), M 1558-1837 (Phil 17). Parish Register of all inhabitants circa 1880 (Inc). *M 1558-1837 in RMI.*

BROOKTHORPE or BROCKTHROP. **OR** CMB 1730 $^+$ *(gap M 1752-6)* (Inc).
   BT 1569 $^+$ (G). **Cop** M (BT) 1617-1756, M (PR) 1756-1812 (Phil 13),
   CMB 1569-1618 Ms (CLG). *M 1612-1811 in RMI.*

BROUGHTON POGIS. – *see Oxfordshire.*

BUCKLAND with LAVERTON. **OR** CMB 1539 $^+$ *(gap M 1754, 1811-12)*, Mar. Lic.
   1839-58 (Inc). **BT** 1599 $^+$ (G). **Cop** M 1539-1808 (Phil 4), CMB 1539-
   1683 (BL), CB 1539-1804, M 1539-1808 Ts I (SG), CB 1551-1709 (SLC).
   M 1539-1812 in RMI.

BULLEY. **OR** CMB 1673 $^+$ *(gap CB 1805, M 1804-12)* (Inc). **BT** 1638 $^+$ (G).
   Cop CMB (PR) 1673-1856, Banns 1815 Mf (SLC).

BURTHORPE. – *see Eastleach Martin.*

CAM. **OR** CMB 1569 $^+$ *(gaps M 1641-48, 1651-54, B 1615-39, 1645-47)* (Inc).
   BT 1599 $^+$ (G). **Cop** M 1569-1812 (Phil 8), M (BT) 1813-1837 Ts
   (Roe 5 – SG and CLG). *M 1569-1812 in RMI. 1813-37 not in RMI but
   in Index to Roe Vol. 5.*

CAM. (Ind). *f 1662. Not at PRO.* **OR** C 1702-1738, 1776 $^+$, B 1878 $^+$
   (Ch Sec).

CAM. (Wes). *f 1826.* – *see* **Dursley Circuit.**

CAMBRIDGE, Bristol Rd. (Bapt. *Now united Bapt and Cong). f 1807. No
   regs known. Not at PRO or Ch Sec. Church closed 1965.*

CAMPDEN, CHIPPING. – *see Chipping Campden.*

CAMSCROSS. *Formed 1837.* **OR** CB 1837 $^+$, M 1838 $^+$ (Inc). *No BT's.*

CERNEY, NORTH. (Gl Dio). **OR** C 1568 $^+$, MB 1574 $^+$ *(gaps CM 1633-1654,
   C 1668-1671, M 1668-1674, 1681-1686, 1696, B 1579-1604, 1631-
   1668)* (Inc). **BT** 1578 $^+$ (G).

CERNEY, SOUTH. **OR** CMB 1538 $^+$ *(gaps CMB 1638-43, CB 1729-30, M 1729-
   1753)* (Inc). **BT** 1578 $^+$ (G). **Cop** CMB (BT) 1578-1608 Ms (CLG).

CERNEY, SOUTH. (Ind). *f 1824. No regs known. Not at PRO or Ch Sec.*

CHACELEY. *Transferred from Worcs 1931.* – *see Worcs.*

CHALFORD, Tabernacle. (Bapt). *f 1740. No pre 1837 regs known. Not at
   PRO or Ch Sec.*

CHALFORD, France Chapel. (Ind). *f 1782.* **OR** ZC 1782-1837, B 1785-1837
   (PRO *cat. under Bisley).*

CHARFIELD. **OR** CMB 1587 $^+$, Mar. Lic. 1802-1853 (9) (GRO). **BT** 1664 $^+$ (G).
   Cop M (BT) 1664-1812 Ts Sep I (Roe 1 – SG and CLG), M (BT) 1813-37
   (Roe 3 – SG and CLG). *M 1664-1837 not in main RMI but in Sep Index
   to Roe Vols. 1-3.*

CHARLTON ABBOTS. **OR** C 1727 $^+$, M 1803 $^+$, B 1742 $^+$ (Inc). **BT** 1660 $^+$ (G).

CHARLTON KINGS. **OR** CMB 1538-1812 *(gaps CB 1755-1759)* (Inc), Mar. Certifs.
   1789, 1827 (2) (GRO). **BT** 1606 $^+$ (G). **Cop** M 1538-1812 (Phil 3).
   M 1538-1812 in RMI.

CHEDWORTH. **OR** CMB 1653 + (*gap M 1690, 1691*) (Inc). **BT** 1617 + (G).
   Cop M 1653-1812 (Phil 2). *M 1653-1812 in RMI.*

CHEDWORTH AND NORTHLEACH. (Ind). (*f Chedworth 1750, Northleach 1778*).
   OR ZC 1799-1836, B 1800-1837 (PRO).

CHELTENHAM, St Mary. **OR** CMB 1558 + (*gap CMB 1654-1675*) (Inc), Mar.
   Lic. 1825-1845 (11) (GRO). **BT** 1604 + (G). **Cop** M 1558-1812 (Phil 7),
   Extracts B 1617-1793 (Misc. Gen. 3 I NS). *M 1558-1812 in RMI.*

CHELTENHAM, Holy Trinity. **OR** 1821 + (Inc). *No BT's.*

CHELTENHAM, St Paul. **OR** 1830 + (Inc). *No BT's.*

CHELTENHAM, St Gregory (RC) *f 1809.* **OR** C 1809-1855 (Inc). *No M or B.*
   Cop C 1809-1855 Ms (Inc).

CHELTENHAM (S of F). **Stoke Orchard Monthly Meeting** (*1668-1755*),
   Gloucester Monthly Meeting (*1755-1854*). *Regs:* Z 1666-1772, M 1665-
   1749, D 1670-1781 (PRO 602).

CHELTENHAM, Portland Chapel House. (Lady Hunt.). *f 1816.* **OR** ZC 1819-
   1837 (PRO).

CHELTENHAM. (Ind). *f 1809.* **OR** ZCB 1810-1837 (PRO).

CHELTENHAM, Tabernacle. (Ind). *f 1836. No regs known. Not at PRO.*
   Chapel no longer exists.

CHELTENHAM, Highbury Chapel. (Ind). *f 1827.* **OR** ZC 1828-1837 (PRO).

CHELTENHAM. (Bapt). *f 1701. No regs known. Not at PRO. Chapel now no*
   longer exists.

CHELTENHAM, Salem, Clarence Parade. (Bapt). *f 1836. No regs known.*
   Not at PRO or Ch Sec.

CHELTENHAM, Bethel. (Bapt). *f 1820. No regs known. Not at PRO.*
   Chapel now no longer exists.

CHELTENHAM CIRCUIT. (Wes). – *see Cheltenham (King St), Cheltenham*
   (*Bethesda*).

CHELTENHAM, King St, Ebenezer Chapel. (Wes). **OR** ZC 1812-1837 (PRO).
   Probably a Circuit register.

CHELTENHAM, Bethesda. (Wes). **Cheltenham Circuit.** *f.c. 1830. Not at*
   PRO. See above entry.

CHELTENHAM. (Prim Meth). **Bristol Circuit.** *f.c. 1830. No regs known.*
   Not at PRO.

CHERRINGTON. **OR** CMB 1568 + (Inc). **BT** 1612 + (G). **Cop** M 1569-1812
   (Phil 12). *M 1569-1812 in RMI.*

CHILDSWICKHAM. **OR** CMB 1560 + (Inc). **BT** 1639 + (G). **Cop** M 1560-1812
   (Phil 4). *M 1560-1812 in RMI.*

CHIPPING CAMPDEN. **OR** CMB 1616 + (Inc). **BT** 1617 + (G). **Cop** M 1616-
   1674 Ms (SOA), M 1717-1837 (Phil Ms). *M 1616-1837 in RMI.*

CHIPPING CAMPDEN, High St. (Bapt). *f 1729.* **OR** C 1729-1766, Z 1785-
   1837 (PRO).

CHIPPING CAMPDEN (S of F). **Stow and Campden Monthly Meeting** (*1668-1790*), **Warwickshire South Monthly Meeting** (*1790 +*). *See Warwickshire* – **Brailes Monthly Meeting.** *No regs known apart from* **Warwickshire South Monthly Meeting** *regs.*

CHIPPING SODBURY. **OR** CB 1661 +, M 1662 + (*gaps CB 1672-87, 1696-1716, 1742-7, M 1665-86, 1688-90, 1692-1714, 1734-47*) (Inc). **BT** 1607 + (G). **Cop** M 1661-1812 (Phil 11), C 1661-1758, Extracts B 1715-1716 Ms (SG), CMB (BT) 1629-1714 Ts I (Roe 4 – SG and CLG), M (BT) 1813-37 Ts (Roe 5 – SG and CLG). *M 1662-1812 in RMI. M 1629-1714 not in RMI but in Index to Roe 4, 1813-1837 in Index to Roe 5.*

CHIPPING SODBURY, Hounds Lane. (Bapt). *f 1656. Not at PRO.*

CHRISTCHURCH (Forest). – *see Dean Forest.*

CHURCHAM. **OR** CMB 1541 + (Inc). **BT** 1600 + (G). **Cop** (PR) CMB 1541-1856 Mf (SLC).

CHURCHDOWN. **OR** CMB 1563 + (*gap 1603-1655*) (Inc). **BT** 1596 + (G).

CHURCH ICCOMB. – *see Iccomb.*

CIRENCESTER, St John the Baptist. **OR** CMB 1560 + (Inc). **BT** 1578 + (G). **Cop** Extracts 1560-1791 (Genealogist NS 16 I), CMB 1560-1700 (GRO), CMB 1560-1637 (CLG).

CIRENCESTER (S of F). **Nailsworth Monthly Meeting. OR** Z 1647-1773, M 1660-1770, B 1659-1775 (PRO 610).

CIRENCESTER, Coxwell St. (Bapt). *f 1639.* **OR** Z 1651-1837, B 1736-1839 (PRO).

CIRENCESTER, Wharf Rd Chapel. (Ind). *f 1830.* **OR** ZC 1828-1836 (PRO).

CIRENCESTER, Gloucester St. (Wes). *f 1808.* **OR** ZC 1811-1837 (PRO).

CLAPTON. – *see Bourton-on-the-Water.*

CLEARWELL, St Peter. **OR** C 1830 +, MB 1856 + (Inc). *No BT's.*

CLEVEDON. (Ind). *f 1826. No regs known. Not at PRO or Ch Sec.*

CLIFFORD CHAMBERS. – *see Warwickshire.* (*M 1538-1812 in RMI*).

CLIFTON. **OR** CM 1538-1844, B 1538-1847 (*gap CMB 1682-1720*), Banns 1767-1951 (CLG). **BT** 1695, 1710, 18, 25-26, 28, 31, 46-49, 51, 56, 59-60, 1773-75, 77-80, 82-84, 86-93, 95, 1859, 61, 62, 65, 68 (B). **Cop** *Extracts in RMI.*

CLIFTON, Hotwell Rd. (Wes). (*Probably* **Bristol South Circuit**). *f 1832.* **OR** ZC 1833-1837 (PRO).

CLIFTON DOWN. (Ind). *f 1662. No regs known. Not at PRO or Ch Sec.*

COALEY. (*commonly spelt* COWLEY). **OR** C 1582-1811, M 1625-1810, B 1569-1811 (Inc). **BT** 1617 + (G). **Cop** M 1625-1812 (Phil 5), CMB 1578-1621 (CLG), M (BT) 1813-1837 Ts (Roe 5 – SG and CLG). *M 1625-1812 in RMI. 1813-1837 not in RMI but in Index to Roe Vol. 5.*

COATES. **OR** CMB 1566 + *(gap M 1792-97)* (Inc). **BT** 1610 + (G).

COBERLEY. (alias CUBBERLEY) (Glo Dio). **OR** CMB 1539 + (Inc). **BT** 1578 +
(G). **Cop** M 1781-1812 (Phil Ms). *M 1780-1812 in RMI.*

CODRINGTON. *– see Wapley.*

CODRINGTON. (Bapt). *f date not known. Not at PRO. No information.*

COLD ASHTON. **OR** CMB 1734 + *(gap B 1789 and 1790)* (Inc).
BT 1606-7, 1609-10, 13, 17-18, 20-25, 28-29, 32, 37-40, 60, 62-64,
1667, 70-71, 74-94, 96-98, 1700-32, 1734-1812 (B), 1813-37 (G).
Cop M (BT) 1813-1837 (ER). *Not in RMI as is stated in Key to
Boyd's Mar. Index. (Error for Cold Aston).*

COLD ASTON. *– see Aston Blank.*

COLEFORD. *Chapelry of Newland until 1872.* **OR** C 1768 + *(gap 1801-3)*,
M 1813 +, B 1784 and 1785 (Inc). **BT** *on Newland returns.*

COLEFORD, Newland St. (Bapt). *f 1799. Not at PRO.* **OR** Z 1786-1837,
D 1850-1863 (Ch Sec).

COLEFORD. (Wes). **Ledbury and Forest of Dean Circuit,** *afterwards* **Forest
of Dean Circuit. OR** C 1838-1854 (PRO). *Probably a Circuit register.
See also Newent.*

COLESBOURNE. **OR** CMB 1632 + *(gaps M 1730-1734, 1753)* (Inc). **BT** 1578 +
(G). **Cop** CMB 1632-1812 (Inc).

COLN ROGERS. **OR** CB 1761 +, M 1755 + (Inc). **BT** 1613 + (G). **Cop** M 1755-
1812 (Phil 12). *M 1755-1812 in RMI.*

COLN ST ALDWYN. **OR** CMB 1650 + *(gap 1728-1774)* (Inc). **BT** 1606 + (G).

COLN ST DENNIS. (ST DENIS or ST DENYS). **OR** C 1561-1755 *(gap 1643-
1664)*, M 1561-1753 *(gaps 1643-1658, 1660-1682, 1754, 1809-12)*,
B 1562-1753 *(gaps 1646-1662, 1664-1676, 1754)*, Mar. Lic. 1813-
1855 (11) (GRO), CB 1756 +, M 1754 + (Inc). **BT** 1570 + (G).

COMPTON ABDALE. **OR** C 1720 +, M 1784 +, B 1722 + *(CMB reg 1784-1812
includes loose copies of C 1720-1812)* (Inc). **BT** 1616 + (G).

COMPTON GREENFIELD. **OR** CMB 1583 + *(gaps CMB 1702-23, M 1805-12)* (Inc).
BT 1693, 1705, 09, 22, 76, 80-84, 87-89, 91, 93, 1796-1812, 1813-
1854 (B). **Cop** *Extracts in RMI.*

COMPTON, LITTLE. *– see Warwickshire.*

CONDICOTE. **OR** CM 1688-1806 *(gap C 1737-1741, M 1737-1751)*, B 1717-1806
(gap 1737-1741) (GRO). **BT** 1612 + (G). **Cop** CMB 1688-1806 Ms (CLG).

CORSE. **OR** CMB 1661 + *(gap CB 1767-1783)* (Inc). **BT** 1578 + (G).
Cop CMB (BT) 1578-1610 Ms (CLG), M (BT) 1662-1837 Ts (ER). *M 1666-
1812 in RMI.*

COUNTERSLIP. (Bapt). *– see Bristol.*

COVER (S of F). **Westbury Monthly Meeting** *disc. by c.1750. No regs
known.*

COW HONEYBOURNE. *Transferred to Worcs. 1931. See Worcs.*

COWLEY, St Mary. **OR** CMB 1676 + (Inc). **BT** 1596 + (G). **Cop** CMB (BT) 1578-1621 Ms (CLG), M 1625-1812 (Phil 5). *Cowley has been sometimes confused with Coaley in records, as the latter was often spelt Cowley.*

COWLEY, St Bartholomew. *– see Coaley.*

CRANHAM. **OR** C 1666-1876, M 1670-1836, B 1666-1812 (GRO), B 1813 + (Inc). **BT** 1616 + (G).

CROMHALL. **OR** CMB 1653 + (Inc). **BT** 1570 + (G). **Cop** M (BT) 1670-1812 Ts Sep I (Roe 1 – SG and CLG), M (BT) 1813-1837 Ts Sep I (Roe 3 – SG and CLG), CMB 1571-1608 Ms (CLG). *M (BT) 1670-1837 not in main RMI but in Sep I to Roe Vols. 1-3.*

CROMHALL. (Ind). *f 1813. Not at PRO. No information.*

CUBBERLEY. *– see Coberley.*

CUTSDEAN *– see Worcs.*

DAGLINGWORTH. **OR** CMB 1561 + (Inc). **BT** 1577 + (G).

DAYLESFORD. *– see Worcs.*

DEAN FOREST, Christchurch. **OR** 1814 + (Inc). *No BT's.*

DEAN FOREST, Holy Trinity. *– see Drybrook.*

DEAN, LITTLE. *– see Littledean.*

DEERHURST. **Peculiar** *of Rector of Deerhurst.* **OR** CMB 1559 + *(gap 1755-1764)* (Inc). **BT** 1578 + (G). **Cop** M (BT) 1672-1837 Ts (ER). *M 1700-1812 in RMI.*

DEERHURST. Moravian Chapel, Apperley. *– see Apperley.*

DIDBROOK. *United with Pinnock-cum-Hyde and Hailes 1738.* **OR** CMB 1558 + *(gap 1761-64)* (Inc). **BT** 1616 + (G). **Cop** CMB 1558-1705 Ms (Inc Toddington).

DIDMARTON. *United with Oldbury-on-the-Hill 1735.* **OR** CMB 1675 +, Mar. Lic. 1792-1804 (6) (Inc). **BT** 1599 + (G). **Cop** M 1675-1812 (Phil 11), M (BT) 1813-1837 Ts (Roe 5 – SG and CLG). *M 1675-1812 in RMI. 1813-37 not in RMI but in Index Roe Vol. 5. See also Oldbury-on-the-Hill.*

DODINGTON. **OR** CMB 1575 + (Inc). **BT** 1578, 1609, 22, 24-25, 28-29, 32, 1636-38, 40, 1661-62, 64, 67, 71-99, 1701-32, 34, 36, 39-41, 43-51, 1762-1804, 1806-12 (B). **Cop** CMB 1578 + (ps) (SG), M (BT) 1661-1837 Ts I ("Roe BT's in Dio of Bristol", BAO and SG), *M (BT) 1661-1837 not in RMI but in Index to "BT's in Dio of Bristol".*

DOOEL. *– see Shipton Moyne.*

DORSINGTON. *Transferred to Warwickshire 1931.* **OR** CMB 1593 + (Inc). **BT** 1599 + (G). **Cop** M 1602-1812 (Phil 3), C 1593- 1641, 1660-1812, M 1602-1640, 1673-1804, B 1571-1641, 1660-1810 (SOA), CMB 1572-1666 (CLG), Extracts CMB 1566-1868 (B'ham Lib). *M 1602-1812 in RMI.*

DOWDESWELL. **Peculiar** *of Rector of Withington.* **OR** CMB 1597 + (*gap M 1751-59*) (*CMB 1575-1597 probably defective*), Mar. Lic. 1774-1804 (6), 1819-1856 (3) (GRO). **BT** 1599 + (G).

DOWN AMPNEY. – *see Ampney, Down.*

DOWNEND. **OR** 1831 + (Inc). *No BT's. See Mangotsfield.*

DOWNEND, Salisbury Rd. (Bapt). *f 1786. Not at PRO. No information.*

DOWNEND. (Parish of Mangotsfield). (Wes). *f 1800.* **OR** ZC 1824-37 (PRO). *Probably a Circuit register.*

DOWN HATHERLEY. **OR** CMB 1563 + (*gaps C 1598, 1738-1739, M 1605-9, 1613-17, 1621-26, 1629-34, 1636-43, 1646-54, 1656-63, 1687-1703, 1737-39, B 1638-39, 1644-45, 1649-53, 1655-1660, 1687-93, 1699-1704, 1738-1739*) (Inc). **BT** 1623 + (G).

DOYNTON. **OR** C 1566 +, M 1568 + (*gap 1678*), B 1567 + (Inc). **BT** 1598, 1602, 05, 08, 12-13, 16-18, 20-26, 28-29, 33, 37-40, 60, 62-63, 1667-68, 72, 1674-1714, 1716-43, 45, 1747-1812 (B), 1814-1837 (G). **Cop** M (BT) 1814-37 Ts I (ER). *Extracts in RMI.*

DRIFFIELD. **OR** C 1561-1810, M 1561-1811 (*gap 1747-1753*), B 1561-1810 (Inc). **BT** 1613 + (G).

DRYBROOK. *Parish formed in 1842 in the Forest of Dean.* **OR** CB 1817 +, M 1845 + (Inc). *No BT's.*

DRYBROOK CIRCUIT. (Bible Christian). *No registers known. Not at PRO or Forest of Dean Methodist Circuit Supt.*

DUMBLETON. **OR** CMB 1738 + (*gap M 1749-1753*) (Inc). **BT** 1602 + (G). **Cop** CMB 1738-1812 (C of A). *M 1738-1812 in Boyd Misc.*

DUNTISBOURNE ABBOTS. **OR** CMB 1683 + (*gap CMB 1715*) (Inc). **BT** 1607 + (G). **Cop** M (BT) 1607-1682, M (PR) 1683-1837 (Phil 12), CMB (BT) 1607-1682 (Inc). *M 1607-1812 in RMI.*

DUNTISBOURNE ROUSE. **OR** CB 1545 +, M 1549 + (*gap 1753 and 1754*) (Inc). **BT** 1570 + (G). **Cop** M 1549-1837 (Phil 17), CMB 1545-1661 Ms (CLG). *M 1549-1837 in RMI.*

DURSLEY. **OR** CMB 1639 + (*gap MB 1655-1663*), Z 1653-8, Mar. Lic. 1843-1880 (28) (GRO). **BT** 1606 + (G). **Cop** M 1639-1812 (Phil 5), M (BT) 1813-1837 Ts (Roe 5 – SG and CLG). *M 1636-1812 in RMI. 1813-1837 not in RMI but in Index to Roe Vol. 5.*

DURSLEY (S of F). **Gloucester Monthly Meeting.** *f 1668, disc. before 1755. No regs known other than Monthly Meeting regs.*

DURSLEY, The Tabernacle. (Ind). *f 1710.* **OR** ZCB 1754-1825 (PRO).

DURSLEY CIRCUIT. (Wes). – *see Dursley, Leonard Stanley, Cam, Eastington Halmore.* **OR** *see Dursley.*

DURSLEY. (Wes). *f 1801.* **OR** ZC 1800-1837, B 1812-1837 (PRO), C 1838-1920 (in Chapel safe). *Probably a Circuit register.*

DYMOCK. **OR** CMB 1538 + , Banns in M reg 1769-1799, Mar. Lic. 19th C
(*several bundles*) (Inc). **BT** 1599 + (G). **Cop** CMB 1538-1790 I
(Ptd B and G.A.S. 1960), CMB 1538-1812 (Inc), CMB 1538-1550 (CLG),
(PR) C 1538-1901, M 1538-1892, B 1538-1901, Banns 1769-1799, 1813-
1856 Mf (SLC). *See also Kempley.*

DYMOCK (RC). *Entries in regs of Little Malvern Court. See Worcs –
Malvern, Little.*

DYRHAM. **OR** CMB 1568 + (Inc), Mar. Lic. 1831-69 (14) (GRO). **BT** Dyrham
and Hinton 1571-78, 1607, 12-13, 16-18, 20, 26, 28-29, 32, 37-40,
1661-65, 67-99, 1701-41, 1743-1812 (B), 1813-37 (G). **Cop** M (BT) 1813-
1837 Ts I (FR). *Extracts in RMI.*

EASTCOMBE, Nr STROUDWATER. (Bapt). *f 1800.* **OR** Z 1797-1824 (PRO).

EASTINGTON, Nr STONEHOUSE. **OR** CMB 1558 + (*gaps M 1659 and 1660*) (Inc).
BT 1578 + (G). **Cop** M 1558-1812 (Phil 13), M (BT) 1813-1837 Ts Sep I
(Roe 5 – SG and CLG). *M 1558-1812 in RMI. 1813-37 not in RMI but
in Index to Roe Vol. 5. See also Alkerton.*

EASTINGTON. (Bapt). – *see Nupend.*

EASTINGTON. (Wes) – *see Alkerton.*

EASTLEACH MARTIN (BURTHORPE or BOUTHROP). **OR** CMB 1538 + (Inc).
BT 1578 + (G). **Cop** CMB 1538-1604 (CLG).

EASTLEACH TURVILLE. **OR** CMB 1654 + (*gaps CB 1749-1778, M 1749-1759*)
(Inc). **BT** 1578 + (G). **Cop** CMB 1578-1640 (CLG).

EBLEY. (Lady Hunt). – *see Randwick.*

EBRINGTON. **OR** CB 1568 + (*gap 1802-1807*), M 1653 + (*gap 1676-1684*) (Inc).
BT 1612 + (G). **Cop** M 1653-1812 (Phil 6), Extracts B 1570-1633 (Ptd),
CB 1568-1812, M 1653-1675, 1684-1784 (SOA).

EDGEWORTH. **OR** C 1554 + (*gap 1736-49, 1765-68*), M 1555 + (*gaps 1700-7,
1745-9*), B 1557 + (*gaps 1743-9*) (Inc). **BT** 1579 + (G). **Cop** M 1554-
1811 (Phil 12).

ELBERTON. **OR** CMB 1763 + (Inc). **BT** 1685, 97, 99, 1710, 18, 1800, 02-09,
1812-51, 1869 (B). **Cop** M (PR and BT) 1683-1837 Ts I (ER).

ELKSTONE. **OR** CMB 1592 + (Inc). **BT** 1578 + (G). **Cop** M 1592-1812 (Phil 6).

ELMORE. **OR** CMB 1560 + (Inc). **BT** 1600 + (G). **Cop** M (BT) 1660-1812
Ts Sep I (Roe 1 – SG and CLG), M (BT) 1813-1837 (Roe 3 – SG and
CLG), CMB 1560-1601 Ms (CLG). *M 1660-1837 not in main RMI but in
Sep Index to Roe 1-3.*

ELMSTONE – HARDWICKE. *With Uckington.* **OR** CMB 1564 + (*gap M 1648-1655*)
(Inc). **BT** 1608 + (G). **Cop** M (BT) 1688-1837 Ts (ER).

ENGLISH BISKNOR. **OR** 1561 + (Inc). **BT** 1586 + (G).

EVENLODE. – *see Worcs.*

EYFORD. – *see Slaughter, Upper.*

FAIRFORD. **OR** C 1617 +, M 1619 +, B 1617 + (Inc). **BT** 1612 + (G).
   Cop M 1619-1837 (Phil 16).

FAIRFORD, The Crofts Chapel. (Ind. *Now united Bapt and Cong*). *f 1744.*
   OR ZC 1787-1837, B 1787-1835 (PRO).

FALFIELD. *Formed from Thornbury 1863.* **OR** C 1814 +, M 1864 +,
   B 1860 + (Inc). **BT** *on Thornbury returns.*

FALFIELD. (Ind). *f 1813. Not at PRO. No information.*

FARMCOTE. *Chapelry of Guiting Power. See Guiting Power.*

FARMINGTON. *Earlier name Thormerton.* **OR** CMB 1613 + (Inc). **BT** 1617 + (G
   Cop CMB 1613-1936 Ms (Inc).

FILKINS. (Bapt). – *see Lechlade.*

FILTON. **OR** CMB 1654 + (*gap M 1755 and 1756*) (Inc). **BT** 1681-1812 (*gaps*
   1687-1707, 1709-1733, 1750-1768, 1778-1788) (B). **Cop** M 1653-1812
   (Phil 13).

FLAXLEY. **OR** C 1562 + (*gaps 1642-44, 1659, 1686-88, 1714-18*), M 1564 +
   (*gaps 1638-1659, 1670, 1672-1680, 1685-87, 1703-5*), B 1566 + (*gaps*
   1646-1657, 1686) (Inc). **BT** 1586 + (G). **Cop** C 1562-1657, M 1562-
   1637, B 1562-1645 (CLG), (PR) 1564-1860 Mf (SLC).

FOREST GREEN. (Ind). – *see Nailsworth.*

FOREST GREEN, UPPER. (Ind). – *see Avening.*

FORTHAMPTON. **OR** CB 1678 +, M 1681 + (Inc). **BT** 1578 + (G). **Cop** M 1681-
   1812 (Phil 1), CMB 1678-1812 (SG C I), CMB (BT) 1578-1606 (CLG),
   CB 1678-1812 (Inc).

FRAMPTON COTTERELL. **OR** CMB 1561 + (*gaps CMB 1640-1656, 1750-1758*)
   (Inc). **BT** 1608, 12, 20-25, 28-30, 36-38, 61, 69, 79-81, 83-85,
   1687-89, 91-94, 1697-1700, 1702-05, 1707-56, 1758-1812 (B), 1813-
   1837 (G). **Cop** M (BT) 1813-37 Ts I (ER). *Extracts in RMI.*

FRAMPTON COTTERELL, Zion Chapel. (Ind). *f 1796.* **OR** ZC 1801-1837 (PRO).

FRAMPTON MANSELL. (Bapt). *f date not known. Not at PRO. No information.*

FRAMPTON-ON-SEVERN. **OR** CMB 1625 + (Inc). **BT** 1606 + (G). **Cop** M 1625-
   1812 (Phil 7), M (BT) 1813-1837 Ts (Roe 5 – SG and CLG). *M 1625-
   1812 in RMI. M 1813-37 not in RMI but in Index to Roe 5.*

FRAMPTON-ON-SEVERN. (Ind). *f 1776.* **OR** C 1777-1837, B 1778-1799 (PRO).

FRENCHAY. *Parish formed from Winterbourne 1836.* **OR** CMB 1834 + (Inc).
   BT 1834-1853 (B).

FRENCHAY. (Pres). *f 1806.* **OR** ZC 1814-1837, B 1806-1837 (PRO *cat. as*
   Winterbourne, Frenchay Chapel).

FRENCHAY MONTHLY MEETING (S of F). *f 1668*. Constituent Meetings: *(all to beyond 1837 unless otherwise stated) Frenchay, Olveston, Thornbury, Sodbury, Kingsweston)(renamed Lawrence Weston), Marshfield (disc. before 1785), Pucklechurch (disc. before 1785), Badminton (disc. before 1785).* Monthly Meeting Regs: OR ZMB 1660-1712 (PRO 585), Z 1776-1837 (594, 595), M 1777-1794 (596), 1797-1834 (597), B 1776-1837 (598-600). Post 1837 regs at Friends' Meeting House, Bristol. *Regs are also known for all Constituent Meetings except Marshfield and Pucklechurch (see under each meeting). Since most of these terminate c. 1775 it is probable no Monthly Meeting regs were kept between 1712 and 1776.*

FRENCHAY. (S of F). Frenchay Monthly Meeting. OR ZMB 1655-1775 (PRO 586).

FRETHERNE. OR C 1631-1812, M 1635-1811, B 1631-1809 (*gaps CMB 1655-1658, M 1751-1753, 1804*). *In C Reg 1721-1796 from 1783 names of childs' maternal grandparents are given* (GRO). BT 1617 + (G). Cop M (BT) 1671-1812 Ts Sep I (Roe 1 — SG and CLG), M (BT) 1813-1837 Ts (Roe 3 — SG and CLG). *M 1671-1837 not in RMI but in Sep Index to Roe 1-3.*

FROCESTER. OR CM 1559 + (*gap 1566-1570 and small gaps between 1640 and 1670*), B 1570 + (*gaps C 1673-81, 1688-89, M 1671-1681, 1754, B 1672-1681*) (Inc). *Some entries for 1673 in Slimbridge Reg.* BT 1602 + (G). Cop M 1559-1837 (Phil 14), CMB 1559-1603 (CLG), CMB 1559-1799 (Glos N and Q 5), Index to B 1570-1671 (Inc), M (BT) 1813-37 Ts (Roe 5 — SG and CLG). *M 1559-1837 in RMI. M (BT) 1813-37 also in Index to Roe Vol. 5.*

GLOUCESTER CATHEDRAL. OR CMB 1661 + (Dean and Chapter). *1661-1666 a few entries only.* BT 1813 + (*none earlier*).

GLOUCESTER, All Saints. *Converted by ordinance of Parliament into part of the Tolsey about 1648. No registers known.* BT 1597, 1604, 1607, 1611, 1616, 1620-5, 1629, 1632, 1636-40 (G).

GLOUCESTER, St Aldate. OR CMB 1572 + (*gap CMB 1646-1755*) (*regs at St John's Church, Gloucester*) (Inc). BT 1619 + (G).

GLOUCESTER. St Catherine. OR CMB 1687 + (*gap M 1813-1867*) (Inc. St Catherine's, Wotton). BT 1571 + (G).

GLOUCESTER, Holy Trinity. *Church pulled down 1798. Parish united with St Nicholas 1648-1660 but now with St Mary de Lode.* OR CB 1557-1758, M 1557-1722 (*gap 1650-1689 — only few entries 1690-1722*) (Inc St Mary de Lode). BT 1613 + (G) — *see also St Mary de Lode.*

GLOUCESTER, St John the Baptist. OR CM 1559 +, B 1558 + (*gaps C 1693-1698, MB 1643-1645 (B 1647) 1660-1672), Z 1653-1659* (Inc). *ZCMB for Commonwealth period scattered between 4 registers.* BT 1570 + (G).

GLOUCESTER, St Mary de Crypt. *United with St Owen.* OR CMB 1653 ⁺
(gaps CB 1692 and 1693, M 1692-1694) (Inc), Mar. Lic. 1857-1874 (
(CLG). BT 1570 ⁺ (G).

GLOUCESTER St Mary de Grace. *United with St Michael 1648 converted
into a magazine for ammunition and demolished 1652. No regs known.*
BT 1613, 1619, 1620, 1632 ⁺ and possibly one or two others at
present unidentified (G).

GLOUCESTER, St Mary de Lode (Wotton). OR CB 1675 ⁺ *(gaps 1694, 1713-
1715),* M 1675 ⁺ *(gaps 1694, 1711-15)* (Inc), Z 1656-7, C 1661 *(1
entry),* M 1656-9 (Chapter Lib. Glos Cath). BT 1606 ⁺ (G).

GLOUCESTER, St Mary Magdalene and St Margaret. OR CB 1790-1812 (CLG).
BT 1813 ⁺ (G).

GLOUCESTER, St Michael. *(With St Mary de Grace since 1648).* OR C 1563
M 1553 ⁺, B 1554 ⁺ (Inc St John Baptist). BT 1602 ⁺ (G).

GLOUCESTER, St Nicholas. OR CMB 1558 ⁺ (Inc). BT 1616 ⁺ (G).
Cop CB 1707-1754 (CLG), M (PR and BT) 1558-1837 Ts I (SG and CLG).

GLOUCESTER, St Owen. *(Taken down 1643 and united with St Mary de Cryp
No regs known.* BT 1610, 1612, 1616, 1617, 1620-8, 1630, 1632 and
1638 (G).

GLOUCESTER, St Peter, Northgate St (RC). *f 1789.* OR C 1855 ⁺,
MD 1856 ⁺ (Inc).

GLOUCESTER MONTHLY MEETING (S of F). *1668-1854.* **Constituent Meetings:**
*Gloucester (1668-1854), Dursley (1668- before 1755), Standcombe
(1668- before 1755), Cheltenham (1755-1854), Tewkesbury (1755-1854)*
OR Z 1652-1771, 1776-1837, M 1666-1724, 1781-1792, 1798-1836,
B 1658-1771, 1797-1837 (PRO 601, 604-609). *Reg No 603 was the
Monthly Meeting register of* **Stoke Orchard Monthly Meeting** *but
after this was discontinued in 1755 the register would appear to
have been used for* **Gloucester Monthly Meeting.** *No registers are
known for the Constituent Meetings.*

GLOUCESTER, Greyfriars, Southgate St. (S of F). **Gloucester Monthly
Meeting** *q.v.*

GLOUCESTER, Southgate St. (Ind). *f 1720.* OR C 1748-1837, B 1786-
1837 (PRO).

GLOUCESTER, St Mary's Square. (Lady Hunt). OR ZC 1790-1837 (PRO).

GLOUCESTER, Barton St Chapel. (Unit and Pres). *f 1699.* OR C 1740-
1836, B 1785-1836 (PRO). **Cop** CMB 1740-1836 (CLG).

GLOUCESTER CIRCUIT. (Wes). – *see Gloucester (Northgate St), Tewkesbur*

GLOUCESTER, Northgate St. (Wes). *f 1770.* OR ZC 1800-1837, B 1830-1837
(PRO). *Probably a Circuit register. See also Tewkesbury.*

GLOUCESTER, Parkers Row, Brunswick Rd. (Bapt). *f 1813. No early regs
known. Not at PRO or Ch Sec.* OR M 1914 ⁺ (Ch Sec).

GLOUCESTER (Jewish). *No Synagogue, but Burial Ground off Organ's Passage, Eastgate St. No regs but copy of some M.I's 1785-1886 (CLG). Names on M.I's 1800-1870 published in C. Roth's "Rise of Provincial Jewry".*

GREAT BADMINTON. – *see Badminton, Great.*

GREAT BARRINGTON. – *see Barrington, Great.*

GREAT RISSINGTON. – *see Rissington, Great.*

GREAT WITCOMBE. – *see Witcombe, Great.*

GREAT WASHBOURNE. – *see Washbourne, Great.*

GRETTON. *Chapelry in Winchcombe. See Winchcombe.*

GUITING POWER (or LOWER GUITING). *Including Chapelry of Farmcote.*
OR CMB 1560 + (Inc). **BT** 1606 + (G). **Cop** M 1560-1812 (Phil 4), CMB 1560-1913 (CLG). *M 1560-1812 in RMI.*

GUITING, TEMPLE (or UPPER GUITING). **OR** 1647 + (Inc). **BT** 1612 + (G). **Cop** M 1676-1771 (Phil 4), CMB 1679-1774 Ms (CLG). *M 1676-1771 in RMI.*

HAILES. – *see Didbrook.*

HALMORE. (Wes). *f 1828.* – *see Dursley.*

HAMPNETT. *United with Stowell 1660.* **OR** CMB 1591 + (*gap M 1680-1684, B 1680, 1681*) (Inc). *Stowell entries from 1660.* **BT** 1575 + (G). **Cop** M 1737-1754 Ptd (Glos N and Q II).

HANHAM. *Chapelry of Bitton until 1842.* **OR** CB 1584-1812, M 1584-1741 (*gaps M 1731, B 1764*) (Inc Bitton), CMB 1813 + (Inc). **BT** *see Bitton.* **Cop** CMB 1584-1681 I (PRS 63). *M 1584-1657 in RMI. See also Bitton and Oldland.*

HANHAM, High St. (Bapt). *f 1714. No regs known. Not at PRO or Ch Sec. Burial ground opened in 1721 closed c. 1935. Some pre 1837 M.I's*

HANHAM. (Ind). *f 1829. Not at PRO. No information.*

HARDWICKE. **OR** CMB 1566 + (Inc). *Some entries in Standish regs.* **BT** 1596 + (CLG). **Cop** M 1566-1812 (Phil 12). *M 1566-1812 in RMI.*

HARESCOMBE. *In parish of Pitchcombe until 1741.* **OR** CMB 1813 + (Inc). *Registers CMB 1741-1812 now missing. See B and G A.S. Trans Vol X pp 87-91.* **BT** 1570 + (G). **Cop** M 1744-1811 (Phil 10 – copy of register now missing). *M 1744-1812 in RMI.*

HARESFIELD. **OR** C 1558 +, M 1565 +, B 1559 + (*gaps M 1620-1628, B 1627 and 1628, CMB 1643-1653, M 1680-1683, B 1736*) (Inc). **BT** 1569 + (G).

HARNHILL, St Michael. **OR** CMB 1730 + (*gap M 1754*) (Inc). **BT** 1630 + (G).

HARTPURY. *Anciently Merewent.* **OR** CMB 1571 + (*gaps CMB 1595-6, M 1744-1753*) Z 1790-1812 (Inc). **BT** 1605 + (G). **Cop** M (BT) 1662-1837 Ts (ER). *M 1662-1812 in RMI.*

HASELTON. – *see Hazleton.*

HASFIELD. **OR** CMB 1559 $^+$ (*gaps C 1621-5, 1642-6, 1648-50,
M 1616-25, 1640-52, B 1621-5, 1636-1652*) (GRO). **BT** 1599 $^+$ (G).
Cop Mf of PR (GRO) M (BT) 1662-1837 Ts (ER). *M 1662-1812 in RMI.*

HATHERLEY, DOWN. – *see Down Hatherley.*

HATHERLEY, UP. – *see Badgeworth.*

HATHEROP. **OR** CMB 1670 $^+$ (Inc). **BT** 1578 $^+$ (G). **Cop** M (BT) 1578-1640
(10 entries) (PR) 1673-1837 (Phil 17), CMB (BT) 1578-1605 (Inc).
M 1673-1837 in RMI.

HAWKESBURY. **OR** CMB 1603 $^+$ (Inc). *Registers include Chapelry of
Tresham until 19th C.* **BT** 1578 $^+$ (G). **Cop** M 1603-1812 (Phil 5),
M (BT) 1813-37 Ts (Roe 5 – SG and CLG). *M 1603-1812 in RMI.
M 1813-37 not in RMI but in Sep Index to Roe Vol. 5.*

HAWKESBURY, Hillsley St (Bapt). *f 1730.* **OR** Z 1785-1837, B 1767-1837
(PRO).

HAWLING, St Edward. **OR** CMB 1677 $^+$ (*gap M 1754*) (Inc). **BT** 1605 $^+$ (G).

HAZLETON. **OR** CB 1597 $^+$, M 1599-1809 (*gap 1745-1753*) (Inc).
B reg 1599-1744 includes a few M. **BT** 1606 $^+$ (G). *See also Yanworth.*

HEMSTED. **OR** CMB 1558 $^+$ (*gap CMB 1662-1708, M 1753-1755*) (Inc).
BT 1603 $^+$ (G).

HENBURY. *Formerly included Chapelries of Redwick and Northwick.*
OR C 1582 $^+$, MB 1590 $^+$ (*gaps C 1651, 52, 1668, MB 1646-1652,
M 1712-1725, B 1668-1677*) (Inc). **BT** 1669-71, 73, 74-79, 81-83,
1685-95, 97-1703, 1705-13, 15-20, 22-25, 27-33, 35-37, 39-40, 42-46,
1748-49, 51-53, 55-56, 57-86, 1788-1859, 1861, 67, 69-1901, 02, 03,
1904, 05-07 (B). *Copy of 1675 with Mangotsfield return.* **Cop** M 1544-
1812 (Phil 16). *M 1544-1812 in RMI. See also Redwick and Aust.*

HEWELSFIELD. **OR** CB 1664-1812, M 1664-1752 (GRO), CB 1813 $^+$, M 1754 $^+$
(Inc). **BT** 1586 $^+$ (G).

HIGHNAM. *Chapelry of Lassington. In Lassington regs. Sep entries
B 1709-1724 in Lassington B reg. See Lassington.*

HILL. **OR** CMB 1653 $^+$ (*gaps C 1743-1756, M 1743-1764, B 1743-1793*).
BT 1571 $^+$ (G). **Cop** M 1653-1812 (Phil 10), M (BT) 1813-37 Ts (Roe 5
SG and CLG). *M 1653-1812 in RMI. M 1813-37 not in RMI but in
Sep Index to Roe Vol. 5.*

HILLESLEY (WOTTON). (Bapt). *f 1730. Not at PRO.* List of Members
1768-1836 (Ch. Sec).

HINTON. – *see Dyrham.*

HINTON ON THE GREEN. *Now in Worcs. See Worcs. (M 1735-1812 in RMI)*

HORFIELD. **OR** CMB 1543 $^+$ (*gap M 1686-1728, 1755*) (Inc). **BT** 1674,
1682-88, 92-93, 95-96, 98, 1700, 1702-03, 09-10, 35, 58, 74-75,
1777-83, 86-91, 98, 1800-26, 27, 28-32, 1839-1853 (B).

HORSLEY. **OR** C 1590 +, M 1591 +, B 1587 + (*gaps C 1675-86, 1773, 1774, M 1641-53, 1670-94, B 1593-1608, 1627-36, 1641-53, 1669-94, 1700-1703, 1773 and 1774*), Mar. Lic. 1833 (Inc). **BT** 1598 + (G).
Cop M 1591-1812 (Phil 12), M (BT) 1813-37 Ts (Roe 5 – SG and CLG), (PR) C 1587-1669, 1680-1772, 1775-1837, M 1587-1881, B 1587-1837 Mf (SLC). *M 1591-1812 in RMI. M 1813-37 not in RMI but in Sep Index to Roe Vol. 5. See also Nailsworth.*

HORSLEY, Shortwood Meeting House. – *see Nailsworth, Shortwood Meeting House.*

HORTON, **OR** CMB 1567 + (*gaps CB 1747, M 1625-59*) (Inc). **BT** 1600 + (G).
Cop M 1567-1812 (Phil 13), M (BT) 1813-37 Ts (Roe 5 – SG and CLG). *M 1567-1812 in RMI. M 1813-37 not in RMI but in Sep Index to Roe Vol. 5.*

HUNTLEY. **OR** CMB 1679 + (*gap M 1806-13*). *Extracts from destroyed regs CMB 1661-9* (Inc). **BT** 1583 + (G). **Cop** M 1583-1837 (Phil 16). *M 1583-1837 in RMI.*

ICCOMB (ICOMBE or CHURCH ICCOMB). **OR** C 1545 +, M 1563 +, B 1602 + (*gap 1727-1730*) (Inc). **BT** 1613 + (WRO). **Cop** M 1563-1812 (Phil 13), CMB (BT) 1613-1700 Mf (SLC). *M 1563-1812 in RMI.*

ILMINGTON. – *see Warwickshire.*

IRON ACTON. **OR** CMB 1570 + (Inc). **BT** 1602, 07-08, 12, 17-18, 20-21, 1624-25, 29-30, 32, 37-41, 1660-63, 65, 68-72, 1674-1736, 38-43, 1745-1812 (B). **Cop** C 1570-1699, M 1570-1687 ps (SG), M (BT) 1660-1837 Ts I (Roe BT's in Dio of Bristol BAO and SG), M (PR and BT) 1660-1837 Ts (CLG sep volume). *M 1660-1837 not in RMI but in Index to Roe's "BT's in Dio of Bristol".*

KEMBLE – *see Wilts. (M 1679-1812 in RMI).*

KEMERTON. – *see Worcs. (M 1575-1812 in RMI).*

KEMPLEY. *Previously with Dymock.* **OR** C 1663 +, M 1666 +, B 1637 + (*gaps 1644-69, 1751 and 1752*) (*entries before 1677 fragments of an earlier register bound in*). **BT** 1583 + (G). **Cop** C 1661-1840, M 1666-1850, B 1637-1643, 1677-1750, 1753-1903 Ts (SG), (PR) C 1677-1857, M 1677-1856, B 1677-1861 Mf (SLC). *See also Dymock.*

KEMPSFORD (KEMSFORD). **OR** CM 1573 +, B 1575 + (*gaps C 1574-97, 1605-1616, 1625-28, 1659-85, M 1573, 1574-1652, 1658-1686, B 1658-59, 1661-71, 1680-85*) (Inc). **BT** 1578 + (G). **Cop** CMB 1653-1700 (Ptd "Regs of Kempsford" F.A. Crisp 1887. *No copy SG*). *M 1653-1700 in RMI.*

KEMPSFORD. (Bapt). *f date not known. Not at PRO. No information.*

KINGSCOTE. **OR** C 1651 +, MB 1652 + *(gaps C 1784-1800, M 1754-56, 1783-1800, B 1780-1800)*, Mar. Lic. 1800-1812 (Inc). **BT** 1578 + (G).
Cop M 1652-1812 (Phil 8), M (BT) 1813-37 Ts (Roe 5 – SG and CLG). *M 1652-1812 in RMI. M 1813-37 not in RMI but in Sep Index to Roe Vol. 5.*

KINGS STANLEY. **OR** CMB 1573 +, Mar. Lic. 1832-1889 (Inc). **BT** 1578 + (G).
Cop M 1573-1812 (Phil 1), CMB 1573-1661 Ms (CLG). *M 1573-1812 in RMI.*

KINGS STANLEY, Middle Yard. (Bapt). *f 1640. Not at PRO. No information.*

KINGSWESTON. (S of F). *Renamed Lawrence Weston.* **Frenchay Monthly Meeting. OR** ZMB 1642-1802 (PRO 587).

KINGSWOOD *(near Wotton under Edge).* **OR** CMB 1598 + *(gap B 1765-1775),* Mar. Alleg. 1822-1828 (Inc). **BT** 1578 + (G). **Cop** M 1598-1812 (Phil 9), M (BT) 1813-37 Ts (Roe 5 – SG and CLG). *M 1598-1812 in RMI. M 1813-37 not in RMI but in Sep Index to Roe Vol. 5.*

KINGSWOOD *(near Wotton under Edge).* (Ind). *f 1662.* **OR** *Not at PRO,* Z 1806 +, C 1807 +, M 1843 +, B 1842 + (Ch Sec).

KINGSWOOD *(near Bristol). Chapel to Bitton. Formed from Bitton 1821.* **OR** C 1823 +, MB 1822 + (Inc). **BT** 1822-1837 (G) *previously on Bitton returns.* **Cop** M (BT) 1822-1837 Ts I (ER). *See also Bitton.*

KINGSWOOD *(near Bristol),* WHITFIELD'S TABERNACLE. (Ind). *f 1668.*
OR ZC 1785-1837 (PRO).

KINGSWOOD *(near Bristol).* (Moravian). *f 1755.* **OR** C 1806-1840, B 1757-1839 (PRO).

KINGSWOOD *(near Bristol).* (Wes). *f 1748.* **OR** ZC 1799-1837. (PRO *cat. as Kingswood School). Probably a Circuit register for the Kingswood Circuit.*

LASBOROUGH. *United with Weston Birt 1868.* **OR** CMB 1827 + (Inc Weston Birt). *No BT's.*

LASSINGTON with HIGHNAM. **OR** C 1655 + *(gaps 1656, 1657),* M 1663-1810 *(gap 1748-54),* B 1662 + (Inc). *Separate entries for Highnam B 1709-1724.* **BT** 1570 + (G). **Cop** CMB 1655-1943 Ms (Inc), (PR) C 1655-1856, M 1655-1883, B 1655-1867 Mf (SLC).

LAWRENCE WESTON (S of F). – *see Kingsweston.*

LEA THE. *Glos Dio but in Herefordshire. See Herefordshire. Not to be confused with The Leigh.*

LECHLADE. **OR** CB 1686 +, Z 1697-1706, M 1738 + *(gaps C 1691-94, B 1687-1694, CB 1707-36, M 1753). C 1686-1757 defective.* (Inc).
BT 1612 + (G).

LECHLADE, Sherbourne St. (Bapt). *f 1819.* **OR** *Not at PRO.* C 1830 + *(including 7 at Filkins in 1835),* D 1832 + *(in minute book),* M 1933 + (Ch Sec).

LECKHAMPTON. OR CB 1709 +, M 1718 + (Inc), Mar. Lic. 19th C (1 Bundle). BT 1601 + (G). Cop CMB 1682-1812 Ms (Inc), Extracts (BT) 1601-1706 (Inc).

LEIGH or LYE, THE. OR C 1569 +, MB 1560 + (gaps C 1639-59, 1665-1677, MB 1640-59, 1664-94, M 1808) (Inc). BT 1599 + (G). Cop C 1569-1732, M 1560-1837, B 1560-1732 (Phil Ms), CB 1569-1836, M 1560-1837 (CLG and Cheltenham Lib), M (BT) 1660-1837 Ts (ER). M 1560-1837 in RMI. Not to be confused with The Lea, which is in Glos Dio but in Herefordshire. See Herefordshire.

LEIGHTERTON. – see Boxwell.

LEMINGTON, LOWER or LEMINGTON PARVA. OR CM 1685 +, M 1701 + (gap M M 1754-1756) (Inc). BT 1571 + (G). Cop M 1701-1812 (Phil 4), CB (BT) 1576-1696, (PR) C 1685-1812, M 1701-1812, B 1685-1810 (SOA), M 1685-1700 (C of A). M (BT) 1576-1696 (PR) 1701-1812 in RMI.

LEMINGTON PARVA. – see Lemington, Lower.

LEONARD STANLEY (or STANLEY ST LEONARDS). OR C 1575 +, MB 1570 + (gap M 1754) (Inc). BT 1578 + (G). Cop M 1570-1812 (Phil 2), C 1575-1600, 1614-1689, B 1571-1812 (Phil Ms). M 1570-1812 in RMI.

LEONARD STANLEY. (Wes). f 1808. Dursley Circuit. OR C 1839-1900 (Minister Dursley). See also Dursley.

LITTLE BARRINGTON. – see Barrington, Little.

LITTLE COMPTON. – see Compton, Little.

LITTLE RISSINGTON. – see Rissington, Little.

LITTLE SODBURY. – see Sodbury, Little.

LITTLE WASHBOURNE. – see Washbourne, Little.

LITTLEDEAN. OR CMB 1684-1812 (Inc). BT 1617 + (G). Cop Mf (GRO) M (BT) 1677-1837 Ts (ER).

LITTLEDEAN. (Ind). f 1797. OR C 1803-1837, B 1821-1837 (PRO).

LITTLETON-ON-SEVERN. OR CMB 1701 + (Inc). BT 1687, 90, 92, 96, 98, 1700, 02-03, 05, 10, 42, 48, 73, 75-76, 82-83, 87-89, 92-1836, 1840-57, 62-66 (B). Cop M (PR and BT) 1684-1837 Ts I (ER). M 1688-1812 in RMI.

LITTLETON WEST. – see Tormarton.

LITTLEWORTH. (Parish of Minchinhampton). (Wes). Stroud Circuit. f 1720. OR ZC 1814-1837 (PRO).

LONG ASHTON. – see Ashton, Long.

LONGBOROUGH. OR CB 1676 +, M 1680 + (gaps M 1753, B 1801, 1802), regs include entries for Sezincote, (Inc). BT 1612 + (G).

LONGHOPE. OR CB 1742 +, M 1745 + (gap M 1753) (Inc). BT 1583 + (G).

LONGHOPE, Zion. (Bapt). f 1810. Not at PRO. No information.

LONG NEWNTON. – see Newnton, Long.

LONGNEY. **OR** CMB 1660 + (Inc). **BT** 1610 + (G). **Cop** M (BT)-1660-1812
Ts (Roe 1 – SG and CLG), M (BT) 1813-1837 Ts Sep I (Roe 3 – SG and
CLG). *M 1660-1837 not in RMI but in Sep Index to Roe 1-3.*

LOWER GUITING. – *see Guiting, Power.*

LOWER LEMINGTON. – *see Lemington, Lower.*

LOWER SLAUGHTER. – *see Slaughter, Lower.*

LOWER SWELL. – *see Swell, Nether.*

LYDBROOK. (Wes). **Ledbury and Forest of Dean Circuit.** *No regs known.
Not at PRO or Forest of Dean Circuit Supt. See Ledbury (Hereford),
Coleford and Newent.*

LYDNEY. **OR** CMB 1678 + (Inc). **BT** 1661 + (G). **Cop** CMB 1678-1812 Ms (CLG)

LYPIATT. – *see Bisley.*

MAISEMORE. **OR** C 1600 +, M 1558 +, B 1538 + *(gaps C 1655-1675, M 1592-
1679)* (Inc). **BT** 1604 + (G). **Cop** CMB 1538-1812 (CLG), M 1557-1812
(Phil 14), C 1600-1663, M 1558-1590, B 1538-1599 (Guildhall Lib.
London), C 1600-1663, M 1556-1591, B 1538-1599 (Glos N and Q 4).
M 1537-1812 in RMI.

MAISEYHAMPTON. – *see Meysey Hampton.*

MANGOTSFIELD. **OR** CMB 1579 + (Inc). **BT** 1670-71, 74-75, 84, 87, 1708,
1722, 35, 39-40, 48-51, 56, 59, 62, 75, 1777-1802, 04-51, 54-58.
Attached to 1675 are copies of Henbury and Westbury on Trym (B).
Cop M (BT) 1762-1837 Ts I (ER). *Extracts in RMI. See also Downend.*

MANGOTSFIELD, Zion. (Ind). *f 1820. No regs known. Not at PRO or
Ch Sec.*

MANGOTSFIELD. (Wes). – *see Downend.*

MARSHFIELD. **OR** CMB 1559 + (Inc). **BT** 1618, 22, 25, 32, 37-38, 46, 55,
1660, 64, 68-72, 74-84, 86, 1689-1812 (B), 1813-37 (G).
Cop CMB 1559-1693 I (Ptd – F.A. Crisp 1893), M (BT) 1813-37 Ts I
(ER). *M 1558-1693 in RMI.*

MARSHFIELD. (Ind). *f 1799.* **OR** ZC 1806-1833 (PRO).

MARSHFIELD (S of F). **Frenchay Monthly Meeting.** *disc. before 1785.
No regs known other than the Monthly Meeting Registers.*

MARSTON SICCA. *(formerly in parish of Clifford Chambers). Civil
Parish is called Long Marston.* **OR** C 1711-1888 *(gap 1750-3),*
M 1681-1837 *(gaps 1750-4, 1810-13),* B 1680-1812, Banns 1831-1950
(Warwick RO). **BT** 1612 + (G). **Cop** M 1680-1812 (Phil 10), CB 1680-
1804 (SOA), CMB 1612-1683 (CLG), CMB (BT) 1612, 1613, 1615, 1623,
1637, 1638, 1662-3, 1665-6, 1669, 1670, 1672, 1677-1702 (Warwick
RO).

MATSON. **OR** CB 1553-1812, M 1553-1809 (CLG). **BT** 1578 + (G).
Cop M 1553-1812 (Phil 3), CMB 1553-1924 Ms (CLG). *M 1553-1812 in
RMI.*

MEREWENT. – *see Hartpury.*

MEYSEY HAMPTON or MAISEYHAMPTON. **OR** CMB 1570 $^+$ *(gaps M 1721-25, 1753 and 1754, B 1721-1730)* (Inc). **BT** 1578 $^+$ (G).

MEYSEYHAMPTON. (Bapt). *f 1639. No registers known. Not at PRO or Ch Sec.*

MICHELDEAN. – *see Mitcheldean.*

MICKLETON. **OR** C 1590 $^+$, MB 1594 $^+$, Mar. Lic. 1822-1867 (12) (Inc). **BT** 1612 $^+$ (G). **Cop** M 1594-1812 (Phil 3), B 1593-1635, Extracts CMB (BT) 1612-1730 (Ptd), CB 1594-1736 (Ptd), CMB 1590-1782 (CLG), C 1590-1640, M 1594-1645, 1657-1812, B 1594-1644 (SOA). *M 1594-1812 in RMI.*

MINCHINHAMPTON. **OR** C 1561 $^+$, M 1566 $^+$, B 1558 $^+$ *(gap CMB 1719, B 1563-1571)*. **BT** 1578 $^+$ (G). **Cop** M 1566-1812 (Phil 11), CB 1566-1661, CMB (BT) 1578-1812 (CLG), M (BT) 1813-37 Ts (Roe 5 SG and CLG). *M 1566-1812 in RMI. M 1812-37 not in RMI but in Sep Index to Roe Vol. 5. See also Nailsworth and Rodborough.*

MINCHINHAMPTON. Tetbury St. (Bapt). *f 1824. Not at PRO. No information.*

MINCHINHAMPTON. (Wes). – *see Littleworth.*

MINSTERWORTH. *(Ancient name Mortune).* **OR** CMB 1633 $^+$ (Inc). **BT** 1575 $^+$ (G). **Cop** M 1633-1837 (Phil 17), CMB 1633-1738 Ms (Inc). *M 1633-1837 in RMI.*

MISERDEN. **OR** CMB 1574 $^+$ (Inc). **BT** 1613 $^+$ (G).

MITCHELDEAN. **OR** CMB 1680 $^+$ *(gaps CB 1715-17, M 1715-19, 1719-52)* (Inc). **BT** 1606 $^+$ (G). **Cop** M 1680-1812 (Phil 9), CMB 1680-1781 (CLG). (PR) CB 1782-1877, M 1754-1836 Mf (SLC). *M 1680-1812 in RMI.*

MITCHELDEAN. (Ind). *f 1662.* **OR** Z CB 1759-1837 (PRO).

MITCHELDEAN. (Wes). **Ledbury and Forest of Dean Circuit.** *No regs known. Not at PRO or Forest of Dean Circuit Supt. See Newent and Coleford.*

MORETON-IN-THE-MARSH. *Annexed to Batsford 1887. Formerly Moreton-Henmarsh.* **OR** CB 1643 $^+$, M 1672 $^+$ (Inc). **BT** 1621 $^+$ (G). **Cop** M 1672-1812 (Phil 5), C 1643-1780 Ts (SG). *M 1672-1812 in RMI.*

MORETON-IN-THE-MARSH. (Ind). *f 1801.* **OR** ZC 1801-1837 (PRO).

MORETON VALENCE. **OR** CB 1681 $^+$, M 1755 $^+$ *(a few M 1681-1768 in CB reg)* (Inc). **BT** 1569 $^+$ (G). **Cop** M (BT) 1569-1578 Ms (CLG), M (BT) 1664-1812 Ts Sep I (Roe 1 – SG and CLG), M (BT) 1813-1837 Ts Sep I (Roe 3 – SG and CLG). *M 1664-1837 not in main RMI but in Sep Index to Roe Vols. 1-3.*

MORTUNE. – *see Minsterworth.*

NAILSWORTH. *Formerly chapelry of Avening.* **OR** C 1794 $^+$ (Inc). *MB pre-1895 in Avening, Horsley and Minchinhampton regs* (Inc). **BT** *on Avening returns.*

NAILSWORTH MONTHLY MEETING (S of F). *f 1668. United to* **Gloucester Monthly Meeting** *1854.* **Constituent Meetings:-** *Nailsworth, Cirenceste Painswick (all 1668-1854), Tetbury (disc. c.1780).* **Monthly Meeting** *Regs:-* ZMB 1649-1778 (PRO 618), Z 1776-1837, M 1775-1784, 1795-1836, B 1776-1794, 1796-1837 (612-617). *Also regs for all constituent meetings except Nailsworth (see under individual meetings).*

NAILSWORTH (S of F). **Nailsworth Monthly Meeting.** *q.v.*

NAILSWORTH. Forest Green Church. (Ind). *f 1687.* **OR** ZC 1776-1837 (PRO).

NAILSWORTH. Shortwood (Newmarket Rd). (Bapt). *f 1715.* **OR** Z 1749-1806 (PRO *cat. under Horsley*), Z 1785-1825, M 1934[+], B pre-1837 *but often only surnames entered and dates of burial not often given. Also CD from 1715 in Members Roll* (Ch Sec – *records at present with Mr. V. Payne*).

NAUNTON. **OR** CB 1540[+], M 1545[+]. *List of inhabitants 1811 in M Reg 1762-1804* (Inc). **BT** 1600[+] (G). **Cop** M 1545-1804 (Phil 15), CMB 1540-1740 Ms (CLG). *M 1545-1804 in RMI.*

NAUNTON and GUITING. (Bapt). *f 1800. No regs known. Not at PRO or Ch Sec.*

NETHER SWELL. – *see Swell Nether.*

NEWENT. **OR** CB 1672[+], M 1673[+] (Inc). **BT** 1597[+] (G). **Cop** (PR) C 1672-1862, M 1673-1837, B 1672-1895 Mf (SLC).

NEWENT (RC). *Entries in regs of Little Malvern Court. See Worcs – Malvern, Little.*

NEWENT. Culvert St. (Wes). *Probably* **Ledbury and Forest of Dean Circuit** **OR** ZC 1818-1837 (PRO). *Possibly the Circuit register of the* **Ledbury and Forest of Dean Circuit.**

NEWINGTON BAGPATH. *United with Kingscote 1842.* **OR** CMB 1686[+] (*gap M 1753*) (Inc) (*regs 1686-1752 damaged 1947*). *Large number of 18th century Marriages of non residents.* **BT** 1578[+] (G). **Cop** M 1599-1812 (Phil 7 and 12), CMB 1686-1752 Mf (CLG), M (BT) 1813-37 Ts (Roe 5 – SG and CLG). *M 1601-1812 in RMI. M 1813-37 not in RMI but in Sep Index to Roe Vol. 5.*

NEWLAND. **OR** CMB 1560[+] (*gaps CMB 1669-1686, M 1799-1812*). *Register CMB 1560-1669 badly damaged, defective 1642-51* (Inc). **BT** 1607[+] (G). **Cop** CMB 1560-1565 (CLG). *See also Bream and Coleford.*

NEWNHAM-ON-SEVERN. **OR** CMB 1547[+] (*gaps CMB 1641-1650*). **BT** 1609[+] (G). **Cop** M (BT) 1661-1812 Ts Sep I (Roe 1 – SG and CLG), (BT) 1813-1837 Ts Sep I (Roe 3 – SG and CLG). *M 1661-1837 not in main RMI but in Sep Index to Roe Vols. 1-3.*

NEWNHAM. (Wes). **Ledbury and Forest of Dean Circuit.** *No regs known. Not at PRO or Forest of Dean Circuit Supt. See also Newent and Coleford.*

NEWNHAM AND BLAKENEY. Tabernacle. (Ind). *f 1823.* **OR** ZC 1823-37 (PRO).

NEWNTON LONG. *– see Wilts.*

NIBLEY, NORTH. *Formerly chapelry of Wotton-under-Edge.* **OR** CMB 1567 + *(gap CM 1683-86)* (Inc), Mar. Alleg. 1786, 1822-3 (14) (GRO). **BT** 1578 + (G). **Cop** M 1617-1837 Ts (CLG), CMB 1567-1812 (Inc), M (BT) 1617-1812 Ts Sep I (Roe 2 – SG and CLG), M (BT) 1813-1837 Ts Sep I (Roe 3 – SG and CLG), M (PR and BT) 1617-1837 Ts I (SG, CLG and Inc). *M 1617-1837 not in main RMI but in Sep Index to Roe Vols. 1-3. See also Wotton-under-Edge.*

NIBLEY, NORTH. Tabernacle. (Ind). *f 1815.* **OR** *Not at PRO.* C 1829-1845, M 1897 +, B 1863 + (Ch Sec).

NIMPSFIELD. *– see Nympsfield.*

NORTH CERNEY. *– see Cerney North.*

NORTH NIBLEY. *– see Nibley North.*

NORTHLEACH with EASTINGTON. **OR** CMB 1556 + *(gaps C 1711-19, 1730-36, M 1670-76, 1727-36, 1775-1812, B 1725-36)* (Inc). **BT** 1620 + (G).

NORTHLEACH. (Ind). *– see Chedworth.*

NORTHWICK. *Chapelry in Henbury. – see Redwick and Northwick.*

NORTON. **OR** CMB 1686 + (Inc). **BT** 1569 (G). **Cop** CMB (BT) 1569-1605 (CLG), M (BT) 1666-1837 Ts (ER).

NOTGROVE. **OR** CMB 1660 + (Inc). **BT** 1590 + (G).

NUPEND (EASTINGTON). (Bapt). *f 1827. Not at PRO. No information.*

NYMPSFIELD. **OR** C 1684 +, M 1679 +, B 1678 + (Inc). *B reg 1678-1753 gives list of "defaults and unchristened children" c. 1695.* **BT** 1578 + (G). **Cop** M (BT) 1813-37 Ts (Roe 5 – SG and CLG), M 1679-1812 (Phil 1 and 12). *M 1679-1812 in RMI; M 1813-37 not in RMI but in Sep Index to Roe Vol. 5.*

NYMPSFIELD. (Bapt). *f 1760 perhaps later. No registers known. Not at PRO or Shortwood Baptist Church.*

ODDINGTON. **OR** C 1619 + *(gap 1675)*, Z 1695 +, M 1685 +, B 1549 + *(gap 1675)* (Inc). *B 1676-7 in C volume.* **BT** 1605 + (G). **Cop** C 1676-1706, M 1685-1706, B 1549-1618, 1676-1706 Ms (CLG), C 1619-1813, M 1685-1812, B 1549-1813 (Royce Mss, Br and Gl Arch Soc. Lib. Gloucester).

OLDBURY-ON-THE-HILL. *United with Didmarton 1735.* **OR** CMB 1567 + *(gaps CMB 1747, CB 1781, M 1752-53)* (Inc Didmarton). **BT** 1596 + (G). **Cop** M 1568-1812 (Phil 11), M (BT) 1813-37 Ts (Roe 5 – SG and CLG). *M 1568-1812 in RMI. 1812-1837 not in RMI but in Index to Roe Vol. 5. See also Didmarton.*

OLDBURY-ON-SEVERN. *See also Thornbury.* **OR** CMB 1538-1740 (Inc Thornbury
BT 1599 + (G). **Cop** M 1538-1733 (Phil 15). *M 1538-1733 in RMI.*

OLDLAND. *Parish formed from Bitton 1861.* **OR** CB 1731 + *(gap B 1764),*
M 1732-1741 (Inc Bitton). *Earlier entries in Hanham regs.* **BT** *see
Bitton.*

OLDLAND. Tabernacle. (Ind). *f 1811. No regs known. Not at PRO or
Ch Sec.*

OLD SODBURY. *– see Sodbury, Old.*

OLVESTON. **OR** C 1561-1812 *(gaps 1658-90, 1710-15, 1718-22, 1743-55),*
M 1579 + *(gaps 1649-93, 1707-15, 1718-33, 1735-40),* B 1561 +
(gaps 1649-1727, 1738-40) (Inc), Mar. Cert. 1783 (BAO). *Some
Quaker Burials 1697-1705 in CM reg.* **BT** 1683-84, 86, 89-92, 98,
1704, 18, 52, 54-55, 59-61, 63-64, 67-81, 1800, 1802-57 (B).
Cop M 1560-1812 (Phil 14), M (BT) 1813-37 Ts I (ER). *M 1560-1812
in RMI.*

OLVESTON (S of F). **Frenchay Monthly Meeting. OR** ZMB 1655-1777 (PRO 588
ZMB 1653-1677 (589).

OVERBURY. *– see Worcs.*

OWLPEN. *United with Uley 1842.* **OR** CB 1687 +, M 1697-1754, C 1677-85
(5) *in CB reg 1687-1764* (Inc). **BT** 1613 + (G). **Cop** M 1687-1897
(Phil 1 and 2), M (BT) 1813-37 Ts (Roe 5 – SG and CLG). *M 1687-
1837 in RMI. 1813-37 also in Index to Roe Vol. 5.*

OXENHALL. *–* **OR** CMB 1665 + (Inc). **BT** 1583 + (G). **Cop** (PR) CM 1665-
1856, B 1665-1950 Mf (SLC).

OXENTON. **OR** CM 1679 +, B 1678 + *(gap CB 1738-1782, M 1738-1754)* (Inc)
BT 1578 + (G).

OZLEWORTH. **OR** CMB 1698 + *(gap CMB 1740)* (Inc). **BT** 1577 + (G).
Cop M 1698-1812 (Phil 12), M (BT) 1813-37 Ts (Roe 5 – SG and CLG).
*M 1698-1812 in RMI. M 1813-37 not in RMI but in Index to Roe
Vol. 5.*

PAINSWICK. **OR** CMB 1547 + *(gaps C 1549, 1555-57, 1628-53, M 1549-50,
1552-57, 1628-53, 1706-9, B 1548-9, 1551-56, 1628-53)* (Inc).
BT 1570 + (G). *See also Sheepscombe and Slad.* **Cop** M 1547-1812
(Phil 8), CMB 1547-1812 Ms (CLG), CMB 1547-1812 Ms (CLG). *M 1547-
1812 in RMI.*

PAINSWICK (S of F). **Nailsworth Monthly Meeting. OR** Z 1647-1790,
M 1658-1786, B 1657-1790 (PRO 611), ZMB 1658-1786 (Grey Friars
Meeting House, Gloucester).

PAINSWICK. Upper Chapel. (Ind). *f 1680.* **OR** ZC 1780-1837 (PRO).

PAINSWICK. New St. (Bapt). *f 1831. Not at PRO. No information.*

PARKEND. *f 1842.* **OR** CB 1822 +, M 1844 + (Inc). *No BT's.*

PAUNTLEY. **OR** CMB 1538 + (Inc). **BT** 1586 + (G). **Cop** CMB 1538-1613 (CLG), CMB 1538-1780 (Inc), (PR) CMB and Banns 1538-1780, CMB 1813-1856, Banns 1824-56 Mf (SLC).

PEBWORTH. — *see Worcs.* (*M 1612-1726 in RMI*).

PINNOCK-CUM-HYDE. — *see Didbrook.*

PITCHCOMBE. **OR** CMB 1709 + (*gaps CMB 1730-32, M 1755*), Mar. Lic. 1800-1884 (20) (Inc). **BT** 1639 + (G). **Cop** M 1709-1742 (Glos N and Q III — Ptd). *See also Harescombe.*

PITCHCOMBE. (Ind). *f 1828.* **OR** C 1828-1837 (PRO).

POOLE KEYNES. — *see Wilts.*

POULTON. *Transferred from Wilts 1844.* **OR** CB 1695 + , M 1703-1756, 1813 + (Inc), *CB reg 1757-1812 contains 4 M.* **BT** 1606-1837 (*gaps 1609-20* except 1615, *1623-1673* except 1635, *1680-96, 1728-1751*) (Salisbury Dio RO).

PRESCOTT. — *see Toddington.*

PRESTBURY. **OR** CMB 1633 + (Inc). **BT** 1601 + (G). **Cop** M 1633-1837 (Phil 15). *M 1633-1837 in RMI.*

PRESTON *near Cirencester.* **OR** CMB 1677 + (*gap M 1754*) (Inc). **BT** 1578 + (G).

PRESTON *near Ledbury.* **OR** CM 1671 + , B 1690 + (Inc). **BT** 1586 + (G). **Cop** C 1665-1856, M 1665-1811, 1819-1832, 1841-1868, B 1665-1866 Mf (SLC).

PRESTON-UPON-STOUR. — *see Warwickshire.* (*M 1541-1812 in RMI*).

PUCKLECHURCH. **OR** CMB 1590 + (*gap CMB 1630-33*) (Inc). **BT** 1596-1600, 1605-06, 08, 12, 18, 20, 22-24, 27-29, 32, 37-38, 60, 63-64, 68-69, 1671, 73-74, 76-81, 83-86, 88-1704, 06-08, 10-14, 1716-1812 (B), 1813-1837 (G). **Cop** M (BT) 1813-37 Ts I (ER). *Extracts in RMI.*

PUCKLECHURCH. (S of F). **Frenchay Monthly Meeting.** *disc. before 1785. No regs known other than Monthly Meeting regs.*

QUEDGELEY. **OR** CMB 1559 + (*gap CMB 1752, M 1753*) (Inc). **BT** 1569 + (G). **Cop** Extracts M 1559-1836 (Phil 1). *M 1559-1837 in RMI.*

QUENINGTON. **OR** CMB 1653 + (*gap M 1755-1767*) (Inc). **BT** 1578 + (G).

QUINTON. (*formerly in parish of Clifford Chambers.* Transferred to Warwickshire 1931). **OR** C 1547-1904, M 1547-1837 (*gaps 1668-1672, 1704-1742*), B 1547-1669, 1672-1886 (Warwick RO). **BT** 1599 + (G). **Cop** M 1548-1812 (Phil 6), CB 1547-1812 (C of A), CMB 1546-1603 (CLG), C 1547-1669, M 1548-1668, B 1547-1671 (SOA). *M 1547-1812 in RMI.*

RANDWICK. **OR** CMB 1662 + (*gap CB 1695-1724, M 1684, 1695-1724, 1766-1769*) (Inc). *Some entries in Standish regs.* **BT** 1607 + (G).

RANDWICK. Ebley Chapel. (Lady Hunt. now Cong). *f 1797.* **OR** ZC 1797-1837 (PRO).

RANGEWORTHY. *Formerly chapelry of Thornbury.* **OR** CMB 1704 [+] *(gap C 1724-33, M 1726-34, 1751, 1754, B 1726-1733 (Inc).* **BT** 1601 [+] (G). **Cop** M (BT) 1663-1812 Ts Sep I (Roe 1 – SG and CLG), M (BT) 1813-1837 Ts Sep I (Roe 3 – SG and CLG). *M 1663-1837 not in main RMI but in Sep Index to Roe Vols. 1-3.*

REDFIELD. *Parish of St. George, Bristol.* (Wes). *f 1815.* **OR** ZC 1820-1837 (PRO).

REDMARLEY D'ABITOT. *Transferred from Worcs 1931. See Worcs.*

REDWICK and NORTHWICK. *Chapelries of Henbury. Now attached to Pilning.* **OR** C 1667 [+], M 1702 [+] (Inc), B 1690-1812 (Inc Henbury). **BT** 1813-15, 19-51, 56-74 (BAO *cat. under Northwick). Earlier BT's on Henbury returns* (B). *See also Henbury.*

RENDCOMBE. **OR** CMB 1566 [+] *(gaps CMB 1638-52, 1658-78, M 1712-1754).* **BT** 1612 [+] (G). **Cop** M 1566-1812 (Phil I), CMB 1566-1660 Ms (CLG). *M 1566-1812 in RMI.*

RISSINGTON, GREAT or BROAD RISSINGTON. **OR** CB 1538-1747, M 1538-1744 *(gap M 1745-6)* (GRO), CMB 1748 [+] (Inc). **BT** 1609 [+] (G). **Cop** M 1538-1913 (Phil 17). *M 1538-1837 in RMI.*

RISSINGTON, LITTLE (or LOWER). **OR** CMB 1543 [+] *(gap M 1750-51, 1754).* **BT** 1599 [+] (G). **Cop** M 1550-1837 (Phil 17). *M 1550-1837 in RMI.*

RISSINGTON, WYCK. **OR** CB 1739 [+], M 1740 [+] *(gap M 1747-1754)* (Inc). **BT** 1605 [+] (G). **Cop** M 1605-1837 (Phil 13). *M 1605-1837 in RMI.*

ROCKHAMPTON. **OR** CMB 1565 [+] *(gap M 1753-1755)* (Inc). **BT** 1606 [+] (G). **Cop** M (BT) 1661-1812 Ts Sep I (Roe 1 – SG and CLG), M (BT) 1813-1837 Ts Sep I (Roe 3 – SG and CLG). *M (BT) 1682-1732, 1753-1812 in RMI, M (BT) 1661-1812 in Sep Index to Roe Vols. 1-3.*

RODBOROUGH, *Formerly chapelry of Minchinhampton.* **OR** CMB 1692 [+] *(gap M 1753)*, Mar. Alleg. 1822-23 (Inc). **BT** 1620 [+] (G). **Cop** M (BT and PR) 1620-1837 (Phil Ms), M (BT) 1813-37 Ts (Roe 5 – SG and CLG). *M 1692-1837 and BT 1620-1700 in RMI. M 1813-37 also in Index to Roe 5.*

RODBOROUGH. The Tabernacle (Calv Meth now Cong). *f 1760.* **OR** ZC 1762-1837, B 1823-1837 (PRO).

RODMARTON. **OR** CB 1605 [+], M 1603 [+] (Inc). **BT** 1578 [+] (G). **Cop** M 1813-37 Ts (Roe 5 – SG and CLG). *Not in RMI. M 1813-37 in Index to Roe Vol.5.*

RUARDEAN. **OR** CMB 1538 [+] *(gaps 1781-1784, M 1727-34, 1753)* (Inc). *A few M 1735-1752 may have been entered at Walford, Herefordshire with which Ruardean was then united.* **BT** 1607 [+] (G). **Cop** CMB 1538-1610 Ms (CLG) Mf of PR (GRO).

RUARDEAN. (Ind). *f 1789.* **OR** ZC 1795-1837, B 1802-1837 (PRO).

RUARDEAN HILL. *(Now called Ruardean Woodside)*. (Wes). **Ledbury and Forest of Dean Circuit.** *No regs known. Not at PRO or Forest of Dean Circuit Supt.*

RUDFORD. *Before 1955 with Upleadon.* **OR** CMB 1729 + *(No entries 1770-79, 1781-83, 1786)* (Inc). **BT** 1583 + (G). **Cop** (PR) C 1729-1812, MB 1729-1856 Mf (SLC). *See also Upleadon.*

RUSCOMBE. (Ind). *f 1828. Not at PRO. No information.*

SAINTBURY. **OR** C 1561 +, M 1585 + *(gap 1747-54)*, B 1603-1811 (Inc). **BT** 1617 + (G). **Cop** M 1585-1812 (Phil 4), Extracts CMB (BT) 1617-1713 (Ptd), C 1561-1777, M 1585-1747, 1755-1812, B 1603-1742, 1776-1811 (SOA). *M 1585-1812 in RMI.*

ST BRIAVELS. **OR** CMB 1664 + *(gap CMB 1733 and 1734)* (Inc). **BT** 1618 + (G).

SALPERTON. **OR** CMB 1629 + *(gap CMB 1644-1665)* (Inc). **BT** 1609 + (G). **Cop** CMB 1629-1812 "of still legible entries". Made 1884 (Inc).

SANDHURST. **OR** CMB 1538 + *(gap M 1788)*, *CMB 1819-21 included in reg 1702-1709* (Inc). **BT** 1570 + (G). **Cop** M (BT) 1661-1837 Ts (ER).

SAPPERTON. **OR** C 1661 +, MB 1662 + *(gap M 1782-4)* (Inc). **BT** 1578 + (G). **Cop** M 1662-1754, 1813-36 (Phil Ms). *M 1662-1754. 1813-36 in RMI.*

SAUL. *Formerly parochial chapelry of Standish.* **OR** C 1573-1808, M 1574-1747, B 1573-1809 *(gaps CB 1688-1711, 1742-60)* (GRO). *Early regs badly damaged by flood but largely legible. CB 1711-1742 at back of 1761-1805 register. Most M before 1798 at Standish, and probably some CB.* **BT** 1576 + (G). **Cop** M (BT) 1663-1812 Ts Sep I (Roe 1 – SG and CLG), M (BT) 1813-1837 Ts Sep I (Roe 3 – SG and CLG), M 1594-1682, 1702-1837 (Phil Ms). *M 1574, 1594-1682, 1702-1837 in RMI. M (BT) 1663-1837 not in RMI but in Sep Index to Roe Vols. 1-3.*

SEVENHAMPTON. **OR** CB 1588 +, M 1605 + *(gap 1732-54)* (Inc). **BT** 1618 +. **Cop** CMB 1588-1808 Ms (CLG), M 1605-1837 (Phil 15), C 1588-1837, B 1590-1837 (Cheltenham Lib). *M 1605-1837 in RMI.*

SEZINCOTE. *Church demolished c. 1700. United with Longborough since c. 1800. See Longborough.*

SHARNCOTE. – *see Shorncote.*

SHEEPSCOMBE. *Chapel of Ease to Painswick from 1821.* **OR** CB 1821 +, M 1845 + (Inc). **BT** *on Painswick returns.*

SHENINGTON. *Transferred to Oxfordshire. See Oxfordshire.*

SHERBORNE. *United with Windrush 1776.* **OR** CMB 1572 + (Inc). **BT** 1571 + (G). *See also Windrush.*

SHIPTON MOYNE. *Formerly Shipton Moyne and Dooel.* **OR** CB 1570 +, M 1587 + *(gap 1753)* (Inc). **BT** 1607 + (G). **Cop** M 1587-1812 (Phil 9), M (BT) 1813-37 Ts (Roe 5 – SG and CLG). *M 1587-1812 in RMI. M 1813-37 not in RMI but in Index to Roe Vol. 5.*

SHIPTON OLIFFE. *United with Shipton Sollars 1776.* **OR** CMB 1666 +, *(gaps 1710, 1722-42)* (Inc). **BT** 1577 + (G).

SHIPTON SOLLARS. – *see also Shipton Oliffe.* **OR** CMB 1653 + *(gaps CMB 1712-42, CB 1754-56)* (Inc). **BT** *on Shipton Oliffe returns.*

SHIREHAMPTON. *Chapelry to Westbury.* **OR** CMB 1727 + *(gap M 1737-1843)* (Inc). **BT** 1845-1873 (B). *Previously on Westbury-on-Trym returns.*

SHORNCOTE. *Formerly in Wilts. United with Somerford Keynes 1881.* **OR** CB 1722-1810, M 1708-1805 *(gap 1755-1761)* (Inc Somerford Keynes) **BT** 1619-1812 *(gaps 1623-1702, (except 1670, 73, 77, 96), 1710-21, 1727-70 (except 1756))* (Dio RO Salisbury).

SHORTWOOD. (Bapt). – *see Nailsworth.*

SHURDINGTON. **OR** CMB 1556 + *(gaps CMB 1557-60, CB 1722-89, M 1722-53)* (Inc), *CMB 1723-1789 in Badgeworth registers. Two paper leaves inserted after 1637 apparently part of register for Up Hatherley and Badgeworth c. 1606-1624.* **BT** 1578 + (G). *See also Badgeworth.*

SIDDINGTON. ST PETER. *United with Siddington St Mary 1778.* **OR** CMB 1687 + (Inc). **BT** 1578 + (G).

SIDDINGTON, ST MARY. *United with Siddington St Peter 1778.* **OR** CB 1686-1779, M 1686-1777 (Inc Siddington, St Peter). **BT** *See Siddington, St Peter.*

SISTON. – *see Syston.*

SLAD. *Formed from Painswick 1844.* **OR** C 1834 +, M 1870 +, B 1836 + (Inc All Saints, Uplands). **BT** *See Painswick.*

SLAUGHTER, LOWER. **OR** CB 1814 +, M 1835 + (Inc). *Earlier entries in regs of Bourton-on-the-Water.* **BT** *on Bourton returns.* **Cop** M 1813-1837 (Phil 17). *M 1813-1837 in RMI.*

SLAUGHTER, UPPER. (Including Eyford). **OR** CMB 1538 + *(gap M 1680-81)* (Inc). **BT** 1605 + (G). **Cop** M 1538-1837 (Phil 17), CMB 1538-1812 Ms (CLG). *M 1538-1837 in RMI.*

SLIMBRIDGE. **OR** CMB 1635 + *(gaps C 1687-1700, 1706-18, 1721-1726, M 1687-1707, 1723-26, B 1714-26)* (Inc). **BT** 1571 + (G). **Cop** M 1747-1812 (Phil 1 and 11), M (BT) 1813-37 Ts (Roe 5 – SG and CLG), M (BT) 1571-1650 (PR). *M 1626-1812 in RMI. M 1813-37 not in RMI but in Sep Index to Roe 5.*

SLIMBRIDGE. (Bapt). *f 1834. Not at PRO. No information.*

SNOWSHILL. *Chapelry held with Stanton.* **OR** CMB 1732 + (Inc). *See also Stanton.* **BT** 1606 + (G). **Cop** M 1593-1603 (Phil 4), CMB 1572-1734 Ms (SG). *M 1593-1603 in RMI.*

SODBURY, CHIPPING. – *see Chipping Sodbury.*

SODBURY, LITTLE. **OR** CMB 1703 + *(gap M 1753)* (Inc). **BT** 1602 + (G). **Cop** M (BT) 1660-1812 Ts Sep I (Roe 1 – SG and CLG), M (BT) 1813-37 Ts Sep I (Roe 3 – SG and CLG), M (PR and BT) 1660-1837 Ts I (SG, CLG and Inc). *M 1673-1812 in RMI, M 1660-1837 in Index to Sep Vol.*

SODBURY, OLD. **OR** CMB 1684-1812 *(gap CMB 1686-94)* (GRO). **BT** 1605 + (G).
Cop M 1684-1812 (Phil 9), CMB (BT) 1605-95 Ts I (Roe 4 – SG and CLG),
M (BT) 1813-37 Ts (Roe 5 – SG and CLG). *M 1684-1812 in RMI. M 1605-1695 not in RMI but in Index to Roe Vol. 4. M 1813-37 in Index to Roe Vol. 5.*

SODBURY, OLD. Chapel Lane. (Bapt). *f 1835. No regs known. Not at PRO or Ch Sec.*

SODBURY (S of F). **Frenchay Monthly Meeting.** *f 1668. Disc. 1869.* **OR**
ZMB 1669-1777 (PRO 591).

SOMERFORD KEYNES. *Transferred from Wilts 1897.* **OR** CMB 1560 + (Inc).
BT 1605, 07, 08, 1620-1838 *(gaps 1623-71, except 1632, 1667; 1671-94 except 1693; 1710-20, 1727-51)* (Salisbury Dio Reg).

SOUTH CERNEY. – *see Cerney South.*

SOUTHROP. **OR** C 1680 + *(gap 1749-52)*, MB 1656 + *(gap 1745-53).* **BT** 1577 +
(G). **Cop** M 1656-1837 (Phil 13). *M 1656-1837 in RMI.*

STANDCOMBE (S of F). **Gloucester Monthly Meeting.** *f 1668. Disc. before 1755. No regs known other than Monthly Meeting regs.*

STANDISH. **OR** CMB 1559 + *(gaps M 1609-19, 1628-54)* (Inc). *Regs contain entries for Hardwick, Randwicke and Saul.* **BT** 1569 + (G). **Cop** M 1559-1812 (Phil 6), CMB 1559-1652 Ms (CLG). *M 1559-1812 in RMI. See also Saul.*

STANLEY PONTLARGE. – *see Toddington.*

STANLEY ST LEONARDS. – *see Leonard Stanley.*

STANTON. *United with Snowshill.* **OR** CB 1735 +, M 1755 + (Inc).
BT 1613 + (G). **Cop** M 1572-1812 (Phil 4), CMB 1572-1734 Ms (Inc).
M 1572-1812 in RMI. See also Snowshill.

STANWAY. **OR** CMB 1573 + *(gap 1714-22)* (Inc). **BT** 1638 + (G).

STAPLETON. **OR** C 1720 +, M 1728 +, B 1738 + (Inc). **BT** 1675-76, 81-86,
1701, 37, 39-40, 42, 44, 47-51, 69-71, 1774-1850 (B). **Cop** *M 1675-1676, 1681-86, 1700-01, 1737-8 in RMI.*

STAUNTON (near Coleford). **OR** CMB 1653 + *(gap 1685-94)* (Inc). **BT** 1584 +
(G). **Cop** (BT) 1820-1891 Mf (SLC), M (BT) 1680-1837 Ts (ER).

STAUNTON (near Ledbury). – *see Worcs.*

STAVERTON *with Chapelry of Boddington.* **OR** C 1538 + *(gap 1674-78)*,
M 1542 + *(gaps 1629-32, 1667-1717, 1794-99)*, B 1538 + *(gap 1674-1717)* (Inc). **BT** 1612 + (G). **Cop** CMB 1538-1784 (CLG).

STINCHCOMBE. **OR** CB 1582 +, M 1583 + *(gap 1754)*, B 1582 + *(gaps 1590-1661, 1665-68)* (Inc). **BT** 1601 + (G). **Cop** M 1583-1753, 1784-1812
(Phil 2 and 6), M (BT) 1813-37 Ts (Roe 5 – SG and CLG). *M 1583-1812 in RMI. M 1813-37 not in RMI but in Index to Roe Vol. 5.*

STOKE GIFFORD. **OR** CMB 1556 + *(gap 1668-1737)* (Inc). **BT** 1678-79, 1710,
1713, 45-54, 57-65 *(gaps)* 68-71, 73-1809, 11-59 (B). **Cop** M (BT)
1748-1837 Ts I (ER).

STOKE ORCHARD. *Chapelry — formerly annexed to Bishop's Cleeve. — see Bishop's Cleeve. Now united with Tredington.*

STOKE ORCHARD MONTHLY MEETING (S of F). *f 1668. Dissolved and constituent meetings joined to* **Gloucester Monthly Meeting** *1755.* **Constituent Meetings:-** *Stoke Orchard* (disc. before 1755), *Cheltenham* (1668-1755), *Tewkesbury* (1668-1755), *Boddington* (1668-pre-1755). **Monthly Meeting regs:-** *PRO reg No 603.* Z 1654-1767, M 1658-1773, B 1660-1784 *appears to be the Stoke Orchard Monthly Meeting register and used by* **Gloucester Monthly Meeting** *after 1755. Constituent Meeting regs exist for Cheltenham and Boddington (q.v.) but not Tewkesbury or Stoke Orchard.*

STOKE ORCHARD (S of F). **Stoke Orchard Monthly Meeting.** *f 1668 disc. before 1755. No regs known apart from Monthly Meeting regs.*

STONE. *Formerly Chapelry of Berkeley.* **OR** C 1594 +, M 1598 + *(gaps 1654-56, 1754),* B 1616 + (Inc). **BT** 1578 + (G). **Cop** M 1594-1812 (Phil 3), M (BT) 1813-37 Ts (Roe 5 — SG and CLG). *M 1594-1812 in RMI. M 1813-37 not in RMI but in Index to Roe Vol. 5.*

STONEHOUSE. **OR** CMB 1558 + (Inc). **BT** 1599 + (G). **Cop** M 1558-1812 (Phil 2), CMB 1558-1603 Ms (CLG), M (BT) 1813-37 Ts (Roe 5 — SG and CLG). *M 1558-1812 in RMI. M 1813-37 not in RMI but in Index to Roe Vol. 5.*

STONEHOUSE. (French Church). **OR** CB 1692-1791 (PRO *cat. under Bristol - Stonehouse*). **Cop** CB 1692-1791 (Hug Soc 20).

STONEHOUSE. (Ind). *f 1812.* **OR** ZC 1824-1837 (PRO).

STOW-ON-THE-WOLD. **OR** CMB 1558 + *(gaps C 1631-79, 1681-88, M 1631-1706, B 1631-1707)* (Inc). **BT** 1610 + (G). **Cop** CMB 1558-1748 Ms (CLG) CMB 1558-1630 (C of A), C 1680-1707 Ms (NLW and Mf SLC).

STOW ON THE WOLD. Sheep St. (Bapt). *f 1715.* **OR** Z 1821-1837 (PRO).

STOW AND CAMPDEN MONTHLY MEETING (S of F). *Established 1668, dissolved 1790 and joined to* **Warwickshire South Monthly Meeting.** *(see* Warwickshire — **Brailes Monthly Meeting**). **Constituent Meetings:-** *Campden, Stow* (both 1668-1790). **Regs:-** Z 1654-1710, M 1661-1773, B 1660-1791 (PRO 1584), Z 1777-1805 (1592), M 1788, 1794 (1589) B 1777-1826 (1594).

STOW ON THE WOLD (S of F). **Stow and Campden Monthly Meeting** (1668-1790). **Warwickshire South Monthly Meeting** (1790-1852) *see* Warwickshire — **Brailes Monthly Meeting,** *disc. 1852. No regs known apart from Warwickshire South Monthly Meeting regs.*

STOWELL. *United with Hampnett 1660. See Hampnett.*

STRATTON. **OR** CMB 1600 + *(gap M 1754)* (Inc). **BT** 1578 + (G). **Cop** CMB 1600-1639 Ms (Cheltenham Lib), Extracts Parish Mag 1912 (CLG).

STROUD. *Formerly a chapelry in Bisley parish.* **OR** C 1624 + , MB 1625 +
  (*gaps M 1643-46, 1649-51, B 1645-47, 1650-51*), Mar. Lic. 1865-
  1894 (Inc). **BT** 1578 + (G). **Cop** *Extracts in RMI.*

STROUD, John St. (Bapt). *f 1824.* **OR** Z 1828-1837 (PRO).

STROUD, OLD MEETING. (Ind). *f 1711.* **OR** C 1712-1837, B 1720-29, 1753-
  1837 (PRO).

STROUD, Bedford St. (Ind). *f 1837. Not at PRO. No information.*

STROUD. (Wes). *f 1763.* **OR** ZC 1813-1837 (PRO). *Probably a Circuit
  register. See also Littleworth.*

STROUDWATER. *— see Eastcombe.*

SUDELEY MANOR. **OR** C 1705-1811, M 1736-1821, B 1854-1908 (GRO), C 1824-
  1930 (*gap 1812-24*), M 1825-1922 (*gap 1822-5, 1838-43*), B 1908 +
  (Inc). *No BT's known.* **Cop** Extracts C 1714-1811, M 1736-1817,
  B 1854-1908 Ms (CLG).

SUTTON UNDER BRAILES. *— see Warwickshire. (M 1578-1812 in RMI).*

SWELL, NETHER. **OR** CMB 1685 + (Inc). **BT** 1605 + (G). **Cop** M 1612-
  1812 (Phil 3), CMB (BT) 1605-1692 Ms (Inc). *M 1612-1812 in RMI.*

SWELL, UPPER. **OR** CMB 1543 + (*gap CMB 1647-1656, M 1751-1753,
  1807-1808*) (Inc). **BT** 1605 + (G). **Cop** CMB 1543-1779 Ms (CLG).

SWINDON. **OR** C 1606 + (*gaps 1608-12, 1621-26, 1648-51, 1658-1661,
  1662-64, 1670-72*), M 1638 + (*gaps 1638-69, 1754-1755*), B 1638 +
  (*gaps 1647-1660, 1662-1669, 1672-1676*) (Inc). **BT** 1570 + (G).
  Cop M 1638-1837 (Phil 1). *M 1638-1837 in RMI.*

SYDE. **OR** CMB 1686 + (Inc). **BT** 1578 + (G). **Cop** M 1686-1812 (Phil 12).
  M 1686-1812 in RMI.

SYSTON OR SISTON. **OR** CMB 1570 + (*gaps CMB 1640, M 1751-53*) (Inc).
  BT 1596-98, 1607-09, 16-17, 19-25, 28-29, 32, 37-40, 60-65, 67-68,
  1670, 72, 1676-1812 (B), 1813-37 (G). **Cop** CMB 1576-1641 (Ptd I),
  CMB 1576-1641 Ts (CLG), M (BT) 1813-37 Ts I (ER). *M 1574-1641 in
  RMI.*

TAYNTON. **OR** CB 1538 + , M 1540 + (*gap 1677*) (Inc). **BT** 1583 + (G).
  Cop (PR) C 1538-1858, M 1540-1856, B 1538-1856 Mf (SLC).

TEDDINGTON. *Transferred from Worcs 1931. See Worcs.*

TEMPLE GUITING. (or UPPER GUITING). *— see Guiting, Temple.*

TETBURY. **OR** CMB 1631 + (Inc). **BT** 1578 + (G). **Cop** M 1631-1812 (Phil
  10). *M 1631-1812 in RMI.*

TETBURY, Lower Meeting. (Ind). *f 1698.* **OR** C 1822-1837 (PRO).

TETBURY (S of F). **Nailsworth Monthly Meeting** *disc. c. 1780.*
  OR ZMB 1692-1771 (PRO 619).

TETBURY, Church St. (Bapt). *f 1721. Not at PRO. No information.*

TETBURY HILL. (Bapt). *— see Avening.*

TEWKESBURY. **OR** CM 1559-1812 *(gaps 1577-1595, 1632-1646, 1648-1652, 1656-1661, 1663-1678)*, B 1595-1812 *(gaps 1609-1633, 1638-1652, 1658-1659, 1661-1664)*, Mar. Lic. 1834-1837 (8) (Inc), C 1813-1847, M 1813-37, B 1813-53 (CLG). **BT** 1570 ⁺ (G). **Cop** CMB 1561-1809 (SOA), Extracts CMB 1571-76, 1638-72 (Ptd). *Extracts in RMI.*

TEWKESBURY (S of F). **Stoke Orchard Monthly Meeting** *(1668-1755)*, **Gloucester Monthly Meeting** *(1755-1854)*. *No regs known apart from Monthly Meeting regs.*

TEWKESBURY. Upper Meeting. (Pres, now Cong). *f 1707.* **OR** ZC 1752-1837 (PRO).

TEWKESBURY. Barton St. (Bapt). *f 1655.* **OR** *Not at PRO.* Z 1787-1836, B 1787-1837, M 1909 ⁺. *Also* D 1755-1841 *in Members' Lists* (Ch Sec).

TEWKESBURY. Tolsey Lane. (Wes). *f 1777. Probably* **Gloucester Circuit.** *Now* **Tewkesbury Circuit.** *No pre-1837 regs known. Not at PRO or Circuit Supt. See Cheltenham (King St).*

THORMERTON. *- see Farmington.*

THORNBURY. *Ancient parish included Falfield, Oldbury-on-Severn and Rangeworthy.* **OR** CMB 1550 ⁺ *(gap CMB 1680-1683)* (Inc). *In CB reg 1768-1812 is index of personal names and pedigrees of local families.* **BT** 1578 ⁺ (G). *See also Falfield, Oldbury-on-Severn and Rangeworthy.* **Cop** M 1550-1812 (Phil 15), M (BT) 1813-37 Ts (Roe 5 – SG and CLG), M (BT) 1664-1684, 1718-1724, 1726-7 (all additions to Phil 15) Ptd. (Gen. Mag. Vol 13 No. 8 Dec 1960). *M 1550-1812 in RMI. 1813-37 not in RMI but in Index to Roe 5.*

THORNBURY (S of F). **Frenchay Monthly Meeting** *– disc. 1847.* **OR** ZMB 1676 1798 (PRO 592).

THORNBURY. (Ind). *f 1720.* **OR** ZC 1796-1837, B 1816-1836 (PRO).

THORNBURY. Gillingstool. (Bapt). *f 1747. No regs known. Not at PRO or Ch Sec.*

TIBBERTON. **OR** C 1661 ⁺, M 1680 ⁺, B 1659 ⁺ (Inc). **BT** 1586 ⁺ (G). **Cop** (PR) CB 1661-1856, M 1680-1856, Banns 1825-56 Mf (SLC).

TIDENHAM. **OR** CMB 1708 ⁺ *(gap CB 1755-92, M 1754-67)* (Inc). **BT** 1609 ⁺ (G) Mf of PR (GRO).

TIMSBURY. Zion. (Ind). *f 1825. Not at PRO. No information.*

TIRLEY. *Formerly Trinley.* **OR** CB 1653 ⁺, M 1655 ⁺ *(gap 1752-53)* (GRO). **BT** 1577 ⁺ (G). **Cop** M 1655-1812 (Phil 14). *M 1655-1812 in RMI.*

TODDINGTON. **OR** C 1652 ⁺, M 1666 ⁺ *(gaps 1688-89, 1716, 1753)* (Inc). Registers include Stanley Pontlarge and Prescott. **BT** 1599 ⁺ (G). **Cop** CMB 1652-1715 Ms (Inc), Extracts CMB 1715-1812 (Inc). *Extracts in RMI.*

TODENHAM. **OR** CMB 1721 ⁺ (Inc). **BT** 1583 ⁺ (G). **Cop** M 1721-1812 (Phil 4), C 1626-39, M 1583-1715, CMB 1721-1812, CMB (BT) 1583-1639 (BL). *M 1721-1812, (BT) 1583-1715 in RMI.*

TORMARTON and WEST LITTLETON. OR CMB 1679 + (Inc). BT 1600, 1606-07,
   1609, 12-13, 17-18, 21-25, 27-29, 32, 37-38, 40, 1660-64, 67-72,
   1675, 78-87, 90-95, 1701, 05-12, 14, 17-32, 34-45, 47-1837 (B).
   Cop M 1600-1812 (Phil 13), M (BT) 1813-37 Ts I (ER). *M 1600-1812
   in RMI.*

TORTWORTH. OR CMB 1592 + (Inc). BT 1578 + (G). Cop M 1620-1812 (Phil
   12), M (BT) 1813-37 Ts (Roe 5 – SG and CLG). *M 1620-1812 in RMI.
   M 1813-37 not in RMI but in Index to Roe Vol. 5.*

TREDINGTON. OR C 1550 + *(gaps 1587-1617, 1637-1707, 1802-1808)*,
   M 1641 + *(gaps 1655-1672, 1726-1743, 1745-1748, 1750-1758)*, B 1541 +
   (gap 1701-1709) (Inc). BT 1599 + (G). Cop M (BT) 1675-1837 Ts (ER).
   M 1675-1812 in RMI.

TRESHAM. – *see Hawkesbury.*

TRINLEY. – *see Tirley.*

TUFFLEY. – *see Gloucester, St Mary de Lode.*

TURKDEAN. OR CM 1572 + *(gap M 1753)*, B 1531 + *(gap 1740)* (Inc).
   BT 1605 + (G). Cop M 1572-1837 (Phil 14). *M 1572-1837 in RMI .*

TWYNING. (TWINING). OR C 1648 +, M 1675 +, B 1656 + (Inc).
   BT 1618 + (G). Cop M 1674-1812 (Phil 13), Mf of PR (GRO), *M 1674-
   1812 in RMI.*

TYTHERINGTON. OR CMB 1662 + (Inc). BT 1606 + (G). Cop M (BT) 1662-
   1812 Ts Sep I (Roe 1 – SG and CLG), M (BT) 1813-1837 Ts Sep I
   (Roe 3 – SG and CLG). *M 1662-1837 not in main RMI but in Sep Index
   to Roe Vols. 1-3.*

UCKINGTON. – *see Elmstone Hardwicke.*

ULEY. OR CMB 1668 + *(gap 1687-91)* (Inc). BT 1599 + (G). Cop M 1668-
   1812 (Phil 2), M (BT) 1813-37 Ts (Roe 5 – SG and CLG). *M 1668-
   1812 in RMI. M 1813-37 not in RMI but in Index to Roe Vol. 5.*

ULEY. Union Chapel. (Ind *now united Bapt and Cong*). *f 1790*. OR ZC 1793-
   1837 (PRO).

UPLEADON. *Before 1955 with Rudford.* OR CMB 1538 + *(gap C 1761-1790)* (Inc).
   BT 1585 + (G). Cop CMB 1538-1604 (CLG). *See also Rudford.*

UPPER GUITING. – *see Guiting Temple.*

UPPER SLAUGHTER. – *see Slaughter, Upper.*

UPPER SWELL. – *see Swell, Upper.*

UPTON CHEYNEY. Zion. (Ind). *f 1834. Not at PRO.* OR C 1868 +, M 1861 +,
   B 1863 + (Ch Sec).

UPTON ST LEONARDS. OR C 1646 + *(gap 1664-71, 1682-87, 1723-35)*,
   M 1649 + *(gaps 1683-87, 1733-35, 1753)*, B 1646 + *(gaps 1663-65,
   1667-73, 1735)* (Inc). BT 1570 + (G), M (BT) 1629-1837 Ts (ER).

WALTON CARDIFF. **OR** C 1677 +, M 1697-1843, *B were at Tewkesbury Ash Church, also CM before 1677* (GRO). **BT** 1686 + (G). **Cop** CM 1697-1812 (C of A).

WAPLEY and CODRINGTON. **OR** CMB 1662 + (Inc). **BT** 1578-79, 1606, 09, 11, 1613, 17, 20, 23, 25, 27-29, 32, 38-40, 64, 67, 69-70, 73-93, 95-97, 1699-1732, 1734-1812 (B). **Cop** M (BT) 1664-1837 Ts I (Roe "BT's in Dio of Bristol" BAO and SG). *M 1664-1837 not in RMI but in Index to Roe's BT's in Dio of Bristol.*

WASHBOURNE, GREAT. **OR** CB 1779-1812, M 1757-1812 (GRO), CMB 1813 + (Inc) **BT** 1632-1700, 1820-1874 (WRO), 1600 + (G). *See notes under Alston, Worcs.* **Cop** 1779-1812 Ms (SOA).

WASHBOURNE, LITTLE. – *see Alston, Worcs. Also Teddington and Dumbleton.*

WELFORD-ON-AVON. *Formerly in parish of Clifford Chambers. Transferred to Warwickshire 1931.* **OR** CMB 1561 + (Inc). **BT** 1605 + (G). **Cop** C 1561 1739, M 1561-1716, 1730-1763 (SOA), Extracts CMB 1561-1689 Ms (PR Vol 1, CN 362324 – B'ham Ref Lib). *M 1561-1716, 1730-1763 in RMI.*

WEST LITTLETON. – *see Tormarton.*

WESTBURY-ON-SEVERN. **OR** CMB 1538 + (*gap M 1547-1557, B 1549-1557*) (Inc) C 1780-1813, 1843-1888, M 1800-1813, 1846-1888, B 1786-1794, 1843-1888 *(Parish Clerk's rough register)* (GRO), Mar. Lic. 1791-93, 1813-40 (GRO). **BT** 1586 + (G). **Cop** B 1538-1664 (C of A), (PR) C 1538 1857, M 1538-1860, B 1538-1883 Mf (SLC and GRO), M (BT) 1670-1837 Ts (ER).

WESTBURY (or FOREST) MONTHLY MEETING (S of F). *f 1668, dissolved c. 1750 and area covered by* **Gloucester Monthly Meeting.** **Constituent Meetings:-** *Westbury-on-Severn, Cover (both disc. by c. 1750). No Monthly Meeting or Constituent Meeting registers known.*

WESTBURY-ON-SEVERN (S of F). **Westbury Monthly Meeting.** – *see above.*

WESTBURY-ON-TRYM. **OR** CMB 1559 + (Inc). **BT** 1667, 69, 72-73, 75-76, 1678-79, 81-82, 84-88, 92-98, 1700-1710, 12, 15-19, 21-23, 25, 1727-29, 30-37, 41, 43-44, 56-71, 73-74, 76-77, 79, 1782-1860 (B). Copy of 1675 with Mangotsfield return. *See also Shirehampton.* **Cop** CMB 1559-1713 I (Ptd 1912). *M 1559-1713, in RMI.*

WESTBURY-ON-TRYM. Portland St Chapel. (Wes). **Bristol North Circuit.** *f 1791.* **OR** ZCB 1793-1837 (PRO), B 1793-1837 (BAO).

WESTCOTE. **OR** CMB 1630 + (*gap M 1740-1757*) (Inc – *B 1672-1730 at end of CMB reg 1630-1739*). **BT** 1605 + (G). **Cop** M 1630-1812 (Phil 14). *M 1630-1812 in RMI.*

WESTERLEIGH. **OR** CB 1693 +, M 1694 + *(gap CB 1797)* (Inc). **BT** 1596, 1605, 07-09, 12, 17, 20-25, 28-29, 37-40, 1660, 1663-65, 1667-68, 1670-72, 74-96, 98-1733, 1735-1812 (B). **Cop** M (BT) 1660-1837 Ts (Roe " BT' s in the Dio of Bristol – BAO and SG), M (PR and BT) 1660-1837 Ts (CLG – Sep volume). *M 1660-1837 not in RMI but in Index to Roe's "BT's in Dio of Bristol".*

WESTERLEIGH. Zion. (Ind). *f 1835. Not at PRO. No information.*

WESTON-ON-AVON. **OR** CMB 1685 + (Inc). **BT** 1713 + (G). **Cop** M 1690-1812 (Phil 4), C 1686-1813, M 1690-1810, B 1685-1812 (SOA). *M 1690-1812 in RMI.*

WESTON BIRT. **OR** CMB 1598 + *(gaps CMB 1640-43, CM 1651-3, C 1678, 1691-94, M 1668-94, B 1651-94). Separate regs for Lasborough. 1827 +* (Inc). **BT** 1610 + (G). **Cop** M 1596-1812 (Phil 6), M (BT) 1813-37 Ts (Roe 5 – SG and CLG). *M 1596-1812 in RMI. M 1813-37 not in RMI but in Index to Roe 5.*

WESTON-SUB-EDGE. **OR** CB 1654 +, M 1663 + (Inc). **BT** 1612 (G). **Cop** M 1612-1812 (Phil 4), Extracts M 1663-1705, B 1658-1708 (Ptd – SG), C 1654-1812, M 1663-1812, B 1657-1812, CM (BT) 1612-1638, B 1612-37 (SOA), Extracts B 1658-1708 (Ptd). *M 1612-1812 in RMI.*

WHADDON. *United with Brookthorpe 1840.* **OR** CMB 1674 + *(gap M 1751-53)* (Inc). **BT** 1617 + (G). **Cop** M 1620-1812 (Phil 13), CMB 1674-1711 (Glos N and Q, IV), CMB 1674-1698 Ms (CLG). *M 1620-1812 in RMI.*

WHEATENHURST. *– see Whitminster.*

WHITESHILL. (Ind). *f 1816. Not at PRO. No information.*

WHITMINSTER (or WHEATENHURST). **OR** CMB 1538 + *(gaps C 1666-1684, M 1638-1698, 1739-54, 1804)* (Inc). **BT** 1571 + (G). **Cop** M (BT) 1660-1812 Ts Sep I (Roe 1 – SG and CLG), M (BT) 1813-1837 (Roe 3 – SG and CLG). *M 1660-1837 not in main RMI but in Sep Index to Roe Vols. 1-3.*

WHITTINGTON. **OR** CMB 1539 + *(gap M 1750-53)* (Inc). **BT** 1602 + (CLG).

WICK. *Parish formed from Abson 1880.* **OR** CMB 1880 + (Inc), CMB 1687-1812 *in Abson regs. Gap CMB 1813-1880.* **BT** 1600-02, 08, 17-18, 1621-25, 28-29, 37-38, 40, 61-65, 67-72, 74-76, 1679-1727, 1729-1812 (B), 1814-36 (G). **Cop** M (BT) 1608-1700 (SOA), M (BT) 1814-36 Ts I (ER). *See also Abson.*

WICK. Zion. (Ind). *f 1836. Not at PRO. No information.*

WICKWAR. **OR** CMB 1689 + (Inc). **BT** 1578 + (G). **Cop** M 1689-1812 (Phil 11), CMB (BT) 1637-1688 Ts I (Roe 4 – SG and CLG), M (BT) 1813-37 Ts (Roe 5 – SG and CLG). *M 1689-1812 in RMI. M 1637-1688 not in RMI but in Index to Roe Vol 4. M 1813-37 in Index to Roe Vol. 5.*

WICKWAR. Lower Chapel. (Ind). *f 1817.* **OR** ZC 1818-1836, B 1818-1832 (PRO).

WIDFORD *(now in Oxfordshire)*. **OR** CB 1751 +, M 1770 + *(gap M 1804-1816)*
(BL). **BT** 1606 + (G). **Cop** C 1751-1830, M 1753-1812, B 1754-1829
Ts (SG — West Oxon Regs 2), 1837-57 (Bod Ms Oxf Dio Papers d. 468).

WILLERSEY. **OR** C 1721-1812 *(gap 1722-1741)*, M 1723-1812 *(gap 1741)*,
B 1727-1812 (Inc). **BT** 1580 + (G). **Cop** M 1723-1812 (Phil 6),
Extracts CMB (BT) 1606-1731 (Ptd), C 1721-1812, M 1723-1754,
B 1727-1812 (SOA). *M 1723-1812 in RMI.*

WINCHCOMBE. **OR** CMB 1539 + *(gap CMB 1640- 1651)* (Inc), Mar. Alleg.
1822 (5) (GRO). **BT** 1620 + (G). **Cop** M 1539-1812 (Phil 9), C 1571-
1812, M 1539-1812, B 1573-1812 Ms (Inc). *M 1539-1812 in RMI.*

WINDRUSH. *United with Sherborne 1776.* **OR** CMB 1586 + *(gaps CMB 1664-
73, CB 1751-52, M 1751-54)* (Inc). **BT** 1605 + (G). *See also
Sherborne.*

WINSON. **Peculiar** *of Rector of Bibury.* **OR** C 1577 +, M 1585 + *(gap
1653-1676)*, B 1602-1812 *(gaps 1610-1629, 1706-1738)* (Inc).
BT *A few only.*

WINSTONE. **OR** CMB 1540 + (Inc). **BT** 1617 + (G). **Cop** M 1540-1837 (Phil
16). *M 1540-1837 in RMI.*

WINSTONE. (Bapt). *f 1822. Not at PRO. No information.*

WINTERBOURNE. **OR** CMB 1600 + *(gap CMB 1691-1696)* (Inc). **BT** 1673 (scrap
of), 1686, 88, 96-97, 1708, 62, 75-76, 79, 1800-60 (B).
Cop M (BT) 1800-1837 Ts I (ER). *M 1600-1812 in RMI. See also
Frenchay.*

WINTERBOURNE. White's Hill. (Ind). *f 1816.* **OR** ZC 1824-1834 (PRO).

WINTERBOURNE. Frenchay Chapel. (Pres). — *see Frenchay.*

WINTERBOURNE (S of F). — *see* **Frenchay Monthly Meeting.**

WITCOMBE, GREAT. **OR** CB 1749 +, M 1749-1754 (Inc). **BT** 1570 + (G).
Cop CMB 1570-1577, 1598-1605 Ms (CLG).

WITHINGTON. **Peculiar** *of Rector of Withington.* **OR** CMB 1609 + (Inc).
BT 1600 + (G).

WOODCHESTER. **OR** CMB 1563 + *(gap CMB 1625-1668)* (Inc). **BT** 1614 + (G).
Cop CMB 1563-1603 (CLG), M 1563-1624, 1669-1836 (Phil Ms). *M 1563-
1624, 1669-1836 in RMI.*

WOODCHESTER. (Bapt). *f 1832. Not at PRO. No information.*

WOODMANCOTE. — *see Bishop's Cleeve.*

WOOLASTON. *With Chapelry of Alvington.* **OR** C 1688 +, MB 1696 + *(gap
M 1730-38, 1756, B 1737).* **BT** *A number of BT's extant, but in
poor condition and cannot be used until repaired.* **Cop** CMB 1587-
1592 (CLG), M 1696-1837 (Phil 14 — includes M 1730-1738 now missing
from OR). *M 1696-1837 in RMI. (Woolaston is often confused with
Woolston). See also Alvington.*

WOOLSTON. **OR** *All records destroyed in Rectory fire 1889.* **BT** 1575 + (G). (*Woolston is often confused with Woolaston*).

WORMINGTON. **OR** CMB 1719 + (*gap M 1754*) (Inc). **BT** 1612 + (G). **Cop** M 1719-1812 (Phil 4), C 1719-1770, M 1719-1811, B 1719-1812 (SOA). *M 1719-1812 in RMI.*

WOTTON. St Catharine. — *see Gloucester, St Catherine.*

WOTTON, St Mary. — *see Gloucester, St Mary de Lode.*

WOTTON-UNDER-EDGE. **OR** CMB 1571 + (*gap C 1586-98*). **BT** 1578 + (G). **Cop** CMB 1659-1715 (C of A), CMB 1571-1715 (Inc), M (BT) 1659-1812 Ts Sep I (Roe 2 — SG and CLG), M (BT) 1813-37 Ts Sep I (Roe 3 — SG and CLG), M (PR and BT) 1571-1812 Ts (with Index to 1571-1837) (SG, CLG and Inc). *M 1659-1837 not in main RMI but in Sep Index to Roe Vols. 1-3. See also Nibley, North.*

WOTTON-UNDER-EDGE. (Bapt). *f 1717.* **OR** Z 1784-1813 (PRO).

WOTTON-UNDER-EDGE. Tabernacle. (Calv Meth now Cong). *f 1772.* **OR** ZC 1772-1837, B 1772-1784 (PRO).

WOTTON-UNDER-EDGE. Old Town Meeting House. (Pres.). *f 1703.* **OR** ZC 1767-1837 (PRO).

WYCK RISSINGTON. — *see Rissington Wyck.*

YANWORTH. *Formerly Chapelry of Hazleton.* **OR** CMB 1695 + (Inc). **BT** 1606 + (G). *See also Hazleton.*

YATE. **OR** CMB 1660 + (Inc). **BT** 1616 + (G). **Cop** M (BT) 1660-1812 Ts Sep I (Roe 1 — SG and CLG), M (BT) 1813-37 Sep I (Roe 3 — SG and CLG), M (PR and BT) 1660-1837 Ts (SG, CLG and Inc). *M 1660-1837 not in main RMI but in Sep Index to Roe Vols. 1-3.*

YATE. North Road. (Bapt). *f date not known. Not at PRO. No information.*

HEREFORDSHIRE

ACKNOWLEDGMENTS

*The Editor gratefully acknowledges the assistance of the follow-
ing persons in compiling this section.*
Mr. A. Shaw Wright, Miss Jancey and Miss Paul of the Herefordshire
County Record Office for assistance in listing deposited and surveyed
registers and in answering numerous queries;
Mr. J.F.W. Sherwood, Librarian Hereford City Library for listing his
holdings;
Mr. F.C. Morgan for assistance with the preface;
Mr. P. Gwynne James, Registrar of the Diocese of Hereford for facili-
ties to examine the Bishop's Transcripts;
Mr. D.C. Owens of the National Library of Wales for supplying in-
formation on Bishop's Transcripts and Marriage Licences;
Miss. D.M. Lloyd for listing surrendered Nonconformist Registers;
Miss. E. Kennard for checking returns at the National Register of
Archives;
Mr. J.R. Cunningham of the Church of Jesus Christ of Latter Day Saints
and Edward Milligan Archivist of Friends' House, Euston, for grant-
ing access to their records, the Archivist of the Catholic Diocese
of Cardiff, the Secretaries of denominational Unions and Associations
and numerous Anglican Clergy, Catholic Parish Priests, Methodist
Circuit Superintendents and Baptist and Congregationalist Ministers and
Secretaries for supplying information.

GENERAL INFORMATION

Record Repositories — (See also list on page xx).

H.R.O. — *Herefordshire Record Office, Shirehall, Hereford.*
(Hours 9.30 - 5.30).
This holds no Parish Registers or Bishop's Transcripts.

H.C.L. — *Hereford City Library, Museum and Art Gallery,*
Broad Street, Hereford.
(Hours 9 - 6.30, Thurs 9 - 5)
This holds about 49 Original Parish Registers.

H. — *Diocesan Registrar at 5 St. Peter's Street, Hereford.*
(Searches by appointment)
This holds all records of the Diocese of Hereford including
the Bishop's Transcripts and Marriage Licences. It also
holds one parish register (Moreton Jefferies). A fee is
normally charged.

For explanation of abbreviations HX and HXX see Bishop's
Transcripts.

N.L.W. *National Library of Wales, Aberystwith.*
(Hours 9.30 - 6, Sat 9 - 5)
This holds the Bishop's Transcripts and Marriage Licences
for 8 parishes in the Diocese of St. David's.

Archbishop's House, Whitchurch, Cardiff.
This holds the Archives of the Roman Catholic Diocese of
Cardiff, but no registers.

Parishes
Ancient Parishes 223
Changes in County Boundaries — only a few minor adjustments have
made.

Original Parish Registers
Most parish registers are still with the Incumbents, though
about 49 are deposited at the City Library, Hereford, and further
deposits are continually being made. One register, that of Moreton
Jefferies is in the Muniment Room of the Cathedral (apply Diocesan
Registrar). The County Archivist is at present in process of listing
all Parish Registers.
The registers of Ledbury enter names of godparents from 1555 until
1576.

At the time of going to press, 7 Herefordshire Parish Registers
have been broken down on to Family Reconstruction forms of the
purpose of demographic analysis. Work on a further nine is in progress.

Bishop's Transcripts.

The whole of the County formed the Archdeaconry of Hereford in
the Diocese of Hereford except for 8 parishes in the Diocese of St.
David's.

Diocese of Hereford (H).

These are kept in the Muniment Room of Hereford Cathedral and
applications to examine them should be made to the Diocesan Registrar,
Diocesan Registry. A fee is usually charged.

They have been sorted into parish bundles until 1812. The majority
start about 1660 and continue to 1812 with only minor gaps which
have been noted in full. The Diocesan Registrar has a detailed list
describing the condition of the transcripts and other details. A few,
though sorted into approximate order of year have not been fully
listed. HX indicates that the period 1754-1812 has been checked and
missing years noted, but not the period 1660-1753. HXX indicates that
both periods are unchecked. In all cases any transcripts dating before
1660 are noted.

The post-1813 Transcripts are arranged by Deaneries, but not
sorted into parishes, listed or checked to discover missing transcripts.

The overall dates of the Deaneries are as follows:-
Archenfield (12 Boxes) 1813-1869
Frome (now Bromyard) (21 Boxes) 1813-1897
Hereford (14 Boxes) 1813-1862
Leominster (15 Boxes) 1813-1891
Ross (10 Boxes) 1813-1897
Weobley (12 Boxes) 1814-1871
Weston (11 Boxes) 1814-1896

There is a separate volume for Hereford Deanery 1815-1816, and
two separate boxes for 1834 and 1835 containing transcripts from
all Deaneries.

Peculiars

Peculiar of Chancellor of Choir of Hereford Cathedral (Little
    Hereford). Normal transcripts. With main series.
Peculiar Prebend of Upper Bullinghope. No transcripts.
Peculiar Prebend of Moreton Magna. Normal transcripts. With main
    series.

Modern Copies of Parish Registers and Bishop's Transcripts.

Very few Herefordshire parishes have been copied. Five have been
printed by the Parish Register Society. (Canon Frome, Fownhope, Ledbury
Munsley, Sarnesfield).

Such manuscript or typescript copies as exist are at the Society
of Genealogists Library or City Library, Hereford. The majority of
transcripts at the latter are extracts only, and these have not been
included if it is known that they are of one family only. The extracts
from 13 parishes made by W.H. Cooke have not been included.

Herefordshire is not included in Boyd's Marriage Index.

Marriage Licences

Hereford Diocese. At Muniment Room, Hereford Cathedral (apply
Diocesan Registrar).
Marriage Bonds (1661-1831) are on files in boxes, Licence Books
(1663-1787) are bound and indexed, but need repair. There are Allega-
tions 1663-1696 and returns of licences (1709-1843). The Allegations
1834-1909 are bound and indexed. Later Allegations are in parcels. A
Microfilm of Extracts from Marriage Licences, 1676-1748 is at Salt
Lake City.

Diocese of St. David's.

There is one Marriage Bond dated 1616 and one dated 1621, but
the main sequence does not commence until 1661. Even for the late 17th
and early 18th centuries the documents are not numerous.

They are divided into two main sections. The documents relating
to the present Diocese of Swansea and Brecon for the period 1661-
1867 are arranged chronologically according to parish in bound
volumes. All the other documents, consisting of loose papers are
arranged chronologically in one sequence.

Roman Catholics

Herefordshire lies within the Roman Catholic Diocese of Cardiff.
There appear to have been four pre-1837 Catholic Chapels or churches
– at Rotherwas, Hereford, Weobley and Courtfield (Goodrich), the
parish priests of the last three holding early registers. The
Rotherwas Church has long been closed. The post-1837 registers are
held by the Vincentian Fathers at Hereford, but the whereabouts of
earlier registers is unknown. Courtfield was a house of the Vaughan
family; the Courtfield registers, held by the parish priest contain
burials for 13 other places. A register dating from 1773-1832 has

been published by the C.R.S. In addition, the early registers of
Little Malvern Court, Worcs. include entries for Bosbury, Colwall,
and Ledbury. No registers are held with the Diocesan Archives.

Baptists

10 Baptist Churches were founded before 1837. Of these, five –
Gorsley, Hereford, Kington, Leominster and Weston-under-Penyard
deposited registers. The last two of these churches go back to the
17th Century, the registers of Leominster dating from 1702 and those
of Weston from 1787. Kington registers date from 1791; the remaining
two from 1831. Of the other five pre-1837 churches, Fownhope has a
particularly interesting register of Baptisms and Admissions dating
from 1806, which includes places of origin. It also includes a few
births from 1826. Garway and Peterchurch hold no registers and no
information has been received from Ross (f.1819) and Ledbury (f.1836).

All the Herefordshire churches were formerly in the Midland
Baptist Association and are now in the Gloucestershire and Hereford-
shire Association. Neither the latter nor the present West Midland
Association holds any registers.

Independents (Congregationalists)

Three independent Churches were founded in 1662, at Gore,Hereford
and Ross. The two former are now in the Hereford District of the
Shropshire Union, the latter in the Cheltenham and Gloucester District
of the Gloucestershire and Herefordshire Union. Hereford deposited
registers from 1690 and Ross from 1732. Two 19th Century foundations,
Pembridge and Whitchurch also deposited registers. The only other
pre-1837 churches still in existence are those of Leominster (f 1829)
and Huntington (f 1804). A manuscript book dating from about 1707 now
in the possession of Eignbrook Congregational Church contains some
baptisms for a former church at Wyebridge. The documents of the Congregational Union of Gloucestershire and Herefordshire are held by
Page & Co, Solicitors, Bristol Chambers, St. Nicholas Street, Bristol
but do not include any registers. No replies have been received
from the Secretaries of the Shropshire Union, or the Hereford District
but it is highly unlikely that any registers are held.

Presbyterians

As far as is known, there were no pre-1837 Presbyterian Churches
in Herefordshire.

Methodists

Wesleyans.

There were three Herefordshire Circuits – two of these Hereford and that of Ledbury and the Forest of Dean came under the Bristol District, the other that of Kington, the Birmingham and Shrewsbury District. In addition, the Ludlow (Salop), Monmouth and Worcester Circuits probably included parts of Herefordshire. Two of the Herefordshire Circuits – Hereford and Kington – deposited registers. It is not known if registers exist for the Ledbury Circuit. (see Modern Methodist Circuits below).

Primitive Methodists

There was only one Circuit centred in Herefordshire, that of Cwm, also known as the Hereford Circuit. The registers were surrendered, as were separate registers for the only other known church, that of Hereford. It is probable that the Circuits of Ludlow (Salop) Presteign (Radnor) and Kidderminster (Worcs) also took in part of Herefordshire.

Methodists New Connection.

There were no churches and no Circuit in Herefordshire, the nearest Circuits being the two Shropshire Circuits and Stourbridge, Worcs.

Modern Methodist Circuits.

Herefordshire now comes within the Birmingham District. The Superintendents of the following Methodist Circuits might be found to hold registers or other records.

All have been circularised, but no replies received.

Hereford
Ledbury
Cwm and Kingstone
Presteigne and Kington
Leominster

Calvinistic Methodists.

Only one pre-1837 church is known, that of Brilley (f.1828) which comes under the Hay (Brecknockshire) District.

Lady Huntingdon's Connexion.

There were only two churches at Hereford (Registers at the P.R.O.) and Cradley. Entries for the latter are found in the registers of Leigh Sinton, Worcestershire, (also deposited).

Society of Friends (Quakers)

The Herefordshire Quarterly Meeting was established in 1668 with the following Monthly Meetings.

Leominster   (1663-1808)
Ross   (1663-1808)

In 1791 *Herefordshire* Quarterly Meeting was united with *Worcestershire* Quarterly Meeting to form the *Herefordshire and Worcestershire* Quarterly Meeting which in turn in 1832 was united with the Wales Half Years' Meeting to form the *Herefordshire, Worcestershire and Wales General Meeting.*

Leominster and Ross Monthly Meetings were united in 1808 to form the Leominster and Ross Monthly Meeting. Hereford Monthly Meeting was united with North Wales Monthly Meeting in 1834 to form the Hereford and Radnor Monthly Meeting, though the Leominster and Ross Registers were continued for Herefordshire.

Registers

Herefordshire Quarterly Meeting Z 1646-1789, M 1677-1786, B 1650-1789 (PRO 631,632).

Herefordshire and Worcestershire Quarterly Meeting Z 1800-1837, M 1800-1836, B 1799-1837 (635-637).

Hereford, Worcestershire and Wales General Meeting. Herefordshire and Worcestershire entries were continued in the previous registers.

Monthly Meeting registers are listed under the individual Monthly Meetings.

Birth and Burial Notes Z 1774-1800, B 1777-1797 for the Herefordshire Worcestershire and Wales General Meeting and Marriage Licences 1795-1799 are at PRO (No. 1472).

The "Digest" at Friends' House, Euston Road, London, N.W.1. lists entries from all surrendered registers.[1]

Moravians

There was a Moravian Church at Leominster (f 1759). Registers at the P.R.O.

Monumental Inscriptions

The Monumental Inscriptions in Hereford Cathedral were published in 1831.

The Woolhope Club has launched a project to copy all Herefordshire Monumental Inscriptions.

Regimental Registers

These cover Births, Baptisms, Marriages and Deaths for the period

---

[1] See general article on Quaker Registers in Vol. 1.

1790-1924 and are at Somerset House, London. They are the original
registers kept by the various regiments. Births and Baptisms are indexed. For Marriages, Deaths and Burials it is preferable, but not
essential to know the regiment. The most likely regiment for Herefordshire Infantrymen was the 36th Regiment of Foot.

Search should also be made of the Guards' Regiments, the Royal
Artillery, the Royal Engineers and the Royal Marines.

Newspapers

Hereford Times 1833 – date

Hereford County Press 1837-40.

Local Societies

The Woolhope Club, Sec. Mr. F.M. Kendrick, 40 Stanhope Street,
Hereford.

Publications: *Transactions* 1852 onwards

*Herefordshire, its Natural History, Archaeology
and History* (1951).

Useful Works of Reference

Audrey H. Higgs, A.L.A. and Donald Wright, F.L.A. *"West Midland
Genealogy"* (Published 1966 under the auspices of the West Midland
Branch of the Library Association). This is a survey of local
genealogical material which is available in the public libraries of
Herefordshire, Shropshire, Staffordshire, Warwickshire and Worcester-
shire. Copies available from A.J. Fox, Esq., F.L.A., Birchfield
Library, Birmingham 20. Price 10/- (11/- Post paid).

*A Select List of Books in the Local Collection of the Herefordshire
County Libraries* (Hereford County Libraries Local History Section
1955).

Duncumb *History of Herefordshire*
G. Strong *The Heraldry of Herefordshire* (1848).

*Visitation of Herefordshire made by Robert Cooke, Clarencieux, in
1569,* Ed. F.W. Weaver 1886.
Heraldic Visitation of Herefordshire 1634.

PARISH LIST

ABBEY DORE. **OR** CMB 1634 $^+$ (*gap 1686-1724*) (Inc). **BT** 1660 $^+$ (H).

ACONBURY. **OR** CMB 1813 $^+$ (Inc). **BT** 1665 $^+$ (*gaps 1667, 68, 1706, 12, 26, 1627, 59*) (H).

ACTON BEAUCHAMP. — *see Worcestershire.*

ALLENSMORE. **OR** CMB 1698 $^+$ (*gap 1728-42*) (Inc). **BT** 1663 $^+$ (*gaps 1668, 1671, 73, 95, 99, 1702, 3, 16, 34, 36, 57, 1806, 07, 10, 11*) (H). **Cop** Extracts from lost register for 1671 (CLH).

ALMELEY. **OR** CB 1596-1812, M 1596-1820 (*gap CMB 1681-1745*), Banns 1792-1821 (CLH), 1813 $^+$ (Inc). **BT** 1660 $^+$ (*gaps 1668, 94, 96, 98, 1700*) (H). **Cop.** *M 1598-1754 in Boyd Misc.*

AMBERLEY. **OR** CMB 1742 $^+$ (Inc). **BT** *on Marden returns.* **Cop** CMB 1596-1681, 1745-1771 Ms Not I (SG).

ASHPERTON. **OR** CMB 1538 $^+$ (Inc). **BT** 1660 $^+$ (*gaps 1663, 69, 1727, 67*) (H).

ASTON. **OR** CMB 1685 $^+$ (Inc). **BT** 1662 $^+$ (*gap 1731*) (H). **Cop** CMB (Phil Ms).

ASTON INGHAM. **OR** CMB 1633 $^+$ (Inc). **BT** 1662 $^+$ (*no gaps*) (H). **Cop** (PR) C 1633-1853, M 1633-1856, B 1633-1881 Mf (SLC), CMB 1633-1737 Mf (NLW).

AVENBURY. **OR** C 1661-1930, M 1678-1931, B 1661-1930, Banns 1754-1812 (CLH). *B 1661-77 entered between years 1760 and 1761.* **BT** 1661 $^+$ (*gaps 1664, 91, 97, 1701*) (H).

AYLTON. **OR** CM 1748 $^+$ (Inc). *No Burials.* **BT** only 1661, 1749, 1750, 53, 1754, 58, 1766 $^+$. Other years on Ledbury returns (H).

AYMESTREY. **OR** C 1568-1894, M 1568-1837, B 1568-1862 (*period 1568-1729 loose sheets only, apparently remains of 2 registers. Almost illegible. Gap CMB 1601-c.1670*), Banns 1755-1812. *All registers after 1812 probably include Leinthall Earls, though only C 1812-1845 is so labelled*) (CLH). **BT** 1660 $^+$ (*gap 1667*) (H).

BACTON. **OR** CMB 1724 $^+$ (Inc). **BT** 1663 $^+$ (*gaps 1706, 18, 28, 86*) (H).

BALLINGHAM. **OR** CMB 1588 $^+$ (Inc). **BT** 1660 $^+$ (*gaps 1661, 69, 89, 1731, 1771*) (H).

BARTESTREE. *Chapel to Dormington.* **OR** CMB 1813 $^+$. **BT** *on Dormington returns.* Separate transcript for 1811 and 1812 (H).

BIRCH, LITTLE. **OR** CB 1557-1812, C 1813-1884, M 1557-1912 (*gap 1741-55*), Banns 1755-1802, Mar. Lic. 1837 (CLH). **BT** 1661 $^+$ (*gaps 1663, 1701, 1737*) (H).

BIRCH, MUCH. **OR** C 1599-1871, M 1599-1837 (*gap 1754-1771*), B 1599-1900, Banns 1771-91, 1809-10, 1813-1818 (CLH). **BT** 1660 $^+$ (*gaps 1663 and 1726*) (H).

BIRLEY. **OR** CB 1757 + (*gap 1778-80*), M 1754 + (Inc). **BT** 1663 + (*gaps 1695, 1701*) (H).

BISHOPS FROME. **OR** CMB 1564 + (Inc). **BT** 1661 + (*gap 1730*) (H).

BISHOPSTONE. **OR** CMB 1727 + (Inc). **BT** 1660 + (*no gaps*) (H).

BLAKEMERE. **OR** CMB 1662-5, 1668, 1670-1753, C 1754-1812, M 1754-1835, B 1754-1812, Banns 1754-7, 1759-91 (CLH), CB 1813 +, M 1837 + (Inc). **BT** 1664 + (*gaps 1668, 69, 1718, 1806, 07, 10, 11*) (H).

BOCKLETON. – *see Worcestershire.*

BODENHAM. **OR** C 1584-1872, M 1584-1837, B 1584-1904 (*gaps CMB 1590-1635, 1644-6, 1647-9, 1656-60, 1665-68*), Banns 1754-1805 (CLH). **BT** 1660 + (*gaps 1661, 69, 91, 1701*) (H).

BOLSTONE. – *see Boulstone.*

BOSBURY. **OR** CMB 1558 + (*gaps CMB 1745-7, M 1750-4*), Banns 1766-1810, 1829 + (Inc). **BT** 1660 + (*gap 1662*) (H).

BOSBURY (RC). *Entries in registers of Little Malvern Court. – see Worcestershire – Malvern, Little.*

BOULSTONE. *Chapel to Holme Lacy.* **OR** CMB 1765 + (Inc). *In Holme Lacy registers until 1727. A separate Boulstone register from 1728 was listed in the P.R. Abstract.* **BT** *on Holme Lacy returns.*

BRAMPTON ABBOTTS. **OR** CB 1561-1812, M 1561-1837 (*gaps 1749-54, 1810-13*), Banns 1754-1810, Mar. Lic. 1807 (CLH). **BT** 1661 + (*no gaps*) (H).

BRAMPTON BRYAN. **OR** CMB 1598 + (*gap 1642-1663*) (Inc). **BT** 1638, 1663 + (*gap 1705*) (H).

BRANTON. – *see Breinton.*

BREDENBURY. **OR** CB 1607-1812, M 1607-1846 (*gaps CMB 1609-11, 1645-60*), Banns 1754-1812 (CLH). **BT** 1660 + (*gaps 1686, 91, 1701, 1706*) (H).

BREDWARDINE. **OR** CB 1723-1890, B 1723-1908 (*gap CB 1767-75, 1795-1813 except for some entries for the following years 1768, 69, 71, 73, 1797, 1804, 1810*), M 1723-1837 (*gap 1751-4*), Banns 1754-1812 (CLH). *(The registers also include Banns and M for Brobury 1760-85, 1797, 1799-1800).* **BT** 1660 + (*no gaps*) (H). **Cop** CMB (BT) 1660-1722 I, CMB 1723-1799 Extracts 1800-1933 Ts (SG), CMB (BT) 1660-1933 (CLH) (PR), CMB 1660-1933 Mf (SLC). *M 1660-1837 in Boyd Misc.*

BREINTON. **OR** CMB 1662 + (*gaps 1728-30, 1784-7*) (Inc). **BT** 1662 + (*gaps 1664, 69, 71, 95, 1718, 87, 1806, 07, 10, 11*) (H).

BRIDGE SOLLARS. **OR** CMB 1615 + (*gaps CMB 1683-96, 1746-54, CB 1754-1761, 1774-91*) (Inc). **BT** 1660 + (*gaps 1727, 1753*) (H). **Cop** CMB 1615-1812 Ts I (SG and Mf SLC), CMB 1615-1716 Ts (CLH).

BRIDSTOW. **OR** CMB 1560 + (Inc). *No BT's traced. Not at H, L or NLW.*

BRILLEY. **OR** CMB 1581 + (*gap 1583-87*) (Inc). **BT** 1660 + (*no gaps*) (H).

BRILLEY. (Calv Meth). **Hay District** (*see Brecknockshire*). *f 1828. Not at PRO. No information.*

BRIMFIELD. **OR** CMB 1566 + (Inc). **BT** 1661 + *(gaps 1666, 67, 1705, 1783)* (H).

BRINSOP. **OR** CMB 1695 + (Inc). **BT** 1660 + *(gaps 1667, 68, 88, 1712)* (H).

BROBURY. **OR** C 1784-1795, 1813-1922, M 1784-1795, 1802-1828, 1836, 1840-1882, B 1784-95, 1813-1907, Mar. Lic. 1827 (CLH), C 1795-1806, Banns and M 1760-85, 1797, 1799-1800 in regs of Bredwardine (CLH). **BT** 1660 + *(gap 1662, 1718)* (H). **Cop** CMB (BT) 1660-1753 I (SG), CMB (BT) 1660-1925 (CLH and Mf SLC).

BROCKHAMPTON. **OR** 1578 + *(gap M 1808-12)* (Inc Bromyard). **BT** 1661 + *(gaps 1663, 4, 6, 8, 9, 70, 75, 1718, 25, 39, 49, 57, 66, 93, 1800-1803, 06, 07, 10, 11)* (H). *Woolhope returns 1666-98 described as with Brockhampton. See Woolhope.*

BROMYARD. **OR** C 1538-1873 *(gap 1646-56)*, M 1545-1869 *(gaps 1651-56, 1730-54)*, B 1545-1866 *(gap 1651-56)*, Banns 1875-1947 (CLH). **BT** 1661 + *(gaps 1695, 1715, 1742)* most in bad condition (H). **Cop** CMB 1545-1643 (Cathedral Lib Hereford), CMB 1700-1726 Ms (CLH).

BROMYARD (S of F). **Leominster Monthly Meeting** *(1668-1808)*, **Leominster and Ross Monthly Meeting** *(1808-1834)*, **Hereford and Radnor Monthly Meeting** *(1834 +)*. *No regs known other than Monthly Meeting regs.*

BROMYARD (Ind). **OR** ZCB 1696-1836 (PRO).

BULLINGHAM (BULLINGHOPE) UPPER. **Peculiar** *Prebend of Upper Bullingham.* **OR** C 1682-1918, M 1682-1837 B 1682-1932, Banns 1754-1813, 1825-1885 *(gaps CMB 1694-1715, CB 1764-1796, M 1813-15)* (CLH). *All registers probably contain entries of residents of Lower Bullingham, Grafton and St Martin's, Hereford, especially after 1813. B 1813-1932 include frequent entries for other Hereford parishes. M 1754-1837, C 1813-1918, B 1813-1932 are all indexed.* **BT** *No BT's traced.*

BULLINGHAM, LOWER and GRAFTON. *Until 1866 both in parish of St Martin's, Hereford. St Martin's church destroyed 1645 and from then until 1845 St Martin's parish annexed to All Saints, Hereford, but many inhabitants of Lower Bullingham and Grafton used church at Upper Bullingham.*

BURGHILL. **OR** CB 1655 + , M 1656 + (Inc). **BT** 1661 + *(gap 1669)* (H).

BURRINGTON. **OR** CB 1541-1812, M 1541-1836 *(gaps CMB 1639-55, M 1810-13)*, Banns 1754-1799 (CLH). **BT** 1660 + (HX).

BYFORD. **OR** CMB 1660 + (Inc). **BT** 1661 + *(no gaps)* (H).

BYTON. **OR** CMB 1763 + or 1780 + (Inc). **BT** 1660 + *(gaps 1704, 1723)* (H).

CALLOW. **OR** CB 1576-1812, M 1576-1835 *(gaps CMB 1636-78, 1738-41, M 1754-64, 1809-13)*, Banns 1764-1809 (CLH). **BT** 1660 + *(gaps 1663, 1664, 91, 92, 93)* (H).

CANON FROME. **OR** CMB 1680 + (Inc Munsley). **BT** 1664 + *(gap 1665)* (H). **Cop** CMB 1680-1812 Ptd (PRS 45), CMB (BT) 1664-1680 (CLH).

CANON PYON. **OR** CMB 1707 + (Inc). **BT** 1662 + *(gaps 1665, 66, 95, 98, 1701, 1739, 1751, 1781, 1806, 07, 10, 11)* (H). **Cop** CMB 1707-1790 (Inc).

CASTLE FROME. **OR** CMB 1719 + (Inc Bishop's Frome). **BT** 1660 + *(gap 1700, 1734)* (H).

CLEHONGER. **OR** CMB 1671 + *(gap CMB 1689-95, 1702-40)* (Inc). **BT** 1670 + *(gaps 1695, 1702, 03, 55, 57, 64, 70, 1806, 07, 10, 11)* (H). **Cop** CMB 1671-1787 Ms and 1764-5 Parchment Ms (CLH), CMB 1671-1787 Ms (CLH).

CLIFFORD. **OR** CMB 1690 + (Inc). **BT** 1662 + *(gaps 1664, 68, 95, 96, 1701)* (H).

CLODOCK. – *including chapelries of Llanveynoe, Craswell and Newton.* **OR** C 1703, 1714-1761 *(includes C at Llanveynoe Chapel 1757)*, CB 1761-1779 *(Llanveynoe, Longtown, Craswell, Clodock)*, 1791 +, M 1714 +, B 1714-1761, 1780 +, Banns 1771-1796 (Inc). **BT** 1687-8, 1713-1810, 1813-39 (with entries for Longtown, Craswell, Llanveynoe and Newton) (NLW – St D).

CODDINGTON. **OR** 1675 + (Inc). **BT** 1660 + *(gap 1808)* (H).

COLLINGTON. **OR** CB 1566-1812, M 1566-1836 *(gaps CMB 1639-42, M 1810-1813)*, Banns 1758-1810 (CLH), *CMB 1566-1639 nearly illegible.* **BT** 1660 + *(no gaps)* (H).

COLWALL. **OR** CMB 1651 + (Inc). **BT** 1660 + *(gaps 1703, 1812). Distinction between the two divisions of Colwall (Bishop's Colwall and Barton) in following years:- 1669 (Barton only), 1671-6, 79, 1694 (Bishop's Colwall only), 1695, 96 (both).*

COLWALL (RC). *Entries in regs of Little Malvern Court. See Worcestershire – Malvern, Little.*

COURTFIELD (RC). – *see Goodrich.*

COWARNE, LITTLE. **OR** CB 1563-1812, M 1563-1813, 1840 + *(gap CMB 1648-66)*, Banns 1954-1957 (Inc Pencombe). **BT** 1660 + *(no gaps except 1664-9 which is included on Ullingswick transcripts)* (H).

COWARNE, MUCH. **OR** 1559 + *(gaps CMB 1644-1663, 1704-7)* (Inc). **BT** 1660 + *(no gaps)* (H).

CRADLEY. **OR** CMB 1560 + (Inc). **BT** 1660 + *(gaps 1694, 1757).* **Cop** CB 1560-1670, M 1560-1733 (C of A).

CRADLEY. – *(Nr Halesowen) – see Worcs.*

CRADLEY (Lady Hunt). – *see Leigh Linton (Worcs).*

CRASWALL. **OR** 1703 + (Inc), C 1761-79 *in Clodock regs.* **BT** *on Clodock returns and on Michaelchurch Eskley returns 1713-31.*

CREDENHILL. **OR** C 1671-1965, M 1671-1837 *(gap 1753-5)*, B 1671-1812, Banns 1824-1941 (CLH), B 1813 + (Inc). **BT** 1662 + *(gaps 1718, 1731, 1734, 35)* (H).

CRODOCK. – *see Clodock.*

CROFT. **OR** CMB 1565 $^+$ (Inc). Separate BT's for 1681, 1691-6, 1698 only. *Other years on Yarpole returns.*

CUSOP. **OR** CB 1709-1812, M 1709-1837 (CLH). *1st register also includes CMB 1698-1709 for Cusop taken from Glasbury reg.* BT 1662 $^+$ *(gaps 1668, 9, 1699, 1702, 04). BT's from March to March even after 1752* (H). *See also Glasbury.*

CWM or **HEREFORD CIRCUIT.** (Prim Meth). **OR** ZC 1828-1837 (PRO). *See also Hereford, Union St.*

DEWCHURCH, LITTLE. **OR** CMB 1730 $^+$ (Inc). **BT** 1660 $^+$ *(gap 1661)* (H).

DEWCHURCH, MUCH. **OR** CMB 1559 $^+$ *(gap 1636-9)* (Inc). **BT** 1661 $^+$ *(gap 1703)* (H).

DEWSALL. **OR** CB 1582-1812, M 1582-1837 *(gap 1809-23)*, Banns 1754-1809 (CLH). **BT** 1672 $^+$ *(gaps 1692-6, 1706, 1768, 70, 71, 94, 96, 1806, 1807, 10, 11)* (H). **Cop** CMB 1582-1787 (CLH).

DILWYN. **OR** CMB 1558 $^+$ *(gap CB 1805-7)* (Inc). **BT** 1660 $^+$ *(gaps 1666, 1668, 69, 94, 1700, 01, 1751)* (H). **Cop** CMB 1558-1639 Ts (SG).

DINEDOR (DYNEDOR). **OR** CMB 1750 $^+$ (Inc). **BT** 1661 $^+$ *(gaps 1664-9, 95, 1806, 7, 10, 11). 1815-16 in Hereford Deanery Vol.* (H).

DOCKLOW. **OR** CMB 1584 $^+$ (Inc). **BT** 1661 $^+$ *(gaps 1678, 81, 84, 87, 91)* (H).

DONNINGTON. **OR** C 1755 $^+$, M 1754 $^+$, B 1765 $^+$ (Inc). **BT** sep trans for 1661, 1701, 1702 only. *Other years on Ledbury returns.* **Cop** C 1755-1840, M 1754-1835, B 1765-1841 Ts I (SG), C 1755-1960, M 1754-1835, 1838-1900, B 1765-1809, 1817-1900 Mf (SLC).

DORMINGTON. **OR** 1690 $^+$ (Inc). **BT** (with Bartestree) 1660 $^+$ *(gaps 1664, 1665, 1669, 1684, 98, 1762)* (H).

DORSTONE. **OR** CB 1733 $^+$, M 1755 $^+$ (Inc). **BT** 1662 $^+$ *(gap 1668)* (H).

DOWNTON ON THE ROCK. **OR** CB 1728-1812 *(gap 1741-3, 1766-8, 1769-81, 1782-4)*, M 1728-1812 *(gap 1749-1757)*, Banns 1757-1812 (CLH), CMB 1813 $^+$ (Inc). **BT** 1605, 1608, 1621, 30, 31, 34, 38, 1660 $^+$ (HXX).

DUCKLOW. – *see Docklow.*

DULAS. **OR** CMB 1770 $^+$ (Inc). **BT** 1818-32, 1834, 1836-7, 1839, 1848-51 (NLW – St D). *1813-14 on Ewyas Harold returns.* **Cop** CMB (BT) 1818-1851 Mf (SLC).

DYNEDOR. – *see Dinedor.*

EARDISLAND. **OR** CMB 1614 $^+$ *(gap M 1759-61)* (Inc). **BT** 1660 $^+$ *(no gaps)* (H).

EARDISLEY. **OR** CMB 1630-1662, 1669 $^+$, Banns 1823-1934 (Inc). **BT** 1660 $^+$ *(no gaps)* (H).

EASTNOR. **OR** CMB 1561 $^+$ (defective 1561-1733) (Inc). **BT** 1660 $^+$ *(gaps 1662, 63, 79, 1701)* (H).

EATON BISHOP. **OR** CMB 1588-1812, Banns 1754-1812, 1823-1909 (CLH). **BT** 1661 $^+$ *(gaps 1695, 1755, 70, 77, 1806, 07, 10, 11). 1815-16 in Hereford Deanery Vol.* (H).

EDVIN LOACH. **OR** CB 1576-1754, M 1576-1832 (*gap 1812-15*), Banns 1755-1812 (CLH), CB 1813+, M 1837+ (Inc), C 1757-1812 in Tedstone Wafer regs. **BT** 1614, 30, 31, 38, 1662+ (*gaps 1666, 81, 1707, 11, 1742, 52*). Period 1754-1812 unchecked. (H). **Cop** M 1813-37 Ts (SG).

EDVIN RALPH. **OR** CB 1651-1812, M 1651-1835 (*gaps 1747-56, 1808-13*), Banns 1756-1808 (CLH). **BT** 1624, 40, 1661+ (*gaps 1662, 1706*) (H). **Cop** M 1813-37 Ts (SG).

EGGLETON. – *see Stretton Grandison.*

EIGNBROOK. – *see Hereford Eign Brook Chapel and also Wyebridge.*

ELTON. **OR** CMB 1657+ (*gap CB 1763-5*) (Inc). **BT** 1662+ (*gaps 1667, 84, 1689*) (H).

EVESBATCH. **OR** CMB 1700+ (Inc). **BT** 1660+ (*no gaps*) (H).

EWYAS HAROLD. **OR** CMB 1734+ (Inc). **BT** 1700-02, 1707-8, 1715-95, 1797-1810, 1813-43, 1845-51 (with Dulas 1813-14) (NLW – St D). **Cop** CMB (BT) 1700-1851 Mf (SLC).

EYE. **OR** CMB 1573+ (Inc). **BT** 1660+ (*gap 1752*) (H). **Cop** CMB 1573-1718 Ms I (SG).

EYTON. **OR** CMB 1682+ (Inc). **BT** 1681-86, 1713, 1714, 1717+ (*gap 1744*) (H).

FAWLEYE. *Chapel to Fownhope.* **OR** 1539+ (Inc). **Cop** CMB 1539-1637 (Ptd).

FELTON. **OR** CMB 1637+ (Inc). **BT** 1660+ (*gaps 1736, 1744*) (H).

FORD (FORDSBRIDGE). **OR** CMB 1742+ (Inc Wellington, Staffs). *No BT's traced.*

FOWNHOPE. **OR** CMB 1560+ (*gap 1668-75 defective 1550-1668*) (Inc). **BT** 1661+ (*gap 1662, 94, 1727*) (H). **Cop** CMB 1560-1673 (Ptd), CMB 1560-1673 Mf (SLC).

FOWNHOPE, OLD WAY. (Bapt). *f 1826.* **OR** *Not at PRO.* Z 1827-1835. *Baptis and admissions (with name of former Church), removals (with destination – includes many emigrants to U.S. and Canada), deaths.* All 1806+ (Ch. Sec).

FOY. **OR** CMB 1570+ (*gap 1604-15*) (Inc). **BT** 1661+ (*gap 1684*).

GANAGREW. **OR** CMB 1743+ (*gap M 1811-13*). Also combined M and Banns reg 1757-1811 for Whitchurch and Ganagrew, (Inc Whitchurch). **BT** 1661+ (*gaps 1663, 65*) (H).

GARWAY. **OR** C 1664-1870, M 1755-1837, B 1664-1943, Banns 1755-93 (CLH). (*M defective 1676-80, gaps 1748, 51, 53, 54, 60*). **BT** 1660+ (*gaps 1786, 1807*).

GARWAY. (Bapt). *f 1817. No regs known. Not at PRO or Ch. Sec.*

GOODRICH. **OR** CMB 1558+, Banns 1822-1870 (Inc). **BT** 1661+ (*gaps 1702, 1703*).

OODRICH, Our Lady Courtfield (RC). *f 1805.* **OR** *Not at PRO.* C 1805 +,
B 1809 + *(Includes Burials for 13 other places. Baptismal register
includes some confirmations and lists of communicants. Some M and B
from 1868 in register of the Congregation)* (Inc). **Cop** C 1773-1832
(Cath R.S. 4).

ORE. (Ind). *f 1662. Not at PRO. No information.*

ORSLEY (or LINTON). (Bapt). *f 1831.* **OR** Z 1831-1837 (PRO).

RAFTON. – *see Bullingham, Lower.*

RENDON BISHOP. **OR** CB 1663-1946, M 1663-1945 *(gap 1754-1790, 1812-38),*
Banns 1790-1812 (CLH). **BT** 1660 + *(gaps 1661, 66)* (H).

AMPTON BISHOP. **OR** C 1670-1854 *(gap 1740-1813),* M 1670-1812 *(gap 1740-
1754),* B 1670-1740, Banns 1754-1812 (CLH), *Register 1670-1740 is
with index.* **BT** 1669 + *(gaps 1672, 94, 1806, 07, 1810, 11)* (H).

AREWOOD. **OR** C 1781-1943, M 1759-1906 *(gaps 1811-13, 1833-39),* B 1781-
1916, Banns 1759-1811, 1824-95 (CLH). *Some entries in Pencoyd regs.*
BT 1772 + *(gaps 1775, 6, 7)* (H). **Cop** CMB 1564-1812 Ptd.
CMB 1671-1812 (Ptd) (CLH).

ATFIELD. **OR** M 1777-1835 *(gap 1808-12),* Banns 1777-1808 (CLH).
BT 1660 + *(gaps 1661-5, 1693, 1698)* (H).

ENTLAND. **OR** C 1558-1859 *(gap 1670-74),* M 1558-1837 *(gap 1643-60,
1670-4, 1812-15),* B 1558-1894 *(gap 1642-60, 1670-4),* Banns 1754-
1812 (CLH). **BT** 1660 + *(gaps 1664, 78, 81, 1702)* (H). **Cop** Extracts
C 1558-1663, M 1558-1661, B 1558-1601 Ms (CLH).

EREFORD CATHEDRAL. *(Parish church for the parish of St John the
Baptist q.v.)*

EREFORD, ALL SAINTS. **OR** CM 1669 +, B 1669-1753, 1757 +, Banns 1756-
1792, 1854-1861, 1916 + (Inc). *Some B after 1813 in registers of
Upper Bullingham.* **BT** 1639, 1662 + *(gaps 1663-9, 71, 89, 95, 1713,
1725, 99, 1806, 07, 10, 11). 1815-16 in Hereford Deanery Vol.* (H).
Cop Extracts CMB 1669-1716 (CLH).

EREFORD, ST JOHN THE BAPTIST. **OR** 1687 + *(CMB 1742-3 defective)* (Inc).
Some B after 1813 in regs of Upper Bullingham. **BT** 1638, 1662 +
*(gaps 1663-9, 1743, 1806, 07, 10, 11). 1815-16 in Hereford
Deanery Vol.* (H).

EREFORD, ST MARTIN. **OR** CMB 1559-1638, 1707 + (Inc). *Church destroyed
1645. No new church built until 1845. From 1645-1845 annexed to
All Saints, Hereford, but many entries during this period,
especially for Lower Bullingham and Grafton in registers of Upper
Bullingham.* **BT** 1672 + *(gaps 1673, 74, 76, 77, 95, 1700-04, 09,
1766, 86, 1806, 07, 1810, 11). 1815-16 in Hereford Deanery Vol.* (H).

HEREFORD, ST NICHOLAS. **OR** 1556 [+], Banns 1754-1812, 1861 [+] (Inc).
Some B after 1813 in regs of Upper Bullingham. **BT** 1629, 1662 [+]
*(gaps 1664-7, 1722, 1806, 07, 10, 11). 1815-16 in Hereford
Deanery Vol.* (H). **Cop** Extract CMB 1667-1700 Ms (CLH).

HEREFORD, ST OWEN. **OR** C 1864 [+], M 1837 [+], B 1851 [+] (Inc), CMB 1626-
1837 (Inc St Peter). *M 1678-1837 in St Peter's regs. Some B after
1813 in regs of Upper Bullingham.* **BT** 1671 [+] *(gaps 1688, 95, 1754,
1757, 1806, 07, 10, 11). 1815-16 in Hereford Deanery Vol.* (H).
Cop Extracts CMB 1679-1699 Ms (CLH).

HEREFORD, ST PETER. **OR** CB 1556 [+] *(gaps C 1622-33, 1664-78, B 1641-
1678),* M 1556 [+] *(gap 1640-1678). M 1678-1812 is with St Owen,
1754-1772 being indexed. Some B after 1813 in regs of Upper
Bullingham.* **BT** 1629, 1670 [+] *(gaps 1695, 1806, 07, 10, 11). 1815-16
in Hereford Deanery Vol.* (H). **Cop** Extracts CMB 1680-1699 Ms (CLH).

HEREFORD (S of F). **Ross Monthly Meeting** *(1668-1808),* **Leominster and
Ross Monthly Meeting** *(1808-1834),* **Hereford and Radnor Monthly
Meeting** *(1834 [+]). No regs known except Monthly Meeting regs.*

HEREFORD. Commercial Rd (Bapt). *f 1829.* **OR** Z 1831-1837 (PRO).

HEREFORD. (Wes). **Hereford Circuit.** *f 1821.* **OR** Z 1821-1837, C 1821-
1854 (PRO), *(probably a Circuit register).*

HEREFORD, Union St (Prim Meth). **Cwm Circuit.** *f 1826.* **OR** ZC 1831-1837
(PRO). *See also Cwm.*

HEREFORD. Eign Brook Chapel (Ind). *f 1662.* **OR** ZC 1690-1836, B 1827-
1835 (PRO). *See also Wyebridge.*

HEREFORD. Berington Street (Lady Hunt Con). *f 1793.* **OR** ZC 1814-1835
(PRO).

HEREFORD, St Francis Xavier, Broad St (RC). *f 1684.* **OR** *Not at PRO.*
C 1799 [+], M 1825-1850 (Inc). **Cop** C 1799-1856, M 1825-1847 Ms (Inc)

HEREFORD, LITTLE. **Peculiar** *of Chancellor of the Choir of Hereford
Cathedral.* **OR** CMB 1725 [+] (Inc). **BT** 1567, 70, 71, 1741 [+] (H).

HOLME LACEY. **OR** CMB 1562 [+] *(defective CMB 1562-1727)* (Inc). *Includes
Boulstone chapelry until 1727.* **BT** (including Boulstone) 1660 [+]
(gap 1699) (H).

HOLMER. **OR** CMB 1712 [+] *(gap CB 1749-1760, M 1749-54),* Banns 1754-1812 (In
Register 1712-1749 includes Huntington Chapelry. **BT** 1638, 1660 [+]
*(gaps 1662-8, 1695, 1700, 01, 39, 1806, 07, 10, 11). With Shelwick
Probably with Huntington 1660-1753. First mentioned 1674, not
noted after 1746. Period 1815-1816 in Hereford Deanery Vol.* (H).
See also Huntington.

HOPE UNDER DINMORE. **OR** C 1701-1900, M 1701-1837, B 1701-1878 *(gaps
CMB 1725-7, M 1798-1813)* (CLH). **BT** 1661 [+] *(gaps 1669, 1725).
M 1660-68 also listed separately, sometimes with more details* (H).

HOPE MANSELL. **OR** 1556 + (Inc). **BT** 1661 + *(gap 1663)* (H).

HOW CAPEL. **OR** 1677 + (Inc). **BT** 1661 + *(gaps 1665, 1685)* (H).

HUMBER. **OR** CMB 1719 + (Inc). **BT** 1660 + *(No gaps)* (H).

HUNTINGTON. (near HOLMER). *Chapelry of Holmer.* **OR** CMB 1718 + (Inc), *CMB 1718-1749 in registers of Holmer.* **BT** 1660-1753 on Holmer returns. *First specifically included 1674 last noted 1746. Separate transcripts for 1718-1722, 1749, 1750 only.* 1754-1812 separate transcripts *(gaps 1766, 71, 74, 1803, 06, 07, 10, 11). 1815-16 in Hereford Deanery Vol.* (H).

HUNTINGTON. (near KINGTON). **OR** CMB 1754 + (Inc). **BT** *1660-1753 on Kington returns (gaps 1661, 1696)* 1754-1812 separate transcripts *(gaps 1760, 1764).*

HUNTINGTON. (near KINGTON). (Ind). *f 1804. Not at PRO. No information.*

KENCHESTER. **OR** CMB 1757 + (Inc). **BT** 1663 + *(gaps 1664, 1706, 1774, 1781)* (H).

KENDERCHURCH. **OR** CMB 1757 + (Inc), CMB 1777-1812 (contemporary copy) (CLH). **BT** 1661 + *(gaps 1662-5, 67, 69, 71, 1711)* (H).

KENTCHURCH. **OR** CB 1686-1812, M 1686-1838 *(gaps 1751-5, 1811-13)*, Banns 1755-1811, 1825-1904 (CLH), CB 1813 +, M 1837 + (Inc). **BT** 1661 + *(gaps 1663, 95, 98, 1700, 01, 02, 29, 90)* (H).

KILPECK. **OR** CB 1678-1812, M 1678-1837, Banns 1812-1837 (CLH), C 1916-1961, M 1837 +, B 1813 + (Inc). *Some Kilpeck entries in Wormbridge regs – see Wormbridge.* **BT** 1661 + *(gaps 1663, 4, 1694)* (H). **Cop** Extracts CMB 1662-1682 Ms (CLH).

KIMBOLTON. **OR** CMB 1565 + *(gap CB 1678-1706)* (Inc). **BT** 1660 + *(no gaps)* (H).

KINGS CAPEL. **OR** CMB 1683 + (Inc). **BT** 1661 + *(gaps 1701, 1744, 1759)* (H).

KINGSHAM. *– see Kinsham.*

KINGSLAND. **OR** CMB 1548 + (Inc). *Period 1548-1563 now exists only as copy in second register.* **BT** 1660 + *(gap 1694)* (H).

KINGSLAND. (Bapt). *f date not known. Not at PRO. No information.*

KINGS PYON. (PION REGIS). **OR** CMB 1538 + (Inc). **BT** 1660 + *(gaps 1669, 1694, 95, 96)* (H).

KINGSTONE (KINGSTON). **OR** CM 1660 +, B 1659 + *(gap M 1749-54)* (Inc). **BT** 1661 + *(gaps 1671, 80, 84, 88, 90, 95, 99, 1731, 1806, 07, 10, 1811). 1815-16 in Hereford Deanery Vol.* (H).

KINGTON. **OR** CMB 1667 + (Inc). **BT** 1660 + *(gap 1668). Period 1660-1753 with Huntington. See also Huntington.* **Cop** Extracts CMB 1667-1729 Ms (CLH and Mf SLC).

KINGTON. The Lower Chapel, Bridge St (Bapt). *f 1805.* **OR** Z 1791-1837 (PRO).

KINGTON. (Wes). **Kington Circuit.** *f 1800.* **OR** ZC 1805-1837 (PRO).
Probably a Circuit register.

KINNERSLEY. **OR** CB 1626-1812, M 1626-1837 *(gaps CMB 1685-1714),*
Banns 1754-92 (CLH). **BT** 1660+ *(gaps 1665, 68, 90, 1719, 1804).*
Transcripts for Letton with 1660, 1792 and 1795. (H).

KINSHAM (or UPPER KINSHAM). **OR** CMB 1594+ *(gap 1715-1778)* (Inc).
BT 1660+ *(gap 1668)* (H).

KNILL. **OR** CMB 1585+ (Inc). **BT** 1661+ *(gap 1668)* (H).

LAYSTERS (LEYSTERS or LEISTERS). **OR** CMB 1703+ *(gap M 1790-1812)*
(Inc Brockleton, Worcs). **BT** 1660+ (HX). **Cop** C 1703-1945, M 1703-
1848 *(gap 1790-1812),* B 1703-1963 Mf (WRO and SLC).

LEA, THE. **OR** CMB 1581-1650, CM 1706+, B 1813+ (Inc). **BT** 1583+
(City Lib. Gloucester). **Cop** CMB 1581-1650, C 1706-1895, M 1706-
1856, B 1813-1856 Mf (SLC).

LEDBURY. **OR** CMB 1556+ (Inc). *C register includes godparents 1556-
1576.* **BT** 1660+ (H). *Includes Donnington and Little Marcle (q.v.).
Some separate transcripts.* **Cop** CMB 1556-1576 I (PRS 18), C 1631-
1743, 1767-1812, M 1585-1620, 1631-1743, 1767, 1812, B 1594-1743,
1767-1812 Ms (SG).

LEDBURY (RC). *Entries in regs of Little Malvern Court. See
Worcestershire – Malvern, Little.*

LEDBURY. (Ind). *f 1700.* **OR** C 1785-1837 (PRO).

LEDBURY. The Homend (Bapt). *f 1836. Not at PRO. No information.*

LEDBURY. (Wes). **Ledbury and Forest of Dean Circuit.** *Possibly the
surrendered register for Newent, Glos. is the Circuit register for
this Circuit.*

LEINTHALL EARLES. **OR** M 1766-1776, 1830-32, 1880+ (CLH), CMB 1591+ (Inc),
C 1812-1845 and probably MB 1812+ in Aymestrey registers.

LEINTHALL STARKES. **OR** CMB 1740+ (Inc). **BT** 1660+ *(gaps 1661-4, 1666-
1672, 1688, 1707)* (H).

LEINTWARDINE. **OR** CMB 1547-1716 *(gaps 1552-60, 1608-15, 1617-30, 1642-
1656)* (CLH). **BT** 1638, 1661+ *(gap 1664).*

LEISTERS. *– see Laysters.*

LEOMINSTER. **OR** CMB 1559+ *(gap CMB 1606-53, defective 1653-77)* (Inc).
BT 1660+ *(gaps 1662, 70, 71, 93, 94, 1705 and part of 1707)* (H).
Cop Extracts CMB 1653-1662 Ms (CLH).

LEOMINSTER MONTHLY MEETING (S of F). *Established 1668 united with*
Ross Monthly Meeting *1808 as* **Leominster and Ross Monthly Meeting.**
Constituent Meetings: Leominster, Bromyard (both 1668-1808),
OR Z 1646-1772, 1778-1806, M 1659-1767, 1777-1810, B 1650-1808
(PRO 646-651).

LEOMINSTER AND ROSS MONTHLY MEETING (S of F). *Established 1808. United 1834 with* **North Wales Monthly Meeting** *as* **Hereford and Radnor Monthly Meeting.** *Constituent Meetings: Leominster, Bromyard, Ross, Hereford (all 1808-1834). Regs: The* **Ross Monthly Meeting** *registers were continued for the* **Leominster and Ross Monthly Meeting.** *See Ross.*

LEOMINSTER (S of F). *– see previous two entries. No other regs known.*

LEOMINSTER. Etnam St Chapel (Bapt). *f 1656.* OR Z 1747-1836, B 1702-1836 (PRO).

LEOMINSTER. South St (Moravian). *f 1759.* OR ZC 1786-1837, B 1784-1837 (PRO).

LEOMINSTER. Broad St Meeting (Ind). *f 1829.* OR ZC 1829-1834 (PRO).

LETTON. OR CMB 1673 + (Inc). BT 1660 + *(gap 1771)* (H). *Transcripts for 1660, 1792, 1795 with Kinnersley returns.*

LEYSTERS. *– see Laysters.*

LINGEN. OR CB 1751 +, M 1754 + (Inc). BT 1660 + *(gap 1661)* (H).

LINTON. OR CMB 1570 + (Inc). BT 1662 + *(gap 1731, 35)*.

LINTON. (Bapt). *– see Gorsley.*

LITTLE BIRCH. *– see Birch, Little.*

LITTLE COWARNE. *– see Cowarne, Little.*

LITTLE DEWCHURCH. *– see Dewchurch, Little.*

LITTLE HEREFORD. *– see Hereford, Little.*

LITTLE MARCLE. *– see Marcle, Little.*

LITTLE SHELSLEY. *– see Worcestershire, Shelsley Walsh.*

LLANCILLO. OR CB 1727-1763, M 1727-1910 *(gaps 1750-6, 1799-1815, 1836-41)* (CLH), B 1784-1811 (CLH *in volume of Walterstone Marriages*), CB 1813 +, M 1913 + (Inc Rowlestone). BT 1707-8, 1714-36, 1738-1809, 1813-23, 1825-8, 1830-3, 1834, 1836, 1837, 1839 (NLW – St D). *(1702-4, 1707-11 on Llancillo returns).* Cop (BT) CMB 1707-1839 Mf (SLC).

LLANDINABO. OR CMB 1596 + *(gap M 1761-9)* (Inc). *Some entries in Pencoyd regs.* BT 1660 + *(gaps 1664, 65, 1768)* (H). Cop CMB 1596-1812 Ptd (CLH).

LLANGARREN. OR CMB 1569 + *(gap 1633-1683)* (Inc). BT 1661 + *(gaps 1702, 1703, 05, 06)* (H).

LLANGUA. *– see Monmouthshire.*

LLANROTHAL. OR C 1740, 1748-1937 *(gap 1802-4)*, M 1740, 1748-1932 *(gap 1802-13)*, B 1740, 1748-1933 *(gaps 1802-4, 1812-15)* (CLH). BT 1663 + *(gaps 1666, 73, 76, 92, 93, 95, 96)* (H).

LLANVEYNO (LLANFEINO). OR CMB 1714 + (Inc), C 1757, 1761-1779 in *Clodock regs.* BT St D *see Clodock.*

LLANWARNE. OR CMB 1675 + (Inc). BT 1660 + (*gaps 1695, 1703, 1731*) (H).

LONGTOWN. OR CMB 1705 + (Inc). *C 1761-79 in Clodock regs.* BT 1799-190?
(NLW – St D). *See also Clodock.*

LUCTON. OR CMB 1711 + (Inc). BT 1662 + (*gaps 1663-81, 1688, 90, 91,
1693-1710, 1713, 24, 32*) (H).

LUDFORD. – *see Shropshire.*

LUGWARDINE. OR C 1538-1900, M 1538-1837, B 1538-1930, Banns 1754-1812
(CLH). *M 1538-1758 entered in middle of C for 1770. B 1780-83 on
last sheet of Volume.* BT 1660 + (*gaps 1661, 69, 1702*) (H).
Cop CB 1538-1783 Ts, M 1538-1758 Ts I (SG and CLH), CMB (BT) 1538-
1783 Mf (SLC). *M 1538-1758 in Boyd Misc.*

LYDE. – *see Pipe and Lyde.*

LYONSHALL. OR C 1682-1874, M 1682-1837, B 1682-1904 (*gaps CMB 1688-
91, 1695-7, part of 1708, CB 1782-1810*), Banns 1754-1882 (CLH).
No BT's traced.

MADLEY. OR CMB 1558 + (Inc). BT 1661 + (*gaps 1662-9, 1694, 1799, 1806
1807, 10, 11*). *1815-16 in Hereford Deanery Vol.* (H). Cop CMB 1566-
1681 (SG D Mss).

MANSELL GAMAGE. OR CMB 1664 + (Inc). BT 1660 + (*gaps 1662, 1701,
1776*) (H).

MANSELL LACY. OR CMB 1714+ (Inc). BT 1660+ (*gap 1664*) (H).

MARCLE, LITTLE. OR CM 1748 + (Inc). *B at Ledbury.* BT Separate transcri
for 1660, 62, 1749, 51, 52, 53, 1754-1812. *For other years see
Ledbury* (H).

MARCLE, MUCH. OR CMB 1556 + (Inc). BT 1660 + (*gap 1728*) (H).

MARDEN. OR 1616 + (Inc). BT 1660, 1661, 1662 (*all perhaps incomplete*)
1670 + (*gaps 1695, 96, 1800, 06, 07, 10, 11*). *1815-16 in Hereford
Deanery Vol.* (H). Cop M 1613-1837 Ts (SG).

MARSTOW. OR CB 1707-1812, M 1707-1836 (*gap 1812-16*) (CLH), CB 1813 +
(Inc). BT 1662 + (*gaps 1703, 06, 16*) (H), M 1813-1837 Ts (SG).

MATHON. (*formerly in Worcs*). – *see Worcs.*

MICHAELCHURCH. (*Chapelry of Tretire*). OR CMB 1586 + (Inc). BT *see
Tretire.*

MICHAELCHURCH ESKLEY. OR 1719 + (*gaps CMB 1732-8, C 1804-8, B 1802-
10*) (Inc). BT 1687-8, 1713-95, 1797-1809, 1813-51 (with entries fo
Crasswall, 1713-31, Newton 1714-27, 1729-30, St Margarets 1713-14)
(NLW – St D). Cop CMB (BT) 1687-1851 Mf (SLC).

MIDDLETON ON THE HILL. OR C 1650 + , MB 1659 + (*gap M 1741-55, 1806-8*)
(Inc). BT 1660 + (*gaps 1668, 69*) (H).

MOCCAS. OR CMB 1673 + (*gap 1735-49*) (Inc). BT 1660 + (*gaps 1666, 1689
(H).

MONKLAND. OR CMB 1582 + (*gap 1598-1600*) (Inc). BT 1660 + (*gap 1714*) (I

ONNINGTON ON WYE. **OR** CMB 1684 + (Inc). **BT** 1660 + *(gap 1661, 2, 4, 79, 1794)* (H).

ORDIFORD. **OR** CMB 1621 + *(gaps CMB 1643-8, 1687-9)* (Inc). **BT** 1661 + *(gaps 1666, 1694, 1744)* (H).

ORETON ON LUGG (MORETON MAGNA). **Peculiar** *Prebend of Moreton Magna.* **OR** CMB 1759 + (Inc). **BT** 1681 + *(gaps 1692, 96, 1701, 06, 17, 48, 1751, 53, 56, 57, 59, 65, 69, 82, 92, 1795-1812)* (H).

ORETON JEFFERIES. **OR** CMB 1711-1855 *(gap 1758-9)* *(Cathedral Lib. Hereford)*. **BT** 1670 + *(gaps 1671, 95, 1736, 42, 69, 70, 1803, 06, 1807, 10, 11)*. *1815-16 in Hereford Deanery Vol.* (H), CMB 1711-1812 (SLC). **Cop** CMB (BT) 1758-9 Ts *(Cathedral Lib. Hereford)*.

UCH BIRCH. – *see Birch, Much.*

UCH COWARNE. – *see Cowarne, Much.*

UCH DEWCHURCH. – *see Dewchurch, Much.*

UCH MARCLE. – *see Marcle, Much.*

UNSLEY. **OR** CMB 1708 + (Inc). **BT** 1662 + *(gap 1671)* (H). **Cop** CMB (BT) 1662-1708, CMB 1708-1812 I(PRS 46 and Mf SLC).

EWTON. **OR** *see Clodock.* **BT** *normally on Clodock returns. On Michaelchurch Eskley returns 1714-27. On St Margaret's returns 1718, 1724.*

ORTON CANON. **OR** CB 1716-1813, M 1716-1836, Banns 1768-1816, 1830 (CLH). **BT** 1661 + *(gaps 1663, 1665-9, 1695, 96, 1802, 05, 06, 07, 09, 10, 1811)*. *1815-16 in Hereford Deanery Vol.* (H). **Cop** CMB (BT) 1661-1715, (PR) 1716-1816 Ms (CLH, SG and Mf SLC).

CLE PYCHARD. **OR** CMB 1773 + (Inc). **BT** 1660 + *(gaps 1662, 1663)* (H).

LDCASTLE. **BT** 1714-17, 1723-1809, 1813, 1817, 1821-38 (NLW – St D) (1702-4, 1707-11 on Rowlestone returns, 1815-16 on Walterstone returns).

RCOP. **OR** CMB 1672 + *(gap M 1811-13)*, Banns 1824 + (Inc). **BT** 1661 + *(no gaps)* (H).

RLETON. **OR** CMB 1565 + (Inc). **BT** 1660 + *(gaps 1668, 1741)* (H).

EMBRIDGE. **OR** CMB 1564 + *(1564-1642 defective)* (Inc). **BT** 1660 + *(gaps 1661, 2, 1739)* (H). **Cop** M 1564-1642 Ts (SG).

EMBRIDGE, Home Missionary Chapel (Ind). *f 1820.* **OR** ZC 1822-1836 (PRO).

ENCOMBE. **OR** CB 1540 +, M 1540-1753, 1755 +, Banns 1755 + (Inc). *(CMB 1540-1725 defective)*. **BT** 1660 + *(gaps 1662, 1729)* (H).

ENCOYD. **OR** CB 1563-1812 *(gap 1738-1784)*, M 1563-1837 *(gaps 1738-1758, 1810-15)*, Banns 1758-1810 (CLH), CB 1813 +, M 1837 + (Inc). **BT** 1660 + *(gaps 1661, 62)* (H). **Cop** CMB 1564-1812, M 1758-1810 (Ptd) *(No copy SG. Copy CLH)*, M 1813-37 Ts (SG).

PETERCHURCH. **OR** CMB 1711 $^+$ *(gaps CB 1751-5, M 1751-77)* (Inc). **BT** 1660 *(gaps 1665, 1702, 1733)* (H).

PETERCHURCH. (Bapt). *f 1820. No regs known. Not at PRO or Ch. Sec.*

PETERSTOW. **OR** CMB 1538 $^+$ (Inc). **BT** 1660 $^+$ *(no gaps)* (H).

PIPE-AND-LYDE. **OR** CMB 1558 $^+$ (Inc). **BT** 1660 $^+$ *(gaps 1664-70, 1695, 1753, 1784, 1806, 09, 10, 11). Lyde specifically included from 1782. 1815-16 in Hereford Deanery Vol.* **Cop** CMB 1558-1812 Ts (SG), CMB 1559-1812 Ms (CLH and Mf SLC). *M 1558-1780 in Boyd Misc.*

PIXLEY. **OR** CM 1745 $^+$ (Inc). *No Burials.* **BT** 1660-1753 *(gaps 1662, 72, 1673, 86, 95, 1700, 01, 09, 11, 13-15, 19, 21, 28, 29, 31-34, 1736-49, 1752). 1754-1812 with Aylton returns (gaps 1757-76, 1784)* (H).

PRESTEIGN. *see Radnorshire.*

PRESTON ON WYE. **OR** CMB 1574 $^+$ *(gap 1642-1667)* (Inc). **BT** 1664 $^+$ *(gaps 1665-8, 71, 95, 1749, 66, 1806, 07, 10, 11). 1815-16 in Hereford Deanery Vol.* (H).

PRESTON WYNNE. **OR** CMB 1671-1723 and possibly also some CB 1723-1809, M 1723-1754 in Withington regs, CMB 1813 $^+$ (Inc). **BT** 1739 $^+$ *(gaps 1752, 55, 1775, 1806, 07, 10, 11). 1660-1738 on Withington returns. 1815-16 in Hereford Deanery Vol.* (H).

PUDLESTON. **OR** CMB 1566 $^+$ *(gap 1707-14)* (Inc). **BT** 1660 $^+$ *(gap 1704)* (H)

PUTLEY. **OR** CMB 1561 $^+$ (Inc). **BT** 1662 $^+$ *(gaps 1665, 66, 71, 95, 1755, 1784, 1806, 07, 10, 11)* (H).

RICHARDS CASTLE. *(now part Hereford, part Salop).* **OR** CMB 1559 $^+$ (Inc). **BT** 1660 $^+$ (HX). **Cop** M 1813-37 Ts (SG *cat. under Salop*), CMB 1558-1812 Ms (SBL), CMB (BT) 1813-1890 Mf (SLC).

ROCHFORD. *Now in Worcs. – see Worcs.*

ROLLSTONE. *– see Rowlestone.*

ROSS-ON-WYE. **OR** CMB 1671 $^+$ (Inc). **BT** 1662 $^+$ *(gaps 1665, 1697)* (H). **Cop** CB 1671-1701, M 1671-1723, B 1671-1708 (CLH).

ROSS-ON-WYE (RC). *Entries in regs of Courtfield, Goodrich.*

ROSS-ON-WYE. Broad St (Bapt). *f 1819. Not at PRO. No information.*

ROSS MONTHLY MEETING (S of F). *Established 1668. United 1808 with Leominster as* **Leominster and Ross Monthly Meeting** *(q.v.). Constituent Meetings: Hereford, Ross (both 1668-1808). Monthly Meeting Regs: Z 1654-1775, M 1661-1775, B 1658-1775 (PRO 654), Z 1776-1812, 1814-37, M 1782-1786, 1799-1834, B 1776-1795, 1797-1837 (PRO 655-660). After 1808 the registers were used for the* **Leominster and Ross Monthly Meeting.**

ROSS (S of F). **Ross Monthly Meeting** *(1668-1808),* **Leominster and Ross Monthly Meeting** *(1808-1834),* **Hereford and Radnor Monthly Meeting** *(1834* $^+$ *). No regs known other than Monthly Meeting regs.*

ROSS. Kyrle Street (Ind). *f 1662*. **OR** CB 1732-1837 (*one B only between 1782 and 1802*) (PRO).

ROTHERWAS (RC). *Church now closed. Registers with the Vincentian Fathers, 101 Belmont Rd, Hereford.*

ROWLESTONE (ROLLSTONE). **OR** CMB 1723-1766, 1813-1837 (CLH), B 1783-1812 (CLH *in volume of Walterstone Marriages*). *No register 1766-1783.* **BT** 1702-4, 1707-11, 1714-21, 1722? 1723-75, 1777-1783, 1785-1795, 1798-1809, 1813-34, 1835? 1836-41 (*with Walterstone, Oldcastle and Llancillo 1702-4, 1707-11*). *See also Oldcastle.*

ST DEVEREUX AND TREVILLE. **OR** CB 1669-1928, M 1669-1836, Banns 1754-1812 (CLH), C 1930 +, M 1836 +, B 1813 + (Inc). *Some St Devereux entries in Wormbridge registers.* **BT** 1660 + (*no gaps*) (H). **Cop** CMB 1669-1812 Ts, CMB (BT) 1660-1669, 1713-1719 Ts I (SG and CLH), Extracts CMB 1662-1682 (CLH). *See also Wormbridge.*

ST MARGARET'S. **OR** CMB 1702 + (*CMB 1702-62 defective*) (Inc). **BT** 1714-95, 1797-8, 1799 or 1800? 1801-3, 1805-9, 1813-51 (*with Newton 1718-1724*) NLW - St D). *On Michaelchurch Eskley returns 1713-14.*

ST WEONARDS. **OR** CMB 1624-1720 (1 entry 1725) (*gaps 1640-2, 1644-8 (except 1646), 1650-54 (except 1653), 1655-9 (except 1657), 1670-1681, 1685-9, 1690-1705, 1716-20*), C 1728-1863, M 1728-1852, B 1728-1876, Banns 1755-1812 (CLH). **BT** 1660 + (*gap 1668*) (H).

SAPEY, UPPER. **OR** CMB 1679 + (Inc). **BT** 1660 + (*gaps 1661, 66, 68, 78*) (H).

SAPEY, LOWER (or SAPEY PITCHARD). *transf to Worcs 1920. - see Worcs.*

SARNESFIELD. **OR** CB 1764-1812, M 1755-1836, Banns 1755-1836 (*gap 1813-1823*) (CLH). **BT** 1660 + (*gaps 1661, 63, 66, 94, 1728, 34, 45*) (H). **Cop** CMB (BT) 1660-1763 (PR), 1764-1897 I (PRS 13).

SELLACK. **OR** CMB 1566 + (Inc). **BT** 1660 + (*gaps 1695, 1701, 1703, 1735*) (H). **Cop** Extracts from oldest register (CLH).

SHELSLEY WALSH or LITTLE SHELSLEY. *- see Worcs.*

SHELWICK. *Chapelry of Holmer. - see Holmer.*

SHOBDEN. **OR** CB 1556-1812, M 1556-1785 (*CMB 1556-1670 defective*) (CLH), CMB 1813 + (Inc). **BT** 1661 + (*gaps 1662, 1743*) (H).

SOLLERS HOPE (or SOLLERSHOPE). **OR** CMB 1695 + (Inc). **BT** 1661 + (*no gaps*) (H).

STANFORD BISHOP. **OR** CB 1699-1812, M 1699-1837 (*gap 1752-4*) (CLH). **BT** 1660 + (*gaps 1666, 82, 1701*) (H). **Cop** M 1813-37 Ts (SG).

STAUNTON ON ARROW. **OR** CMB 1558 + (Inc). **BT** 1642, 1660 + (*gaps 1667, 1668*) (H).

STAUNTON ON WYE. **OR** CMB 1677 + (Inc). **BT** 1660 + (*gap 1718*) (H).

STOKE BLISS. *Now in Worcs. - see Worcs.*

STOKE EDITH. **OR** CMB 1538 + (Inc). **BT** 1660 + (*gaps 1669, 1701*) (H). **Cop** C 1660-1840, M 1660-1838, B 1660-1837 Ts (SG).

STOKE LACY. **OR** CMB 1567 $^+$ (Inc). *Some entries for 1688 in Avenbury regs.* **BT** 1662 $^+$ (*no gaps*) (H).

STOKE PRIOR. **OR** CMB 1678 $^+$ (Inc). (*gap M 1831-7. Some M in CB register 1802-12*). **BT** 1661 $^+$ (*gaps 1665, 66, 68, 69, 88, 1722*) (H).

STRETFORD. **OR** CMB 1720 $^+$ (Inc). **BT** 1660 $^+$ (*gaps 1661, 1666, 1710*) (H).

STRETTON GRANDISON (with EGGLETON). **OR** CMB 1558 $^+$ (Inc). **BT** 1660 $^+$ (*gaps 1661, 1662*) (H).

STRETTON SUGWAS. **OR** CMB 1753 $^+$ (Inc). **BT** 1660 $^+$ (*gaps 1662, 3, 6, 1694*) (H).

SUTTON, ST MICHAEL. **OR** CB 1593 $^+$, M 1593-1811, 1813 $^+$, Banns 1755-1811 (Inc). **BT** 1663 $^+$ (*gaps 1664, 66, 68, 69, 72, 1718, 1728, 43, 1784, 1812*) (H).

SUTTON, ST NICHOLAS. **OR** C 1813 $^+$, M 1763 $^+$, B 1813 $^+$ (Inc). (*The majority of Burials now take place in Sutton St Michael.*) **BT** 1660 $^+$ (*gaps 1667, 1707*) (H). **Cop** Extracts CMB 1591-1810 (Geneologist 7).

TARRINGTON. **OR** CMB 1561 $^+$ (*gaps 1563-5, 1611-13*) (Inc). **BT** 1661 $^+$ (*gaps 1664, 69, 98, 1739*) (H). **Cop** CMB 1561-1812 Ms (SG). *M 1562-1812 in Boyd Misc.*

TEDSTONE DELAMERE. **OR** CMB 1690 $^+$ (Inc). **BT** 1660 $^+$ (*gaps 1661, 62, 1726*) (H). **Cop** M 1813-37 Ts (SG).

TEDSTONE WAFER. **OR** C 1729-1812 (*gap 1759-63*), M 1729-1836 (1753-1808 with Banns) (*gaps 1814-36*), B 1729-1759 (CLH), CB 1813 $^+$, M 1837 $^+$ (Inc). *C 1757-1812 includes Edvin Loach.* **BT** 1660 $^+$ (*gaps 1661, 1681, 1698, 1742*) (H). **Cop** M 1813-37 Ts (SG).

THORNBURY. **OR** CMB 1538 $^+$, Banns 1755-1811, 1824-1893 (Inc). **BT** 1660 $^+$ (*gap 1711*) (H). **Cop** CMB 1538-1812 (Ptd Revd S Dodderidge 1905).

THRUXTON. **OR** CMB 1582 $^+$ (*gap 1638-1674*) (Inc). **BT** 1672 $^+$ (*gaps 1695, 1699, 1755, 59, 1791, 1806, 07, 10, 11*). *1815-16 in Hereford Deanery Vol.* (H).

TIBERTON (or TYBERTON). **OR** CMB 1672 $^+$ (Inc). **BT** 1670 $^+$ (*gaps 1671, 1689, 91, 92, 95, 1719, 27, 44*). *1815-16 in Hereford Deanery Vol.* (H).

TITLEY. **OR** CB 1570-1812, M 1570-1899 (CLH), CB 1813 $^+$ (Inc). **BT** 1660 $^+$ (*no gaps*) (H). **Cop** CMB 1570-1714 (BM).

TRETIRE AND MICHAELCHURCH. **OR** CB 1586-1812, M 1586-1942 (*gaps CMB 1646-9, 1677-80, 1685-7, 1688-90, 1710-12, M 1752-5*) (CLH). **BT** 1660 $^+$ (*gaps 1662, 1729*) (H).

TREVILLE. – *see St Devereux.*

TURNASTONE. **OR** CMB 1678 $^+$ (Inc). **BT** 1671 $^+$ (*gaps 1672, 73, 1701, 174?*

TYBERTON. – *see Tiberton.*

ULLINGSWICK. **OR** CMB 1561 $^+$ (Inc). **BT** 1660 $^+$ (*no gaps*). *BT's for 1664-1669 include Little Cowarne.*

UPPER BULLINGHAM or BULLINGHOPE. – *see Bullinghope, Upper.*

UPPER SAPEY. – *see Sapey, Upper.*

UPTON BISHOP. **OR** CMB 1571 $^+$ (*gap CMB 1644-7*) (Inc). **BT** 1660 $^+$ (*gaps 1663, 1674*) (H). **Cop** M 1571-1882 (F. T. Habergalls, "Records of Upton Bishop").

VOWCHURCH. **OR** CMB 1642 $^+$ (Inc). *Perhaps only from 1754. No information received.* **BT** 1670 $^+$ (*gaps 1678, 1679, 1700*) (H).

WACTON. **OR** CM 1660-1877 (*gaps CMB 1661, 1666, 1674, 1687, 1692, 1694-6, 1726, 1728, 1735, 1736, 1754-1771, M 1772-1813, 1836-8*) (CLH). *Burials at Bromyard.* **BT** 1660 $^+$ (*gaps 1662, 1688, 1692, 1766*) (H).

WALFORD-ON-WYE. **OR** CMB 1663 $^+$ (Inc). **BT** 1661 $^+$ (*no gaps*) (H).

WALTERSTONE. **OR** C 1761-1813, M 1777-1835, B 1786-1813 (CLH), CB 1813 $^+$, M 1839 $^+$ (Inc). *One volume of M 1783-1810 contains also Burials for Llancillo 1784-1811 and for Rowlestone 1783-1812.* **BT** 1712-1809, 1813-18, 1820-37 (*with Oldcastle 1815-1816*) (*on Rowlestone returns 1702-4, 1707-11*). *See also Rowlestone and Oldcastle.*

WELLINGTON. **OR** C 1559-1897, M 1559-1838, B 1559-1935 (*gaps CMB 1707-1735 except 1731, CB 1774-8, 1794-6, M 1812-14*), Banns 1754-1812, 1823-1883 (CLH). **BT** 1660 $^+$ (*gaps 1661, 1669, 1705-8, 1730*) (H).

WELSH BICKNOR. **OR** CMB 1600 $^+$ (Inc). **BT** 1661 $^+$ (*gaps 1662-4, 1667-72, 1701-3, 1723-4, 1726, part of 1757*) (H).

WELSH BICKNOR, COURTFIELD (RC). – *see Goodrich.*

WELSH NEWTON. **OR** C 1798-1894 (*gap 1809-13*), M 1758-1837, B 1808-1914 (*gap 1809-13*), Banns 1750-1812 (CLH). **BT** 1660 $^+$ (*gaps 1700, 1713*) (H).

WEOBLEY. **OR** C 1635-1885, M 1635-1836, B 1635-1862 (*gaps CMB 1637-1653, 1655-82, CB 1685-87, M 1685-1732*), Banns 1754-1806 (CLH). **BT** 1660 $^+$ (*gaps 1670, 1679, 1702*) (H).

WEOBLEY, St Thomas of Hereford. Kempton Rd (RC). *f 1834.* **OR** C 1787 $^+$, M 1845 $^+$, D 1874 $^+$ (Inc).

WESTHIDE. **OR** CMB 1575-1636, 1660 $^+$, Banns 1756-1812, 1857 $^+$ (Inc). **BT** 1660 $^+$ (*gaps 1661, 1669, 1697, 1808*) (H).

WESTON-UNDER-PENYARD. **OR** C 1568-1914, M 1569-1812, Banns 1786-1799, 1907-1948, B 1568-1812 (*gaps M 1628-30, CMB 1641-46, except 1643, CB 1768-1808*) (CLH). **BT** 1662 $^+$ (*gap 1735*) (H).

WESTON-UNDER-PENYARD. Ryeford Chapel (Bapt). *f 1662.* **OR** Z 1787-1837, B 1791-1836 (PRO).

WESTON BEGGARD. **OR** CMB 1587-1753 (*gaps 1604-6, 1644-58* except 1651, 1655, 56, *1660-2, 1669-72* except 1671) C 1754-1928, M 1754-1932, B 1754-1812 (*gaps CB 1776-8, M 1811-13, 1884-1905*), Banns 1754-1811, 1815-1932 (CLH). **BT** 1660 + (*gaps 1661, 1669, 1706, 1740*) (H).

WHITBOURNE. **OR** CMB 1588 + (Inc). *M 1588-1754 defective.* **BT** 1660 + (*gap 1716*) (H).

WHITCHURCH. **OR** CB 1813 +, M 1761 +, Banns 1761-1812, 1823 +. *Also combined register for Whitchurch and Ganarew M and Banns 1757-1811.* (Inc). *Earlier registers destroyed by floods.* **BT** 1660 + (*gap 1694*) (H). **Cop** CB 1633-1814, M 1633-74, 1761-1838. *Ts of register since destroyed* (Hereford RO).

WHITCHURCH. Doward Chapel (Ind). *f 1819.* **OR** C 1820-1833 (PRO).

WHITNEY ON WYE. **OR** C 1740-1894, M 1740-1835, B 1740-1812 (CLH).

WIGMORE. **OR** CMB 1572 + (Inc). **BT** 1660 + (*gaps 1703-5, 1712, part of 1758*) (H).

WILLERSLEY. **OR** CMB 1764 + (Inc). **BT** 1675 + (*gaps 1676, 77, 1679-1708, 1728, 30, 35-7, 1739-40, 42, 43, 1748-51, 1804*) (H).

WINFORTON. **OR** CMB 1690 + (Inc). **BT** 1660 + (*gaps 1701, 1702*) (H).

WITHINGTON. **OR** CMB 1671 +, *CMB 1671-1723 perhaps also CB 1723-1809, M 1723-1754 with Preston Wynne.* **BT** 1660 + (*gaps 1665, 1787, 1801, 1802, 06, 07, 10, 11*). *1815-16 in Hereford Deanery Vol.* (H).

WOLFERLOW. **OR** CMB 1629 + (*gap M 1809-12*) (Inc). **BT** 1660 + (*gaps 1706, 1725*) (H).

WOOLHOPE. **OR** CMB 1558 + (*defective 1650-1662*) (Inc). **BT** 1638, 1666 + (*gaps 1733, 1806, 07, 10, 11*). *1666-1698 described as with Brockhampton. 1815-16 in Hereford Deanery Vol.*

WORMBRIDGE. **OR** CMB 1611-1752 (CLH), C 1813 +, M 1838 +, B 1813 +, Banns 1880 + (*includes entries for Wormbridge, St Devereux, Treville and Kilpeck*) (Inc). **BT** 1664 + (*gaps 1673, 84, 88, 92*) (H). **Cop** CMB 1611-1812 I Ts (SG and CLH), Extracts 1662-1682 Ms (CLH). *M 1612-1812 in Boyd Misc.*

WORMSLEY. **OR** CMB 1595 + (*gap M 1782-5*) (Inc). *Perhaps only from 1749. No information received.* **BT** 1660 + (*gaps 1662, 1667, 1702*) (H).

WYEBRIDGE. (Ind). *f.c. 1707 closed. Some C in Ms book in possession of Minister, Eignbrook Congregational Church.*

YARKHILL. **OR** C 1559-1876, M 1559-1836, B 1559-1913 (*gaps C 1621-5, 1736-48* (except 1738), *M 1621-4, 1672-87, 1736-49* (except 1738), *B 1671-5, 1736-48* (except 1738)), Banns 1754-1812, 1824-1918 (CLH). **BT** 1661 + (*gap 1757*) (H). **Cop** M 1813-37 Ts (SG).

YARPOLE. **OR** CMB 1561 + (*gaps B 1676-8, MB 1715-18*). **BT** 1661 + (*gaps 1666, 67, 68, 85, 93, 1700, 02*) (H).

YAZOR. **OR** CMB 1621 + (*gap CMB 1711-15*) (Inc). **BT** 1660 + (*gaps 1668, 1804*) (H).

OXFORDSHIRE

ACKNOWLEDGMENTS

The Editor gratefully acknowledges the assistance of the following persons in compiling this section:-

Mr. J.S.W. Gibson for preparing the list of typescript and manuscript copies, for considerable assistance in compiling the preface, and checking the proofs; Mr. T. Daish for listing the returns of parish registers made for the National Register of Archives; Captain J.A.S. Trydell for listing the Bishop's Transcripts; Mr. M. Barratt, of the Bodleian Library, Oxford, for clearing up numerous queries and for assistance in compiling the preface; Mr. F. Leeson for listing surrendered Nonconformist Registers; Mr. B. Trinder for supplying information on unsurrendered Nonconformist registers; Father McEvilly, Archivist of the Catholic Diocese of Birmingham for supplying information on Catholic Registers; Mr. P.J. Birkitt, Clerk of the Oxfordshire County Council for supplying information on Microfilms and Quaker Registers in his custody; Mr. J.R. Cunningham of the Church of Jesus Christ of Latter Day Saints and Edward Milligan of the Society of Friends for granting access to their records, and numerous librarians, Anglican Clergy, Catholic Parish Priests officials of Oxford Colleges and Nonconformist Ministers and Church Secretaries for supplying information.

GENERAL INFORMATION

Record Repositories (*see also list on page xx*).

Bod. — *The Bodleian Library, Oxford. (Department of Western Mss).*
(Hours 9 - 7 (10 pm in full term), Sat 9 - 1)
This holds the Bishop's Transcripts and is the official
Diocesan repository for Parish Registers.

O.R.O. — *The Oxfordshire County Record Office, County Hall, Oxford.*
(Hours Mon-Fri 9 - 1, 2.15 - 5)
This holds much other material, but no Registers or Trans-
cripts, except for Microfilms of six parishes and a number
of registers, birth and burial notes etc. of the Banbury
Monthly Meetings.

A.H.B. — *Archbishop's House, Bath Street, Birmingham 4.*
This holds the Archives for the Catholic Diocese of
Birmingham including 4 Oxfordshire Catholic Registers.

G.L. — *Guildhall Library, Basinghall Street, London, E.C.2.*
(Hours Mon-Sat 9.30 - 5).
This holds copies of the late Mr. W.H. Challen's transcripts
of Oxfordshire registers.

S.L.C. — *The Genealogical Society of the Church of Jesus Christ of*
Latter Day Saints, Salt Lake City, Utah.
This holds Microfilms of about half of the Bishop's Trans-
cripts and of many Oxfordshire registers.

Other Abbreviations used in this Section (*see also list on page xxiii*)

J.G. — Copies in the possession of *Mr. J.S.W. Gibson, Humber House,*
Bloxham Banbury, Oxon.

Parishes

Ancient Parishes 217 (14 in the City of Oxford)

Changes in County Boundaries

Only minor adjustments have been made. Caversfield and Towersey
have been transferred from Bucks. Shenington and Widford from

Gloucestershire, Grimsbury Hamlet (in Banbury parish) from Northants, Ibstone, Lillingstone Lovell, Stokenchurch and Achampstead (chapelry of Lewknor) to Bucks and Caversham to Berks.

Parish Registers

The information on Original Registers has been taken mainly from the lists compiled for the National Register of Archives, copies of which are at the N.R.A., Chancery Lane, London, E.C.4. and at the Bodleian Library, Oxford (Ref. R7 62/1-2). Registers of about fifty Oxfordshire parishes are now deposited at the Bodleian and are listed in detail in file R7 3/11. To search any of these, it is necessary to register as a Bodleian reader.

102 parishes or just under half the total have registers beginning in the 16th Century, including 17 in 1538 or 1539, 10 in the 1540's and 18 in the 1550's. The first Marriage entry in the register of Chalgrove dates from 1531. Original paper registers survive in a few parishes including Banbury, the registers of which are being published by Banbury Historical Society.

At the time of going to press five Oxfordshire Parish Registers have been broken down on to Family Reconstitution forms for the purpose of demographic analysis. Work on a further ten is in progress and eight others projected.

Chapels of the Oxford Colleges*

As far as is known only six Colleges hold registers of Baptisms, Marriages or Burials. Of these, Christ Church was the Cathedral and Merton the parish church of the parish of St. John the Baptist until the latter was amalgamated with St. Peter-in-the-East. Two others – Wadham and New College have Burial registers, a partial copy of the former being at the Bodleian. Information on Burials in the chapels of All Souls and Oriel (and perhaps some other College Chapels) may be gleaned from College Records.

The three most interesting registers are, however, those of Christ Church, Magdalen and St. John's. These end in 1753 and consist almost entirely of Marriages. A practice seems to have begun towards the end of the 17th Century, by which Fellows holding Oxford College Livings performed marriages of their parishioners in their College Chapels instead of in the Parish Churches. This custom became more common during the first half of the 18th Century. Thus, the Magdalen registers have entries from various Oxford parishes and from villages and hamlets all over North Berks, South Oxfordshire, and even

---

* The greater part of the information below is taken from the article on the subject by Miss Gabrielle Lambricke, Oxoniensia vol. 25. 1960.

West Bucks. There are 24 entries from Cumnor, 22 from Woolton, 9 from Dorchester, 7 from South Hinksey, 6 from Brill, 5 from Yarnton[*] and two or three from many other parishes. All the Cumnor entries and at least five of those of South Hinksey do not appear in the parish registers. 15 out of 18 weddings in the Woolton register described as having taken place at Magdalen College are not in the Magdalen College Register. Yarnton register has 5 Marriages in the 1740's described as in Magdalen College Chapel, but 5 different ones appear in the Magdalen College Register. Thus, entries seem to have been made, sometimes in the College Register, sometimes in the Parish Register and occasionally in both.

In the St. John's Register, there were 200 Marriages between 1695 and 1752 including 28 entries each from Kirtlington (Oxon) and Fyfield (Berks). In those of Christ Church entries for couples from Oxfordshire and Berkshire villages became more numerous in the 18th Century. There are 30 entries of Cassington couples between 1708 and 1754. This is the more curious since in the 18th century the villages in North Berkshire were not in the Diocese of Oxford, but that of Salisbury.

It is known that Marriages took place in the chapels of other Colleges — for Eynsham at New College, for Headington at Trinity, for Kidlington and Great Milton at Exeter, for Stadhampton and Chiselhampton at All Souls and for Hampton Poyle at Queen's. All date between 1725 and 1754. No registers exist for these colleges and doubtless they were never kept, but the Fellows entered them in the relevant parish register on their next visit to the parish. It seems highly probable, therefore, that many marriages escaped entry in any register.

The practice came to an abrupt end with the passing of the Hardwicke Act in 1753.

Bishop's Transcripts

The Diocese of Oxford was formed in 1542 and included almost all parishes in the County, although the Peculiars listed below were wholly or partly exempt from the Bishop's Jurisdiction. All transcripts are at the Bodleian Library unless otherwise stated. The reference numbers given in the text should, unless otherwise stated, all be preceded by "Ms Oxf Dio Papers". In general, Transcripts do not survive consecutively before about 1720, with the exception of a few parishes formerly in the Peculiars of Banbury, Dorchester and Thame. Many parishes have a few stray years about 1670, 1680 and 1700.

---

[*] Cumnor, Woolton and South Hinksey are in Berks, Dorchester and Yarnton in Oxfordshire and Brill in Bucks.

After 1720, though in many parishes large numbers of odd years are missing, major gaps are rare. In this list only gaps of 4 years or more have been indicated. The full details will be found in Canon Oldfield's Parochial Index in the Bodleian Library (R7 60) a copy of which is at the National Register of Archives, Chancery Lane.

Peculiars

All transcripts which have survived are now in the Bodleian, but they were originally scattered among the Oxford, Berks and Bucks Archdeanery and the Oxford and Lincoln Diocesan records.

Peculiars of the Dean and Chapter of Lincoln

Banbury, Cropredy etc. – (Actually 4 separate Peculiars but they always had the same official, and may be regarded as one unit). Banbury and its Hamlets, Cropredy and its chapelries, Claydon, Mollington, Wardington, Horley and Hornton, and King's Sutton, Northants. A fairly complete series of Transcripts exists.

Thame – (Thame and its Hamlets, Great Milton, Sydenham and Tetsworth. Also Towersey in Bucks). Some or all of the transcripts survive for each parish.

Langford – (Langford and Little Faringdon). Transcripts exist for most years.

Other Peculiars

Dorchester Abbey – (Dorchester, Benson, Chiselhampton, Clifton, Hampden, Drayton St. Leonard, Marsh Baldon, Nettlebed, Pishill, Stadhampton, Toot Baldon, Warborough). A complete series, though some parishes have larger gaps than the average.

Monks Risborough – (Peculiar of Archbishop of Canterbury). Included in Oxfordshire, Newington and its Chapelry Britwell Prior, Transcripts at Bodleian Library.

Modern Copies of Parish Registers and Bishop's Transcripts

Printed

Few registers have been printed, there being only two volumes of Phillimore Marriages. The Banbury Historical Society are publishing Banbury Registers. A few other registers have been printed at various times. Copies of printed registers are at the British Museum, the Society of Genealogists' Library and the Genealogical Society, Salt Lake City unless otherwise stated.

Typescript and Manuscript.

Mr. J.S.W. Gibson (Humber House, Bloxham, Banbury) has copied about a third of the Marriage registers in the County, some from the Bishop's Transcripts. The Society of Genealogists has already received copies of most of his work, and will eventually receive it all. This includes some complete registers of parishes in the North of the County. The volume numbers given after Society of Genealogists' copies refer to the four manuscript volumes of Marriages unless otherwise stated. The remainder are the volumes of North Oxfordshire registers.

The *Bodleian Library* has a sizeable miscellaneous collection. The references given should be preceded by "Ms. Top. Oxon". These include some made by W.H. Challen (also in the Guildhall Library, London), some manuscript copies of Oxford City registers made by Cokayne and of Shipton-under-Wychwood, Culham and Stanton Harcourt made by Canon Oldfield.

The *Banbury Borough Library* has a few copies of North Oxon Registers made by the Banbury Historical Society, but these are all duplicated in the Society of Genealogists' own Library.

Microfilms

The Church of Jesus Christ of Latter Day Saints is in the process of microfilming the transcripts, and copies of these microfilms are at the Society of Genealogists (on permanent loan from the Bodleian Library) and at the Genealogical Society of the Church, Salt Lake City, Utah, U.S.A. Although the filming has been completed as far as the letter "M" (Great Milton) details have been given in this index only as far as Fritwell. This is because the standard of film from "F" to "M" was doubtful, and the Society of Genealogists has so far received copies only to Fritwell. However, it is understood that filming will recommence at "M" rather than "F". There are also at Salt Lake City microfilms of the Phillimore Manuscripts, of some other copies and of a few original Oxfordshire registers. The Oxfordshire Record Office holds microfilms of 6 parishes deposited by the British Records Association, Records Preservation Section, but it will not be possible to use the films without the prior permission of the incumbent, and the permission of the Bodleian Library to use their microfilm reader.

Marriage Index

Oxfordshire is not included in Boyd's Marriage Index as a separate unit, but parts of 36 parishes are in the miscellaneous volumes. A comprehensive 25 year period index of 65,000 marriages from all transcribed marriage registers has been compiled by Mr. Couzens and is now completed, but is awaiting typing, after which

copies will de deposited at the Society of Genealogists' Library and
the Bodleian Library, Oxford.

Marriage Licences

The Bishop and Archdeacon of Oxford had concurrent powers of
granting Marriage Licences which were formally recognised in 1737
Ms Oxf. Dioc. Papers c 266, f 35 V). There are, therefore, two main
series of Marriage Bonds, Allegations and Affidavits for Oxfordshire,
both of which are held by the Bodleian Library, Oxford. In addition,
licences were granted by the Officials of the Peculiar Jurisdictions.
The Bodleian holds also the greater part of these, though some are at
Buckinghamshire Record Office (see C below). The full details of all
three series are listed in Section II 6 of the lists of the Diocesan
records in R7 3/11.

Diocesan Series, 1613-1850 (Ms Oxf. Dioc. Papers d 22-d 97), 1850-
1857, (c 819-822), 1858- present (c 823-870, c 2127-8).

Up to 1850 these are arranged alphabetically by the Bridegrooms'
surnames. Within each letter of the alphabet the order is approxi-
ately chronological. Few documents have survived for *1728-1735.* There
are a few Diocesan Bonds and Allegations of 1623 in Ms Archd. Papers
Oxon c 126.

Between 1850 and 1857 Affidavits are somewhat confused being
arranged, sometimes in Surname order and sometimes in years. From
1857 they are arranged chronologically. An index to the Diocesan series
to 1850 is in progress. (Bod. R6. 155 b).

Archidiaconal Series, 1618-1856 (Ms Archd. Papers Oxon c 450-629)
1930-52 (d 30-58).

These are arranged by years and up to 1856, within each year
alphabetically by the Bridegrooms' surnames. (Ms Archd. Papers Oxon
c 126) (S.C. No. 25939) contain a few Bonds and Affidavits which have
strayed from the main series.

The Bodleian Library holds a photographic reproduction (R6 155/3-
4) of a 19th Century index to this series to 1856 as well as a Microfilm of it. (Ms Film 231), the original index being in the possession
of the Diocesan Registrar Messrs Franklin Ltd., 14, King Edward Street,
Oxford. Further photostat copies are in the Society of Genealogists'
Library, the National Register of Archives, Chancery Lane, and
Banbury Borough Library. Papers for all the years now missing between
1667 and 1849 were in existence when the index was compiled. No
Affidavits appear to have survived for the period 1857 to 1929.

103

C   *Peculiars. (For parishes within the Peculiars see Bishop's Transcripts above).*

Bonds and Allegations for Marriages within the Lincoln Peculiars up to 1736 are at the Bodleian Library arranged alphabetically by Bridegrooms' surnames. From 1736 (except for Langford) they are at the Buckinghamshire Record Office, Aylesbury, where they are filed with the Buckinghamshire Archidiaconal Series. These post-1736 Bonds and Affidavits are included in A.H. Plaisted's typescript *"Index to Buckinghamshire Marriage Bonds and Allegations"* copies of which are at the Society of Genealogists' Library, the Bodleian and the Buckinghamshire Record Office.

183 stray bonds for the Banbury, Thame, Dorchester and Monks Risborough Peculiars (as well as Aylesbury, the Court of the Archdeacon of Bucks and a list for Bierton) were formerly at Somerset House with the wills, and are still filed at the Bodleian with the Probate records of the Oxon, Berks and Bucks Peculiars (Ref. Ms Wills Peculiars 85). A calender of these was prepared by Mr. George Sherwood and published in the Berks, Bucks and Oxon Archaeological Journal Vol. II 1896. An offprint of this article and of the index which appeared in the next issue is at the Society of Genealogists, boxed with the Bucks tracts.

Details – *Lincoln Peculiars*

Banbury, Cropredy etc. Bonds and a few Allegations 1668-1736 (Mss Archd. Papers Oxon b 54-57. Stray Bonds 1617-1735 with Wills. All from 1736 at Bucks R.O.

Thame Bonds and a few Allegations 1624-1737 (Ms Archd. Papers Oxon. b 83-86). Stray Bonds 1617-1735 with Wills. All from 1736 at Bucks R.O.

Langford Bonds and Affidavits 1676-1814 (Ms Archd. Papers Berks c 196) A reproduction of a 19th Century Index is held by the Bodleian Library Society of Genealogists and the National Register of Archives.

Other Peculiars

Dorchester Bonds, Allegations and **Affidavits** 1625 – 1836 (Ms Archd. Papers Oxon b 67-71, c 302). Stray Bonds 1626-1735 with Wills.

Monks Risborough Bonds 1681 – 1716 (Ms Archd. Papers Berks c 201). Stray Bonds 1626-1735 with Wills.

Roman Catholics

Oxfordshire lies within the Roman Catholic Diocese of Birmingham. There were six separate chaplaincies of the 18th Century Oxford

Mission at Holywell Manor, Sandford-on-Thames, Britwell Prior, Haseley Court, Overy near Dorchester and Waterperry. Registers are known for only two of these – Britwell Prior and Waterperry. Two other 18th Century important chapels were at Heythrop and Tusmore Park (an estate of the Fermor family). A Heythrop register beginning in 1753 is held by the Parish Priest at Chipping Norton and Heythrop Marriages 1729-30 are in the registers of Revd. Monox Hervey at Archbishop's House, Westminster (published by C.R.S.). Archbishop's House, Birmingham holds registers of Hardwick and the Northamptonshire chapels of Overthorpe and Warkworth as well as a copy of a register containing Tusmore Park entries from 1714 taken from an altar missal at Hethe Chapel.

There were at least three other 18th Century foundations: Kiddington, Stonor, and St. Aloysius, Oxford. The registers of Kiddington are held by the Parish Priest of Radford and those of Stonor are at the P.R.O. No registers are known for St. Aloysius, although the Parish Priest holds the Waterperry registers.

The 19th Century foundations were St. Clement's Oxford, the successor church to Waterperry; Banbury, the successor church to Overthorpe and Warkworth; and Chipping Norton, the successor church to Heythrop. Banbury used the existing registers, and it is possible that Chipping Norton did also – Chipping Norton's own registers do not start until 1879. No registers are known for St. Clement, Oxford. The Registers of Britwell Priory, Kiddington and Waterperry have been printed by the Catholic Record Society. The Diocesan Archivist holds a Confirmation Register of Vicars Apostolic from 1786-1816 which covers the whole of the Midland District.

Baptists

17 Baptist Churches founded before 1837 have been listed. Four (Chipping Norton, Coate, Hook Norton and New Road, Oxford) were 17th Century foundations, Burford was founded about 1700 and the remainder probably between 1800 and 1837. The only surrendered registers were from Chipping Norton; Coate; New Road, Oxford and Burford and also from Sydenham (founded 1821). Of these that of Coate is especially interesting as it begins as early as 1647. The Minister of Hook Norton holds registers from 1772. No registers are known for the 6 closed churches of Swerford, Tadmarton, Wigginton, West Bar, Banbury, South Bar, Banbury and Commercial Road, Oxford or for Little Tew. No information has been received from the Church Secretaries of the remaining four.

105

Independents (Congregationalists)

18 Independent churches are known to have been founded before 1837. Three (Bicester, Witney and Rotherfield Grays) were founded in the 17th Century; two more in the 18th Century (Thame and Banbury) and the remainder between 1800 and 1837. Ten surrendered registers, but for two of these (Banbury and Bicester) registers earlier than those surrendered are held by the Churches. The Rotherfield Grays surrendered register begins in 1685. No registers are held by the Secretaries of two of the remaining eight churches, and no informatio has been received from the other six. Neither the Berks, South Oxon and South Bucks congregational Union, nor the Secretaries of its constituent districts holds registers. The records of George Street Church, Oxford (f. 1832 closed 1932) are at Mansfield College, Oxford but it is not known if these include registers.

Presbyterians and Unitarians

Three pre-1837 registers are known, all surrendered. The Presbyterian Registers of Banbury (now Banbury Unitarian Church) and for Bloxham and Milton begin in 1816 and 1789 respectively. Baptisms for two years for Witney are in the register which appears in the catalogue of surrendered registers under Taunton, Somerset. This was clearly the personal notebook of a minister which he took with him from place to place. A duplicate of the Banbury Register is held by the minister.

Methodists

Wesleyans

The whole of the County appears to have been covered in 1837 by five Circuits in the Oxford District viz. Oxford, Witney, Banbury, Watlington and Chipping Norton. The Brackley (Northants) Circuit may possibly have covered a few villages in the North of the County, thoug this is doubtful. The Banbury Circuit covered Warwick and Kenilworth until between 1810 and 1816 and still included the Warwickshire churches of Tysoe, Oxhill and Northend in 1837. All five of the circuit churches surrendered registers, so in the case of Oxfordshire the surrendered Wesleyan registers probably represent all in existenc It would seem to have been customary in Oxford, for copies to have been made when the registers were surrendered. Two of these copies ar certainly in existence, for Banbury (at the Methodist Church) and for Oxford (at Bodleian Library) and there may be others. The Banbury register does not include the Kenilworth and Warwick areas. In addition to the five circuit registers, a sixth register, that of Biceste beginning in 1820 was also surrendered. Bicester was presumably in the Oxford Circuit, but doubtless kept a separate register because of the distance from Oxford. It is possible that Bicester entries before 1820 may be found in the Oxford register.

Primitive Methodists

There were only two Circuits in Oxfordshire: those of Banbury and Witney, though doubtless the Reading and Wallingford circuits, and perhaps that of High Wycombe included parts of Oxfordshire. Witney registers from 1835 were surrendered, but none from Banbury. The Methodist Church, Banbury holds a register for the Banbury Circuit, but this was originally a register for the Welton, Northants (near Daventry) circuit and the first Banbury entries appear only in 1842.

Methodist New Connexion

No pre 1837 churches in Oxfordshire are known.

Lady Huntingdon's Connexion

Three churches are known. The register of Goring was surrendered. No reply has been received from the Church Secretary of South Stoke. Banbury Independent Church was part of Lady Huntingdon's Connexion c. 1807-1810. The registers were surrendered.

Society of Friends (Quakers)

The Oxfordshire Quarterly Meeting was established in 1688 with the following Monthly Meetings:-

Oxford afterwards Witney
Banbury
Warborough

In 1790 the Oxfordshire Quarterly Meeting was joined to the Berkshire Quarterly Meeting to form the Berks and Oxford Quarterly Meeting.

In 1810 Warborough Monthly Meeting was united with Reading Monthly Meeting to form the Reading and Warborough Monthly Meeting (see Berks). The Reading Monthly Meeting registers have been added under the two meetings concerned.

Registers

The majority of pre-1837 registers were surrendered, though a number of records of the Banbury Monthly Meeting and its constituent meetings are now at the Oxfordshire Record Office.

Oxfordshire Quarterly Meeting. ZM 1776-1796, B 1778-1796 (PRO 52-55).

Berks and Oxon Quarterly Meeting. ZMB 1796-1837 (PRO 56-60).

Oxfordshire entries for the period 1790-1796 are in the Oxon Quarterly Meeting registers which continued in use for the combined Quarterly Meeting until 1796.

The Monthly Meeting Registers are listed under the names of the Monthly Meetings. Birth notes 1760-1796 and Burial notes 1776-1796 for the Berks and Oxon Quarterly Meetings are at the PRO (1449-1450).

A "Digest" (i.e. consolidated abstracts arranged alphabetically) of all surrendered registers is held at Friends' House, Euston Road, London, N.W.1.

Regimental Registers

These cover Births, Baptisms, Marriages and Deaths for the period 1790-1924 and are at Somerset House, London. They are the original registers kept by the various regiments. Births and Baptisms are indexed. For Marriages, Deaths and Burials it is preferable, but not essential to know the regiment. The most likely regiment for Oxfordshire Infantrymen was the 52nd Regiment of Foot.

Search should also be made of the Guards' Regiments, the Royal Artillery, the Royal Engineers and the Royal Marines.

Monumental Inscriptions

Printed

The only printed volume devoted specifically to M.I's is " Oxfordshire M.I's from the Mss of A. Wood and others " (Ed. Sir T. Phillips 1825). For M.I's up to about 1700, "Wood and Rawlinson's *Parochial Collections* (Ed. F.N. Davis, Oxfordshire Record Society Vols 2, 4, 11 (1920, 1929)) is useful. The Oxford City M.I.'s in Churches and College Chapels are transcribed in some detail in Wood's *History of Oxford.* Thame M.I.'s are in the *"History of Thame"* (1883). Brasses will be found in the "Oxford Journal of Monumental Brasses " Vol. 1-2 pt 3 1897-1900; 1900-1912.

Typescript and Manuscript

The Bodleian Library holds no single collection of copies, but many are scattered through miscellaneous Oxfordshire collections and Church notes. In the Society of Genealogists' Library, there is a very good series of virtually all the Oxfordshire church M.I.'s compiled by Whitmore in two manuscript volumes entitled *Church Notes.*

ewspapers

Jackson's Oxford Journal 1753-1898. Incomplete series at Bodleian ibrary and British Museum Newspaper Library, Colindale. An Index of art of Jackson's Oxford Journal is in course of preparation with a iew to eventual publication in some form by Oxford City Libraries.

Oxford City and County Chronicle (afterwards *Oxford Chronicle* and *Berks and Bucks Gazette*) 1837 onwards. There were no other newspapers f which a consecutive series survives.

Full details of all Oxfordshire newspapers are given in Cordeaux nd Merry's *Bibliography (see General works of reference below)*.

ublishing Societies

Oxfordshire Record Society, c/o Bodleian Library, Oxford. Record Series 1919 to date.

Oxford Historical Society, 59 Five Mile Drive, Oxford. Publications 1-101, 1885-1936. New Series 1939- date.

Oxford Architectural and Historical Society, c/o Ashmolean Museum, Oxford. (Publications; Proceedings New Series 6 vols 1860-1900; Oxoniensia 1936 onwards). The Oxford University Genealogical and Heraldic Society was amalgamated with the Architectural and Historical Society in 1841. It produced 5 Annual reports (Proceedings 1835-39).

Banbury Historical Society, c/o Banbury Borough Library. Magazine "Cake and Cockhorse". Publications 1959 onwards. It is publishing the Banbury Parish Registers and is active in parish register transcription.

Oxfordshire Archaeological Society (formerly *North Oxfordshire Archaeological Society*), 59 Five Mile Drive, Oxford. — Transactions, reports publications etc. 1853 onwards. Magazine Top. Oxon. 1958 onwards.

Other Local Societies

(The Rural Community Council, 20 Beaumont Street, Oxford acts as a co-ordinating body for Local Societies).

Bicester Local History Circle, Lammas Cottage, Launton Road, Bicester, Oxon.

General Works of Reference

Cordeaux, E.H. *and* Merry, D.H. *A Bibliography of printed works relating to Oxfordshire*.......Oxford, Clarendon Press, 1955. This is extremely comprehensive, and obviates the necessity of giving a full bibliography here. It lists a large number of useful local histories, many with genealogical material.

The Victoria County History of the County of Oxford. 8 v. 1939-1964.

Williams, W.R. *The Parliamentary History of the County of Oxford.* 1213-1899 with Biographical and Genealogical Notices 1899.

Faulkner. *History of Parish Registers with remarks on a few of the registers of North Oxfordshire* (**Trans.** N. Oxf. Arch. Soc. 1853-1855 p 101-111).

McClatchey, Diana. *Oxfordshire Clergy, 1777-1869*: a Study of the Established Church and of the role of its Clergy in Local Society. Oxford, Clarendon Press, 1960.

Lamborn, E.A. Greening. *The Armorial Glass of the Oxford Diocese, 1250-1850*. London, Oxford University Press (for the Berkshire Archaeological Society), 1949.

Local Histories

A large number of Oxfordshire local histories have been printed, the full list up to 1955 being given in Cordeaux and Merry.

CKHAMPSTEAD. *(Chapelry of Lewknor). Now transferred to Bucks. See Lewknor.*

DDERBURY. **OR** CB 1598 [+], M 1598-1837 (Inc). **BT** 1670-1856 *(gaps 1671-1679, 1684-1733)*, (C 567, 475, d 192). **Cop** M 1598-1840 Ts (SG), B 1598-1840 (Alpha) Ts (SG N. Oxon Reg 1 and Bod d 233), Index to B 1598-1810 (Inc), CMB (BT) 1670-1822, 1826-1869 Mf (SLC and SG).

DDERBURY (S of F). **Banbury Monthly Meeting.** *f 1668. disc. 1910.*
OR Z notes 1839-51, B notes 1842-61, 1868-69, B notes
Adderbury and Banbury) 1820-1880 (ORO).

DWELL. **OR** CMB 1539 [+] (Inc). **BT** 1639-1866 *(gaps 1640 - 74, 1676-1720, 1793-1801, 1807-11)*, (C 475). **Cop** M 1539-88, 1639-43, 1671-1753, Ts (SG), CB 1539-1812, M 1539-1753 Ts (Bod d 289 and GL), M 1754-1809 (Phil Ms), CMB (BT) 1639-1851 Mf (SLC and SG), M 1539-1588, 1639-1809 (SLC). *M 1540-1809 in Boyd Misc.*

LBURY. **OR** CB 1653-1812, M 1653-1837, Z 1639-1702, Banns 1754-1805, 1823-1923 (Bod). **BT** 1680-1866 *(gaps 1682-1720, 1738-43, 1750-56)*, (C 476). **Cop** CMB (BT) 1680-1851 Mf (SLC and SG).

LKERTON. **OR** C 1545-1741, M 1546-1739, B 1544-1742 (Bod), C 1742 [+], M 1742-1803 *(gap 1764-1783)*, B 1742-1812, Banns 1784-1803 (Inc Shenington), B 1813 [+] (Inc Alkerton). **BT** 1720-1873 *(gaps 1754-58)*, (c 476, 60, 165). **Cop** M 1546-1742 Ts (JG), CMB (BT) 1720-1851 Mf (SLC and SG), CMB Extracts 1547-1670 (SG), M (BT) 1720-1836 Ms (SG Vol. 1).

LVESCOT. **OR** CM 1662 [+], B 1663 [+] *(gap M 1754-1783)* (Inc). **BT** 1721-1877 *(gap 1732-1812)*, (C 477, d 295). **Cop** CMB (BT) 1721-1851, Mf (SLC and SG).

LVESCOT (S of F). **Oxford Monthly Meeting.** *f 1709. disc. 18th C. No regs known apart from Mo Mg regs.*

MBROSDEN. **OR** C 1611-1752, M 1611-1754, B 1611-1745 *(gaps M 1638-1671, 1673-1681, B 1639-1654, 1656-1664, 1670-1684 (Bod)*, CB 1752 [+], M 1754 [+] (Inc). **BT** 1685-1865 *(gaps 1690-99, 1702-19, 1830-33)*, (C 477, 478). **Cop** M 1611-37, 1662-72, 1682-1837 Ts (SG), CMB (BT) 1685-1851 Mf (SLC and SG).

MBROSDEN, Bethel (Ind). *f 1825. No early regs known. Not at PRO or Ch Sec.* ZCB 1927 [+], M 1929 [+], D 1926 [+] (Ch Sec). *See also Blackthorn.*

RDLEY with FEWCOTT. **OR** CMB 1758 [+] *(gaps M 1812-14, 1836-38)*, Banns 1758-1811 (Inc). **BT** 1681-1872 *(gaps 1682-1700, 1702-12, 1714-19)*, (C 478, d 200). **Cop** CMB (BT) 1822-1851 Mf (SLC and SG), M (BT) 1713, 1723-1836 Ms (SG Vol. 3).

ASCOT-UNDER-WYCHWOOD. **OR** CMB 1566 [+] (*gaps C 1655-1677, M 1655-1753*),
   Banns 1754-1812, 1823 [+] (Inc). **BT** 1721-1866 (C 479). **Cop** CMB (BT)
   C 1721-1851 Mf (SLC and SG).

ASTHALL. **OR** CMB 1704 [+] (Inc). **BT** 1667-1877 (*gaps 1671-1683, 1685-172(*
   and odd years), (C 479, 480). **Cop** CMB (BT) 1667-1851 (SLC and SG).

ASTON (RC). *Entries in Britwell Prior regs.*

ASTON, NORTH. **OR** CMB 1678 [+] (*gaps C 1784-88, B 1784-1812*), Banns
   1824 [+] (Inc). **BT** 1722-1853 (*gaps – odd years*), (C 567). **Cop** CMB (B
   1722-1853 Mf (SLC and SG), M (BT) 1725-1836 Ms (SG Vol. 2).

ASTON ROWANT with KINGSTON BLOUNT. **OR** CMB 1554 [+] (*gaps CMB 1573-1580*)
   (Inc). **BT** 1639-1871 (*gaps 1641-1681, 1686-1713*), (c 480, 481).
   Cop M 1554-1754 Ts (SG), CB 1554-1805, M 1555-1754 Ts (Bod d 289
   and GL), CMB (BT) 1639-1871 Mf (SLC and SG), M 1555-1812 (SLC),
   M 1555-1812 in Boyd Misc.

ASTON STEEPLE. – *see Steeple Aston.*

BALDON, MARSH. **Peculiar** *of Dorchester Abbey.* **OR** C 1559 [+], M 1582 [+],
   B 1586 [+] (*gaps M 1724-28, 1734-53*) (Inc). **BT** 1662-1814 (*gaps 1738-
   1744, 1781-1786, 1799-1803*) (Ms Archd. Papers Oxon b 72). Odd year
   between 1764 and 1814 and 1815-65 (Ms Oxf Dio Papers c.558, 559).
   Cop CMB (BT) 1662-1702, 1764-1851 Mf (SLC and SG).

BALDON, TOOT. **Peculiar** *of Dorchester Abbey.* **OR** C 1579 [+], MB 1599 [+]
   (*gap M 1733-53*), Banns 1823 [+] (Inc). **BT** 1662-1854 (*gaps 1739-44 a*
   odd years) (1662-1764 and some odd years between 1764 and 1814
   Ms Archd. Papers Oxon b 72. Other years 1764-1814 and 1815-1856 Ms
   Oxf Dio Papers c.621). **Cop** CMB (BT) 1662-1856 Mf (SLC and SG).

BALDWYN BRIGHTWELL. – *see Britwell Baldwin.*

BALSCOTE. **OR** *In Wroxton regs.* **BT** 1726-1820 (*gaps 1731-4, 1737-42,
   1751-87, 1806-12*) (with Wroxton c.640). 1822-53 (c.481).
   Cop CMB (BT) 1813-1820, 1822-53 Mf (SLC and SG). *See also Wroxton.*

BAMPTON. **OR** CB 1538 [+], M 1538-1791, Z 1653-1660 (Inc). *CMB almost ill
   before 1570.* **BT** 1680-1879 (*gap 1684-1720*), (c.482, d 209-11).
   Cop CMB (BT) 1680-1855 Mf (SLC and SG).

BAMPTON. (Bapt). – *see Coate.*

BAMPTON ASTON. **OR** post 1837. **BT** 1843-65 (d 212). **Cop** CMB (BT) 1843-
   1865 Mf (SLC and SG).

BAMPTON JEW. **OR** post 1837 (Inc). **BT** 1842-1878 (d 212). **Cop** CMB (BT)
   1842-78 (SLC and SG).

BANBURY. **Peculiar** *of Dean and Chapter of Lincoln.* **OR** C 1558-1898,
   M 1558-1837, B 1558-1962 (*gap C 1654-1660*), Banns 1653-1659,
   Z 1653-1661 (Bod). **BT** 1606-1734 (*gap 1607-61*) (b.114), 1735-1813
   (Mss. Archd. Papers Bucks c.160/1-2, 161/1-2, 162/1). **Cop** CB 1558-
   1723, M 1558-1837 (Ptd. Banbury Historical Society, 5 vols) CB
   1723-1837 Ms & Ts (JG), CMB (BT) 1735-1851 Mf (SLC and SG), CMB
   1558-1812 Mf (ORO).

BANBURY (RC). **OR** C 1771-1827 *formerly Overthorpe and Warkworth* (AHB). **Cop** C 1771-1827 Ms (SG).

BANBURY, WEST BAR (Strict Bapt). *f 1829. Now defunct. No regs known. Not at PRO.*

BANBURY, SOUTH BAR (Strict Bapt). *f 1834. Now defunct. No regs known. Not at PRO.*

BANBURY. Great Meeting House Fair (Pres. *Now Christchurch Unitarian Church*). **OR** ZC 1816-1837 (PRO), ZC 1816-1930 (Minister).

BANBURY. Church Lane (Ind. Lady Hunt. Conn. c.1807-10). *f 1787.* **OR** C 1794-1806 (Banbury Cong Church), ZC 1814 [+] (Banbury Cong Church), ZC 1807-1837 (PRO).

BANBURY. Church Lane (Wes). *f 1804.* **OR** ZC 1805 [+] (Marlborough Rd. Meth. Church, Banbury), ZC 1805-1837 (PRO). *Includes whole of Banbury Circuit except Warwick and Kenilworth Areas.* **Cop** C 1805-1837 (Banbury Lib).

BANBURY CIRCUIT. (Prim Meth). *Register used previously for the Welton, Northants Circuit.* (*No Banbury entries before 1842*) Marlborough Rd, Methodist Church, Banbury).

BANBURY (LADY HUNT CONN.).— *see Banbury (Ind).*

BANBURY MONTHLY MEETING (S of F). *f 1668.* **Constituent Meetings:** *Adderbury (1668-1910), Banbury (1668* [+]), *Hook Norton (1705* [+]), *Sibford (1668* [+]), *South Newington (1668-1825, 1893-1911).* **Monthly Meeting Registers:** Z 1632-1837, M 1662-1769, 1776-1792, 1796-1837, B 1655-1837 (PRO 84-89), Z 1632-1837, M 1648-1837, B 1655-1837 (*copies made in 1826 because originals badly damaged*) (ORO), ZMB 1776-1792, Z notes 1827-37, 1885-1908, D notes 1828-38, B notes 1827-39, 1880-1898. Letters and forms re. M 1895-1904 (ORO). **Cop** Z 1632-1868, M 1655-1868, B 1648-1894 (Alpha) (ORO cat. AV/1-3), ZMB c.1660-1837 (Alpha) Ts (JG).

BANBURY (S of F). **Banbury Monthly Meeting.** **OR** Z notes 1837-1884, D 1836-1846, B notes (Adderbury and Banbury) 1820-80, D notes (Banbury and Sibford) 1846-1859 (ORO).

BARFORD, ST JOHN. **OR** CMB 1695 [+] (Inc). **BT** 1669-1866 (*gaps 1671-1720, 1728-32, 1738-1807*), (c.483). **Cop** CMB (BT) 1669, 1721-3, 1727, 1733-7, C 1808-1840 Ts (SG N. Oxon Reg 1) CMB (BT) 1669-1852 Mf (SLC and SG), M (OR) 1695-1753 Ms (JG).

BARFORD, ST MICHAEL. **OR** CB 1813 [+], M 1755 [+] (Inc). **BT** 1721-1852 (*gaps – odd years*), (c.483). **Cop** CB 1813-1849, M 1755-1849 Ts (SG), M (BT) 1721-1742, CB 1721-1727 Ms (JG), CMB (BT) 1721-1852 Mf (SLC and SG).

BARTON. – *see Steeple Barton and Westcott Barton.*

BECKLEY. **OR** CB 1813 [+], M 1837 [+], Banns 1754-1812, 1823 [+] (Inc). **BT** 1678-1878 (*gaps 1680-1720, 1733-1742, 1752-56, 1758-1762, c.413, 414*), *sep BT's for Horton-cum-Studley 1721-4, 1737-8.* **Cop** CMB (BT) 1678-1851 Mf (SLC and SG).

BEGBROKE. **OR** CMB 1665[+], Banns 1823[+] (Inc). **BT** 1721-1865 (*gap 1724-1728*), (c.484, 485). **Cop** CMB (BT) 1721-1809, 1813-1853 Mf (SLC and SG).

BENSINGTON. (Ind). *f 1800*. **OR** ZC 1835-36 (PRO).

BENSON. **Peculiar** *of Dorchester Abbey*. **OR** CB 1565-1812, M 1569-1812 (Berks RO), CMB 1813[+] (Inc). **BT** 1661-1877 (*gaps 1693-96, 1835-1852 and odd years*), (b.73, c.485). **Cop** CMB (BT) 1661-1858 Mf (SLC and SG), M 1569-1812 Ts (SG), CMB 1565-1812 Mf (SLC and Berks RO).

BERRICK PRIOR. - *see Newington* (*Nr. Wallingford*).

BERRICK SALOME. **OR** C 1609-1769, M 1615-1755, B 1616-1790 (Inc Chalgrove). **BT** 1639-1877 (*gaps 1641-1668, 1671-1683, 1686-1695, 1698-1719, 1733-1742, 1748-1766, 1794-1800*), (c.485). **Cop** CMB (BT) 1639-1853 Mf (SLC and SG).

BICESTER. **OR** CMB 1539[+] (Inc). **BT** 1680-1879 (*gaps 1687-98, 1702-20*), (c.486-488, d.221/2). **Cop** M 1539-1840, CB 1813-1840 I Ts (SG). CMB (BT) 1680-1834 Mf (SLC and SG), CMB 1539-1812 Mf (ORO) C 1758-1812 Ms (Bod).

BICESTER, Market End, Water Lane (Ind). *f 1690*. **OR** ZC 1786-1837, B 1786-1835 (PRO), C 1695-1745, M 1695-6 (Ch.Sec). **Cop** C 1695-1745, M 1695-6 Ts (SG).

BICESTER. (Wes). *f 1816*. **OR** ZC 1820-36 (PRO).

BINSEY, ST MARGARETS. **OR** CMB 1791[+] (Inc St Frideswide's, Oxford). **BT** 1805-1866 (*gap 1806*), (d.226). **Cop** CMB (BT) 1805-1866 Mf (SLC and SG).

BIX. **OR** CMB 1577[+], Banns 1754-1812 (Inc). **BT** 1639-1877 (*gaps 1641-79, 1687-1720*), (c.488). **Cop** CMB (BT) 1639-1852 Mf (SLC and SG).

BLACK BOURTON. **OR** CMB 1542[+] (*gap CMB 1721-57*) (Inc). **BT** 1678-1874 (*gaps 1682-1720, 1865-1873 and odd years*), (c.489). **Cop** CMB (BT) 1678-1853 Mf (SLC and SG).

BLACKTHORN. (Ind). *f 1825. Not at PRO. No information.*

BLADON. **OR** C 1543[+], MB 1545[+] (*gap M 1693-94*), Banns 1756[+] (Inc). **BT** 1684-1856 (*gaps 1686-1720, 1733-37*), (c.489, 490). **Cop** CMB (BT) 1684-1856 Mf (SLC and SG).

BLETCHINGDON. **OR** C 1561[+], MB 1559[+], Banns 1754-1812, 1823[+] (Inc). **BT** 1713-1865 (*gaps 1715-1720, 1836-1845*), (c.491, d.227, 228). **Cop** CMB (BT) 1713-1865 Mf (SLC and SG), M (BT) 1713, 1721-1835 Ms (SG Vol. 3).

BLOXHAM with MILCOMBE. **OR** CMB 1630[+], Banns 1754-1800, 1823[+] (Inc). **BT** 1669-1871 (*gap 1671-1720*), (c.491, 493). **Cop** C 1630-1660, M 1630-1745 Ts (JG), CMB (BT) 1669-1811, 1851-1871 Mf (SLC and SG), M (BT) 1746-1836, C (BT) 1813-1837 Ms (SG Vol. 1). *See also Milcombe.*

BLOXHAM, Hawk Rd. (Bapt). *f 1808. Not at PRO. No information.*

LOXHAM and MILTON (Pres). **OR** ZC 1789-1837 (PRO).

ODICOTE. **OR** CMB 1563 + (gaps CB 1802-12, M 1754-1836) (Inc). **BT** 1721-
1864 (gap 1732-1734), (c. 493, 494). **Cop** C 1563-1840, M 1564-1750,
1837-40, B 1567-1840 Ts (SG N. Oxon Reg 1), CMB (BT) 1813-1852
Mf (SLC and SG). Marriages were at Adderbury 1754-1836.

OURTON, GREAT. – see Cropredy.

RADWELL. – see Broadwell.

RITWELL BALDWIN. **OR** 1705 +, M 1705-1836, B 1705-1812 (Inc). **BT** 1639-
1870 (gaps 1641-95, 1698-1720 and odd years), (c. 495, d. 236 b).
Cop M 1547-1709 Ms – Snell Col. Vol. 18 p. 12 (SG under Berks),
M 1547-1812 (Phil Ms), CMB (BT) 1639-1812 Mf (SLC and SG), M 1575-
1812 (SLC), M 1547-1812 in Boyd Misc.

RITWELL PRIOR. Chapelry of Newington (Peculiar of Monk's Risborough)
until 1867 when it was transferred to Britwell Salome. No OR.
BT 1604-5, 1632-39 (with church accounts), (Ms Archd. Papers Oxon
c. 143 fol 6-12), 1812 (c. 495). **Cop** CMB (BT) 1604-39, 1812 (SLC
and SG).

RITWELL PRIOR (RC). Chaplaincy of Oxford Mission. **OR** C 1765-88
(St Aloysius, Oxford). **Cop** C 1765-1788 ptd (CRS Vol. 13).

RITWELL SALOME. **OR** CB 1574 +, M 1574-1834 (gap 1766-87), Banns
1823 + (Inc). **BT** 1696-1868 (gaps 1698-1720 and odd years), (c. 495,
496). **Cop** M 1575-1812 (Phil Ms), CMB (BT) 1696-1852 Mf (SLC and SG).
M 1575-1812 in Boyd Misc. See also Britwell Prior above.

RIZE NORTON. **OR** C 1548-1896, M 1569-1837, B 1568-1877 (gaps C 1549-
1551, 1555-57, 1569-83, 1597, M 1580-85, 1589-97, 1667-71), Banns
1812-14 (Bod). **BT** 1682-1877 (gaps 1684-1720, 1731-34, 1739-45),
(c. 496, 497). **Cop** M 1569-1837 Ts (SG), CMB (BT) 1696-1852 Mf (SLC
and SG).

ROADWELL (BRADWELL). **OR** CMB 1538 + (Inc). See also Filkins and
Holwell. **BT** 1721-1860 (gaps 1813-44 and odd years), (c. 495).
Cop CMB (BT) 1721-1752 Mf (SLC).

ROUGHTON. **OR** CMB 1683 + (Inc). **BT** 1680-1904 (gaps 1682-1721, 1729-
1734 and odd years), (c. 498). **Cop** M 1683-1840 Ts (JG), CMB (BT)
1680-1852 Mf (SLC and SG).

ROUGHTON POGIS (or POGGS). **OR** CMB 1557-1710 (In mutilated condition – depos in Bank), CMB 1743 + (gap M 1814-37) (Inc). **BT** 1721-
1868 (odd year gaps), (c. 499, d. 237). **Cop** CMB (BT) 1721-1852
Mf (SLC and SG).

UCKNELL. **OR** CMB 1653 +, Banns 1754-1812, 1824 + (Inc). **BT** 1700-1877
(gaps 1702-20, 1814-26 and odd years), (c. 499). **Cop** CMB 1653-1840
Ts I (SG), CMB (BT) 1700-1852 Mf (SLC and SG).

URDRUP. – see Swalecliffe.

BURFORD. **OR** CMB 1612 + (Ind). **BT** 1684-1860 (*gap 1686-1720*), (c.500, 501, 502). **Cop** C 1612-1858, M 1612-1888, B 1612-1937 Ts (SG), CMB (BT) 1684-1860 Mf (SLC and SG).

BURFORD, Witney St (Bapt). *f 1700.* **OR** Z 1809-35, B 1831-37 (PRO).

BURFORD (S of F). *f 1668.* **Oxford**, *afterwards* **Witney Monthly Meeting** *disc. 1855. No regs known apart from Monthly Meeting Registers.*

BURTON, GREAT (Ind). − *see Wroxton.*

CADMORE END. − *see Bucks.*

CASSINGTON. **OR** CB 1653 +, M 1653-1837, Banns 1824 +. Index, M and Banns 1673-1837 (Inc). *30 Marriages between 1708 and 1754 in M register Christ Church, Oxford.* **BT** 1721-1865 (*gap 1749-1752*), (c.502), 503). **Cop** M 1673-1837 (Phil 2), CMB (BT) 1721-1852 Mf (SLC and SG). *M 16 1675 in Boyd Misc.*

CAVERSFIELD (formerly BUCKS). **OR** CB 1764 +, M 1755 + (*gaps CB 1811-13, M 1811-15, 1836-8*), Banns 1823 + (Inc). **BT** 1807-1865 (1807-1826 with Bucks pprs. e.162), (d.242). **Cop** CB 1813-1840, M 1754-1840 Ts I (SG), CMB (BT) 1807-1865 (SLC and SG).

CAVERSHAM. (*now part of Reading, Berks*). **OR** CMB 1597 + (Inc). **BT** 1639-1882 (*gaps 1641-1669, 1671-81, 1684-89, 1692-98, 1701-20*), (c.503, 504, d.243, 244). **Cop** CMB (BT) 1639-1859 Mf (SLC and SG).

CHADLINGTON. **OR** CMB 1567 + (Inc). **BT** 1669-1851 (*gaps 1671-1720, 1814-1829, 1832-1850*), (c.143). **Cop** CMB (BT) 1669-1851 Mf (SLC and SG).

CHALGROVE. **OR** CB 1538 +, M 1531 + (*gap CMB 1676-1701*) (Inc). **BT** 1639-1874 (*gaps 1641-1669, 1671-1683, 1686-1720, 1758-66, 1795-1800*), (c.505, 506). **Cop** CMB (BT) 1640-1853 Mf (SLC and SG), CB 1538-1637 M 1531-1637 Ms (Bod).

CHARLBURY. **OR** C 1559-1860, M 1559-1848, B 1559-1863 (*gap M 1644-51, 1658-60, 1780-96*), Banns 1754-1778 (Bod). **BT** 1669-1851 (*gaps 1672-1679, 1686-1719, 1831-50*), (c.506, 507). **Cop** CMB (BT) 1670-1851, 1867-1886 Mf (SLC and SG), M (PR) 1559-1764 Ms (SG Vol. 4).

CHARLBURY (S of F). *f 1668.* **Oxford**, *afterwards* **Witney Monthly Meeting** *closed 1918. Later particular meeting opened. No pre-1837 regs known apart from Monthly Meeting Registers.* **Cop** B 1867-1886 Mf (SLC and SG).

CHARLTON-ON-OTMOOR. **OR** C 1567 +, MB 1567-1813 (*gap M 1679-1753*) (Inc) **BT** 1700-1890 (*gap 1701-1720*), (c.507, 508). **Cop** CMB (BT) 1700-1854 Mf (SLC and SG).

CHARLTON. (Ind). *f 1827. No regs known. Not at PRO or Ch.Sec. No Burial ground.*

CHASTLETON. **OR** C 1586 +, M 1573 +, B 1572-1779 (*gap M 1754-55, 1812-13* Banns 1824 + (Inc). **BT** 1682-1874 (*gaps 1683-1720, 1785-1800*), (c.508, 509). **Cop** CMB (BT) 1682-1852 Mf (SLC and SG).

HECKENDON. **OR** CB 1719 $^+$, M 1756 $^+$, Banns 1756-1810, 1824 $^+$ (Inc).
BT 1639-1871 (*gaps 1641-1721, 1731-36, 1814-18*),(c.509, 510).
Cop CMB (BT) 1639-1813, 1819-1860 Mf (SLC and SG).

HESTERTON. **OR** CMB 1538 $^+$ (*gaps CMB 1595-1603, 1645-1662*), Banns
1755-1812, 1827 $^+$ (Inc). **BT** 1684-1871 (*gaps 1685-1699, 1701-17,
1732-37*),(c.510). **Cop** M 1538-1837 Ts (SG), CMB (BT) 1684-1855
Mf (SLC and SG).

HINNOR. **OR** C 1581-1705, MB 1621-1705 (*gaps C 1610-20 and others*)(Inc).
BT 1716-1871 (*gap 1813-1835*), (c.511, d.256). **Cop** M 1622-1754,
B 1622-25 Ts (SG), M 1754-1812 Ts Alpha (SG), C 1581-1609, 1621-
1812, M 1622-1754, B 1622-1812 Ts (Bod d.290), CB 1581-1837,
M 1622-1812 Ms (Alpha) (Inc), CMB (BT) 1836-1855 Mf (SLC and SG).
M 1622-1754 in Boyd Misc.

HINNOR. (Ind). *f 1803.* **OR** ZC 1804-37, B 1815 (PRO).

HIPPING NORTON. **OR** CMB 1560 $^+$ (Inc). **BT** 1669-1856 (*gaps 1671-9,
1682-1720*), (c.512, 513). **Cop** M 1560-1837 (Phil 1), CMB (BT) 1669-
1856, 1869-1885 Mf (SLC and SG). *M 1626-1675 in Boyd Misc.*

HIPPING NORTON. New St (Bapt). *f 1694.* **OR** Z 1767-1830 (PRO).

HIPPING NORTON. (Wes). *f 1796.* **OR** ZC 1814-1837 (PRO).

HIPPING NORTON (S of F). **Oxford**, *afterwards* **Witney Monthly Meeting**
*f 1668. disc 1910. No regs known apart from Monthly Meeting
Registers.*

HIPPING NORTON, Holy Trinity (RC). *f 1836. Not at PRO.* **OR** CM 1879 $^+$,
D 1880 $^+$ (*Inc holds C register for Heythrop beginning 1753*).

HISLEHAMPTON. **Peculiar** *of Dorchester Abbey.* **OR** CMB 1762 $^+$ (Inc).
For earlier regs see Stadhampton. **BT** 1663-1833 (*gaps 1680-1698,
1702, 1714, 1716-1768, 1771-3, 1815-19, 1822-30*), (c.513 1769-1833).
Cop CMB (BT) 1769-1833 Mf (SLC and SG).

HURCHILL. **OR** CB 1630-1765, M 1631-1765 (Bod), CB 1765 $^+$, M 1754 $^+$ (Inc).
BT 1630-1837 (*gaps 1670-1718, 1727-1733, 1814-1841, 1855-1871 and
odd years*), (c.513). *Some with Sarsden.* **Cop** M (BT) 1754-1837,
CB 1765-1812, C 1812-1904 (Bod), M 1631-1837 Ts (SG), C 1765-1904,
M 1631-1837, B 1765-1812 Ms (Bod c.233, d.176-8, 220), CMB (BT)
1630-1904 Mf (SLC and SG).

LANFIELD. **OR** CMB 1633 $^+$ (Inc). **BT** 1721-1871 (*gaps 1731-36, 1805-1870*),
(c.514). **Cop** CMB (BT) 1721-1852 Mf (SLC and SG).

LAYDON. **Peculiar** *of Dean and Chapter of Lincoln.* **OR** CB 1569-1812,
M 1569-1836 (*gaps C 1692-4, 1723-4, MB 1605-31, 1647-1660, M 1670-
1685, 1722-1754*), Banns 1759-99, 1811, 1814, 1819 (Bod). *Some M
in Cropredy regs.* **BT** 1605-1734 (*gaps 1606-62, 1701-4 and many odd
years* (b.114 fol.18), 1736-1812 (with Bucks Mss. c.162).
Cop M 1569-1604, 1631-47, 1660-70, 1685-1722, M (BT) 1722-54),
M (PR) 1754-1837 Ts (JG), CMB 1569-1691 (Inc), CMB (BT) 1605-1851
Mf (SLC and SG).

CLIFTON HAMPDEN. **Peculiar** *of Dorchester Abbey.* **OR** CB 1578 [+], M 1578-
1836 (*gap CMB 1684-1714*), Banns 1755-1832 (Inc). **BT** 1621, 1662-
1874 (*gaps 1693-1701 and odd years*), (c.515). **Cop** CMB 1578-1837
Ms (Inc), CMB (BT) 1621, 1662-1764, 1813-1866 Mf (SLC and SG).

COATE. *Parish of Bampton.* (Bapt). *f 1657.* **OR** Z 1647-1836, B 1657-
1837 (PRO).

COGGES. **OR** C 1661-1783, M 1655-1755, B 1653-1783, Z 1653-1659 (Bod).
CB 1813 [+], M 1754 [+], Banns 1824 [+] (Inc). **BT** 1721-1865 (*gap 1731-173*)
(c.505, 506). **Cop** M 1655-1755 Ts (SG), CMB (BT) 1721-1852 Mf (SLC
and SG).

COMBE (LONG). **OR** C 1646-1705, CMB 1813 [+] (Inc). *All other registers*
before 1813, destroyed by fire 1918. **BT** 1669-1851 (*gaps 1671-1720,*
1786-1790, 1793-1800, 1821-1829, 1845-1850), (c.516, 517).
Cop M 1654-1692 Ts (SG), CB 1647-1757, M 1654-92 (Bod c.339),
CMB (BT) 1669-1851 Mf (SLC and SG), CB 1647-1757, M 1654-92 Mf of
copy at Bod (SLC and SG).

CORNWELL. **OR** CMB 1662 [+] (Inc). **BT** 1669-1874 (*gaps 1671-1722, 1724-173*
1733-39, 1767-1770, 1772-1776, 1779-1790, 1866-1869 and odd years)
(c.517). *(For B see Churchill).* **Cop** CMB (BT) 1669-1853 Mf (SLC and

COTE. (Bapt). – *see Coate.*

COTTISFORD. **OR** CB 1610 [+], M 1651 [+], Banns 1826 [+] (Inc). **BT** 1678-1865
(*gaps 1685-1699, 1701-1720, 1816-1829*), (c.517). **Cop** CMB (BT) 1678-
1852 Mf (SLC and SG), M (BT) 1678, 1700, 1724-1815, 1836 Ms (SG
Vol. 3).

COWLEY, ST JAMES. **OR** CMB 1678 [+] (Inc). **BT** 1721-1874 (*gap 1729-1736*),
(c.518, 519). **Cop** CMB (BT) 1721-1853 Mf (SLC and SG).

CRAWLEY. – *see Hailey.*

CROPREDY. **Peculiar** *of Dean and Chapter of Lincoln.* **OR** CMB 1538 [+]
(*gap CB 1755-1812*) (Inc) – *see also Claydon and Wardington.*
BT 1605-1859 (*gap 1672-1675*), (d.114, c.519, d.267), (1735-1812 with
Bucks Ms c.163). **Cop** MB 1654-1719, C 1654-1701 Ms (very bad) (SG),
CMB (BT) 1664-1812 Mf (SLC and SG), M 1538-1837 Ts (JG), CB 1538-
1571, C 1654-1701, B 1654-1719 Ts (JG).

CROWELL. **OR** CMB 1594-1782 (Inc). **BT** 1639-1871 (*gaps 1641-1669, 1671-*
1720, 1731-1737 and many odd years), (c.520). **Cop** CMB 1602-1903 (A)
Ms (SG), M 1602-1837 (Phil 1), C 1594-1782, M 1602-1765, B 1602-
1782 Ts (Bod d.290). Index to regs (Bod c.372), C 1594-1782 (GL),
CMB (BT) 1639-1852 Mf (SLC and SG), CMB (BT) 1639-1871 Ms (Bod
d.290). *M 1651-1675 in Boyd Misc.*

CROWMARSH GIFFORD. **OR** CMB 1576 [+] (*gap C 1685-1737*) (Inc). **BT** 1639-
1852 (*gaps 1641-1689, 1692-1720*), (c.520, 521). **Cop** C 1576-1685,
1737-1840, M 1576-1836, B 1576-1840 Ms (SG and Bod), CMB 1576-1840
Mf of above copy (SLC and Berks RO), CMB (BT) 1639-1852 Mf (SLC
and SG). *M 1755-1813 in Boyd Misc.*

UDDESDON and WHEATLEY. **OR** CB 1541-1812, M 1542-1754 (*gaps C 1654-1719,*
MB 1654-94, 1700-20, M 1744), Banns 1754-1826 (Bod), CB 1813 [+],
M 1755 [+] (Inc). *See also Wheatley.* **BT** 1724-1851 (*gaps 1731-1736,*
1791-1794, 1830-1850), (c. 521, 522). **Cop** C 1541-1739, M 1542-1699,
1721-54, B 1542-1699 Ts (SG). *Wheatley only* C 1628-1699 Ts (SG),
CMB (BT) 1724-1851 Mf (SLC and SG).

ULHAM. **OR** CB 1648 [+], M 1659 [+], Banns 1813 [+] (Inc). **BT** 1721-1869
(*gap 1733-1736*), (c. 522, 523). **Cop** CB 1648-1812, M 1648-1754 Ms bad
(SG), M 1648-1840 (Alpha) Ts (SG and Inc), CMB 1648-1917 Alpha Ms
(Bod c. 222), CMB (BT) 1721-1852 Mf (SLC and SG).

UXHAM. **OR** CM 1577 [+], B 1736 [+] (*gap C 1788-1812*), Banns 1754 [+] (Inc).
BT 1639-1865 (*gaps 1641-1681, 1687-1720, 1736-38*), (c. 523, 524).
Cop CMB (BT) 1639-1865 Mf (SLC and SG).

EDDINGTON. **OR** C 1631-1902, M 1631-1959, B 1631-1883, (*gaps M 1652-3,*
1785-87), Banns 1754-1803, 1823-72, 1876-1929 (Bod). **BT** 1669-1865
(*gaps 1672-79, 1684-1720, 1847-50, 1852-1863*), (c. 525, d. 271).
Cop CB 1631-1794, M 1631-1754 Mf (SLC, ORO and SG), CMB (BT) 1669-
1858 Mf (SLC and SG), M (BT) 1669-70, 1680, 1682, 1722-1837 (with
gaps) Ms (SG Vol. 2).

ORCHESTER. **Peculiar** *of Dorchester Abbey.* **OR** CMB 1638 [+] (Inc). *9*
Marriages between 1728 and 1754 in M register of Magdalen College,
Oxford. **BT** 1602, 1624, 1661-1872 (*gaps 1694-98, 1738-1741, 1821-32*
and odd years), (c. 525). **Cop** CMB (BT) 1661-1816 Mf (SLC and SG).

RAYTON. (near BANBURY). **OR** CB 1577 [+], M 1578 [+] (*gaps CB 1688-1725,*
M 1688-1721), Banns 1831 [+] (Inc). **BT** 1721-1874 (*gaps 1728-35 and*
many odd years), (c. 526). **Cop** Extract CMB 1586-1660 (SG), CMB (BT)
1721-1859 Mf (SLC and SG), M 1578-1837 Ms and Ts, CB 1654-1688 Ts (JG).

RAYTON, ST LEONARD. (near DORCHESTER). **Peculiar** *of Dorchester Abbey.*
OR CB 1568 [+], M 1755 [+], Banns 1824 [+] (Inc). **BT** 1662-1857 (*gaps 1683-*
1688, 1693-1698, 1738-1741 and odd years), (c. 526, d. 273).
Cop CMB (BT) 1767-1857 Mf (SLC and SG).

UCKLINGTON. **OR** C 1560 [+], MB 1580 [+] (*gaps 1662-1812, M 1651-95,*
B 1661-77, 1746-1812), Banns 1754 [+] (Inc). **BT** 1721-1906 (*gaps 1792-*
1794) (*1813-1848 badly damaged*), (d. 275, c. 526). **Cop** CMB (BT) 1721-
1865 Mf (SLC and SG), C 1550-1880, MB 1580-1880 Index form (*includ-*
ing names in missing registers). (Ptd.).

DUNS TEW. **OR** CMB 1654-1695 (illeg), CB 1747 [+], M 1813 [+] (*gap CB 1755-*
1812), Banns 1754 [+] (Inc). **BT** 1669-1867 (*gap 1671-1720*), (c. 526,
d. 527). **Cop** CMB (BT) 1669-1852 Mf (SLC and SG), M (BT) 1670, 1741-
1837 (with gaps) Ms (SG Vol. 2).

EASINGTON. **OR** *Early registers destroyed.* **BT** 1639-1865 (*gaps 1641-1668,*
1671-1720, 1726-1739, 1751-1759, 1765-1774, 1777-1787, 1790-1800,
1803-1810), (c. 527). **Cop** CMB (BT) 1639-1865 Mf (SLC and SG).

ELSFIELD. **OR** CMB 1686 [+] (*gap M 1805-1812*), Banns 1766-1816, 1822 [+] (Inc)
BT 1670-1874 (*gaps 1671-1719, 1731-1744, 1747-1752, 1763-1772,
1774-1779, 1792-1796, 1800-1805*), (c. 527, 528). **Cop** CMB (BT) 1670-
1852 Mf (SLC and SG).

EMMINGTON. **OR** CMB 1539 [+], Banns 1810 [+] (Inc). **BT** 1639-1883 (*gaps 1641
1683, 1686-89, 1691-1720 and odd years*), (c. 528, 529). **Cop** M 1539-
1632, 1715-1809 Ts (SG), C 1539-1647, 1715-1812, M 1539-1632, 1715
1809, B 1542-1635, 1715-1812, Banns 1810-69 Ts (Bod d. 290 and GL),
CMB (BT) 1639-1840 Mf (SLC and SG). *M 1539-1837 in Boyd Misc.*

ENSTONE. **OR** CMB 1558 [+] (*gap CMB 1626-1654*) (Inc). **BT** 1670-1839
(*gaps 1671-1720, 1730-33*), (c. 529, 530). **Cop** C 1558-1841, M 1558-
1837, B 1558-1852 (*gap CMB 1626-1654*) Ts (SG and SLC), CMB (BT)
1670-1839 Mf (SLC and SG).

EPWELL. **OR** C 1577 [+], M 1580 [+], B 1584 [+] (Inc Swalecliffe). **BT** 1722-187
(*gaps 1729-1734, 1753-60, 1763-1804*), (c. 530, 143, d. 281) (*1763-1803
on Swalecliffe BT's*). **Cop** C 1577-1653, 1718-34, M 1580-1675, 1707
1727, B 1584-1642, 1720-30 Ts (Bod. Poor copy), C 1577-1730, M 1580
1731, 1754-1777, B 1584-1728 (Phil Ms), CMB 1754-1777 (C of A),
C 1577-1837, M 1580-1675, 1707-1837, B 1584-1837 Ts (SG N. Oxon
Reg 2), CMB (BT) 1722-1853 Mf (SLC and SG), C 1577-1685, M 1580-
1731, 1754-1777 Ts (SLC). *M 1580-1800 in Boyd Misc.*

EWELME. **OR** CMB 1599 [+] (Inc). **BT** 1670-1900 (*gaps 1671-1683, 1686-1720,
1779-1785,1875-1888*),(c. 530, d. 283). **Cop** CMB (BT) 1670-1852
Mf (SLC and SG).

EWELME (RC). – *Some entries in Britwell Prior Registers.*

EYNSHAM. **OR** CB 1653 [+], M 1665 [+] (Inc). **BT** 1725-1862 (*gaps – odd years
from 1754-1786*), (c. 531, 532, d. 284). **Cop** M 1665-1837 (Phil 2),
CMB (BT) 1725-1844 Mf (SLC and SG). *M 1653-1675 in Boyd Misc.*

EYNSHAM, Lombard St. (Bapt). *f 1818. Not at PRO, No information.*

FARINGDON, LITTLE. **Peculiar** *of Langford, Diocese of Lincoln –
Chapel of Ease. 1870.* **BT** 1865-98 (d. 286). **Cop** CMB (BT) 1865-98
Mf (SLC and SG). *See also Langford.*

FEWCOTT. – *see Ardley.*

FIFIELD. **OR** 1712-1812, M 1754 [+], B 1712 [+] (Inc). **BT** 1669-1851 (*gaps
1672-1720, 1731-1735 and odd years*), (c. 532, 143). **Cop** CMB (BT)
1669-1851 Mf (SLC and SG).

FILKINS. (*Chapel of Broadwell*). **OR** B 1813 [+] (Inc Broadwell).

FINGEST. – *see Bucks.*

FINMERE. **OR** CMB 1560 [+], Banns 1754 [+] (Inc). **BT** 1684-1853 (*gaps 1690-
1699, 1702-20*), (c. 538). **Cop** CMB (BT) 1684-1853 Mf (SLC and SG),
M (BT) 1700, 1728-1837 Ms (SG Vol. 3).

FINSTOCK. **OR** CMB 1842 [+] (Inc). **BT** 1847-1851 (d. 288). **Cop** CMB (BT)
1847-51 Mf (SLC and SG).

OREST HILL. **OR** CB 1564 [+], M 1564-1812 (*gaps CM 1684-99, B 1684-1813*), Banns 1825 [+] (Inc). **BT** 1564-1869 (*gaps 1684-1720, 1731-37*), (c. 533, 534). **Cop** CMB (BT) 1564-1683, 1721-1852 Mf (SLC and SG).

RINGFORD. **OR** CMB 1598 [+] (*gap CMB 1737-1750*), Banns 1823 [+] (Inc). **BT** 1680-1871 (*gaps 1682-1699, 1702-1720*), (c. 534, 535). **Cop** CMB (BT) 1680-1856 Mf (SLC and SG), M (BT) 1721-1837 Ms (SG Vol. 3).

RITWELL. **OR** CMB 1558 [+] (Inc). **BT** 1713, 1720-1881 (*gaps 1788-1791, 1794-1803, 1814-1829, 1866-1869*), (c. 535). **Cop** C 1558-1695, M 1558-1837, B 1558-1697 Ts (SG), CB 1558-1695, M 1558-1702 Ms (Bod Ms Top Oxon c. 293 and c. 239), CMB 1558-1691 Mf (SLC and SG), CMB (BT) 1713-1865 Mf (SLC and SG).

ULBROOK. **OR** CMB 1615 [+] (Inc Burford). **BT** 1720-1858 (c. 535, 536), *1740-41 on Burford returns.* **Cop** CB 1615-1840, M 1615-1837 Ts (SG West Oxon Reg Vol. 2).

ARSINGTON. **OR** CMB 1562 [+], Banns 1754-1812, 1823 [+] (Inc). **BT** 1679-1868 (*gaps 1681-1720, 1733-1744, 1748-1764, 1846-1849*), (c. 536, 537).

LYMPTON. **OR** CMB 1567-1657 (Bod Ms Top Oxon b. 22 Summ. Cat. No. 29293), CMB 1667-1812 (Inc). **BT** 1719-1871 (*gaps 1726-28, 1731-35, 1747-62 and odd years to 1865*), (c. 537, 538). **Cop** CB 1567-1812, M 1567-1754 Ptd.

ODINGTON. **OR** CB 1678-1812, M 1679-1834 (*gaps C 1758, 1805, M 1757-1759, 1812, 1814-16, 1818, 1821-4, 1832-3*), (Bod), CB 1813 [+], M 1838 [+], Banns 1825 [+] (Inc). **BT** 1700-1874 (*gaps 1702-1717, 1766-1805*), (c. 538). **Cop** CB 1678-1840, M 1678-1837 I Ts (SG).

ORING. **OR** CMB 1643 [+] (*gaps CMB 1684-88, 1731-34, 1736-38, 1742-5*) (Inc). **BT** 1639-1851 (*gaps 1641-81, 1686-1721, 1732-1756, 1834-50*), (c. 538, 539, d. 289). *See also Goring Heath.*

ORING (Lady Hunt Con). *f 1786.* **OR** ZC 1790-1834 (PRO).

ORING HEATH, St Bartholomews (Alnuts) Chapel. **OR** CB 1742-1832, M 1743-1752 (Inc Goring). **BT** On Goring returns. **Cop** CB 1742-1832, M 1743-1752 Ms (SG). *See also Goring.*

REAT HASELEY. − *see Haseley Great.*

REAT MILTON. − *see Milton Great.*

REAT ROLLRIGHT. − *see Rollright Great.*

REAT TEW. − *see Tew Great.*

AILEY. (near WITNEY). **OR** CB 1797 [+] (Inc). *Earlier entries in Witney Registers. Some Hailey entries also in registers of Cogges and Oxford St Martin).* **BT** 1769-1854 (with Witney) (*gaps 1773-1779, 1782-1790, 1793-1853*), (c. 633-4), 1813-1882 (d. 292-3).

AMPTON GAY. **OR** CMB 1621 [+] (Inc). **BT** (*19th C transcripts badly damaged by damp*), (d. 296).

HAMPTON POYLE. **OR** C 1540-1777, M 1545-1754, B 1544-1769 (*gaps C 1574-1597, M 1553-1596*) (Bod), Banns 1755-99 (Inc). **BT** 1721-1865 (*gaps 1726-29, 1762-66, 1778-1783, 1785-1800*), (c. 539). **Cop** M 1545-1754 Ts (SG). *See also Kidlington.*

HANBOROUGH. **OR** CMB 1560[+] (*gaps C 1790-1812, M 1753-55, 1774-1812*), Banns 1755-1831 (Inc). **BT** 1721-1851 (*gaps 1784-1829, 1831-1850*), (c. 540). **Cop** M 1560-1837 (Phil 2). *M 1651-1675 in Boyd Misc.*

HANWELL. **OR** CMB 1586[+] (*gap B 1755-1812*), Banns 1824[+] (Inc). **BT** 1721-1883 (*gap 1783-85*), (c. 540, 541). **Cop** CB 1586-1754, M 1586-1837 Ts (JG).

HARDWICK (with TUSMORE). **OR** CMB 1758[+] – *earlier entries in Hethe and Souldern registers.* **BT** 1739-1865 (*gaps 1740-43, 1746-1754, 1760-63, 1777-1782*), (c. 541, d. 298). **Cop** M (BT) 1755, 1758, 1764, 1767-76, 1813-37 Ms (SG Vol. 3).

HARDWICK (RC). **OR** 1810-1836 (AHB). *See also Tusmore Park (RC) and Hethe (RC).*

HARPSDEN. **OR** CMB 1558[+] (Inc). **BT** 1639-1877 (*gaps 1641-1684, 1686-1720*) (c. 143, 541). **Cop** M 1563-1754 Ts (SG), CB 1558-1836, M 1558-1754 Ts (Bod d. 283).

HASELEY, GREAT. **OR** C 1538-1859, M 1538-1837, B 1538-1866 (*gaps M 1658-1660, B 1660, 1674-1677*), Banns 1776-1812 (Bod). **BT** 1721-1851 (*gap 1836-1850*), (c. 541, 542). **Cop** M 1538-1837 Ts (SG).

HASELEY, GREAT – HASELEY COURT (RC). *Chaplaincy of Oxford Mission. No regs known. Some entries in Britwell Prior registers.*

HEADINGTON. **OR** C 1681-1848, M 1694-1837, B 1683-1900 (*gaps M 1715-16, 1742-43, 1794*), Banns 1823-1889 (Bod). **BT** 1678-1853 (*gaps 1680-1720, 1733-37*), (c. 542, 543, d. 300). **Cop** Extracts 1598-1680, complete 1694-1837 Ts (SG).

HENLEY-ON-THAMES. **OR** Z 1558-1706, C 1653[+], MB 1558[+] (*gap M 1684-1753*) Banns 1653-1683 (Inc). **BT** 1639-1851 (*gaps 1640-1683, 1691-1720, 1726-1737, 1831-50*), (c. 544, c. 545, d. 303-4). **Cop** CMB 1558-1653 I Ts (SG).

HENLEY-ON-THAMES. (Ind). – *see Rotherfield Grays.*

HENLEY-ON-THAMES (S of F). **Warborough Monthly Meeting** (*1668-1810*). **Reading and Warborough Monthly Meeting** (*1810-1873*). *disc. 1873. No regs known apart from Monthly Meeting Registers* (**Reading Monthly Meeting Registers**. Z 1650-1836, M 1683-1773, 1779-1835, B 1660-1837 (PRO 75-83, 1506)).

HETHE. **OR** CB 1678[+], M 1753[+] (*gap CB 1802-12*), Banns 1754-1812 (Inc). **BT** 1678-1874 (*gaps 1680-99, 1702-20*), (c. 545, 546, d. 305 – also c. 75 fol. 17, c. 143 fol. 25). **Cop** M (BT) 1700, 1721-1837 Ms (SG Vol. 3). *See also Hardwick.*

HETHE (RC). **OR** 1836-1859 (AHB). *See also Tusmore Park (RC) and Hardwick (RC).*

HEYFORD, LOWER. **OR** CMB 1539 ⁺, Banns 1754-1812, 1823 ⁺ (Inc). **BT** 1680-1877 (*gaps 1690-99, 1702-12, 1715-20*), (c. 546, d. 305, d. 306).
Cop CMB 1539-1840 Ts (JG).

HEYFORD, UPPER or WARREN. **OR** CMB 1557 ⁺ (*gaps M 1812-36, B 1778-1784*) (Inc). **BT** 1680-1851 (*gaps 1701-19, 1730-34, 1772-6, 1820-1850*), (c. 546). **Cop** M (BT) 1682, 1685, 1700, 1722-1819 Ms (SG Vol. 3).

HEYTHROP. **OR** CMB 1607 ⁺ (Inc). **BT** 1668-1833 (*gaps 1670-1722, 1788-1792*), (c. 546, 547). **Cop** M (BT) 1668-9, 1723-1833 Ms (SG).

HEYTHROP (RC). **OR** C 1753 ⁺ (Inc Holy Trinity Cath. Ch. Chipping Norton).

HINKSEY, NORTH and SOUTH. – *see Berks.*

HOLTON. **OR** CB 1633-1794, M 1633-1754 (Bod), CB 1795 +, M 1755 ⁺ (Inc). **BT** 1680-1863 (*gaps 1682-1719*), (c. 547).

HOLWELL. *Chapel of Broadwell.* **OR** M 1813-1837 (Inc Broadwell) *Previous entries in Broadwell regs.* **BT** 1851-1877 (*gap 1852-57*), (d. 308). *See also Broadwell.*

HOLYWELL MANOR (RC). *Chaplaincy of Oxford Mission. No regs known.*

HOOK NORTON. **OR** C 1566 ⁺, M 1813 ⁺, B 1643 (*gap C 1662-1723*) (Inc). **BT** 1669-1874 (*gap 1672-1720*), (c. 548, d. 308, 309). **Cop** M (BT) 1669-1670, 1721-8 (PR) 1729-1837 Ms (SG Vol. 1).

HOOK NORTON. (Bapt). *f 1645. Not at PRO.* **OR** Z 1772 ⁺, M 1844 ⁺, B 1841 ⁺ (Manse, Hook Norton).

HOOK NORTON (S of F). **Banbury Monthly Meeting.** *f 1705. No regs known other than Monthly Meeting Registers.*

HORLEY. **Peculiar** *of Dean and Chapter of Lincoln.* **OR** CMB 1538 +, Banns 1815 + (Inc). (*M with Hornton 1754-1812*). **BT** 1605-1877 (*gaps 1669-1674, 1686-1691*), (b. 114 fol 52, 62), (1736-41 with Bucks Mss c. 163). **Cop** Extracts CMB 1558-1666 (SG), M 1538-1837 Ts (JG). *See also Hornton.*

HORNTON. (*Chapelry of Horley.* **Peculiar** *of Dean and Chapter of Lincoln.* **OR** CB 1703 ⁺, M 1703-1753, 1813 ⁺, Banns 1785-1812 (Inc Horley). *M 1754-1812 in Horley regs.* **BT** 1605-1877 (*gaps 1670-75, 1677-80, 1706-8, 1711-15*), (b. 114) (1739-1877 with Bucks Mss c. 164, b. 155, d. 310). **Cop** M 1703-1754, 1813-37 Ts (JG). *See also Horley.*

HORSEPATH. **OR** CMB 1561 ⁺ (Inc). **BT** 1721-1866 (*gap 1733-36*), (c. 548, d. 311). **Cop** CMB 1561-1837 I Ts (SG and Bod).

HORTON cum STUDLEY. *In parish of Beckley.* **OR** *See Beckley.* **BT** 1721-4, 1737-8 (with Beckley BT's).

IBSTONE or IPSTONE. – *Transferred to Bucks. See Bucks.*

ICKFORD. – *See Bucks.*

IDBURY. **OR** CB 1762 ⁺, M 1754 ⁺, Banns 1823 ⁺ (Inc Fifield). **BT** 1669-1851 (*gap 1671-1720*), (c. 549, d. 317). *See also Swinbrook.*

IFFLEY. **OR** CMB 1572 $^+$ (*gap M 1653-1692*), Banns 1823 $^+$ (Inc). **BT** 1721-1875 (*gap 1727-1742*), (c.549, d.317). **Cop** M 1574-1812 (Phil Ms). *M 1574-1812 In Boyd Misc.*

IPSDEN. **OR** C 1560-1876, M 1569-1837, B 1569-1812, Banns 1755-1811 (Boc **BT** 1639-1851 (*gaps 1641-1683, 1687-1721, 1731-35, 1829-1850*), (c.550). **Cop** M 1569-1840 Ts (SG), C 1560-1860, MB 1569-1860 (Ms Bod Ms Top Oxon c.39).

IPSDEN. (Ind). – *see Stoke Row.*

IPSTONE. *Transferred to Bucks. See Bucks.*

ISLIP. **OR** CMB 1590 $^+$ (*gaps C 1650-54, 1681-82, M 1641-4, 1657-63, 1678-94, 1754-93, B 1771-93*) (Inc). **BT** 1678-1852 (*gaps 1683-1699, 1702-1720, 1823-25, 1831-3, 1840-9*), (c.550, 551).

KELMSCOT. **OR** CMB 1560 $^+$ (Inc Broadwell). **BT** 1740-1859 (with Broadwell (*gaps 1746-63, 1766-1773, 1801-34*), (c.551, d.321).

KENCOT. **OR** CMB 1584 $^+$ (*gap M 1791-1813*) (Inc). **BT** 1721-1806 (*gap 1732 1735*), (c.551).

KIDDINGTON. **OR** CB 1573 $^+$, M 1576 $^+$, Banns 1755-1812, 1824 $^+$ (Inc). **BT** 1722-1871 (*1814-71 badly damaged by damp*) (*gaps 1795-1800, 1823 1832*), (c.552, d.322, 323). **Cop** M 1576-1837 Ts (SG), CB 1573-1721, M 1576-1837 Ms (Northants RO). *M 1576-1837 in Boyd Misc.*

KIDDINGTON (RC). **Cop** 1788-1840 (Ptd) (CRS Vol. 17).

KIDLINGTON. **OR** C 1579-1812, M 1574-1754, B 1574-1812 (*gap C 1654-1662*) (Bod), CB 1800 $^+$, M 1755 $^+$ (Inc Hampton Poyle). **BT** 1670-1870 (*gaps 1671-79, 1682-1720, 1732-38*), (c.552, d.324, d.325). **Cop** M 15' 1754 Ptd (Oxford Hist. Socy. 24), Extracts M 1587-1816, B 1576-181: Ms (SG). *See also Hampton Poyle.*

KINGHAM. **OR** CMB 1663 $^+$ (*gap M 1736-1754*), Banns 1755 $^+$ (Inc). **BT** 1669-1851 (*gaps 1672-1720, 1797-1800, 1803-9, 1839-50*), (c.553).

KINGSEY. – *see Bucks.*

KINGSTON BLOUNT. – *see Aston Rowant.*

KIRTLINGTON. **OR** CB 1558-1599, M 1558-1698 (*gaps M 1644-61, B 1648-60*), (Bod), CB 1813 $^+$, M 1754 $^+$, Banns 1824 $^+$ (Inc). *28 Marriages betwee 1695 and 1754 in M. Register of St John's College, Oxford.* **BT** 1678-1853 (*gaps 1680-1720*) (c.554). **Cop** M 1558-1698 Ts (SG), CMB 1558-1699 (C of A), CMB 1558-1699 Ts (Inc), M (BT) 1678, 1720-1837 Ms (SG Vol 3).

LANGFORD and LITTLE FARINGDON. **Peculiar** *of Langford, Partly in Berks.* **OR** CB 1538 $^+$, M 1580 $^+$ (*gap M 1730-1752*) (Inc). **BT** 1675-1803 (Ms Arch. Papers Berks c.198), 1813-1884 (d.329). *See also Faringdon, Little.*

LAUNTON. **OR** C 1648 $^+$, M 1671 $^+$, B 1681 $^+$ (*gap CB 1752-1812*) (Inc). **BT** 1700 1866 (*gaps 1702-18, 1849-62*), (c.555, 556). **Cop** M 1671-1837 Ts (SG'

LAUNTON. (Ind). *f 1807. Not at PRO. No information.*

EAFIELD. *(Chapelry of Shipton-under-Wychwood)* **OR** C 1784 [+] *(gap C 1813-1843)* (Inc). *Not licenced for M until 1853.* **BT** 1786-1902 *(gap 1787-1800, 1807-1811)*, (c. 556, d. 332). *See also Shipton-under-Wychwood and Wilcote.*

EIGH, NORTH. **OR** CMB 1573 [+] *(gaps CB 1662-1671, M 1662-1753, 1814-1836)*, Banns 1824 [+] (Inc). **BT** 1684-1884 *(gaps 1686-1720, 1859-1865)*, (c. 567, 568, d. 359).

EIGH, SOUTH. **OR** CMB 1612 [+] (Inc). **BT** 1721-1864 (c. 603).

EWKNOR. **OR** CMB 1666 [+] (Inc). *(with Chapelry of Ackhampstead).* **BT** 1670-1851 *(gaps 1671-1720, 1745-47, 1819-34, 1838-50)*, (c. 556, d. 334). **Cop** CB 1666-1760, M 1666-1754 Ts (SG and Bod d. 290), M 1754-1812 (Phil Ms), M 1666-1812 (SLC). *M 1666-1812 in Boyd Misc.*

LITTLE FARINGDON. – *see Faringdon, Little.*

LITTLE MILTON. – *see Milton, Little.*

LITTLE ROLLRIGHT. – *see Rollright, Little.*

ILLINGSTONE LOVELL. *(now in Bucks).* **OR** CMB 1558 [+] (Inc). **BT** 1678-1888 *(gaps 1680-1699, 1702-20)*, (c. 559, d. 335). **Cop** CMB 1558-1840 Ts (SG).

LITTLEMORE. **OR** CMB 1836 [+] (Inc). **BT** 1848-1871 (d. 336).

LOWER HEYFORD. – *see Heyford, Lower.*

MAPLEDURHAM. **OR** CMB 1627 [+] (Inc). *(Early regs lost except fragment, B 1580-82 in Eton Coll. Lib).* **BT** 1639-1877 *(gaps 1641-69, 1671-89, 1692-1717)*, (c. 557, 558, d. 340).

MAPLEDURHAM (RC). – *Some entries in Britwell Prior regs.*

MARSH BALDON. – *see Baldon Marsh.*

MARSH GIBBON. (Ind). *f 1828. Not at PRO. No information.*

MARSTON. **OR** CMB 1653 [+] (Inc). **BT** 1722-1871 *(gaps 1733-68)*, (c. 558, d. 347).

MERTON. **OR** CB 1635 [+], M 1739 [+] *(mostly in Exeter Coll. Chap. to 1751)* *(gap C 1641-51)*, Z 1655-1688, 1718-1732, Banns 1754-1814 (Inc). **BT** 1721-1877 *(gaps – odd years)*, (c. 559, d. 348). **Cop** CMB (BT) 1721-1837 Ts (SG). *M 1729-1837 in Boyd Misc.*

MIDDLETON STONEY. **OR** CMB 1598 [+], Banns 1756-1803 (Inc). **BT** 1678-1865 *(gaps 1687-1717, 1733-37, 1745-1753)*, (c. 560). **Cop** M (BT) 1679-80, 1685, 1718, 1721-1830 Ms (SG Vol. 3).

MILCOMBE. **OR** C 1562-1766, M 1562-1711, B 1562-1719 (Inc Bloxham). *Subsequent entries in Bloxham regs.* **BT** 1811 only (with Bloxham BT's). **Cop** Extracts (PR) 1563-1627 (Bod), C 1562-1766, M 1562-1711, B 1562-1719 Ts (JG). *See also Bloxham.*

MILTON, GREAT. Peculiar *of Thame.* **OR** CMB 1550 [+] (Inc). **BT** 1604-1794 *(gaps 1606-64, 1668-73, 1692-1717)* (with Bucks Mss c. 164), 1638-1798 *(gap 1640-1735)* (with Bucks Mss c. 165), 1798-1857 (Ms Oxf. Dio. Papers c. 560, c. 561, d. 728). **Cop** M 1550-1840 Ts (SG), CMB 1550-1840 I only (Inc). *See also Milton, Little below.*

MILTON, LITTLE. **OR** CMB 1844 + (Inc) (*previously in Great Milton parish*) BT 1798-1812 with Great Milton (transcripts damaged).

MILTON (Pres). – *see Bloxham.*

MILTON-UNDER-WYCHWOOD, High St. (Bapt). *f 1837.* **OR** *No early regs know Not at PRO.* DB 1872 + only (Ch. Sec.).

MILTON-UNDER-WYCHWOOD (S of F). *f 1668.* **Oxford,** *afterwards* **Witney Monthly Meeting** *disc. 1813. No regs known apart from Monthly Meeting Registers.*

MINSTER LOVELL. **OR** CB 1813 +, M 1754 + (Inc). **BT** 1667-1865 (*gaps 1671-1679, 1686-1720, 1844-55 and odd years*), (c. 154, 561, 562).

MIXBURY. (*now with Finmere*). **OR** CMB 1645 + (*gap M 1755-1812*), Banns 1754-1811, 1824 + (Inc). **BT** 1721-1851 (c. 562). **Cop** M 1654-1812 (Phil Ms and Mf SLC), M (BT) 1725-1837 Ms (SG Vol. 3), *M 1657-1675, 1703-1812 in Boyd Misc.*

MOLLINGTON. (*formerly partly in Warwickshire*). **Peculiar** *of Banbury.* **OR** C 1562-1813, M 1565-1837, B 1565-1813 (*gaps M 1716-1724, 1755-1758*), Banns 1789-1792, 1824-1910 (Bod). ·BT 1664-1851 (*gap 1736-1812*), (b. 59). **Cop** M 1565-1840 Ts (JG), CMB 1562-1729 (Bod and Inc)

MONGEWELL. **OR** CB 1682-1812, M 1682-1806, Banns 1682-1806 (Bod). **BT** 1682-1878 (*gaps 1684-1720, 1776-81 and odd years*), (c. 563). **Cop** M 1682-1812 Ts (SG).

NETHER WORTON. – *see Worton, Nether.*

NETTLEBED. **Peculiar** *of Dorchester Abbey.* **OR** CMB 1653 + (*gaps C 1805-1812, M 1725-1740, 1750-1783, B 1721-1725*), Banns 1818 + (Inc). **BT** 1662-1874 (*gaps 1705-9, 1725-41, 1744-6 and odd years*), (c. 563, 564).

NETTLEBED. (Ind). *f 1834. Not at PRO. No information.*

NEW HINKSEY. – *see Berks.*

NEWINGTON. (near WALLINGFORD). **Peculiar** *of Monks Risborough.* **OR** CMB 1572 + (*gap M 1737-1812*) (Inc) *including Berrick Prior to 1736 and Britwell Prior to 1867.* **BT** 1604-1723 (Bod with Berks Mss c. 203), 1736-1828 (With Bucks Mss c. 165). *See also Britwell Prior).*

NEWINGTON, SOUTH. (near BANBURY). **OR** CMB 1538 +, Banns 1823 + (Inc). **BT** 1669-1877 (*gap 1671-1720*), (c. 564, 565). **Cop** CMB 1538-1840 Ts (JG), CMB 1538-1812 Mf (SLC and ORO).

NEWINGTON, SOUTH (S of F). **Banbury Monthly Meeting.** *f 1668, disc 1825 re-opened 1893, disc 1911. No regs known other than Monthly Meeting Registers).*

NEWNHAM MURREN. **OR** CM 1685 +, B 1678 + (Inc). **BT** 1721-1851 (*gaps 1729-1740, 1830-50*), (c. 565). **Cop** CM 1685-1840, B 1678-1835 Ts (SG), CMB 1678-1835 Mf (Berks RO and SLC).

NEWTON PURCELL and SHELSWELL. OR CMB 1681 [+], Banns 1755-1812 (Inc). BT 1637-1882 (*gap 1638-1686*), (c.565, 566). Cop M (BT) 1700, 1721-1837 Ms (SG Vol. 3).

NOKE. OR C 1574-1785, M 1574-1754, B 1574-1784 (*gaps M 1651-1666, B 1651-1666* (Inc). BT 1721-1871 (*gaps 1772-1777, 1779-1786*), (c.154, 566).

NORTH ASTON. — *see Aston North.*

NORTH LEIGH. — *see Leigh North.*

NORTH STOKE. — *see Stoke North.*

NORTHMOOR. OR CB 1653 [+], M 1654 [+], Banns 1790-1812, 1827 [+] (Inc). BT 1682-1854 (*gaps 1684-1719, 1818-27, 1838-42*), (c.568, 569). Cop M 1654-1837 (Phil 2), CB 1653-1899, M 1654-1840 Ms (SG), *M 1654-1675 in Boyd Misc.*

NUFFIELD. OR CMB 1570 [+] (Inc). BT 1639-1864 (*gaps 1642-83, 1692-1720, 1825-1831*), (c.569). Cop CMB 1570-1779 (Inc).

NUNEHAM COURTNEY. OR CMB 1715 [+] (*gaps C 1766-90, M 1790-1815*), Banns 1764-1784, 1823 [+] (Inc). BT 1721-1874 (*gaps 1733-36, 1739-43*), (c.570).

ODDINGTON. OR C 1704-1812, M 1704-1754 (Inc). BT 1700-1889 (*gap 1702-1720*), (c.570, 571).

OVEREY. (near DORCHESTER) (RC). *Chaplaincy of Oxford Mission. No regs known. Some entries in Britwell Prior regs.*

OVERTHORPE and WARKWORTH (RC). OR C 1771-1827 (AHB).

OVER WORTON. — *see Worton Over.*

OXFORD, CHRIST CHURCH (Cathedral). OR C 1633 [+], M 1642 [+], B 1639 [+] (College Librarian). BT *None.* Cop C 1633-1865, M 1642-1754, B 1639-1865 (Bod Ms Top Oxon 169), CMB 1640-1840 (C of A) (BM), M 1642-1754 (Misc. Gen. and Her. 2nd Ser. Vol. 2, pp 236, 251, 268, M 1642-1754 Ts (SG), B 1642-1882 (SLC).

OXFORD, ALL SAINTS. OR CMB 1559 [+], Banns 1823 [+] (Inc). BT 1559-1812. Cop CB 1559-1812, M 1559-1754 Ms (Bod c.172 and C of A).

OXFORD, HOLYWELL ST CROSS. — *see Oxford, St Cross.*

OXFORD, ST ALDATE. OR CMB 1678 [+], Banns 1754 [+] (Inc). BT 1721-1895 (*gap 1733-37*), (c.571, 572, d.366).

OXFORD, ST CLEMENT. OR CB 1666-1812, M 1666 [+] (*gap M 1762-1816*) (Inc), Banns 1877-1921 (Bod). BT 1724-1895 (*gaps 1732-38, 1745-47*), (c.574, d.368, 369).

OXFORD, ST CROSS. OR CMB 1653 [+] (Inc), Banns 1798-1939 (Bod). BT 1721-1846, 1851, 1874 (*gap 1723-30*), (c.575, d.364, 365).

OXFORD, ST EBBE. OR CMB 1558 [+] (Inc), Banns 1798-1939 (Bod). BT 1720-1851 (*gaps 1832-36, 1841-50*), (c.576, 577, d.371, 372).

OXFORD, ST GILES. **OR** C 1576 [+], M 1599 [+], B 1605 [+] (Inc). **BT** 1721-1865
(c.577, 578, d.373). **Cop** C 1576-1768, M 1599-1754, B 1605-1768
Ts SG and Bod d.299 and Ms Bod c.169). *M 1599-1775 in Boyd Misc.*

OXFORD, ST JOHN THE BAPTIST. **OR** C 1687-1892, M 1687-1888
B 1813-1900, B (St Cross Burial Ground) from 1848 (Library, Merton
College). *See also Merton College. Parish united to that of
St Peter in the East about 1900.* **BT** No BT's recorded. **Cop** Extracts
from PR 1813, 1874 (Bod), C 1722, M 1695-1722, B 1696-1748 Ts (SG).
In Great Card Index (SG).

OXFORD, ST MARTIN. **OR** CMB 1562 [+] (*gaps C 1686-1691, MB 1580-98, 1681-
1694*) (Inc). **BT** 1721-1894 (c.579, d.374).

OXFORD, ST MARY MAGDALEN. **OR** C 1602-1870, M 1602-1886
B 1602-1946, Banns 1823-1914 (Bod). **BT** 1721-1856 (*gap 1729-37*),
(c.580, d.375, 376). **Cop** M 1726-1754 Ts (SG), M 1764-1837 Ms (JG),
CMB 1602-1726 Ms (Bod c.171 and C of A).

OXFORD, ST MARY THE VIRGIN. **OR** CB 1599-1812, M 1599-1877 (*gaps M 1648-
1649, 1651-61, B 1651-55, 1657-59*), Z 1694-1706, 1769-1812, Banns
1755-1823 (Bod). **BT** 1599-1865 (c.580, 581). **Cop** CMB 1599-1865
Ms (Bod c.170 and C of A).

OXFORD, ST MICHAEL'S at the North Gate. **OR** C 1558 [+], M 1619 [+], B 1629 [+]
(*some gaps*) (Inc). **BT** 1722-1883 (*gap 1730-37*), (c.581, 582, 583).
Cop C 1558-1758, M 1616-1753, B 1616-1759 Ts (GL, Inc and Bod d.288
M 1616-1753 in Boyd Misc.

OXFORD, ST PETER in the East. **OR** CB 1559-1673, M 1559-1671, (*gap B 165
1659*) (Bod), CMB 1672 [+] (Inc). **BT** 1559-1866 (*gap 1733-37*), (c.584,
585, d.383, 384). **Cop** CMB 1559-1865 (Ms Bod c.168, 169 and C of A).

OXFORD, St Peter le Bailey. **OR** C 1580 [+], M 1563 [+], B 1585 [+] (*gaps C 164
1658*), *M 1645-1661, B 1649-1662*) (Inc). **BT** 1721-1899 (c.584, d.379,
381, 382).

OXFORD, ST THOMAS. **OR** C 1655 [+], MB 1667 [+] (*gaps M 1779-1836, B 1766-
1812*), Banns 1778 [+] (Inc). **BT** 1679-1851 (*gaps 1682-1720, 1830-1850*)
(c.585, 586, d.385).

OXFORD, Commercial Rd (Bapt). *No regs known − not at PRO − Now no
longer exists.*

OXFORD, New Road Chapel (Ind. Now Bapt). *f 1721.* **OR** Z 1784-1837,
B 1786-1836 (PRO).

OXFORD, George Lane (Ind). *f 1832. Closed 1932.* **OR** C 1833-1835 (PRO).

OXFORD, New Inn Hall St (Wes). *f 1760.* **OR** ZC 1812-37, B 1818-37 (PRO),
C 1812-1942 (Bod). (*Almost certainly Circuit Registers*).

OXFORD, Bull St (Prim Meth). *Not at PRO.* **OR** C 1839-1961 (Bod) *registe
for whole former Prim. Meth. Oxford Circuit.*

XFORD MONTHLY MEETING (S of F). *estab. 1668. Title changed to* Witney
Monthly Meeting *during 18th C.* Constituent Meetings: *Alverscot
(1709 - 18th C), Burford (1668-1855), Charlbury (1668-1918),
Chipping Norton (1668-1910), Faringdon, Berks (1791-1880), Milton
(1668-1813), Oxford (1668 - 18th C), Witney (1668-1890).*
Registers: Z 1657-1774, 1776-1795, 1797-1837, M 1662-1776, 1795-
1833, B 1659-1837 (PRO 90, 92-97). *Register 91, described in
Nonconf. Cat. as Witney Monthly Meeting is actually Vale Monthly
Meeting. No separate registers known for any of the Constituent
Meetings.*

XFORD (S of F). Oxford Monthly Meeting. *f 1668. disc. 18th C. No
separate regs known.*

XFORD, ST ALOYSIUS, Woodstock Rd (RC). *f 1785. Not at PRO. (Inc.
holds regs of Waterperry RC Church, C 1700-1793), (but no later
pre-1837 registers).*

XFORD, ST CLEMENTS (RC). *f 1793 as successor to Waterperry RC Church.
Demolished 1910. Successor Church is St Edmund and St Frideswide,
Greyfriars. No regs at PRO or with Inc of Greyfriars.*

XFORD COLLEGES. *– See also under Original Registers in County Preface.*

LL SOULS. *No registers. Sir Edmund Chester's "Monumental Inscriptions
in All Souls College" (privately printed, copy in Bodleian gives
details of Burials where any information has survived.*

HRIST CHURCH. *Also the Cathedral. See beginning of list of Oxford
parishes.*

ESUS. *No registers. College used the Church of St Michael at the
North Gate for CM. B in Holy Cross Churchyard or Cemetery.*

MAGDALEN. OR M 1728-1754 *(Librarian).* BT None. Cop M 1728-1754 Ms
(Bod Ms Top Oxon c.172 fol 349), M 1728-1754 Ts (SG).

MERTON. *Chapel used until late 19th Century as Parish Church for
parish of St John the Baptist.* OR *See Oxford, St John the Baptist.*
Cop B in the College chapel 1617-1900 *taken from M.I's and from the
1813-1900 Burial Register.* (Appendix 3 of Ancient Monuments in
Merton College Chapel – pub Oxford 1964).

NEW COLLEGE. OR B 1813-1903 *(19 entries altogether, 7 before 1837)*
(Librarian).

ORIEL. *No registers. Some B in the Chapel recorded in College Records.
See "The Provosts and Fellows of Oriel College, Oxford" (pub OUP).*

ST JOHNS. OR M 1695-1752 (200 entries). One C, Very few B. Cop CMB 1690-
1752 Ptd (Misc Gen et Her. 5th Ser Vol. 1 Pt 4), CMB 1690-1752 Ts (SG).

WADHAM. OR B 1583-1676 (Librarian). Cop Extracts 1583-1676 (Bod Ms
Wood D 5 Summ Cat 8524).

No registers are known for any of the other colleges founded before
1837, viz:- BALLIOL, BRASENOSE, CORPUS CHRISTI, EXETER, HERTFORD,
LINCOLN, PEMBROKE, QUEEN'S, TRINITY, UNIVERSITY, WORCESTER.

PIDDINGTON. **OR** CMB 1654 [+], Banns 1754-1795, 1823 [+] (Inc). **BT** 1678-186?
(*gap 1686-1720*), (c.587). **Cop** M 1702-1837 Ts (SG) CMB 1654-1812 (In?
See also Ambrosden.

PISHILL. **Peculiar** *of Dorchester Abbey.* **OR** CMB 1763-1783 (fragmentary
remains), CMB 1783 [+] (*gap CMB 1810-1813*) (Inc). **BT** 1666-1813
(Oxon b.79), 1768-1862 (Ms Oxf Dio Papers c.588).

PYRTON. **OR** CB 1568-1812, M 1568-1754 (Bod), CB 1813 [+], M 1754 [+] (Inc).
BT 1568-1877 (*gap 1715-1720*), (c.588, 589). **Cop** M 1568-1812 (Phil 1)
M 1651-1675 in Boyd Misc.

ROLLRIGHT, GREAT. **OR** CMB 1560 [+] (*gaps M 1709-1716, 1756-1812*), Banns
1755-1816, 1823 [+] (Inc). **BT** 1667-1865 (*gap 1670-1721*), (c.589, 590).
Cop M (BT) 1668-9, 1722-1837 Ms Vol. 4 (SG).

ROLLRIGHT, LITTLE. **OR** C 1813 [+], M 1754 [+], B 1783 [+] (*gaps M 1794-1813,
1829-1840, B 1811-1814*), Banns 1754, 1823 [+] (Inc). **BT** 1721-1875
(*gaps 1737-39, 1745-48, 1761-6, 1777-1782, 1784-1791*). (c.590).
Cop M (BT) 1721-1829 Ms Vol. 4 (SG).

ROTHERFIELD GREYS. **OR** C 1568 [+], MB 1592 [+] (*gaps C 1720-1764, M 1720-
1787*), Banns 1754-1783 (Inc). **BT** 1670-1859 (*gaps 1671-1683, 1686-
1698, 1701-1720*), (c.590, 591).

ROTHERFIELD GREYS. (Ind). *f 1662.* **OR** ZC 1719-1837, B 1685-1837 (PRO).

ROTHERFIELD PEPPARD. **OR** CMB 1754 [+] (Inc). **BT** 1639-1854 (*gaps 1641-
1669, 1671-1683, 1686-1689, 1692-1721*), (c.592).

ROUSHAM. **OR** CMB 1544 [+] (Inc). **BT** 1678-1877 (*gaps 1681-1719, 1726-29*),
(c.593).

SALFORD. **OR** C 1762 [+], MB 1755 [+], Banns 1823 [+] (Inc). **BT** 1669-1865
(*gaps 1671-79, 1682-1718, 1730-34*), (c.594).

SANDFORD, ST MARTIN. **OR** CMB 1695 [+] (Inc). **BT** 1738-1883 (c.594, 595,
d.411), M (BT) 1738-1837 Ms (SG Vol. 2).

SANDFORD-ON-THAMES. **OR** CMB 1572 [+], Banns 1754 [+] (Inc). **BT** 1771-1865
(c.595).

SANDFORD-ON-THÁMES (RC). *Chaplaincy of Oxford Mission. No regs known.*

SARSDEN. **OR** CMB 1575-1719 (Bod). **BT** 1575-1886 (*gaps 1671-1719, 1866-
66 and many odd years*), (c.596, d.412, 413). **Cop** M 1575-1840 Ts (S?
CM 1575-1919, B 1575-1869 Ms (Bod c.233, d.176-8).

SHELSWELL. – *see Newton Purcell.*

SHENINGTON. (*formerly in Glos*). **OR** CB 1721 [+], M 1813 [+], Banns 1753-
1812, 1823 [+] (Inc). **BT** 1578 [+] (City Lib Gloucester).

HIFFORD. OR CMB 1783 + (gaps M 1812, 1836-37), Banns 1783-1811, 1823 + (Inc Bampton Aston). *Earlier regs destroyed by damp.* BT 1721-1855 (gaps 1726-1732, 1748-1812) (c. 596).

HILTON. OR CB 1662 +, M 1672 + (gap M 1680-1754), Banns 1827 + (Inc). BT 1721-1877 (c. 596, 597).

HIPLAKE. OR CB 1672 +, M 1644 + (gap M 1653-1672), Banns 1754 + (Inc). BT 1639-1901 (gap 1641-1715) (c. 597, 598, d. 419). Cop CMB 1672-1791 Ms (Inc).

HIPTON-ON-CHERWELL. OR CMB 1653 +, Banns 1754 + (Inc). BT 1757-1865 (gaps 1763-66, 1782-86, 1806-12) (c. 598). Cop M 1538-1840 Ts (SG W. Oxon Regs Vol. 2).

HIPTON-UNDER-WYCHWOOD. OR CMB 1538 +, Banns 1823 + (Inc). BT 1669-1917 (gaps 1671-1720, 1878-1898) (c. 599, d. 419, 420, 421). Cop M 1538-1840 (alph) Ts (SG), CMB 1538-1919 (alpha) Ms (Bod c. 240-2). *See also Leafield.*

HIRBURN. OR CMB 1587 + (Inc). BT 1639-1877 (gaps 1641-1677, 1680-1717) (c. 600). Cop M 1590-1753 Ts (SG), C 1587-1780, M 1590-1753, B 1598-1780 Ms (Bod c. 295).

HORTHAMPTON. OR C 1646-1812, M 1663-1836, B 1773-1811, Banns 1754-1813 (Bod). BT 1670-1851 (gaps 1672-1684, 1686-1720, 1728-1735, 1838-50) (c. 600, 601).

HUTFORD. OR CMB 1698 + (Inc Swalecliffe). BT 1728-1866 (gaps 1728-1736, 1753-56) (c. 601). Cop CMB 1698-1840 Ts (SG N. Oxon Regs Vol. 2).

SIBFORD (S of F). **Banbury Monthly Meeting.** OR Z 1685-1784, B 1689-1773, Z notes 1841-1904, D notes (Banbury and Sibford) 1846-59, B notes (Sibford Graveyard) 1840-1890, B notes (Sibford Gower) 1865-80, B notes (Sibford Ferris) 1893-1904 (all ORO).

SIBFORD FERRIS. − *see Swalecliffe.*

SIBFORD GOWER. − *see Swalecliffe.*

SOMERTON. OR CM 1660 +, B 1627-1647, 1660 +, Z 1695-1706, 1758-1781, Banns 1812, 1823 + (Inc). BT 1700-1874 (gaps 1702-1720, 1775-1778, 1792-1798, 1867-1873) (c. 601, 602). Cop M (BT) 1722-1837 Ms (SG Vol. 3).

SONNING. − *see Berks.*

SOULDERN. OR CMB 1667 +, Banns 1754 + (Inc). BT 1700-1879 (gaps 1702-1720, 1731-1734, 1773-1779, 1785-1803) (c. 602, 603, d. 427). Cop M 1667-1840 Ts (SG). *See also Hardwick.*

SOUTH HINKSEY. − *see Berks.*

SOUTH LEIGH. − *see Leigh, South.*

SOUTH STOKE. − *see Stoke, South.*

SOUTH WESTON. − *see Weston, South.*

SPELSBURY. **OR** CB 1539 +, M 1540 + *(gaps C 1753-1806, B 1807-1812)*, Banns 1823 + (Inc). **BT** 1669-1866 *(gaps 1671-1680, 1683-1719, 1729-1733, 1736-1740, 1857-1863)* (c.604). **Cop** M 1540-1654 (Phil Ms and Mf SLC), CMB 1539-1752 (Inc). *M 1540-1651 in Boyd Misc.*

STADHAMPTON *(with Chislehampton until 1761)*, **Peculiar** *of Dorchester Abbey.* **OR** CB 1556-1819, M 1567-1768 *(gap M 1763-1767)* (Bod), CB 1813 +, M 1763 +, Banns 1824 + (Inc). **BT** 1662-1833 *(gaps 1664-66, 1699-1710, 1739-1742, 1747-59, 1762-70, 1814-19)* (b.74, Fol.19, c.605). **Cop** M 1567-1812 Ts (SG) *with Chislehampton to 1761* (SG), CMB 1567-1762 Ts (Bod and Inc).

STANDLAKE AND YELFORD. **OR** CMB 1559 + *(gaps C 1733-1773, B 1670-1812)* Z 1653-1656 (Inc). **BT** 1669-1874 *(gaps 1671-1720, 1773-76 and odd years)* (c.605, d.430). **Cop** CMB 1559-1959 Ts (SG), CMB 1559-1669 Ms (SG), M 1559-1837 (Phil 2). *M 1651-1675 in Boyd Misc. See also Yelford.*

STANTON HARCOURT. **OR** C 1567-85, 1602-11, 1655 +, M 1569-85, 1602-11, 1655 +, B 1570-85, 1602-11, 1655 + (Inc). **BT** 1721-1900 *(gaps 1806-1812, 1893-99)* (c.605, 606, d.432). **Cop** M 1570-1837 (Phil 2), CMB 1567-1840 (alpha) (Ms Bod c.203), C 1567-1852, M 1569-1870, B 1570-1837 Ms (SG). *M 1653-1675 in Boyd Misc.*

STANTON ST JOHN. **OR** CM 1654 +, B 1654-1812 *(gap CMB 1706-1712)* (Inc). **BT** 1738-1840 *(gap 1834-1839)* (c.606). **Cop** M 1660-1837 Ts Alph (SG). Index to M 1660-1837 Ms (Bod).

STEEPLE ASTON. **OR** C 1543 +, MB 1538 +, Banns 1824 + (Inc). **BT** 1721-1880 *(gaps odd years)* (c.607-8). **Cop** CMB (BT) 1721-1859 Mf (SLC and SG), M (BT) 1721-1837 Ms (SG Vols 2 and 3).

STEEPLE BARTON. **OR** CMB 1678 + (Inc). **BT** 1721-1867 (c.608, 609). **Cop** M (BT) 1725-1836 Ms (SG Vol. 2), CMB (BT) 1721-1852 Mf (SLC and SG).

STOKE, NORTH. **OR** CB 1740-1812, M 1744-53, 1813-35 (Bod), CMB 1740 + (Inc). **BT** 1639-1851 *(gaps 1641-1720, 1733-39, 1821-26, 1828-50)* (609, 610). **Cop** M 1744-53, 1813-35 M (BT), 1721-1812 Ts (SG).

STOKE, SOUTH. **OR** CMB 1557 + *(gap B 1785-1812)* (Inc). **BT** 1639-1877 *(gaps 1641-1683, 1686-1720, 1727-39, 1767-1770).*(c.610, d.436). *See also Woodcote.*

STOKE, SOUTH. (Lady Hunt Conn). *f 1821. Not at PRO. No information.*

STOKE LYNE. **OR** CMB 1665 +, Banns 1754-1812, 1823 + (Inc). **BT** 1725-1811 *(gaps 1701-1717, 1739-1758)* (c.609, d.435). **Cop** M (BT) 1713, 1718, 1721-1836 Ms (SG Vol. 3).

STOKE ROW, IPSDEN. (Ind). *f 1815.* **OR** ZC 1818-33 (PRO).

STOKE TALMAGE. **OR** CB 1760-1812, M 1759, 1819-1837 (Inc). **BT** 1670-1866 *(gaps 1671-1720)* (f.237, c. 611). **Cop** M 1754-1812 (Phil Ms and Mf SLC). *M 1756-1812 in Boyd Misc.*

STOKENCHURCH (*Transferred to Bucks*). **OR** CMB 1707 + (*gap B 1793-1812*) (Inc). *Regs at Bank. 7 days notice needed.* **BT** 1670-1872 (*gaps 1671-1677, 1680-1713, 1716-20*) (e.611, 612, d.436). **Cop** CMB 1670-79 Ms (SG).

STOKENCHURCH (RC). *Some entries in Britwell Prior regs.*

STOKENCHURCH (Ind). *f 1823.* **OR** C 1830-1836 (PRO).

STONESFIELD. **OR** CMB 1571 + (*gaps C 1658-1663, 1810-12, M 1650-61, B 1652-62, 1810-13*) (Inc). **BT** 1721-1877 (*gaps 1786-90*) (c.612, d.437). **Cop** C 1571-1657, MB 1571-1651 (C of A and Inc).

STONOR (RC). **OR** C 1758-1840, M 1759-88, 1795-1837, B 1758-1839 (PRO).

STRATTON AUDLEY. **OR** C 1696-1874, M 1696-1841, B 1696-1950 (*gap M 1752-1754*), Banns 1757-1811, 1825-1896 (Bod). **BT** 1678-1877 (*gaps 1680-1684, 1687-1699, 1702-17*) (c.613, d.439). (*1843-1877 damaged*). **Cop** M 1696-1754, 1813-37, M (BT) 1754-1812 Ts (SG).

SUMMERTOWN. **OR** CMB 1833 + (Inc). **BT** 1833-1866.

SWALCLIFFE (SWALECLIFFE). **OR** C 1558 +, M 1566 +, B 1577 + (Inc). **BT** 1721-1877 (*gaps 1729-1734, 1856-63*) (c.614, d.444, 445). **Cop** C 1558-1840, M 1566-1840, B 1577-1840 Ts (SG N. Oxon Regs Vol. 2).

SWERFORD. **OR** CB 1577 +, M 1813 + (*gap B 1746-1812*), Banns 1755-1812, 1823 + (Inc). **BT** 1670-1877 (*gaps 1671-1721*) (c.614, 615). **Cop** CMB 1746-1812 Ms (JG), M (BT) 1670, 1722-54, 1813-37 Ms (SG Vol. 4).

SWERFORD (Bapt). *Church now owned by Methodists. No regs known. Not at PRO. Entries probably in regs of Hook Norton – parent church.*

SWINBROOK. **OR** CMB 1662-1837 (Bod). **BT** 1667-1804 (*gaps 1671-1720, 1730-1737*) (c.154, e.615, d.447, 448). **Cop** M 1685-1837 Ts (SG), M 1685-1837 Ptd (*Genealogical Quarterly Vol. XXV No. 2*).

SWYNCOMBE. **OR** C 1573-1801, M 1568-1730, B 1568-1800 (*gaps M 1624-1653, B 1730-1757*) (Bod), M 1800 +, B 1813 + (Inc). **BT** 1641-1867 (*gaps 1641-1677, 1680-1684, 1692-1720, 1732-1757*) (c.615, 616). **Cop** M 1568-1730 Ts (SG).

SYDENHAM. **Peculiar** of *Thame*. **OR** CMB 1705-1754 (Inc). **BT** 1605-1734 (*gaps 1606-1675, 1713-1722, 1724-1732*) (d.448), 1736-1812 (Bucks Mss – Bucks 165/2). **Cop** CMB (BT) 1676-1734 Ms (SG). *M 1678-1715 in Boyd Misc.*

SYDENHAM (Bapt). *f 1821.* **OR** ZD 1821-36 (PRO).

TACKLEY. **OR** CMB 1568 + (*gap M 1654-1670*), Banns 1754 + (Inc). **BT** 1669-1889 (*gaps 1671-1683, 1686-1721*) (c.616, 617, d.448).

TADMARTON. **OR** CB 1548 +, M 1755 + (Inc). **BT** 1680-1874 (*gaps 1684-1720, 1731-36, 1865-67*) (c.617, 618). **Cop** CB 1813-1837, M 1754-1837 Ms (JG), Extracts CMB 1551-1650 (SG).

TADMARTON (Bapt). *Church originally Methodist. No regs known. Not at PRO. Probably Tadmarton entries in regs of Hook Norton, parent church.*

TAYNTON. **OR** CMB 1538-1754 *(gaps C 1692-1702, M 1603-1617, 1692-1725, B 1603-1617, 1686-1702* (Bod). **BT** 1680-1874 *(gaps 1684-1720)* (c.618 619). **Cop** CMB 1538-1837 Ts I (SG).

TETSWORTH. **Peculiar** *of Thame.* **OR** C 1604-1752, M 1625-1752, B 1653-1752 (Bod), CMB 1753 + (Inc). **BT** 1605-1734 *(gaps 1606-1669, 1691-1718)* (c.165, d.450), 1736-8, 1742-1814, 1834-9 (with Bucks Mss Bucks c.666). **Cop** M 1625-1812 (Phil Ms and Mf SLC). *M 1625-1812 in Boyd Misc.*

TETSWORTH (Ind). *f 1820. Not at PRO. No information.*

TEW, GREAT. **OR** CMB 1606 + *(gap CMB 1692-1712)*, Banns 1829 + (Inc). **BT** 1669-1876 *(gaps 1671-1720)* (c.619, 620, d.450). **Cop** M 1606-1756 Ms (SG), M (BT) 1754-1836 Ms (SG Vol. 2). *M 1606-1756 in Boyd Misc.*

TEW, LITTLE (Bapt). *f 1778. No regs known. Not at PRO or Ch Sec.*

THAME. **Peculiar** *of Thame.* **OR** 1601-1812, M 1601-1837 *(gap CMB 1654-1656)*, Banns 1754-1760 (Bod). **BT** 1667-1818 *(gaps 1671-1675, 1694-99, 1702-1706, 1709-11)* (c.165, d.451, d.502, 452, 453) *(1736-1818 with Bucks Mss – Bucks c.166-168).* **Cop** M 1601-1760 Ts (SG), Extracts CMB 1601-1784 (Ptd), CB (BT) 1667-1714, M 1667-1723, 1733-4 Ms (SG). *M 1667-1734 in Boyd Misc.*

THAME (RC). *Some entries in Britwell Prior regs.*

THAME (Bapt). *f 1825.* **OR** Z 1826-37 (PRO).

THAME (Ind). *f 1750. Not at PRO. No information.*

TOOT BALDON. – *see Baldon Toot.*

TOWERSEY. *(Formerly in Bucks).* – *see Bucks.*

TUSMORE. – *see Hardwick.*

TUSMORE PARK (RC). **OR** 1718-1795 (Reg of Fermon Family) (AHB). See also Hardwick (RC) and Hethe (RC).

UPPER HEYFORD. – *see Heyford, Upper.*

WARBOROUGH. **Peculiar** *of Dorchester Abbey.* **OR** CMB 1538 + (Inc). **BT** 1662-1871 *(gaps 1691-1711, 1732-35, 1739-42)* (b.80, c.621, 622)

WARBOROUGH MONTHLY MEETING (S of F). *f 1668. United to* **Reading Monthl Meeting** *1810.* **Constituent Meetings:** *Abingdon, Berks (1791-1810), Henley (1668-1810), Turville Heath, Bucks (1668-18thC), Wallingford, Berks (1725-1810), Warborough (1668-1810).* **Monthly Meeting Registers:** Z 1652-1835, M 1664-1774, 1780-1789, 1798-1836, B 1666-1835 (PRO Nos 67-73). *No separate registers known for any of the constituent meetings.*

WARBOROUGH (S of F). **Warborough Monthly Meeting** (*1668-1810*), **Reading and Warborough Monthly Meeting** (*1810-1865*) *disc. 1865. No regs known apart from Monthly Meeting regs.* (**Reading and Warborough Monthly Meeting Registers:** Z 1650-1836, M 1683-1773, 1779-1835, B 1660-1837 (PRO 75-83, 1506)).

WARDINGTON. **Peculiar** *of Banbury.* **OR** CMB 1603-1695 (*gap M 1636-1647*), Z 1644-1695 (Bod), CMB 1695 + (Inc). *Some M at Cropredy from 1573.* **BT** 1605-1735 (*gap 1671-1675*) (b.114, 59, c.622), 1736-1812 (with Bucks Mss – Bucks c.168). **Cop** M 1603-1840 Ts (JG).

WARREN HEYFORD. – *see Heyford Upper.*

WARPSGROVE. – *see Chalgrave.*

WATERPERRY. **OR** C 1538-1667, 1711-89, M 1538-1667, 1712-1812, B 1539-1689, 1702-89, Banns 1754-1812 (Bod), C 1790 +, MB 1813 + (Inc). **BT** 1670-1856 (*gaps 1671-77, 1682-1720*) (c.622, 623). **Cop** M 1538-1812 Ts (SG).

WATERPERRY (RC). *Chaplaincy of Oxford Mission.* **OR** 1700-1793 (Inc St Aloysius RC Church, Woodstock Rd, Oxford). **Cop** 1700-1793 (CRS Vol. 7).

WATERSTOCK. **OR** CB 1580-1812, M 1583-1812 (Bod), CMB 1813 + (Inc). **BT** 1670-1897 (*gaps 1671-77, 1682-1719, 1852-55 and odd years*) (c.623, 624). **Cop** M 1583-1812 Ts (SG).

WATLINGTON. **OR** CB 1635-1812, M 1635-1754 (*gaps C 1654-1669, 1732-48, M 1652-1660, 1732-53, B 1729-47*), Z 1653-1660 (Bod). **BT** 1678-1853 (*gaps 1686-1720, 1732-36, 1784-87*) (c.624, 625, d.464, 465). **Cop** M 1635-1731 Ts (SG), M 1635-1731 (Phil Ms and Mf SLC). *M 1638-1731 in Boyd Misc.*

WATLINGTON. (RC). *Some entries in Britwell Prior regs.*

WATLINGTON. (Wes). *f 1824.* **OR** ZC 1824-37 (PRO).

WENDLEBURY. **OR** CMB 1579 + (Inc). **BT** 1680-1877 (*gaps 1682-85, 1688-1712, 1715-20*) (c.626, d.465). **Cop** M 1579-1840 Ts (SG).

WESTCOTT BARTON. **OR** CM 1559 +, B 1559-1812 (*gaps M 1678-1704, 1754-1816*), Banns 1757-1811, 1824 + (Inc). **BT** 1719-1872 (c.626). **Cop** CMB (BT) 1719-1853 Mf (SLC and SG), M (BT) 1730-1836 Ms (SG Vol. 2).

WESTON, SOUTH. **OR** C 1586 +, M 1559 +, B 1558 + (Inc). **BT** 1639-1866 (*gaps 1641-83, 1686-1720, 1738-1757, 1771-1781, 1793-1800, 1802-1804*) (c.627). **Cop** C 1586-1747, M 1559-1747, B 1558-1745 Ms (SG and Ts Bod d.290), M 1558-1810 (SLC). *M 1559-1812 in Boyd Misc.*

WESTON-ON-THE-GREEN. **OR** CMB 1591 + (*gaps CMB 1673-1694, M 1743-1812, Z 1591-1672, 1695-1742*), Banns 1755-1812 (Inc). **BT** 1721-1866 (*gaps 1731-37, 1813-29*) (c.627, d.466). **Cop** M (BT) 1721, 1740-1812 Ms (SG Vol. 3).

WESTWELL. **OR** C 1602 +, M 1576 +, B 1577 +, Banns 1756-1811, 1824 + (Inc). **BT** 1697-1865 (*gaps 1698-1720, 1786-88*) (c.628). **Cop** C 1602-1701, M 1576-1700, B 1577-1631, 1661-2, 1671-1701 Ts (SG).

WHEATFIELD. **OR** C 1722 +, M 1733 +, B 1722-1819 (*gap M 1745-1812*), Banns 1757-1812 (Inc). **BT** 1639-1866 (*gaps 1640-1721, 1755-58, 1764-72*) (c.628). **Cop** M 1593-1812 (Phil Ms and Mf SLC). *M 1614-1812 in Boyd Misc.*

WHEATLEY. **OR** CMB 1813 + (Inc). **BT** 1797-1812 (with Cuddesdon) (c.629). *(gap from 1812). See also Cuddesdon.*

WHITCHURCH. **OR** CMB 1596 + (Inc). **BT** 1639-1877 (*gaps 1641-1683, 1687-1720*) (c.629, 630, 631). **Cop** CMB 1596-1812 (Ptd).

WIDFORD. *(Formerly in Glos.). – see Glos.*

WIGGINTON. **OR** CMB 1558 + (*gap B 1799-1812*), Banns 1754-1812, 1823 (In **BT** 1670-1874 (*gaps 1671-1720*) (c.631, 632). **Cop** M 1670, 1721-1838 Ms (SG Vol. 1).

WIGGINTON. (Bapt). *Church now closed. No regs known. Not at PRO. Probably entries in regs of Hook Norton, parent church.*

WILCOTE. **OR** CB 1755-1812 (*a few entries only*), 1813 +, M 1755 +, Banns 1755 (Inc Ramsden), CMB 1700-1708 (Bod – with Cogges records **BT** 1813-1866 (d.468). **Cop** M 1755-1837, CB 1813-37 existing casual entries 1755-1812 Ts (SG – West Oxon Regs Vol. 2). *See also Leafield and Shipton-under-Wychwood.*

WITNEY. **OR** C 1551 +, M 1604 +, B 1583 +, Banns 1754-1798, 1823 + (Inc **BT** 1682-1855 (*gaps 1684-1720*) (c.632, 634, d.475-479).

WITNEY (Ind and Bapt). *f 1662.* **OR** ZC 1804-19, 1823-36 (PRO).

WITNEY (Wes). *f 1800.* **OR** ZC 1803-37 (PRO). *Almost certainly a Circuit register.*

WITNEY. Corn St Chapel. (Prim Meth). *f 1827.* **OR** ZC 1835-37 (PRO).

WITNEY. (Pres). **OR** C 1761-62 in register of Taunton, Somerset (PRO).

WITNEY MONTHLY MEETING (S of F). – *see* **Oxford Monthly Meeting.**

WITNEY (S of F). *f 1668.* **Oxford,** *afterwards* **Witney Monthly Meeting.** *Disc. 1890. No regs known apart from Monthly Meeting regs.*

WOLVERCOTE. **OR** CMB 1596 +, Banns 1823 + (Inc). **BT** 1721-1869 (*gaps 1731-38, 1752-55*) (c.635, d.481). **Cop** CMB 1596-1670 (Inc), Extracts CMB 1596-1650 (Ptd). *M 1596-1647 in Boyd Misc.*

WOOD EATON. **OR** C 1539-1814, M 1539 +, B 1539-1816, Banns 1760 + (Inc) **BT** 1721-1868 (*gaps 1732-42, 1749-1754, 1798-1800, 1808-11*) (c.635)

WOODCOTE. **OR** *In South Stoke registers until 1846.* **BT** 1791-2 (with South Stoke). (d. 483). *See also Stoke, South.*

WOODSTOCK. **OR** CMB 1651 + (*gaps C 1703-25, 1796-1803, M 1703-12, 1716-1722, 1737-1754, B 1726-1735, 1796-1803*), Banns 1653-1702, 1754-1821 (with I) (Inc). **BT** 1682-1861 (*gaps 1684-1779*) (c.636. 637, d.483).

WOODSTOCK. High St (Bapt). *f 1825. Not at PRO. No information.*

WOOLVERCOT. – *see Wolvercote.*

WOOTTON-BY-WOODSTOCK. **OR** CMB 1564 + (Inc). **BT** 1669-1881 *(gaps 1671-77, 1680-3, 1686-1720, 1867-70)* (c.637, 638, 639). **Cop** M 1564-1837 (Phil 1). *M 1651-1675 in Boyd Misc.*

WORTON, NETHER. **OR** CMB 1784 + (Inc). **BT** 1751-1866 (1751-1763 with Over Worton) *(gaps 1752-54, 1764-1776, 1778-1812)* (c.639). **Cop** C 1561-1775, 1784-1812, M 1599-1775, 1784-1812, B 1560-1568, 1601-1759, 1784-1812 Mf (SG and ORO), M (BT) 1813-1830 Ms (SG Vol. 2).

WORTON, OVER. **OR** CB 1813 + (Inc). **BT** 1721-1866 *(gaps 1732-4, 1765-68, 1795-8, 1805-12 and many odd years)* (c.639). *1756-7, 1771 with Nether Worton.* **Cop** CMB 1628-1812 Mf (SG and ORO), M (BT) 1721-1835 (with Nether Worton 1756-7, 1771) (with gaps) Ms (SG Vol. 2).

WROXTON WITH BALSCOTE. **OR** CB 1548-1552, M 1552-1821 (Inc). **BT** 1670-1865 *(gaps 1672-9, 1684-1720, 1731-34)* (c.640, 143). **Cop** Extracts CMB 1553-1656 (SG), M (BT) 1680-82, 1721-1837 Ts (SG Vol. 1), M 1552-1753 Ts.

WROXTON AND GREAT BURTON. (Ind). *f 1819.* **OR** 1823-37 (PRO). *See also Polesworth, Warwickshire.*

YARNTON. **OR** CMB 1569 + (Inc). *5 marriages between 1728 and 1754 in M register of Magdalen College, Oxford.* **BT** 1723-1874 *(gaps 1730-36, 1784-88, 1792-95)* (c.641). **Cop** M 1569-1837 (Phil 2). *M 1651-1675 in Boyd Misc.*

YELFORD. **OR** C 1813 + (Inc Standlake). **BT** 1751-1906 *(gaps 1752-87, 1792-95, 1803-11, 1852-55)* (c.641). *See also Standlake.*

SHROPSHIRE

ACKNOWLEDGMENTS

*The Editor gratefully acknowledges the assistance of the follow-
ing persons in compiling this section.*

Miss. Mary C. Hill, Shropshire County Archivist for supplying information, answering many queries and for assistance in writing the County
Preface;

The late Mr. J.L. Hobbs and Mr. M.F. Messenger, successive
Librarians of Shrewsbury Borough Library for supplying information,
and the latter for reading the preface and offering many useful
comments and suggestions;

Mr. M.J. Mildren for compressing information on Original Registers
into the required form;

Mr. F.M. Barrell for checking the holdings of the Society of
Genealogists, checking dates or Original Registers and for dealing with
numerous queries;

Mr. F. Leeson for listing surrendered Nonconformist registers and for
checking against the returns at the National Register of Archives;

Mrs. E. Kennard for further work on the returns at the National
Register of Archives;

Mr. P.D.A Harvey, Assistant Keeper, Department of Manuscripts,
British Museum for supplying information on Bishop's Transcripts for
the Bridgnorth Peculiar;

Mr. E. Coker for listing the Bishop's Transcripts at Lichfield;

Mr. D.C. Owens of the National Library of Wales for supplying information on Bishop's Transcripts and Marriage Licences;

Mr. J.R. Cunningham of the Church of Jesus Christ of Latter Day
Saints and Mr. E. Milligan, Archivist of Friends' House, Euston,
London for granting access to their records;

Revd. R.H. Hewitt and Mr. B. Trinder for supplying information on
Methodist Churches;

Mr. P. Gwynne James, Registrar of the Diocese of Hereford for
facilities to examine the Hereford Bishop's Transcripts;

Revd. F. Rice, Bishop's Secretary, Catholic Diocese of Shrewsbury;

The Secretaries of Baptist and Congregationalist Unions and Associa-
tions and numerous Librarians, Catholic Parish Priests, Methodist
Circuit Superintendents, Baptist, Congregationalist and Unitarian
Ministers and Secretaries for supplying information.

GENERAL INFORMATION

Record Repositoires (See also list on page xx)

S.R.O. — *Salop Record Office. Shire Hall, Abbey Foregate, Shrewsbury* (*moved from old Shire Hall in April 1966*).
(*Hours 9 - 1, 2 - 5 Sat closed*)
This holds an increasing number of original parish registers

S.B.L. — *Shrewsbury Borough Library and Museum, Castle Gates, Shrewsbury.*
(*Hours 9.30- 8 p.m.*)
This holds original registers of 10 Shropshire parishes transferred from Hereford City Library and printed, manuscript or microfilm copies of almost all parish registers of the county. It also holds 8 volumes of George Morris's *"Shropshire Genealogies,"* 9 volumes of Joseph Morris's *"Genealogical Manuscripts relating to Shropshire,"* 3 volumes of T. Hardwick's *"Pedigrees of the Heraldic Visitation of Shropshire"* and 1 volume of R.C. Turton's *"Shropshire Pedigrees"*. A list of their holdings of Wills and Marriage Settlements has been printed (R.E. James 1958).

Shrewsbury Corporation, Borough Archives, Guildhall, Dogpole, Shrewsbury.
(*Hours 9.30- 5 Sat 9.30 - 12*)
This holds considerable records but no parish register material.

H. — *Hereford Cathedral Muniment Room.*
This holds the Hereford Diocesan Archives including the Bishop's Transcripts and Marriage Licences. To consult, apply to Diocesan Registrar, 5 St. Peter's St, Hereford.
(*for explanation of abbreviations HX and HXX see Bishop's Transcripts*)

L. — *Lichfield Joint Record Office, Bird St., Lichfield, Staffs.*
(*Hours 10 - 1, 2.15 - 5 (Sat 10 - 12.30 by special arrangement*
This holds the Archives for Lichfield Diocese including Bishop's Transcripts and Marriage Licences. *No searches are permitted during August unless arrangements are made no later than 15th July preceding. Fees are charged for the*

examination of Bishop's Transcripts and Marriage Licences.

L.C.L.   – *Lichfield Cathedral Library.*
This holds a few Bishop's Transcripts and Marriage Licences for Peculiars. This is not open for searchers, but on written application to the Diocesan Registrar arrangements may be made for documents to be inspected at the Diocesan Registry.

N.L.W.   – *National Library of Wales, Aberystwyth, Cardiganshire, Wales.*
(Hours 10 - 5)
This holds the Bishop's Transcripts and Marriage Licences for the parishes in the Diocese of St. Asaph, and one Shropshire Nonconformist register.

Council House, Shrewsbury (apply Bishop's Secretary).
This holds the Archives of the Catholic Diocese of Shrewsbury, but no registers.

B.M.   – *British Museum, Department of Manuscripts, London W.C.1.*
(Hours 10 - 4.45) A reader's ticket is necessary.
This holds the Bishop's Transcripts for the Bridgnorth Peculiar up to 1812.

G.L.C.   – *The Genealogical Society of the Church of Jesus Christ of Latter Day Saints, Salt Lake City, Utah, U.S.A.*
This holds microfilms of registers deposited at the Salop Record Office and of the genealogical manuscript material at the Shrewsbury Borough Library.

Other Abbreviations used in this section. (See also list at front of this volume).

S.P.R.S.– Shropshire Parish Register Society printed volumes.

Ancient Parishes 229

Changes in County Boundaries.

Only minor changes have been made since 1800. In 1844, *Halesowen* was transferred from Salop to Worcestershire, and *Farlow* from Hereford to Salop. *Mucklewick*, a township of Hyssington parish (Co. Mont) was amalgamated with *Shelve* parish (Co. Salop) in 1884. In 1895 *Tittenley* was transferred from Cheshire to Salop, parts of *Ludford* from Hereford to Salop, parts of *Leintwardine* from Salop to Hereford, and *Sheriffhales* from Staffs to Salop. There are two Ecclesiastical parishes still split by the County Boundary, *Richard's*

Castle (Salop and Hereford) which has two civil parishes, and *Llanymynech* (Salop and Mont). *Woore* Ecclesiastical parish includes part of *Mucklestone* (Staffs), the parish from which it was taken in 1841.

Original Parish Registers

This list gives only the starting dates of Baptisms, Marriages and Burials and any major gaps before 1837. Duplicate and overlapping registers have therefore been ignored, but full details will be found in *Shropshire Parish Documents*[1]. The details given are still substantially accurate. A few registers lost in 1903 have since been found, and some others, present in 1903 have disappeared. In one parish, three registers covering 1716-1859 were reported missing in 1956, but discovered six years later in a farmhouse. In another case, a register already lost in 1831 has been found in private hands and presented to Salop Record Office. Five parishes (*Chetton, Munslow, Pontesbury, Rushbury and Shipton*) have registers dating back to 1538; seventeen others begin before 1558 and another seventeen in 1558-9.

Many Shropshire registers were almost totally neglected during the Civil War, and notes to this effect were included in some registers. On the other hand, some parishes (*e.g. Clun, Shrawardine, Kinlet, Stirchley and Stoke St. Milborough*) started new registers during the Commonwealth period and kept them with reasonable diligence. Both the County Record Office and Shrewsbury Borough Library have been appointed by the Bishop of Lichfield as the Diocesan Record Office for the Archdeaconry of Salop. The latter holds the registers of only ten parishes but new deposits are continually being made at the County Record Office.

Bishop's Transcripts

At the beginning of this Century, Shropshire was divided Ecclesiastically between the Dioceses of *Hereford* (South), *Lichfield* (North) and *St. Asaph* (North West). In addition, three parishes were in the Diocese of *Worcester*. When the Church of Wales was established, all Deaneries along the Welsh Border had the option whether to join the new church or to stay with the Church of England, and Oswestry Deanery (including parishes of Oswestry, Melverley, St. Martin and Selattyn) opted to stay, and was then transferred from St. Asaph to Lichfield. Bishop's transcripts exist for these four parishes both at Lichfield and at the National Library of Wales those at the latter being odd years probably overlooked at the time of the transfer. A few other minor adjustments have been made since.

---

[1] Published 1903 by Salop County Council. Copies still obtainable from Salop Record Office on payment of postage.

Two parishes have been transfered from Hereford to Lichfield and fifteen parishes from Lichfield to Hereford.

Diocese of Hereford.

These are kept in the Muniment Room of Hereford Cathedral. All applications to examine the Hereford Bishop's Transcripts should be made to the *Diocesan Registrar*. A fee is usually charged.

They have been sorted into Parish Bundles until 1812. The majority start about 1660 and continue to 1812 with only minor gaps. The Diocesan Registrar holds a catalogue which gives full details of dates and condition of some of the transcripts. Where the exact dates have been listed and all missing years noted, parishes are followed by the simple abbreviation *"H"*. *"HX"* indicates that the period 1754-1812 has been checked and all missing years noted, but not the period 1660-1753. *"HXX"* indicates that both periods are unchecked. In all cases, any transcripts dating before 1660 are noted. In many parishes there is one only (1638). The transcripts are kept in boxes. The post-1813 transcripts are arranged by Deaneries, but not sorted into parishes, listed or checked to discover missing transcripts. The overall dates of the Deaneries are as follows:-

Burford	(10 boxes)	1813-1870
Clun	(9 boxes)	1813-1871
Ludlow	(10 boxes)	1813-1873
Pontesbury	(10 boxes)	1813-1871 and 1896
Stottesdon	(6 boxes)	1813-1879
Wenlock	(12 boxes)	1813-1868

In addition, there are boxes for 1834 and 1835 containing transcripts from all deaneries, a miscellaneous box for 1834 and a box containing transcripts for Bridgnorth and Shrewsbury Cemeteries 1855-1871. Apart from the Bishop's Transcripts proper, registers of deaths exist for 1682 and 1685.

Hereford Peculiar.

Chancellor of the Choir of Hereford Cathedral (Ashford Carbonell). Normal transcripts with the main series.

Diocese of Lichfield.

At the *Joint Record Office, Bird St., Lichfield* except for some of the Peculiars which are at *Lichfield Cathedral Library*. The dates given are overall dates only and must not be taken as an indication that the series is complete, though gaps of ten years or more have been noted. In general they begin in the 1660's and continue to dates between 1855 and 1880. The transcripts have not been fully sorted and fresh transcripts may come to light, which may alter the gaps in some cases. In 1693, it is probable that the Bishop instructed incumbents to fill in all gaps in the transcripts and many lists were made covering the years 1660-1693 except for years where separate transcripts existed.

The transcripts of the parishes transferred from the Diocese of St. Asaph have not been examined since they arrived.

Lichfield Peculiars.

When printed registers started in 1813, all incumbents were instructed to made their returns to the Diocesan Registry[2], so there is a complete series for the Lichfield Peculiars from that date. The previous transcripts, where known, are however elsewhere. (see below)

Bridgnorth and the Royal Free Chapelry of St. Mary Magdalene

(Peculiar of Dean and Chapter of Lichfield Cathedral).

Parishes: - St. Mary Magdalen and St. Leonard in Bridgnorth Alverley, Claverley, Quatford and Bobbington[3], Staffs. The transcripts from 1636 to 1812 are at the *British Museum* (Add Mss. 28735 to 28740) except for two isolated transcripts of Claverley and Quatford for 163 and 1635 respectively at the Lichfield Cathedral Library. Those for *St. Mary Magdalen* and *Bobbington* start in 1662. The post-1813 Transcripts are at Lichfield Diocesan Registry.

Buildwas Abbey.

Parishes: - Buildwas only – no transcripts known before 1813. Post-1813 transcripts at Lichfield Diocesan Registry.

Royal Free Chapel of Shrewsbury St. Mary.

Parishes: - Albrighton, Astley[4], Clive, St. Mary Shrewsbury. Transcripts from 1708 to 1755 were sent to St. Mary's where they were kept with the parish records. They are described in *Shropshire Parish Documents* as *Files of Parchment Membranes* and are now at the Shropshire Record Office, with the Parish Register of St. Mary's.

Post-1813 transcripts are at Lichfield Diocesan Registry.

Prees.

Parishes in Shropshire: - Prees, Calvershall, and Whixhall – transcripts in *Lichfield Cathedral Library* up to 1812; there after in *Diocesan Registry*.

On written application to the Diocesan Registrar, transcripts at Cathedral Library will be brought to the Diocesan Registry for searche to consult there.

---

2   See General Preface on Bishop's Transcripts.
3   Not Bovington as is stated in "Wills and their Whereabouts"
4   Astley, Shropshire not Astley, Warwickshire as is erroneously stated in "Wills and their Whereabouts".

Diocese of St. Asaph.

At the *National Library of Wales.* The transcripts are far from
complete. The gaps have been listed and in general, extend for a period
of from one to five or six years. The condition of the transcripts
is generally satisfactory. As mentioned above, the National Library
of Wales still holds transcripts for a few odd years for four of the
Oswestry Deanery parishes transferred from St. Asaph to Lichfield.

Modern Copies of Parish Registers and Bishop's Transcripts

Registers to 1812 have already been printed by the *Shropshire
Parish Register Society* for 146 Anglican Parishes, 22 Nonconformist
churches and 5 Roman Catholic Churches. Transcripts of the registers
of 69 other parishes are deposited at *Shrewsbury Borough Library,*
and the *Shropshire Archaeological Society* has now microfilmed all remaining registers to 1812 and the greater number to 1837. The microfilms are kept with the transcripts and both are available to students.
The Church of Jesus Christ of Latter Day Saints has microfilmed
the registers at the Shropshire Record Office. The *Society of
Genealogists* holds relatively few typescript or manuscript copies.

Consolidated Indexes

Boyd's Marriage Index (Copies S.G. and S.L.C.).

This has separate volumes devoted to Shropshire and covers
marriages from 127 parishes for various periods but mostly to 1812
or to 1837. The exact dates included are indicated under each parish.
It is based almost entirely on the printed Shropshire Parish Register
Society volumes. An *index of the manuscript copies at Shrewsbury
Borough Library* has been prepared by Mr. K. Hotchkiss. This index is
in 37 manuscript note books and is available to searchers at the
Library.

Marriage Licences

Diocese of Hereford – at *Muniment Room, Hereford Cathedral. Apply
Diocesan Registrar.*
The Marriage *Bonds* (1660-1831) are on files in boxes; *Licence Books*
(1603-1787) are bound and indexed but need repair. The *Licence
Allegations* (1834-1909) with Affidavits are bound and indexed. Later
Allegations are in parcels.

Dicoese of Lichfield – at *Lichfield Diocesan Registry.*
The Marriage *Bonds* and *Allegations* and (after 1824) the
Affidavits for Marriage Licences in the Registry are arranged by

years for the whole Diocese: either a year is divided alphabetically
(e.g. A-K, L-Z) into two bundles or there is one bundle for the year.
The Bonds available are as follows:-

Prior to 1660: only a few Bonds are extant.

1660-1670: a number of Bonds extant, but probably not complete.

1670 onwards: nearly all the Bonds sworn during this period are
believed to be extant.

In each bundle the Bonds etc. for the whole Diocese (except
Peculiars) arranged in quasi alphabetical order, i.e. the initial
letters of the surname of the male party to the proposed marriage is
the governing factor, and all Bonds and Allegations with the same
initial letter are placed together: thus to search for a marriage of
"William Smith and Hannah Brown in the year 1794, the bundle L-Z
1794 would first be located, and the "S" would be found all together
in the bundle. It would be necessary to search all the "S"s but not
outside the "S"s in normal circumstances. If a Bond which was
practically certain to exist was not discovered in its correct place,
a search could then be made through the whole bundle, but it is
believed that such misplacements are rare. The bundles have not been
kept in good order of recent years, and the task of reorganising
their storage is at present being under-taken, but may take some
time. The work of sorting the documents in the Registry has shown
that a fairly large number of Bonds etc. have become separated from
their bundles. The task of replacing these will take a considerable
time, and therefore failure to locate a Bond and Allegation does not
necessarily mean that it is not in existence or that it is not deposited in the Registry. About 10% of the Allegations have not yet
been sorted. At least three weeks' notice should be given to the
Registrar of the year and surname of the male party to the marriage.
Bonds, Allegations and Affidavits may be inspected at the Registry
by approved searchers by appointment (at least *14 days' notice* having
previously been given).

*Lichfield Peculiars (for parishes covered see Bishop's Transcripts
above).*

The bonds etc. sworn in respect of licences issued out of the
former Peculiar Courts are not included in the Diocesan Bonds, but
some are in the Registry under separate storage. Those for the
peculiars of the *Dean & Chapter* are kept in the *Cathedral Library*,
but there is no catalogue or list. The Cathedral Library is not open
to searchers, and applications to inspect the bonds should be made to
the Diocesan Registrar.

Bridgnorth – Some Bonds and Allegations for the Peculiar of
Bridgnorth may be in the Cathdral Library, Lichfield.

Shrewsbury St. Mary – There are some 17th and 18th Century
arriage Licences and Bonds among the records of St. Mary's deposited
, the Shropshire Record Office. Possibly also some in Diocesan
egistry.

Buildwas – Possibly in Diocesan Registry.

Prees – Probably in Cathedral Library.

ocese of St. Asaph – at *National Library of Wales.*
    There is one marriage Bond for each of the years 1616, 1675, 1678,
d 1685, and two each for 1687 and 1689. From 1690 onwards, there is
greater number of Documents and the series continues until 1938.

man Catholics

Shropshire now lies within the Roman Catholic Diocese of
rewsbury. During the penal period, there were a number of Catholic
aplaincies – at Shrewsbury (Moat Hall, home of Berington family),
wport (Longford Hall, home of Talbot family), Acton Burnell (Smythes),
owden Hall (Plowdens), Mawley Hall (Blounts), Whiteladies, Madeley
rookes), Shifnal (Lords Stafford) and Ditton Priors. No registers
e known for Shifnal, and Madeley registers do not begin until after
37. Registers exist, however, for the others, and have been printed
the Shropshire Parish Register Society, with a long and detailed
eface by F.F.J. Vaughan on the History of Catholicism in Shropshire.
e *Newport* Register has also been printed by the Catholic Record
ciety.
    In 1830 a church was established at Wellington, but the registers
not begin until 1853.
    There are no registers with the Diocesan Archives at the Council
use, Shrewsbury.
    Archbishop's House, Bath Street, Birmingham 4 holds a Confirmation
gister of Vicars Apostolic, which covers the whole Midland District
cluding Shropshire.

ptists

12 Baptist Churches in Shropshire before 1837 have been listed. Of
ese, 8 surrendered registers and two of these, Bridgnorth and
rewsbury, have been printed by the Shropshire Parish Register Society.
hose of Shrewsbury began in 1766). No registers are known for
llington (founded in 1807) and no information has been received on
e remaining three. All these Shropshire churches are in the West
dland Association which, however, holds no registers. *Works of
ference*: Revd. I. Williams *300 Years of Baptist Witness in Netherton
orcs) and thereabouts.* (Copy at S.G.) This includes many references

to Shropshire Baptist families.

Independents (Congreational ists)

No less than 34 pre-1837 Independent Churches have been listed.
Of these 20 surrendered registers, seven of which have been printed
by the Shropshire Parish Register Society in their Nonconformist
volume. These include Bridgnorth and Shrewsbury where the churches
date from 1662 (the registers starting in 1769 and 1767 respectively)
The Shropshire Parish Register Society have also printed the
registers of *Oldbury Chapel*, which is now in Worcestershire. The
printed *Llanyblodwel* register is interesting as the maiden names of
mothers are given. No other registers have been located at the
Churches, only two replies having been received from Church Secretaries to questionnaires. All twelve about which there is no information were, however, 19th century foundations. All churches are in
the Shropshire Congregational Union, from which no reply has been
received, but it is most unlikely that any registers are held.
Works of Reference: E. Elliott. *History of Congregationalism in
Shropshire (1898)*.

Presbyterians and Unitarians

There were three 17th century foundations at Shrewsbury, (now
Shrewsbury Unitarian Church) Wem and Whitchurch. The registers starting in 1692, 1755 and 1708 respectively are at the P.R.O. and have
been printed by the Shropshire Parish Register Society.
Works of Reference

J. Reavley. *Presbyterianism in Shrewsbury and District 1647-1925*.
R.S. Robson. *Presbyterianism in Shrewsbury a revival of 1662*.
Shrewsbury Chronicle March 6th 1914 et seq.

Methodists

Wesleyans.

In 1837 there were four Shropshire Methodist circuits in the
District of Birmingham and Shrewsbury – Shrewsbury, Madeley,
Wellington and Ludlow and a fifth, Whitchurch, was in the Liverpool
District. Between them they probably covered the whole of the county,
though the east and south east part may have come under the circuits
of Wolverhampton (Staffs) and Stourport & Stourbridge (Worcs). It is
also possible that parts of Shropshire were included in Rhayader and
Llanbister (Radnorshire) and Stafford. Oswestry was the church of
the Severn Valley Mission and was not covered by any of the Shropshir
Circuits. All five of the circuit head churches deposited registers,
and one may assume that these were probably circuit registers. It

ould seem, however, that some of the individual churches in the
Madeley Circuit kept separate registers as three others are known
besides Madeley – for Broseley (surrendered) Ketley Bank (with minister)
and Shifnal (with minister). It is possible that there may be duplicate
entries in the Madeley register. In the *Wellington* circuit, besides
Wellington, registers are known for Wrockwardine Wood and Wombridge
(both surrendered) and St. George's Oakengates (with Circuit Superintendent of Oakengates & Shifnal Circuit). In the *Ludlow* circuit,
besides Ludlow, registers are known for Clee Hill and Ditton Priors
(both surrendered). Oswestry kept a separate register (surrendered).
Where individual churches are known they have been listed under the
relevant circuit as well as individually.

Primitive Methodists.

In 1837, there were the following Shropshire circuits: Wrockwardine
Wood, Shrewsbury, Ludlow, Prees, Bishop's Castle and Oswestry. Four
of these surrendered registers and a register for Wrockwardine Wood
is held by the Circuit Superintendent of the present Ellesmere Circuit.
These are the only registers so far known and may almost certainly be
taken as circuit registers. It is possible that the Bishop's Castle
register may be held in the circuit safe of the present Bishop's
Castle & Clun circuit. Information has been received on only five
other pre-1837 Primitive Methodist Shropshire churches, at Maesbury,
Babbins Wood, Bagley and Houghton (all Oswestry circuit), and Braden
Heath (probably Prees circuit).

Methodist New Connexion.

There were only two pre-1837 circuits in Shropshire, Dawley
Green & Madeley, and Shrewsbury. Both surrendered registers and
these are the only Shropshire registers known. From its description
in the catalogue the first is clearly a circuit register, and with
safety one may assume that the Shrewsbury register was as well. Parts
of Shropshire were probably also covered by the Wolverhampton (Staffs)
and possibly by the Stourbridge (Worcs) Chester (Cheshire) and Hanley
(Staffs) circuits.

Present Methodist Circuits.

Information has been received from the Circuit Superintendents
of

Oakengates & Shifnal.	Registers of St. George's, Shifnal and Ketley Bank in churches.
Madeley and Dawley.	No pre-1837 registers known to be in churches.
Wem and Prees Green.	No pre-1837 registers in churches.
Ellesmere.	Wrockwardine Wood register at Ellesmere church.
Oswestry.	No pre-1837 registers in churches.
Llanymyrech.	No pre-1837 registers in churches.

No information has been received from the circuit superintendents of Minsterley, Bishops Castle & Clun, Ludlow, Craven Arms and Church Stretton, Leintwardine or Knighton, Radnorshire.

Works of Reference.
W. Phillips *Early Methodism in Shropshire* (1896)
Revd. W.E. Morris *History of Methodism in Shrewsbury and District.*

Calvinistic Methodists

There appear to have been at least three Shropshire churches (now in the Montgomery and Salop Presbytery), two at Oswestry (at the P.R.O.) and one at Shrewsbury (at the National Library of Wales) all with registers beginning 1812-13.

Society of Friends (Quakers)

Shropshire was covered not by a separate Quarterly Meeting but by the *Shropshire Monthly Meeting* under the jurisdiction of the *North Wales Quarterly Meeting.* In 1797 the North and South Wales Quarterly Meetings were united to form the *Wales Half Year's Meeting,* which in 1832 was itself united with the Herefordshire and Worcestershire Quarterly Meeting to form the *Hereford Worcestershire and Wales Quarterly Meeting.*

The Constituent Meetings of the Shropshire Monthly Meeting were Shrewsbury, Broseley (afterwards Coalbrookdale), New Dale, and perhap Ruyton in the 11 Towns.

Registers.
North Wales Quarterly Meeting Z 1777-1796 (PRO 639) B 1777-1797 (642, 643) No M. register is known.

Wales Half Yearly Meeting. The registers of the South Wales Quarterl Meeting Z 1784-1820 (640), B 1791-1820 (644) include the whole of Wales and Shropshire after 1797. Then Z 1820-1837 (641), M 1800-1834 (638) B 1820-1837 (645).

Shropshire Monthly Meeting. Regs Z1656-1837, M 1657-1762, 1795-1834, B 1659-1838 (703-709) M 1657-1765, B 1661-1776 (1558). It seems likely that the latter part of *Broseley* Marriage register 1691-1794 in fact covered the whole Monthly Meeting (See Broseley) M 1838-1941 at Worcs R.O.

Copies.
Shropshire Monthly Meeting surrendered registers have been printe by the *Shropshire Parish Register Society.* Digests (i.e. abstracts of

11 entries arranged alphabetically)[5] covering the whole period from
656 to 1838 of all surrendered registers for the Herefordshire,
rcestershire and Wales General Meeting are at *Friends' House*,
uston Rd, London, N.W.1. and at the Worcestershire Record Office.
rcestershire Record Office also holds a copy of Births, Marriages
d Burials for the Shropshire Monthly Meeting for the period 1656 to
38. Marriages from Shropshire Monthly Meeting Surrendered Registers
57-1754 are in Boyd. (see General Preface on Quaker Registers)

irth Notes 1774-1800, *Burial Notes* 1777-1797, and *Marriage Licences*
795-1799 for the Herefordshire, Worcestershire and Wales Quarterly
eeting are at the P.R.O. (No. 1472). Birth Notes 1832-1891, Burial
otes 1827-1896 and Marriages 1838-1841 for the Shropshire Monthly
eeting, and Birth Notes 1880-1909, Burial Notes 1872 to 1933 and
arriages 1936-1952 for the Worcestershire and Shropshire Monthly
eeting are held by the Worcestershire Record Office.

rvingites

There is a surrendered register for an Irvingite Church at
ridgnorth.

egimental Registers

These cover Births, Baptisms, Marriages and Deaths for the period
790-1924 and are at Somerset House, London. They are the original
egisters kept by the various regiments. They are indexed, and to
earch this index, one does not need to know the Regiment. For
arriages, Deaths and Burials, it is preferable, though not essential
o know the regiment. The most likely regiment for infantrymen was
3rd Regiment of Foot. Search should also be made of the Guards'
egiments, the Royal Artillery, the Royal Engineers and the Royal
arines.

onumental Inscriptions

rinted.   M. Stephenson. Monumental Brasses in Shropshire.
anuscript.   Shrewsbury Borough Library has two manuscript notebooks
    of monumental inscriptions. Ms. No 310 "Monumental Inscriptions at
    several Shropshire Churches" and Ms. No 217 Revd. E. Williams
    "Monumental Inscriptions at Barrow, Benthall, Broseley, Wenlock
    etc."

For a description of these Digests see General Article on Quaker Registers
in Vol.1.

Newspapers

Shrewsbury Chronicle 1772-date (S.B.L.) 3 copies for 1773, 4, 5, 1776-1799, 1829 – date (B.M.N.L.)

Salopian Journal 1794-1843 (continued as Eddowes Journal (843-53) (S.B.L. & B.M.N.L.)

Salopian Magazine 1815-17 (B.M.N.L. and S.B.L.)

Publishing Societies

Shropshire Parish Register Society 1898 onwards.

Shropshire Archaeological Society Sec. H. Beaumont, Esq, M.A.
Silverdale, Severn Bank, Shrewsbury (absorbed the Salop and North Wales Natural History and Antiquarian Society). Transactions vols 1-11, 2nd series vols 1-12, 3rd series vols 1-10, 4th series vols 1-12, 5th series vol 46 onwards 1878-date.

Other Local Societies

Bridgnorth and District Historical Society, Dudmaston, Bridgnorth

Caradoc and Severn Valley Field Club Sec. Mrs. A. Benger, Rivington, Sundorne Rd, Shrewsbury. Transactions I vol 1869 then new series 1893 onwards.

Offa Antiquarian Society, Oswestry. Joint Secretaries: H. Jones, Esq., Borough Librarian, Borough Library Oswestry and G. Griffiths, Esq., Llys Hill, Middleton Rd., Oswestry.

General Works of Reference

Audrey H. Higgs A.L.A. and Donald Wright F.L.A. "West Midland Genealogy" (Published 1966 under the auspices of the West Midland Branch of the Library Association). This is a survey of local genealogical material which is available in the public libraries of Herefordshire, Shropshire, Staffordshire, Warwickshire and Worcestershire. Copies available from A.J. Fox Esq., F.L.A. Birchfield Library, Birmingham 20. Price 10/- (11/- Post paid).

A Select List of Books about the County in the Shrewsbury Public Library and the Shropshire County Library (Available from S.B.L. price 6d.)

Shrewsbury – A list of Books and Articles about the Town (Available from S.B.L. price 6d).

Victoria County History vol 1 (1908).

Shropshire County Records 1-17 1910-17.

Shropshire Notes and Queries vols 1-3 new series vols 1-8 3rd series vols 1-2 Nov 1884-March 1887.

Kittermaster Shropshire Arms and Lineages. Compiled from the Heralds
    Visitations etc. 1869.
Armorial Bearings of Shropshire Families (from George Morris's Ms)
    (1924).
W. Watkins-Pitchford Shropshire Hearth Tax Roll of 1672 (1949).
G.F. Matthews Shropshire Probates in the P.C.C. 1700-1749.
R.W. Eyton Antiquities of Shropshire 12 vols. (1854-60).
Blakeway – Sheriffs of Shropshire (1831) Continuation by Hughes.

Local Histories etc

*More comprehensive lists of Local Histories will be found in the two
book lists above. Some of the more interesting for the genealogist
are : -*
Albrighton, History of J.B. Blakeway (contains extracts from
    registers etc.)
Ludlow Churchwardens' Accounts 1540-1750.
Oswestry Records of Corporation of-Ed.S Leighton (contains genea-
    logical material).
Shrewsbury History of, with Pedigrees, plates views etc. by H. Owen
    and J.B. Blakeway – 2 vols 1825.
Shrewsbury-Burgess Roll ed. Forrest (1924).

3DON. **OR** CMB 1554 + *(many small gaps until 1749)*, Banns 1754-1813, 1827 + (Inc). **BT** 1638, 1660 + *(gaps 1661, 1668, 69, 1779, 1794)* (H). **Cop** CB 1561-1812, M 1561-1838 (SPRS 19).

2TON BURNELL. **OR** CMB 1568 + *(gap 1667-93)* (Inc). **BT** 1630-1810, 1813-1856 (L) *now Hereford*. **Cop** CB 1568-1812 M 1568-1838 (SPRS 19).

2TON BURNELL (RC). **OR** C 1769 + (Inc). **Cop** C 1769-1838 (SPRS Nonc. Vol).

2TON ROUND. **OR** CMB 1713 + (Inc). **BT** 1638, 1660 + (HX). **Cop** CMB 1713-1812 Ms (SBL).

2TON SCOTT. **OR** CMB 1690 +, Banns 1866 + (Inc). **BT** 1638, 1660 + *(gaps 1661, 1692, 1705, 26, 36, 40)* (H). **Cop** CMB 1690-1812 Ms (SBL).

DDERLEY. **OR** CMB 1692 +, Banns 1824 + (Inc). **BT** 1680-1876 (L). **Cop** CMB 1692-1812 (SPRS 4). *M 1692-1812 in Boyd.*

LBERBURY. **OR** CM 1564-1812, B 1564-1779 *(gap B 1779-1813)*, Banns 1754-1812 (SBL) CMB 1813 +, Banns 1824-1850 (Inc). **BT** 1660 + *(gap 1661, 2, 1702, 1786)* (H). **Cop** CMB 1564-1812 (SPRS 6 and 7). *M 1564-1812 in Boyd. See also Wollaston, Great.*

LBRIGHTON, Nr Shrewsbury. **Peculiar** *Royal Free Chapel of Shrewsbury St Mary.* **OR** CMB 1674 + *(gap M 1790-1852)*, Banns 1858 + (Inc). **BT** 1708-1813 described as *"Files of Parchment Membranes"* (SRO with Shrewsbury St Mary Parish Registers) 1813-1866 (L). **Cop** CMB 1649-1812 (SPRS 1), CMB (BT) 1708-1813 (SRO and SLC). *M 1684-1812 in Boyd.*

LBRIGHTON, Nr Wolverhampton. **OR** CMB 1555-1812 *(gap CMB 1653-1660)* (SRO) CMB 1813 + (Inc). **BT** 1676-1810, 1813-1856 (L). **Cop** CMB 1555-1812 (SPRS 3), Extracts CMB 1813-1894 (Ptd). *M 1555-1812 in Boyd.*

LVELEY. **Peculiar** *Deanery of Bridgnorth.* **OR** CMB 1561 +, Banns 1754-1809, 1894 + (Inc). **BT** 1636-1812 (B.M. Add. Ms 28737) 1813-1837 (L). **Cop** CMB 1561-1812 Ms (SBL), CMB (BT) 1636-1735 Ms Sep I (SG). *M (BT) 1662-1750 in Boyd.*

SH MAGNA. *Formed from Whitchurch 1849.* **OR** CMB 1837 +, M 1845 + (Inc). **BT** 1841-1868 (L).

SHFORD BOWDLER. **OR** CMB 1630 + (Inc). *Early years in poor condition.* **BT** 1638, 1660 + *(gap 1757, 1795)* (HX). **Cop** CMB 1602-1837 Ms I (SG and SBL). *(Copy made before loss of entries 1602-1630).*

SHFORD CARBONELL. **OR** CMB 1653 +, Banns 1813 + (Inc). **BT** 1638, 1670 + *(gaps 1672, 73, 77-79, 81, 84, 88-9, 91, 97-8, 1701-2, 1716, 1740, 1742, 49, 1752, 55, 1803)* (H). **Cop** CB 1653-1812 M 1653-1841 Mf No 10 (SBL).

ASTLEY. **Peculiar** *Royal Free Chapel of Shrewsbury St Mary.* **OR** CMB 1695
(gaps CB 1795-1801, M 1812-1830), Banns 1754-1812 (Inc). **BT** 1708-
1812 described as *"Files of Parchment Membranes"* (SRO with
Shrewsbury St Mary dep regs.) 1313-1859 (L). **Cop** CMB 1692-1812
(SPRS 5), CMB (BT) 1708-1812 Mf (SRO and SLC). *M 1726-1812 in Boyd*

ASTLEY ABBOTS. **OR** CMB 1561 + *(gap CMB 1653-8, 1671-94)* (Inc).
BT 1660 + *(gaps 1671, 2, 1680, 92, 1708, 17)* (H). **Cop** CMB 1561-165
1659-1670, 1695-1812, M 1813-1837 Ms (SBL).

ASTON BOTTERELL. **OR** CMB 1559 +, Banns 1754-1812, 1824 + (Inc).
BT 1638, 1660 + (H). **Cop** CMB 1559-1812 Ms (SBL).

ASTON EYRE. *See Morville.*

ASTON ON CLUN. Mill St (Bapt) *f 1830. Not at PRO. No information.*

ATCHAM. **OR** CMB 1621 + *(gap B 1638, 1644-1657)* (Inc). **BT** 1619-1810,
1813-1871 (L). **Cop** CB 1619-1812 M 1619-1837 (SPRS 14). *M 1619-183?
in Boyd.*

BADGER (or BAGSORE). **OR** CMB 1713 + *(gap M 1754-57)*, (Banns 1840 + (Inc
BT 1602, 1622, 38, 40, 1660 + (HX) *now Lichfield diocese.*
Cop CMB (BT) 1660-1713 (PR) 1713-1836 (SPRS 16). *M 1662-1836 in
Boyd.*

BAGLEY. (Prim Meth) *f 1827.* **Oswestry Circuit.** *No regs known. Not at
PRO or Ellesmere Meth Circuit Supt.*

BARROW. **OR** C 1660-1726 (SBL) CMB 1727 + (Inc). **BT** 1660 + (HX).
Cop CMB 1727-1812 Ms (SBL).

BASCHURCH. **OR** CMB 1600 +, Banns 1754-1812, 1823 + (Inc) – *included
Little Ness after about 1740.* **BT** 1630-1869 *(gap 1637-1663)* (L).
Cop CMB 1600-1812 Ms (SBL).

BATTLEFIELD. **OR** CMB 1665 + *(gap M 1811-14, 1830-40)* (Inc). **BT** 1630-184
(gap 1637-1658) (L). **Cop** CMB 1665-1812 (SPRS 14 and 19). *M 1665-
1775 in Boyd.*

BECKBURY. **OR** CMB 1661 +, Banns 1755-1812 (Inc). **BT** 1610, 1620, 22, 28
38, 1660 + (HX) *now L. diocese.* **Cop** CB 1738-1812, M 1738-1854 Ms
(SBL).

BEDSTONE. **OR** CMB 1719 + *(gap M 1810-14)*, Banns 1756-1810, 1826 + (Inc
BT 1638, 1660 + (HX). **Cop** CMB 1719-1812 (SPRS 5). *M 1720-1812 in
Boyd.*

BENTHALL. **OR** CMB 1640 + *(gap M 1722-56)*, Banns 1823 + (Inc) *previous
entries in Much Wenlock registers.* **BT** 1638, 1660 + (HX).
Cop CMB 1640-1812 Ms (SBL) CMB 1558-1638. *(Transcript of Much
Wenlock Regs relating to Benthall)* (Inc).

BERRINGTON. **OR** CMB 1559-1812, Banns 1754-1812 (SRO) CMB 1813 +, Banns
1853 + (Inc). **BT** 1630-1882 (L) *now Hereford.* **Cop** CMB 1559-1812,
M 1559-1837 (SPRS 14). *M 1561-1837 in Boyd.*

BETTWS-Y-CRWYN. **OR** CMB 1695 + (*gap CMB 1741-44, 1783-85*), Banns 1759-98 (Inc). **BT** 1638, 1660 + (HX). **Cop** CB 1695-1812, M 1695-1798 Ms (SBL) CMB 1695-1812 P/S (NLW) M 1754-1798 (NLW).

BILLINGSLEY. **OR** CMB 1626-1812 (*gap CB 1732-39, M 1732-61*) (SRO) CMB 1813 +, Banns 1828 + (Inc). **BT** 1639, 1660 + (*gaps 1672, 1702, 1742*) (H). **Cop** CMB 1625-1812 (SPRS 5). *M 1628-1812 in Boyd.*

BISHOPS CASTLE. **OR** CMB 1559 +, Banns 1823 + (Inc). **BT** 1638, 1660 + (HXX). **Cop** CMB 1559-1812 Ms (SBL).

BISHOPS CASTLE CIRCUIT. (Prim Meth). *No information. Not at PRO.*

BISHOPS CASTLE. (Ind). *f 1810.* **OR** ZC 1814-1837 (PRO).

BITTERLEY. **OR** CMB 1658 + (*gap CMB 1735-37*) (SBL). **BT** 1660 + (HXX). **Cop** CMB 1658-1812 (SPRS 4). *M 1658-1812 in Boyd.*

BOBBINGTON. **Peculiar** *Deanery of Bridgnorth. See Staffs.*

BOLAS, GREAT. (or BOLAS MAGNA). **OR** CMB 1582 +, Banns 1755-1808, 1824 + (Inc). **BT** 1673-1868 (L). **Cop** CMB 1582-1812 (SPRS 13). *M 1584-1812 in Boyd.*

BONINGALE. (or BONNINGHALL). **OR** CMB 1698-1941 (*gap M 1750-58, 1834-7*) (SRO), (*Banns 1826 + (Inc) missing at last inspection*). **BT** 1661-1875 (L). **Cop** CMB 1698-1812 (SPRS 3), CMB 1698-1837 Mf (SRO and SLC). *M 1698-1812 in Boyd.*

BRADEN HEATH. (Prim Meth) *f 1832* **Press Circuit.** *No regs known. Prob in Prees Green regs.*

BRIDGNORTH – ST LEONARD. **Peculiar** *Deanery of Bridgnorth.* **OR** CMB 1556 +, Banns 1754-98 (Inc). **BT** 1636-1812 (B.M. Add. Ms 28735) 1813-1835 (L). **Cop** M (BT) 1636-1812 I Ms (SG) CMB 1556-1812 Ms (SBL). *M 1636-1812 in Boyd.*

BRIDGNORTH – ST MARY MAGDALEN. **Peculiar** *Deanery of Bridgnorth.* **OR** CMB 1610 + (*irreg 1645-1649*), Banns 1754-1808, 1876 + (Inc). *Many CB for Civil War period in Bridgnorth St Leonard's registers.* **BT** 1662-1725 (B.M. Add. Ms 28736) 1813-1835 (L). **Cop** M (BT) 1662-1725 Ms M (SG) CMB 1610-1812 Ms (SBL). *M 1665-1725 in Boyd.*

BRIDGNORTH. (Wes). *f.c. 1793.* **See Madeley Circuit.**

BRIDGNORTH – WEST CASTLE ST (Bapt). *f 1700.* **OR** ZB 1779-1836 (PRO). **Cop** ZB 1779-1838 (SPRS Nonc. Vol).

BRIDGNORTH (Invingite). **OR** C 1835-1840 (PRO).

BRIDGNORTH – STONEWAY CHAPEL. (Ind. Now United Meth and Cong). *f 1662.* **OR** C 1769-1836, B 1822-37 (PRO). **Cop** C 1765-1812 (SPRS Nonc. Vol).

BROMFIELD. *See also Halford.* **OR** CMB 1559-1685 (paper reg to 1617) (*gap 1685-1691*) CMB 1691-1731 (SRO) CMB 1732 +, Banns 1824 + (Inc). **BT** 1660 + (*gap 1755*) (HX). **Cop** CMB 1559-1685 (SRO), CMB 1559-1812, (SPRS 5). *M 1559-1812 in Boyd.*

BROSELEY. OR CMB 1570 + (gap CMB 1720-22, CB 1756-66), Banns 1846 +
(Inc). BT 1638, 1660 + (HXX). Cop CMB 1570-1750 I (Ptd I 2 vols)
(SBL), CMB 1751-1797 Ms (SBL). M 1571-1750 in Boyd.

BROSELEY (S of F) renamed COALBROOKDALE. Shrewsbury Mo. Mg. (See
preface). OR Z 1684-1777, M 1691-1794, B 1701-1777 (PRO 702).
Cop Z 1684-1777, M 1691-1794, B 1701-1777 Mf (SBL Mf No 14).

BROSELEY (Wes). Madeley Circuit. OR ZC 1819-1837 (PRO).

BROSELEY (Ind). f 1837. Now closed. No regs known. Not at PRO or Union
Sec.

BROSELEY OLD CHAPEL BIRCHMEADOW. (Particular Baptist). f 1741.
OR Z 1794-1837 (PRO). Cop C 1794-1835 (SPRS Nonc. Vol).

BROUGHTON. OR CMB 1705 +, Banns 1754-1835 (Inc). Register 1705-1774
mutilated and largely indecipherable. BT 1630-1856 (gap 1635-1659)
(L). Cop CMB 1705-1811, Extracts 1586-1683 (SPRS 1). M 1586-1812 in
Boyd.

BROUGHALL. (Ind). f 1819. Not at PRO. No information.

BUCKNELL. OR CMB 1598 + (gaps CMB 1618-1637, 1643-52, 1675-1703) (Inc
BT 1638, 1660 + (HX). Cop CMB 1598-1617, 1638-1642, 1653-1674,
1704-1812 Ms (SBL).

BUILDWAS. Peculiar of Buildwas Abbey. OR CMB 1665 +, Banns 1755-1812,
1824 + (Inc). BT 1813-1868 (L). No earlier BT's traced. Cop CB 1665
1812, M 1665-1837 (SPRS 14). M 1665-1837 in Boyd.

BURFORD. OR CMB 1558 +, Banns 1797 + (Inc). BT 1660 + (HX).
Cop CMB 1558-1812 (SPRS 16), CMB 1559-1684 (Genealogist, 2). M 1559
1812 in Boyd.

BURWARTON. OR CMB 1575 + (Inc). BT 1637, 38, 1660-1753, 1755 (period
1754-1812 missing except 1755) (HX). Cop CMB 1575-1812 Ms (SBL).

CAINHAM. – see Caynham.

CALVERHALL. (Corra). Peculiar of Prees. OR C 1778-1813, B 1771-1805
(SRO), C 1813 +, M 1844 +, B 1815 + (Inc). BT 1791-1807 (LCL),
1810-1869 (L). Cop C 1778-1813, B 1771-1805 Mf (SBL Mf No 1 and
SLC).

CARDESTON. (or CARDISTON). OR CMB 1706 + (gap M 1754-56, B 1754-1877)
(SBL). BT 1614, 1620, 1623, 1663 + (HXX). Cop CMB (BT) 1663-1703.
CMB 1706-1816 (SPRS 5). M 1663-1812 in Boyd.

CARDINGTON. OR CMB 1598 + (gap CMB 1636-48), Banns 1824 + (Inc).
BT 1660 + (HXX). Cop CMB 1598-1812 Ms (SBL).

CAYNHAM. OR CMB 1558 +, Banns 1754-1812 (Inc). BT 1660 + (HXX).
Cop 1558-1837 Mf No 9 (SBL).

CHELMARSH. OR CMB 1557 + (gaps B 1812-14), Banns 1754-1812, 1823 +
(Inc). BT 1660 + (HXX). Cop CMB 1557-1812 (SPRS 3). M 1558-1812 in
Boyd.

HESWARDINE. OR CMB 1558 + *(gaps C 1812-43, B 1812)*, Banns 1754-1812
(Inc). BT 1673-1861 (L). Cop M 1558-1662 Ms (SG), CB 1558-1662 Ms
and 1663-1812 Ts (SBL), CMB 1653-1812 Mf (SLC). *M 1556-1662 in Boyd.*

HETTON, with GLAZELEY, DEUXHILL and LOUGHTON. OR CMB 1538-1812 (SRO).
Sep CMB for Deuxhill and Glazeley 1634-1714. BT 1638, 1660 + (HXX).
Cop CMB 1538-1812 Ms (SBL). *See also Glazeley and Loughton.*

HETWYND. OR CMB 1585 +, Banns 1824 + (Inc). *There appear to be no
burials after 1808.* BT 1679-1810, 1813-1868 (L). Cop CMB 1585-
1837 Ts (SBL), CMB 1585-1837 Mf (SBL Mf No 5).

HILDS ERCALL. OR CMB 1569 + *(gap CMB 1679-1728)*, Banns 1755-1813
(Inc). BT 1681-1810, 1813-1869 (L). Cop C 1569-1874, M 1569-1837,
B 1569-1905 Mf (SBL Mf No 3).

HIRBURY. OR CMB 1629 +, Banns 1789-1812 (Inc). BT 1660 + (HXX).
Cop CMB 1629-1812 (SPRS 8). *M 1629-1812 in Boyd.*

HIRBURY. MARTON CHAPEL (Ind). *f 1829.* OR ZB 1829-36 (PRO).

HIRBURY. (Bapt). OR Z 1827-1834 (PRO).

HURCH ASTON. *Chapel to Edgmond.* OR CMB 1620 + (Inc). BT 1681-1859 (L).
Cop C 1620-1843, M 1620-1837, B 1620-1872 Mf (SBL Mf No 7).

HURCH PREEN. OR CMB 1680 +, Banns 1758-1812 (Inc Hughley). BT 1605,
1614, 22, 31, 38, 40, 1660 + (HXX). Cop CMB 1680-1813 (SPRS 16).
M 1680-1812 in Boyd.

HURCH PULVERBATCH. – *see Pulverbatch.*

HURCH STRETTON. OR CMB 1661 +, Banns 1754-1811 (Inc). BT 1638,
1660 + (HXX). Cop CMB 1661-1812 (SPRS 8). *M 1663-1812 in Boyd.*

LAVERLEY. Peculiar *Deanery of Bridgnorth.* OR CMB 1568 +, (Inc),
Banns 1800-1894 (SRO). BT 1636-1812 (B.M. Add. Ms 28739) 1634 (L),
1702 (H), 1813-1836 (L). Cop CB 1568-1812, M 1568-1837 (SPRS 10)
I to CMB 1568-1884 Ms (SRO), Banns 1800-37 Mf (SRO and SLC). *M
1568-1837 in Boyd.*

LEE – ST MARGARET. OR CMB 1721 + *(gap CB 1755-1758)*, Banns 1754-1812,
1824 + (Inc). BT 1638, 1660 + (HX). Cop CMB 1634-1812 Ms (SBL).

LEEHILL (CLEE HILL). (Wes). Ludlow Circuit. OR ZC 1796-1829, B 1803-
1829 (PRO). *Since 1829 ZC entered at Ludlow.* Cop ZCB 1802-1829
(SPRS Nonc. Vol).

CLEOBURY MORTIMER. OR CMB 1601 + *(gap CMB 1637-1648)*, Banns 1754-1812,
1823 + (Inc). *Oldest register beginning 1601 very illegible.*
BT 1638, 1660 + (HXX). Cop CMB 1601-1812 (SPRS 9). *Early part of
SPRS copied from George Morris's Ms extracts. M 1601-1812 in Boyd.*

CLEOBURY NORTH. OR CMB 1680 + (Inc). BT 1637, 1660 + (H). Cop CB 1680-
1812, M 1680-1752 Ms (SBL).

CLIVE. (*Chapelry*). **Peculiar** *Royal Free Chapel of Shrewsbury St Mary*.
OR CB 1671 +, M 1671, 1713, 1852 +, Banns 1877 + (Inc). BT 1708, 17!
(described as *"Files of Parchment Membranes"* (SRO with Shrewsbur;
St Mary Parish Registers) 1813-1868 (L). **Cop** CMB 1671-1812 (SPRS 7
CMB (BT) 1708-1755 Mf (SRO and SLC). *M 1671, 1713, 1714 in Boyd.*

CLIVE. (Ind). OR C 1831-37 (PRO *cat. under Hadnall and Clive*).
Cop C 1831-7 (SPRS Nonc. Vol).

CLUN. OR CMB 1653 + (*gap C 1796-1813*) (Inc). BT 1660 + (HXX).
Cop CMB 1653-1812 Ms (SBL).

CLUNBURY. OR CMB 1574 + (*gap CMB 1654-1660, CB 1793-95, M 1730-1754)*
Banns 1754-1812 (Inc). BT 1660 + (HXX), **Cop** CMB 1574-1812 (SPRS 2
and 38), CMB 1813-1840 Ms (SG). *M 1574-1812 in Boyd.*

CLUNGUNFORD. OR CMB 1559 +, Banns 1823-63 (Inc). BT 1638, 1660 + (HXX)
Cop CMB 1559-1812 Ms (SBL).

COALBROOKDALE (S of F). – *see Broseley.*

COALBROOKDALE. (Wes). *f.c. 1786.* – *see* **Madeley Circuit.**

COALFORD. (Wes). *f.c. 1825.* – *see* **Madeley Circuit.**

COCKSHUTT. OR C 1772 +, B 1776 +, M 1860 + (*M prior to 1860 at Ellesme.*
(Inc). BT 1797-1877 (L). **Cop** C 1772-1801, B 1776-1812 Ms (SBL).

COLD WESTON. OR C 1693 +, M 1689 +, B 1692 + (Inc Hopton Cangeford).
BT 1663 + (*gap 1779*) (HX). **Cop** C 1693-1812, M 1689-1829, B 1692-
1833, CMB (BT) 1663-1691 (SPRS 20).

CONDOVER. OR CMB 1570 + (Inc). BT 1630-1870 (L) *now Hereford Dio.*
Cop CMB 1570-1812 (SPRS 6). *M 1570-1812 in Boyd.*

CONDOVER. (Ind). – *see Dorrington and Lythe Hill.*

CORELEY. OR CMB 1543 + (*CMB 1543-1740, very poor condition, partly
illegible*), (*gaps CMB 1644-50, M 1754-1813*), Banns 1823 + (Inc).
BT 1638, 1660 + (HXX). **Cop** CMB 1543-1812 Ms (SBL).

COUND. OR CMB 1608 + (Inc). BT 1632-1868 (L) *now Hereford Dio.*
Cop CMB 1562-1812 (SPRS 2). (*Period 1562-1608 covering register no
missing taken from George Morris's Ms extracts.*) *M 1562-1812 in
Boyd.*

CRESSAGE. *Chapelry to Cound.* OR CM 1722 (*gap C 1754-1813, M 1812-41*) (
B before 1841 at Cound. BT 1660-1805, 1813-1872 (L) *now Hereford D*
Cop CMB (Extract) 1605-1631, CMB 1722-1812 (SPRS 2 and 27). (*Perio
1605-1631 covering register now missing taken from George Morris's
Ms extracts.*) *M 1701-1775 in Boyd.*

CULMINGTON. OR CMB 1579-1894 (*gaps CMB 1644-69, M 1812*), Banns 1754-
1899 (SRO). BT 1660 + (HX). **Cop** CMB 1575-1812 Ms (SBL), CMB 1579-
1837 Mf (SRO and SLC).

DAWLEY. (Wes). *f.c. 1825. – see* **Madeley Circuit.**

DAWLEY GREEN and MADELEY CIRCUIT. (Meth New Connexion). OR ZC 1829-1835 (PRO). *Covers whole circuit consisting of Dawley, Madeley and Shifnal.*

DAWLEY, LITTLE. (Wes). *f.c. 1837. – see* **Madeley Circuit.**

DAWLEY MAGNA. OR CMB 1666 +, Banns 1755-1812, 1823-30, 1843 + (Inc). BT 1673-1871 (L). Cop CB 1666-1812, M 1666-1837 (SPRS 18). *M 1666-1837 in Boyd.*

DEUXHILL and GLAZELEY. *– see Glazeley and Chetton.*

DIDDLEBURY. OR CMB 1583 + *(gap CMB 1598-1683 except B 1678-1679).* Banns 1822 + (Inc). BT 1660 + (HXX). Cop CMB 1583-1812 (SPRS 15). *M 1583-1600 in Boyd.*

DITTON PRIORS. OR CMB 1673 + *(gap M 1812-1837),* Banns 1834-45, 1861 + (Inc). BT 1638, 1660 + *(gap 1672, 1736)* (H). Cop CMB 1673-1812 Ms (SBL).

DITTON PRIORS. St Michael, Middleton (RC). *f 17th C. Perhaps registers with Bridgnorth parish priest.*

DITTON PRIORS. (Wes). *prob* **Ludlow Circuit.** *f 1801.* OR C 1801-1834 (PRO cat. as Priors Ditton). Cop 1801-1834 (SPRS Nonc Vol).

DODINGTON. *– see Whitchurch, Dodington Chapel.*

DONINGTON. OR CMB 1556 + *(gap M 1755),* Banns 1756-1813, 1824-47, 1869 + (Inc). BT 1661-1812, 1813-1879 (L). Cop CMB 1556-1812 (SPRS 3). *M 1556-1812 in Boyd.*

DONNINGTON WOOD. Queens Rd (Bapt). *f 1820. No regs known before 1937. Not at PRO or Ch. Sec.*

DORRINGTON and LYTHE HILL. Parish of Condover (Ind). *f 1806.* OR ZC 1808-1837 (PRO). Cop ZC 1808-1837 (SPRS Nonc. Vol).

DOVASTON (Ind). *f 1826. Not at PRO. No information.*

DOWLES. *– now in Worcs.* OR CMB 1572 + (Inc). BT 1614, 1631, 1638, 1660 + (HXX). Cop CMB 1572-1812 (B'ham Lib), Extracts CMB 1596-1683 (Burton's History of Bewdley).

DRAYTON IN HALES. *– see Market Drayton.*

DUDLESTON. OR C 1693-1887, M 1693-1752, B 1693-1910 *(gap CB 1752-1770)* (SRO), M 1813 + (Inc Ellesmere). BT 1664-1810 *(gap 1674-1685)* 1813-1852 (L). Cop C 1693-1837, M 1732-1757 Mf (SBL), CB 1813-1829 Mf (SRO and SLC).

DUDLESTON HEATH. (Wes). **Whitchurch Circuit.** *f 1816. Prob in regs of Whitchurch q.v.*

EASTHOPE. OR CMB 1624 + *(defective 1792-4, gap M 1811-1816, 1830-1840),* Banns 1755-1811 (Inc). BT 1605, 8, 14, 20, 22, 28, 31, 38, 40, 1660 + (HXX). Cop CB 1624-1812, M 1624-1811, 1816-1830 (SPRS 19).

EATON CONSTANTINE. **OR** C 1684-1812, M 1684-1811 (SRO). *B. were at Leighton.* **BT** 1665-1810 (*gap 1784-1796*) 1813-1874 (L). **Cop** CMB 1684-1812 (SPRS 13). *M 1684-1812 in Boyd.*

EATON UNDER HEYWOOD. **OR** CMB 1688 +, Banns 1754-83, 1823 + (Inc). **BT** 1638, 1660 + (HXX). **Cop** CB 1688-1812, M 1688-1837, CMB (BT) 1660 1837, Extracts CMB 1581-1687 (SPRS 19).

EDGMOND. **OR** CMB 1669 + (Inc). **BT** 1673-1810, 1813-1879 (L). **Cop** CMB 1669-1812 (SPRS 13). *M 1676-1812 in Boyd. See also Church Aston.*

EDGTON (EDGDON). **OR** CMB 1722 + (*gap M 1773-8, and 1813*) (Inc). **BT** 1660 + (H). **Cop** CMB 1722-1812 (SPRS 3). *M 1722-1811 in Boyd.*

EDSTASTON. **OR** CB 1712 +, M 1850 + (Inc). *For earlier regs see Wem.* **BT** 1745-1829 (*gap 1749-1762, 1776-1800*) (L). **Cop** CMB 1712-1812 (SPRS 9 and 10). *M 1712-1775 in Boyd.*

ELLESMERE. **OR** CMB 1654 + (*gap M 1692-1707, B 1692-1713*), Banns 1822-1850 (Inc). **BT** 1630-1880 (*gap 1637-1659*) (L). **Cop** CB 1654-1812, M 1654-1837 Ms (SBL).

ELLESMERE. (Ind). *f 1786.* **OR** ZC 1788-1837 (PRO). **Cop** ZC 1787-1811 (SPRS Nonc. Vol).

ERCALL HIGH or MAGNA. – *see High Ercall.*

EYTON-UPON-THE-WILDMOORS. **OR** C 1698 + (*gap 1813*), M 1756 +, Banns 1853 + (Inc). *B in Wellington regs.* **BT** 1701-1898 (L). **Cop** CMB 1698-1812 (SBL).

FARLOW. *transf. from Herefordshire 1844.* **OR** C 1813 +, MB 1858 + (Inc). *F earlier entries see Stottesdon.* **BT** *on Stottesdon returns.*

FELTON, WEST. **OR** CB 1628 +, M 1694 + (*gap C 1653-82, B 1653-78*) (Inc). **BT** 1630-1865 (L). **Cop** C 1628-1653, 1682-1812, M 1628-1812, B 1628-1653, 1678-1812 Ms (SBL).

FITZ. **OR** CMB 1559 + (*1559-1774 some leaves missing*) (Inc). **BT** 1630-1810 (*gap 1638-1658*), 1813-1868 (L). **Cop** CMB 1559-1812 (SPRS 4). *M 1564-1812 in Boyd.*

FORD. **OR** CMB 1569 (*6 entries*), 1590 + (*gap B 1761*) (Inc). **BT** 1605, 08, 1631, 39, 1660 + (*gap 1794*) (HX). **Cop** CMB 1569, 1590-1812 (SPRS 1 and 29). *M 1569-1812 in Boyd.*

FRANKTON (Ind). *f 1834. Not at PRO. No information.*

FRODESLEY. **OR** CMB 1547 + (*gap M 1812-15*) (Inc). **BT** 1632-1809, 1813-1862 (L) *now Hereford Dio.* **Cop** CMB 1547-1812 (SPRS 4). *M 1547-1812 in Boyd.*

GABOWEN, Preeshenlle Chapel (Ind). – *see Whittington.*

LAZELEY. **OR** CMB 1634-1714 (*gap 1669-1693*), B 1678-1724 (Inc Chetton) (*gap CMB 1720-1735*), CMB 1736-1812 (*includes Loughton B 1804-5*) (SRO), CB 1813 +, M 1814 + (Inc Glazeley). **BT** 1597, 99, 1602, 04, 1610, 14, 22, 23, 31, 37, 38. *All probably Deuxhill and Glazeley though only the first few say so. Remainder headed Deuxhill;* 1660-1753 sep returns for Deuxhill and Glazeley (*gaps 1666-73, 1676-79*); 1754-1812 combined return (H). **Cop** CMB 1654-1812 (SPRS 5). *M 1659-1812 in Boyd. See also Chetton.*

REAT BOLAS. – *see Bolas Great.*

REAT DAWLEY. – *see Dawley Magna.*

REAT HANWOOD. – *see Hanwood Great.*

REAT NESS. – *see Ness Great.*

REAT UPTON. – *see Upton Magna.*

REAT WOLLASTON. – *see Wollaston Great.*

REETE. **OR** CMB 1714 + (*gap M 1813, 1834-39*), Banns 1755-1812, (*1823 + missing at last inspection*) (Inc). **BT** 1630, 31, 1663 + (HXX). **Cop** (BT and PR) CMB 1663-1812 (SPRS 5). *M 1666-1812 in Boyd.*

RIMPO. (Ind). *f 1831.* **OR** C 1833-36 (PRO).

RINSHILL. **OR** CB 1592 +, M 1595 + (*gap M 1811-15*) (Inc). **BT** 1630-1853 (L). **Cop** CMB 1592-1812 (SPRS 2). *M 1595-1812 in Boyd.*

ABBERLEY. **OR** CMB 1670 + (*gap M 1736-55, 1812, CB 1736-1793, B 1813*), Banns 1755-1811 (Inc). **BT** 1614, 20, 30, 38, 1660 + (HXX). **Cop** Extracts 1573-1802 Ptd (Shrop Arch Soc Ser I Vol VIII), CMB 1573-1812 (SPRS 5). (*Period 1573-1670 covering register now missing taken from Morris's Ms Extracts and Shrop Arch Soc Trans.*) *M 1600-1812 in Boyd.*

ADNALL. **OR** C 1783 +, M 1857 +, B 1813 +, Banns 1857 (Inc). **BT** 1659-1662, 1664 only, 1813-1869 (L). *There appear to be no BT's between 1664 and 1813. Reason unknown.* **Cop** Extracts 1751-1892 (Ptd Shrop Arch Soc Ser 2 Vol IV), C 1732-1763, 1783-1827, B 1808-37 (SBL).

ADNALL. (Ind). **OR** ZC 1798 (2 *entries*), 1801-1837 (PRO). **Cop** ZC 1798-1837 (SPRS Nonc Vol).

ALESOWEN. (*Formerly part Worcs, part Salop. Transf to Worcs 1844*). – *see Worcs.*

ALFORD (HAWFORD) and DINCHOP. *Formerly Chapelry of Bromfield.* **OR** CMB 1597-1759 (SBL), CB 1813 +, M 1844 + (Inc). **BT** 1660 + (*gap 1767*) (HX). **Cop** CMB 1597-1759 Ts (SBL). *See also Bromfield.*

ALSTON. **OR** CMB 1686 + (Inc Whittington). **BT** *probably on Whittington returns* (St A). *Now Lichfield Dio.* **Cop** CMB 1686-1897 (SPRS 1). *M 1699-1826 in Boyd.*

HANWOOD GREAT. **OR** C 1813 +, M 1874 +, B 1837 + (Inc). **BT** 1605, 08, 38, 1660 + (HX). **Cop** CMB 1559-1763 (SPRS 1). (*Copy of register now lost. But period 1559-1641 defective – register almost illegible when copied.*) *M 1561-1754 in Boyd.*

HARLEY. **OR** CMB 1745 +, Banns 1891 + (Inc). **BT** 1631-1810 (*gap M 1638-1684*) 1813-1853 (L) *now Hereford Dio.* **Cop** CMB (Extracts) 1590-1724, CMB 1745-1812 (SPRS 2 and 23). (*Period 1590-1724 covering 2 registers now lost – from Morris's Ms Extracts.*) *M 1601-1812 in Boyd.*

HAUGHTON. (Prim Meth) **Oswestry Circuit.** *f 1833. Demolished 1966. No separate registers known. Not at PRO or Ellesmere Meth Circuit Supt*

HAWFORD. – *see Halford.*

HEATH. – *see Stoke St Milborough.*

HIGH ERCALL or ERCALL MAGNA. **OR** CMB 1585 + (*gap CMB 1652*), Banns 1754-1804, 1820 + (Inc). *Including B of Rodington and Waters Upton 1679-1684, 1686-8.* **BT** 1631-1870 (*gap 1632-1659*) (L). 1630, 1632-4, 1636, 1663-4 (BM Add Ms 32344). **Cop** CB 1585-1812, M 1585-1837 (SPRS 20).

HIGHLEY (HIGLEY). **OR** CMB 1551 + (*gap CMB 1749-1756*) (Inc). **BT** 1637, 1638, 1660 + (HX). **Cop** CMB 1551-1812 Ms (SBL).

HINSTOCK. **OR** CMB 1695 + (*gap CB 1738-1757, M 1738-55*), Banns 1755-1812 (Inc). **BT** 1673-1868 (L). **Cop** CMB 1695-1837 Mf (SBL, Mf No 8).

HODNET. **OR** CMB 1656-1700 (Inc). **BT** 1630-1849 (L). **Cop** Extracts from lost reg CMB 1539-1659 (SBL), CMB 1656-1812 (SPRS 11). *M 1540-1812 in Boyd.*

HODNET. Wollerton Chapel (Ind). *f 1800.* **OR** ZC 1814-37 (PRO).

HOLDGATE. **OR** M 1662-1796, B 1662 +, Banns 1824 + (Inc). *No C. (Gap M 1796-1837).* **BT** 1660 + (HX). **Cop** M 1662-1796, B 1662-1837 Mf (SBL)

HOPE BAGOT. **OR** CMB 1714 + (*gap CB 1742-54, M 1742-1823*) (Inc). **BT** 1660 + (HXX). **Cop** CB 1714-1812, M 1714-1837 (SPRS 20).

HOPE BOWDLER. **OR** CMB 1564 + (*gap C 1780-83, B 1780-1813, M 1812-1813*), Banns 1755-1811 (Inc). **BT** 1638, 1660 + (HXX). **Cop** CMB 1564-1837 Ms (SBL).

HOPESAY. **OR** CMB 1678 +, Banns 1754-1812, 1823 + (Inc). **BT** 1660 + (HX). **Cop** CMB (BT) 1660-1677 (PR), CB 1678-1812, M 1678-1837 (SPRS 14 and 18). *M 1662-1837 in Boyd.*

HOPTON CANGEFORD. **OR** CMB 1788 + (*gap C 1811-16, M 1811-22, 1834-38, B 1811-15*) (Inc). *No BT's traced. (Hereford Dio.)* **Cop** CMB 1790-1812 (SBL).

HOPTON CASTLE. **OR** CMB 1538 + (*gap M 1733-1755*), Banns 1755-1812 (Inc) **BT** 1660 + (HXX). **Cop** CMB 1538-1812 (SPRS 2 and 40). *M 1549-1812 in Boyd.*

OPTON WAFERS. **OR** CMB 1729 + , Banns 1824 + (Inc). **BT** 1608, 27, 30, 1660 + (HXX). **Cop** CMB (BT) 1638, 1661-1728 (*gap 1691-7*) (Inc), CMB (BT) 1638, 1661-1728, (PR) 1729-1812 (SPRS 9). *M 1638-1812 in Boyd.*

ORDLEY. **OR** CMB 1686 + (*gap CB 1756-1813, M 1812*), Banns 1754-1811 (Inc). **BT** 1634-1869 (L). **Cop** CMB Extracts 1656-1686 and CMB 1686-1812 (SPRS 7). *M 1656-1812 in Boyd.*

ORSEHAY. (Wes). *f.c. 1838. – see* **Madeley Circuit.**

UGHLEY. **OR** CMB 1576 + (*gap CMB 1679-81, M 1753-58, B 1813*), Banns 1758-1812 (Inc). **BT** 1638, 1660 + (HXX). **Cop** CMB 1576-1812 (SPRS 1 and 41). *M 1582-1812 in Boyd.*

GHTFIELD. **OR** CB 1557-1812, M 1557-1809 (*gaps CMB 1625-55*), Banns 1755-1809, 1823-1927 (SRO) Notes of ZD 1668-1765 (SRO), CMB 1813 + (Inc). **BT** 1682-1830 (L). **Cop** CB 1557-1812, M 1557-1809, Banns 1755-1809, 1823-1837 Mf (SBL, SRO and SLC).

RONBRIDGE. *formed in 1845 from Madeley.* **OR** C 1837 +, M 1838 +, B 1846 + (Inc).

EMBERTON. **OR** CMB 1659 +, Banns 1840 + (Inc), Banns 1823-34 (Inc Sutton Maddock). **BT** 1674-1859 (L). **Cop** CMB 1659-1812 Ms (SBL).

ENLEY. **OR** CMB 1682 + (*gap CMB 1687-92, CB 1812, M 1772, 1813*), Banns 1773-1812 (Inc). **BT** 1631-1810, 1813-1867 (L) *now Hereford Dio.* **Cop** CMB 1682-1812 (SPRS 2). *M 1690-1812 in Boyd.*

ETLEY. **OR** C 1838, M 1840, B 1839 *formed in 1838 from Wellington.* **OR** C 1838 +, M 1840 +, B 1839 + (Inc). *No BT's.*

ETLEY BANK HILL TOP. (Wes). *f 1814.* **Oakengates and Shifnal Circuit.** **OR** C 1817 + (Revd. G. Wallis, Sutherland House, Ketley).

INLET. **OR** CMB 1657 + (*1657-1705 in bad condition*) (Inc Neen Savage). **BT** 1660 + (HX). **Cop** CMB 1657-1840 (SPRS 17), CMB 1657-1705 (Inc Neen Savage). *M 1651-1837 in Boyd.*

INNERLEY. **OR** CMB 1677 +, Banns 1827 + (Inc). **BT** 1662-1840 (L). **Cop** CMB 1677-1812 (SPRS 3). *M 1677-1812 in Boyd.*

INNERSLEY or KYNNERSLEY. **OR** CMB 1691 + (*gap M 1788-93, 1836*), Banns 1754-88, 1825 + (Inc). **BT** 1676-1869 (L). **Cop** CMB 1691-1812 Ms (SBL).

NOCKIN. **OR** CMB 1661 + (*gaps C 1762-94, M 1755, 1812, B 1762-1817*), Banns 1756-99 (Inc). **BT** 1637-1846 (L), 1686, 1690, 1809, 1828 (NLW – St A). **Cop** CMB 1661-1812 (SPRS 3). *M 1679-1812 in Boyd.*

NOCKIN HEATH. (Wes) *f 1831. prob in* **Shrewsbury Circuit** *before 1837. Now in* **Llanymynech Circuit.** *No regs known. Not at PRO or Circ. Superint.*

YNNERSLEY. *– see Kinnersley.*

AWLEY BANK. (Wes). *f.c. 1837. – see* **Madeley Circuit.**

LEEBOTWOOD. **OR** CMB 1548 + (*gap CMB 1631-58*), Banns 1754-1821 (Inc Longnor). **BT** 1632-1810 (*gap 1637-1658*) 1813-1856 (L) *now Hereford Dio.* **Cop** CMB 1548-1812 (SPRS 5). *M 1547-1812 in Boyd.*

LEE BROCKHURST. **OR** CMB 1566-1706, (Inc kept at Birm and Counties Bank Wem), CMB 1715 + (Inc). **BT** 1630-1810, 1813-1866 (L). **Cop** CMB 1566-1838 (SPRS 19).

LEIGHTON. **OR** CB 1661-1812, M 1661-1811 (SRO), CB 1813 +, M 1814 + (In **BT** 1631-1810 (*gap 1637-1660*) 1813-1868 (L). **Cop** 1661-1812 (SPRS 14 *M 1661-1837 in Boyd.*

LEINTWARDINE. *– see Herefordshire.*

LILLESHALL. **OR** CMB 1653 + (*gap M 1660-1693*) (Inc). **BT** 1675-1924 (L). **Cop** C 1653-1831, M 1653-1660, 1693-1788, B 1653-1836 Ms (SBL), M 1788-1837 Mf (SBL Mf No 11). *See also St George's, Oakengates.*

LINLEY. **OR** C 1859 + (Inc). *MB at Broseley.*

LITTLE NESS. *– see Ness, Little.*

LITTLE WENLOCK. *– see Wenlock, Little.*

LLANFAIR WATERDINE. (*now in Radnorshire*). **OR** CMB 1593 + (*gap CMB 172. 1724, CB 1782-84*), Banns 1823 + (Inc). **BT** 1660 + (*gap 1778*) (HX). **Cop** CMB 1593-1812 Ms (SBL).

LLANYBLODWEL. **OR** CMB 1695 +, Banns 1755-1812, 1826 + (Inc). **BT** 1662-1850 (L). **Cop** CMB 1695-1812 (SPRS 3). *M 1599-1812 in Boyd. See als Moreton.*

LLANYBLODWEL – Smyrna Chapel (Ind). *f 1825.* **OR** ZC 1825-36 (PRO). **Cop** ZC 1825-1836 (SPRS Nonc. Vol). *Maiden name of mother given.*

LLANYMYNECH. (*Part Salop, part Montgomery*). **OR** CMB 1666 + (*gaps CMB 1767-73, M 1797-1813*) (Inc). **BT** 1662-1857 (L). **Cop** CMB 1666-1812 (SPRS 8). *M 1683-1812 in Boyd.*

LONG STANTON. *– see Stanton Long.*

LONGDON UPON TERN. **Peculiar. OR** CMB 1692 + (*gaps M 1754-58, 1810-14*) (Inc). **BT** 1809-1879 (L). *No BT's before 1809 traced.* **Cop** CMB 1692 1812 (SPRS 2). *M 1781-1812 in Boyd.*

LONGFORD. **OR** CMB 1558 + (*gap CMB 1603-54, 1699-1703, B 1791-1813*) (Inc). **BT** 1674-1868 (L). **Cop** CMB 1558-1812 Mf (SBL Mf No 5).

LONGNOR. **OR** CM 1586 + (Inc). *B at Leebotwood Churchyard.* **BT** 1669-181 (*gap 1694-1744, 1783-1804*) 1813-1854 (L) *now Hereford Dio.* **Cop** CMB 1586-1812 (SPRS 5). *M 1584-1812 in Boyd.*

LOPPINGTON. **OR** CMB 1654 +, Banns 1755-1815 (Inc). **BT** 1558-1810, 1813 1864 (L). **Cop** Extracts CB 1650-1748, M 1607-1742 Ptd (Shrop Arch Soc Ser I Vol VIII), C 1654-1858, M 1654-1841, B 1654-1891 Mf (SBL Mf No 6).

LORD'S HILL and SNAILBEACH (Bapt). *f 1818. Not at PRO. No informatio*

OUGHTON. *Formerly in Parish of Chetton.* OR C 1821 *(gap 1858-62),*
  M 1838 + *in Wheathill regs,* (Inc Wheathill), B 1804-5 *in Glazeley*
  regs, (Inc Glazeley). BT *on Chetton returns.*

UDFORD. OR CMB 1643 + *(gap CMB 1744-5),* Banns 1838-77 (Inc).
  BT 1660 + *(gap 1779)* (HX). Cop C 1643-1838, M 1643-1812, B 1643-1837
  Ms (SBL).

UDLOW. OR CMB 1558 +, Banns 1754-1788 (Inc). BT 1660 + (HXX).
  Cop CMB 1558-1812 (SPRS 13 and 14). *M 1558-1812 in Boyd.*

UDLOW CIRCUIT. (Wes). – *see Ludlow, Broad St Chapel; Clee Hill; Ditton*
  Priors.

UDLOW. Broad St Chapel (Wes). OR ZC 1815-37 (PRO). *Perhaps a Circuit*
  register. See also Clee Hill, Ditton Priors.

UDLOW. Old St Chapel (Prim Meth). OR ZC 1825-37 (PRO). *Almost*
  certainly a Circuit register.

UDLOW. Corve St and Old St (Ind). *f 1736.* OR ZC 1802-36, B 1826-36
  (PRO). Cop ZCB 1802-1836 (SPRS Nonc. Vol).

YDBURY, NORTH. OR CMB 1563 + *(few entries 1642-47)* (Inc). BT 1660 +
  (HX). Cop CMB 1563-1812 Ms (SBL).

YDHAM. OR CMB 1596 + *(gap CM 1660-90, B 1660-1679)* (Inc). BT 1638,
  1660 + (HX). Cop CMB 1596-1812 (SPRS 3). *M 1596-1812 in Boyd.*

YTHE HILL and DORRINGTON. (Ind). – *see Dorrington.*

MADELEY. OR CMB 1645 + *(gaps CMB 1690-95, CB 1719-1726, M 1719-1728)*
  (Inc). BT 1638, 1660 + *(gaps 1759, 1765, 1767, 1781, 1791)* (HX).
  Cop C 1645-1838, M 1645-1837, B 1645-1833 Ms (SBL). *See also*
  Ironbridge.

MADELEY. St Mary, High St (RC). *f 1784.* OR ZC 1843 +, M 1849 +,
  D 1853 + (St Mary's Cath. Ch. Shifnal).

MADELEY CIRCUIT. (Wes). *Madeley, (Fletcher Chapel) f.c. 1786.*
  Madeley Wood (f 1818), Coalbrookdale (f.c. 1786), Coalford (f.c.
  1825), Bridgnorth (f.c. 1793), Broseley (f.c. 1795), Dawley
  (f.c. 1825), Little Dawley (f.c. 1837), Lawley Bank (f.c. 1837),
  Horsehay (f.c. 1838), Much Wenlock (f date not known).
  Regs. Madeley, Coalbrookdale and Horsehay. OR C 1838 + (Circ. Supt.
  Manse, Ironbridge). Madeley Wood. OR ZC 1818-1837 (PRO).
  Broseley. OR ZC 1819-1837 (PRO). *No other regs known.*

MADELEY. (Meth New Conn). – *see* Dawley Green and Madeley Circuit.

MADELEY WOOD. (Wes). Madeley Circuit. *f 1818.* OR ZC 1818-37 (PRO).

MAESBURY (Ind). *f 1831. Not at PRO. No information.*

MAESBURY, Bethesda (Prim Meth). *f 1834* Oswestry Circuit. *See Oswestry*
  (Prim Meth).

MAINSTONE. OR CMB 1604 + *(gap CMB 1641-48).* BT 1638, 1660 + (HX).
  Cop CMB 1590-1812 Ms (SBL).

MARKET DRAYTON (DRAYTON IN HALES). OR CMB 1558 + (gap CMB 1657-1659), Banns 1754-89 (Inc). BT 1682-1876 (L). Cop C 1558-1831, M 1558-1837, B 1558-1841 Mf (SBL Mf Nos 3 and 4).

MARKET DRAYTON. (Ind). OR ZC 1776-1836 (PRO). Cop ZC 1776-1836 (SPRS Nonc. Vol).

MARTON-IN-CHIRBURY. (Ind). – see Chirbury, Marton Chapel.

MAWLEY HALL. St Mary (RC). OR ZC 1763-1824, M 1770-1811, D 1771-1814 (Parish Priest, Cleobury Mortimer – St Peter's, East Hamlet, Ludlow Cop ZC 1763-1824, M 1770-1811, D 1771-1814 (SPRS Nonc. Vol).

MELVERLEY. OR CMB 1723 + (gap M 1812), Banns 1754-1811 (Inc). BT 1662-1850 (L), 1694, 1751, 1780, 1837, 1844 (ST A – NLW) now Lichfield. Cop CMB 1723-1812 (SPRS 1 and 24). M 1724-1812 in Boyd.

MEOLE BRACE. OR CMB 1681 + (Inc). BT 1638, 1660 + (HX) now Lichfield Dio. Cop CMB (BT) 1660-1681, CB (PR) 1681-1812, M 1681-1837 (SPRS 18).

MIDDLE. OR CMB 1617 + (gap CMB 1645-1681), Banns 1800 + (Inc). BT 1632-1810, 1813-1852 (L). Cop CB 1541-1812, M 1541-1837 (SPRS 19 (Earlier register copied by SPRS now missing.) M 1541-1837 in Boyd.

MIDDLETON PRIORS. St Michael (RC). – see Ditton Priors.

MIDDLETON SCRIVEN. OR CMB 1728-1812 (SRO), C 1815 +, M 1813 +, B 1814 Banns 1754-1811, 1866 + (Inc). BT 1604, 31, 37, 38, 1660 + (gap 1784) (HX). Cop CMB 1728-1812 (SPRS 5). M 1734-1812 in Boyd.

MILSON. OR CM 1706 +, B 1678 + (gap M 1812-16), Banns 1756-1809 (SBL), BT 1638, 1660 + (HX). Cop CMB 1678-1812 (SPRS 16), M 1678-1848 (SRO M 1708-1812 in Boyd.

MINDTOWN or MYNDTOWN. OR C 1813-1829 (SRO), C 1830 +, M 1813-1829, 1854 +, B 1813 + (Inc). BT 1608, 1630, 31, 34, 38, 1660 + (HX). Cop CMB 1630-1812 (C of A), (copy of lost register), M 1813-1829 Mf (SRO and SLC). See also Norbury.

MINSTERLEY (Ind). – see Westbury, Minsterley Chapel.

MONK HOPTON. OR CMB 1698 (gap M 1835-39), Banns 1882 + (Inc). BT 1638, 1660 + (HX). Cop CMB 1698-1812 (SPRS 3). M 1700-1812 in Boyd.

MONTFORD. OR CMB 1661 +, Banns 1755-1812, 1824 + (Inc). BT 1630-1860 (L). Cop CMB 1662-1812, Extracts 1573-1664 (SPRS 7). (Extracts from lost register 1559-1664 from Ms Extracts by Wm. Mytton, but first of these extracts is 1573.) M 1573-1812 in Boyd.

MORE. CB 1569-1950, M 1569-1837 (gap CB 1807-9), Banns 1826-1951 (SRO). BT 1660 + (HX). Cop CMB 1570-1812 (SPRS 2 and 34), Banns 1826-1951 Mf (SRO and SLC). M 1574-1812 in Boyd.

ORETON. *Formed 1861 from parish of St Oswalds, Oswestry and Llanyblodwel.* **OR** CB 1823 +, M 1861 + (Inc), CB 1827-52 (in St Oswalds, Oswestry regs). **BT** *see Oswestry, St Oswald.*

ORETON CORBET. **OR** CMB 1580 +, Banns 1754-1812 (Inc). **BT** 1631-1881 (L). **Cop** CMB 1580-1812 (SPRS 1 and 39). *M 1580-1812 in Boyd.*

ORETON SAY. **OR** CMB 1690 +, Banns 1754-1812, 1823-77 (Inc). **BT** 1634-1888, *(gap 1635-1682)* (L). **Cop** CMB 1690-1812 (SPRS 8). *M 1690-1812 in Boyd.*

ORVILLE (MORVEILD). **OR** CMB 1562 + (Inc). **BT** 1638, 1660 + *(including Chapelry of Aston Eyre)* (HX). **Cop** CMB 1562-1812 Ms (SBL).

OUNSLOW. *- see Munslow.*

UCH WENLOCK. *(included Benthall to 1638).* **OR** CMB 1558 + *(few entries 1655-1660)* (Inc). **BT** 1660 + (HXX). **Cop** Extracts 1558-1698 Ptd (Shrop Arch Ser I Vol XI), CMB 1539-1560 Ptd (Harlesborne Tenby 1861), CMB (Benthall entries) 1558-1638 (Inc Benthall), CMB 1558-1812 Mf (SBL).

UCH WENLOCK. (Wes). *- see* **Madeley Circuit.**

UNSLOW (MOUNSLOW). **OR** CMB 1538 + *(gap CMB 1632-37)*, Banns 1754-1812, 1823 + (Inc). **BT** 1638, 1660 + (HX). **Cop** CMB 1538-1812 (SPRS 15). *M 1538-1812 in Boyd.*

YDDLE. *- see Middle.*

YNDTOWN. *- see Mindtown.*

ANTMAWR. (Ind). *f 1830. Not at PRO. No information.*

EEN SAVAGE. **OR** CMB 1575 +, Banns 1754-1812, 1846 + (Inc). **BT** 1638, 1660 + (HX). **Cop** CMB 1575-1812 (SPRS 17). *M 1575-1812 in Boyd.*

EEN SOLLARS. **OR** CMB 1656-1708 (SRO), CMB 1708 + (Inc). **BT** 1638, 1660 + *(gap 1761)* (HX). **Cop** CMB 1678-1812 (SPRS 16), M 1678-1851 Ms (SRO), CMB 1656-1708 Mf (SBL Mf No 1 and SLC). *M 1710-1851 in Boyd.*

EENTON. **OR** CMB 1558 + *(gap CMB 1810-13)*, Banns 1824 + (Inc). **BT** 1637, 1638, 1660 + *(gap 1788)* (HX). **Cop** CMB 1558-1805 (SPRS 3). *M 1558-1812 in Boyd.*

NESS GREAT or NESTRANGE. **OR** CMB 1589 + *(gap 1664-76)* (Inc). **BT** 1630-1810, 1813-1873 *(gap 1637-1659)* (L). **Cop** CB 1589-1812, M 1589-1837 (SPRS 20).

NESS, LITTLE. *Became Chapelry of Baschurch about 1740.* **OR** CMB 1605-1737 (Inc Baschurch). *Entries after 1737 in Baschurch regs.* **BT** 1660-1742 *(gap 1705-1717)* (L). *On Baschurch BT's after 1742.* **Cop** CMB 1605-1737 Ms (SBL).

NEW DALE (S of F). **Shrewsbury Monthly Meeting.** *Closed 1844. No regs known apart from Monthly Meeting registers.*

NEWPORT. **OR** CMB 1569 + *(gap CMB 1734-1750)*, Banns 1754-1838 (Inc). **BT** 1679-1885 (L). **Cop** CB 1569-1812, M 1569-1893 Ms (SBL).

NEWPORT, St Peter and St Paul (RC). *f 1650.* OR C 1785 + (Inc).
Cop C 1785-1846 (Cath R.S. 13), C 1785-1837 (SPRS. Nonc Vol).

NEWPORT. (Ind). *f 1765.* OR ZC 1814-37 (PRO).

NEWTOWN. OR CB 1779 +, M 1865 + (Inc). *Formed from Wem 1861.* BT 1673-1810, 1813-1873 *(gap 1776-1796)* (L). Cop CB 1779-1812 (SPRS 9 and 10).

NORBURY. *Chapelry of Mindtown.* OR C 1560-1948, M 1560-1837 *(gap 1813)*, B 1560-1781, Banns 1823-1932 (SRO), B 1813 + (Inc). BT 1638, 1660 + (HX). Cop CB 1560-1812, M 1560-1789 (SPRS 19), CM 1560-1837, B 156 1781 Mf (SRO and SLC).

NORTH LYDBURY. – *see Lydbury North.*

NORTON-IN-HALES. OR CMB 1575-1813 *(gap M 1737-1754),* Banns 1754-1812, 1824 + (SRO). BT 1681-1805, 1813-1855 (L). Cop CMB 1575-1880 (SPRS 18). *M 1573-1836 in Boyd.*

OAKENGATES, St Georges. – *see St Georges, Oakengates.*

OLDBURY. *(near Bridgnorth).* OR CMB 1582 + *(gap B 1813),* Banns 1835 + (Inc). BT 1631, 32, 37, 1660 + (HX). Cop CMB 1582-1812 (SPRS 16). *M 1583-1812 in Boyd.*

OLDBURY. *parish of Halesowen (Old Dissenting Chapel). Now in Worcestershire. See Worcs.*

ONIBURY. OR CMB 1577 + *(gap CB 1770-1773)* (Inc). BT 1660 + (HXX). Cop CB 1577-1812, M 1577-1836 (SPRS 18). *M 1577-1836 in Boyd.*

OSWESTRY, St Oswald. *Formerly St Asaph Dio. Now Lichfield.* OR CMB 1558 +, Banns 1843 +, CB for Moreton 1827-52 (Inc). BT 1662-1860 (L), 1662, 1670, 1674, 1679-80, 1683-6, 1690, 1722-7, 1731, 1735, 1751, 1763, 1833-6, 1861-7 (St A – NLW). Cop CMB 1558-1812 (SPRS 4-7). *M 1551-1812 in Boyd.*

OSWESTRY, Salop Rd (Bapt). *f 1806. Not at PRO. No information.*

OSWESTRY, Pant Chapel (Ind). *f 1822.* OR ZC 1829-36 (PRO).

OSWESTRY, Old Chapel (now Christchurch) (Ind). *f.c. 1651.* OR ZC 1779-1837, B 1813-37 (PRO). Cop ZCB 1780-1811 (SPRS Nonc. Vol).

OSWESTRY (Prim Meth). OR ZC 1830-37 (PRO). *Almost certainly a circuit register.*

OSWESTRY (Croesoswallt) ZION (SEION) WELSH CHAPEL. (Calv Meth). *f 1813.* OR ZC 1821-37 (PRO).

OSWESTRY. Carneddau Chapel (Calv Meth). *f 1797.* OR ZC 1813-37 (PRO *listed under Montgomery).*

OSWESTRY. (Wes). *Severn Valley Mission. Not attached to a circuit. Now closed.* OR ZC 1812-36 (PRO). Cop C 1812-1815 (SG).

PANT. (Ind). – *see Oswestry, Pant Chapel.*

PETTON. **OR** CMB 1695 $^+$ *(gaps CB 1767-73, 1810-13, M 1837)*, Banns 1758-1812, 1825 $^+$ (Inc). **BT** 1631-1862 (L). **Cop** CMB 1677-1812 Ms (SBL).

PITCHFORD. **OR** CMB 1558 $^+$ *(gap M 1754-56, 1834-38)*, Banns 1780-1812 (Inc). **BT** 1630-1878 (L) *now Hereford Dio.* **Cop** CMB 1558-1812 (SPRS 1 and 31), CMB 1543-1581 p/s (NLW Ms 9041 E). *M 1558-1812 in Boyd.*

PLOWDEN, St Francis (RC). **OR** C 1826 $^+$ (Inc). **Cop** C 1826-1837 (SPRS Nonc Vol).

PONTESBURY. **OR** CMB 1538 $^+$ *(gap B 1813-1886)*, Banns 1791-1985 (Inc). **BT** 1638, 1660 $^+$ (HXX). **Cop** CMB 1538-1812 (SPRS 12), M 1813-1882 Ms (SBL). *M 1538-1812 in Boyd.*

PONTESBURY. (Bapt). *f 1828.* **OR** Z 1828-37 (PRO).

PONTESBURY. (Ind). *f 1836. Not at PRO. No information.*

PREES. **Peculiar** *Prebend of Prees.* **OR** CB 1597 $^+$ *(gap B 1654-1661)*, M 1654 $^+$, Banns 1756-1803 (Inc). **BT** 1669-1809 *(gaps 1673-4, 1678-80, 1748-9)* (LCL), 1810-75 (L). **Cop** C 1597-1837, M 1654-1837, B 1597-1648, 1653-1813 Ts (SBL). *See also Whixhall.*

PREES GREEN. (Prim Meth). **Prees Circuit.** *Now* **Wem and Press Green Circuit.** **OR** ZC 1824-37 (PRO). *Almost certainly reg of Prees Prim Meth Circuit.*

PREES. Whixhall Chapel (Ind). *– see Whixhall.*

PREES. (Ind). *f 1800. Not at PRO. No information.*

PRESTON GOBALDS. **OR** CMB 1601 $^+$ *(gap M 1750-55)*, Banns 1755-1812 (Inc). **BT** 1630-1868 (L). **Cop** CB 1560-1812, M 1560-1837 (SPRS 21), Extracts CMB 1560-1622 Ptd (Shrop Arch Soc Ser 2 Vol VIII).

PRESTON GOBALDS, Zions Hill. (Ind). **OR** ZC 1827-36 (PRO).

PRESTON ON THE WEALD MOORS (or WILD MOORS). **OR** CMB 1693 $^+$ *(gap M 1833-39)* (Inc). **BT** 1668-1868 (L). **Cop** CB 1693-1812, M 1693-1833 Mf (SBL).

PRIORS DITTON. *– see Ditton Priors.*

PRIORS LEE. Chapel to Shifnal. **OR** C 1813 $^+$, M 1837 $^+$, B 1867 $^+$ (Inc). *Entries prior to 1813 at Shifnal).* **BT** 1808-1880 (L).

PULVERBATCH. **OR** CMB 1542 $^+$ *(gap M 1812)* (SBL). **BT** 1638, 1660 $^+$ (HX). **Cop** CMB 1542-1812 Ms I (SG) and Ts (SBL), C 1542-1812, M 1542-1848, B 1541-1887 Ms (SRO).

QUATFORD. **Peculiar** *Deanery of Bridgnorth.* **OR** CMB 1602 $^+$ *(gap M 1811-14, 1835-38) (1602-1714 out of order)* (Inc). **BT** 1635 (L), 1636-1811 (B.M. Add Ms 28740), 1813-1836 (L). **Cop** CB 1577-1812, M 1577-1835 Ms (SBL), CMB Extracts 1636-1811 Ms (SG). *M (BT) 1665-1700 in Boyd.*

QUATT MALVERN and QUATT JARVIS. **OR** CMB 1672 $^+$ (Inc). **BT** 1662-1871 (L). **Cop** CMB 1672-1812 Ms (SBL).

RATLINGHOPE. **OR** C 1813-1898, M 1755-1837, B 1813-1878 (SRO), C 1794-
1813 (*allegedly with Inc, but not seen in 1963 inspection*).
BT 1638, 1660 + (HX). **Cop** CB 1794-1813, M 1755-1813 (SPRS 5),
CB 1813-37, M 1755-1837 Mf (SRO and SLC).

RICHARDS CASTLE. *Now part Hereford and part Salop – see Herefordshire.*

RODINGTON. **OR** CMB 1678-1738 (SRO), CMB 1739 + (*gap M 1755*) (Inc),
1679-84, 1686-8 *in High Ercall regs. Separate lists* (Inc High
Ercall). BT 1631-1868 (*gap 1638-1653*) (L). **Cop** CMB 1678-1837
(SPRS 21), CMB 1678-1812 Ms (SBL), CMB 1678-1738 Mf (SRO and SLC).

RUITON. – *see Ryton.*

RUSHBURY. **OR** CMB 1538 + (*gaps CMB 1545-60, 1574-76, 1647-50, 1678-84*)
(Inc). BT 1660 + (HX). **Cop** CMB 1538-1812 Ms (SBL).

RUYTON-IN-THE-ELEVEN-TOWNS. **OR** CMB 1719 +, Banns 1760-1812, 1823-76
(Inc). BT 1630-1860 (*gap 1636-1659*) (L). **Cop** CMB 1719-1809 (SPRS 5)
M 1719-1812 in Boyd.

RUYTON-IN-THE-ELEVEN-TOWNS (S of F). – *see Preface.*

RUYTON-IN-THE-ELEVEN-TOWNS (Ind). *f 1833. Not at PRO. No information.*

RYTON (RUITON By BECKBURY). **OR** CM 1663-80 (*loose leaves from a lost
reg*), B 1678-1717 (*defective*), CMB beginning 1724 and ending variou
dates in 18th century – very defective, C 1770 +, M 1755 +, B 1813
Banns 1755-1812 (Inc). BT 1672-1868 (L). **Cop** C 1678-1839, M 1678-
1864, B 1678-1872 Ms (SBL).

ST GEORGES, OAKENGATES. *Parish formed 1861 from Shifnal, Lilleshall
and Wrockwardine Wood.* **OR** C 1806 +, M 1838 +, B 1813 +, Banns 1889
(Inc). *No B T 's.*

ST GEORGES, OAKENGATES. (Wes). **Wellington Circuit,** *now* **Oakengates** *and*
Shifnal Circuit. OR C 1830 + (Circuit Supt.).

ST MARTINS. **OR** CMB 1601 + (Inc). BT 1663-1849 (L), 1679, 1685, 1731,
1763 (St A – NLW) *now Lichfield.* **Cop** CB 1579-1812, M 1579-1837
(SPRS 8). *M 1579-1837 in Boyd.*

SELATTYN. **OR** CMB 1556 + (Inc). BT 1662-1860 (L), 1755-6, 1861-5, 1874
(St A – NLW) *now Lichfield.* **Cop** CMB 1556-1812 (SPRS 1 and 58),
Extracts CMB 1557-1841 (Shrop Arch Soc Ser 2 Vol XI). *M 1559-1812
in Boyd.*

SHAWBURY. **OR** CMB 1561 + (*gap CMB 1597-1618*), Banns 1754-1804, 1812 +
(Inc). BT 1630-1810, 1813-1853 (L). **Cop** Extracts 1561-1711 Ptd
(Shrop Arch Soc I, VII), C 1551-1844, M 1551-1837, B 1551-1862 Mf
(SBL).

SHEINTON. **OR** CMB 1711 + (*gap M 1834-37*), Banns 1754-1812 (Inc).
BT 1637-1810, 1813-1866 (*gap 1638-1662*) (L) *now Hereford.*
Cop CMB 1658-1812 (SPRS 2 and 28). *M 1658-1812 in Boyd.*

IELVE. OR CB 1584-1811, M 1584-1838 *(gap M 1742-1754)* (SRO), CB 1813 +,
M 1838 + (Inc). BT 1598, 99, 1605, 1614, 20, 1638, 1660 + (HX).
Cop CB 1584-1812, M 1584-1837 Ms (SBL), CB 1584-1811, M 1584-1838
Mf (SRO and SLC).

IERIFFHALES. − *transferred from Staffs.* OR CMB 1557 + (Inc). BT 1670-
1809, 1813-1859 *(gap 1679-1693)* (L). Cop CMB 1557-1812 (SPRS 7).
M 1551-1812 in Boyd.

IIFNAL. OR CMB 1678-1812, Banns 1754-1806, 1824-1938, M. Lic. 1759-
1923 (SRO). BT 1672-1868 (L). Cop CB 1678-1812, M 1678-1837 Ms
(SBL), CMB 1678-1812 Mf (SRO and SLC), CB 1813-1842 Mf (SBL). *See
also Priors Lee and St George's, Oakengates.*

HIFNAL. (Wes). **Oakengates and Shifnal Circuit.** OR C 1837 + (Manse,
Shifnal).

HIFNAL. Ashton St (Bapt). OR Z 1811-36 (PRO).

HIFNAL. (Meth New Connexion). − *see* **Dawley Green and Madeley Circuit.**

HINETON. − *see Sheinton.*

HIPTON. OR CB 1538-1812, M 1538-1807 *(gap CMB 1648-1656)* (SRO),
CMB 1813 + (Inc). BT 1603, 08, 20, 22, 23, 29, 38, 40, 1660 + *(gaps
1794, 97, 1804)* (HX). Cop CMB 1538-1812 (SPRS 1 and 22), CMB 1538-
1648 (SRO). *M 1538-1812 in Boyd.*

HRAWARDINE. OR CMB 1645 +, Banns 1759-1812 + (Inc). BT 1630, 31, 38,
1660 + *(gaps 1794, 95)* (HX), 1851-1864 (L) *now Lichfield Dio.*
Cop CMB 1645-1812 Ptd (Shrop Arch Soc Ser 2 Vol VII) Ms (SBL).

HREWSBURY ABBEY. Holy Cross. OR CMB 1541 + *(gap B 1650-78)*, Banns
1795 + (Inc). BT 1630-1880 *(gap 1635-1659)* (L). Cop Extracts 1542-
1854 Ptd (Shrop Arch Soc Ser I Vol I), C 1541-1853, M 1541-1591,
1662-1812, B 1541-1591, 1662-1812 Ms (SBL), M 1813-1858, B 1813-
1837 Mf (SBL Mf No 15).

SHREWSBURY. St Alkmund. OR CMB 1559 + (Inc). BT 1630-1871 *(gap 1637-
1658)* (L). Cop C 1559-1858, M 1559-1837, B 1559-1854 Ms (SBL).

SHREWSBURY. St Chad. OR C 1616-1874, M 1616-1895, B 1616-1922, Banns
1823-1898 (SRO). BT 1631-1855 *(gap 1638-1658)*(L). Cop CMB 1616-1812
(SPRS 15, 16, 17). *M 1616-1812 in Boyd.*

SHREWSBURY. St George. OR CM 1837 +, Banns 1879 + (Inc). BT 1841-
1864 (L).

SHREWSBURY. St Giles. OR B 1825 + (Inc) *used by Shrewsbury people who
wanted private funeral. Used regularly from 1836. Parish formed
1857.*

SHREWSBURY. St Julian. OR CMB 1559 + (Inc). BT 1630-1872 *(gap 1637-
1662)* (L). Cop Extracts CMB 1559- 1812 Ptd (Shrop Arch Soc Ser I
Vol X), C 1559-1833, M 1559-1837, B 1559-1840 Ms (SBL).

SHREWSBURY. St Mary. **Peculiar** *Royal Free Chapel.* **OR** CM 1584-1812,
B 1584-1839 (to 1856 at St Michael's) (*gaps CB 1732-55, M 1732-
54*), Banns 1803-40, 1901-44 (SRO), CM 1813 + (Inc). **BT** 1663-1755
described as *"Files of Parchment Membranes"* (SRO with Shrewsbury
St Mary deposited regs), 1813-1840 (L), 1839-1840 described as
"loose parchment sheets" (SRO), 1853-1856 (L). **Cop** CMB 1584-
1812 (SPRS 12), CM 1584-1812, B 1584-1839, Banns 1803-40 Mf (SRO
and SLC), C 1813-1847, M 1813-1837, B 1813-1848 Mf (SBL). *M 1584-
1812 in Boyd.*

SHREWSBURY, St Michael. **OR** B 1830-1856 (SRO), CM 1854 + (Inc). *Closed
for B.* **Cop** B 1830-1856 Mf (SRO and SLC).

SHREWSBURY. St Mary (RC). *f before 1720.* **OR** C 1775 + (Inc). **Cop** C
1775-1837 (SPRS Nonc Vol).

SHREWSBURY (S of F). **Shropshire Monthly Meeting.** – *see Preface.*

SHREWSBURY. Claremont St (Bapt). *f 1620.* **OR** Z 1766-1836 (PRO).
Cop Z 1766-1808 (SPRS Nonc Vol).

SHREWSBURY. High St (Pres. now Unitarian). *f 1662.* **OR** C 1692-1837
(PRO). *Includes C for Wem.* Z 1692-1962, M 1842-1897 (Ch Sec).
Cop C 1692-1812 (SPRS Nonc Vol).

SHREWSBURY. (Meth New Connexion). **OR** ZC 1834-37 (PRO). *Almost
certainly a circuit register.* **Cop** ZC 1834-7 Mf (SBL).

SHREWSBURY. Swan Hill Chapel (Ind). *f 1767 by secession from High St.*
OR ZC 1767-1857, B 1767-1854 (PRO). **Cop** ZCB 1767-1812 (SPRS Nonc
Vol).

SHREWSBURY. Bayston Hill (Ind). *f 1834. Not at PRO. No information.*

SHREWSBURY. Longden (Ind). *f 1836. No regs known. Not at PRO or
Ch Sec.*

SHREWSBURY. Castle Court (Prim Meth). **OR** ZC 1822-37 (PRO) (*almost
certainly a Circuit Register*). **Cop** ZC 1822-1837 Mf (SBL).

SHREWSBURY CIRCUIT. – *see Shrewsbury St John's Chapel. A church also
at Treflach Wood, but no other regs known.*

SHREWSBURY. St John's Chapel (Wes). **Shrewsbury Circuit.** **OR** ZC 1812-
37 (PRO), (*perhaps the register of the Shrewsbury Circuit*).
Cop ZC 1812-37 Mf (SBL).

SHREWSBURY. Hills Lane Ch. afterwards St Davids (Calv Meth). **OR** C 181
1829 (NLW).

SIBDON CARWOOD. **OR** CMB 1582 + (*gap M 1835-38*) (Inc). **BT** 1598, 1605,
1614, 22, 30, 34, 1660 + (HX). **Cop** CMB 1582-1812 (SPRS 2 and 20).
M 1583-1812 in Boyd.

SIDBURY. **OR** CMB 1560 + (*gap CMB 1623-58, 1717-31*) (Inc). **BT** 1599,
1604, 08, 14, 23, 24, 37, 38, 1660 + (*gaps 1672, 78, 1742*) (H).
Cop CMB 1560-1812 (SPRS 1). *M 1560-1812 in Boyd.*

SILVINGTON. **OR** CMB 1716-1837 *(gap CMB 1749-52, M 1812-38)* (SRO), CB 1813+, M 1838+ (Inc). **BT** 1660+ *(gaps 1761, 1781)* (HX). **Cop** CMB 1716-1812 Mf (SBL and SLC).

SMETHCOTE. **OR** CMB 1609+, Banns 1754-1811 (Inc). **BT** 1630-1868 (L) *now Hereford Dio.* **Cop** CMB 1609-1811 (SPRS 1 and 26). *M 1613-1812 in Boyd.*

SNAILBEACH. (Bapt). – *see Lord's Hill.*

SNEAD. *County Montgomery but now with Lydham.* **OR** CMB 1618+ *(gap B 1812-15)*, Banns 1758-1802, 1823+ (Inc). **BT** 1605, 08, 14, 31, 1660+, (1754-1812 unchecked) (H).

STANTON LACY. **OR** CMB 1561+, Banns 1754-1800, 1837+ (Inc). **BT** 1638, 1660+ (HX). **Cop** CMB 1561-1812 (SPRS 4). *M 1561-1812 in Boyd.*

STANTON, LONG. **OR** CMB 1568-1734 (fragment), CMB 1734+ *(gap M 1754-1813)* (Inc). **BT** 1638, 1660+ *(gap 1808)* (H). **Cop** CMB 1568-1812 Ms (SBL), M 1568-1836 Ms (SRO).

STANTON on HINE HEATH. **OR** CMB 1655+ *(CMB 1655-80 in bad state)* *(gap M 1751-54, C 1798-1813)*, Banns 1754-1812 (Inc). **BT** 1636-1888 *(gap 1636-1655)* (L). **Cop** CMB 1655-1861 Mf (SBL Mf No 5).

STAPLETON. **OR** CMB 1635-1812 *(gap CMB 1747)* *(1635-1746 delapidated)* (SRO), CMB 1813+ (Inc). **BT** 1630-1810, 1813-1853 (L) *now Hereford Dio.* **Cop** CMB 1546-1812 (SPRS 1 and 35). *M 1546-1812 in Boyd.*

STIRCHLEY. **OR** CMB 1658-1923 (SRO). **BT** 1679-1876 (L). **Cop** CMB 1658-1812 (SPRS 5), CMB 1658-1837 Mf (SRO and SLC).

STOCKTON. **OR** CMB 1558+, Banns 1754-1812 (Inc). **BT** 1664-1811, 1813-1878 (L). **Cop** CMB 1558-1837 Mf (SBL Mf No 8).

STOKE ON TERN. **OR** CMB 1654-1724, C 1837+, M 1813+, B 1877+ (Inc), CB 1717-1812 *(almost completely illegible)* (SRO). *Other registers destroyed 1881.* **BT** 1668-1810, 1813-1890 (L). **Cop** Extracts M 1654-1700 Ms (SG), Extracts CB 1717-1812 (SRO). *M 1662-1699 in Boyd.*

STOKE ST MILBOROUGH (MILBURGH). **OR** CMB 1654+ *(gap CMB 1690-92, 1735-49, CB 1776, M 1812)*, Banns 1754-1812 (Inc). *Includes Heath entries.* **BT** 1664+ *(gaps 1668, 1672)* (H). **Cop** CB 1654-1812, M 1654-1837 (SPRS 19).

STOKESAY. **OR** CMB 1558+ *(gap CMB 1642-1729, M 1729-1754, 1 entry 1652, 1 entry 1654)* (Inc). **BT** 1660+ *(gap 1784)* (HX). **Cop** CB 1558-1812, M 1558-1837 (SPRS 17). *M 1561-1837 in Boyd.*

STOTTESDON. **OR** CMB 1565+ (CMB Farlow to 1754, CB to 1780), Banns 1754-1807, 1824-49 (Inc). **BT** 1660+ (HXX). **Cop** CMB 1565-1813 Ms (SBL). *See also Farlow.*

STOWE. **OR** MB 1576-1640, 1663-1723, M 1755-1811 (SBL), CB 1724-1807, 1813+, M 1724, 1813-35, 1838+, Banns 1825+ (Inc). **BT** 1603, 22, 30, 38, 1660+ (HX). **Cop** CMB 1576-1811 Ms (SBL).

SUTTON by SHREWSBURY. **OR** C 1769 +, M 1838 +, B 1847 + *(1 M for 1756, gap C 1809-13)* (Inc Meole Brace). *No B T 's traced. Hereford Dio.* **Cop** Extracts CMB 1709-1868 Ptd (Shrop Arch Soc Ser 4, Vol V), C 1709-1868, M 1709-1870, B 1709-1853 Ms (SBL).

SUTTON MADDOCK. **OR** CMB 1559 + *(gap 1646-79)*, Banns 1823-74, Banns for Kemberton 1823-34 (Inc). **BT** 1673-1878 (L). **Cop** CMB 1559-1812 Ms (SBL).

TASLEY. **OR** CMB 1563 + *(gap CMB 1777-1813, B 1813-15)* (Inc). **BT** 1599, 1608, 14, 20, 23, 31, 34, 37, 38, 41, 1660 + (HX). **Cop** CMB 1563-1813 (SPRS 1). *M 1564-1812 in Boyd.*

TIBBERTON. **OR** CMB 1719 +, *(gap M 1812-43)* (Inc). **BT** 1681-1810, 1813-1856 (L). **Cop** CMB 1719-1812 (SPRS 13). *M 1719-1753 in Boyd.*

TILSTOCK. *formed from Whitchurch in 1844.* **OR** CB 1836 +, M 1846 + (Inc) CB 1797-1812 *(separate entries for Tilstock in Whitchurch Regs).* **BT** 1836-1868 (L). **Cop** CB 1797-1812 from Whitchurch Regs (Inc Tilstock).

TITTENLEY. *Transf. from Cheshire 1895. – see Cheshire.*

TONG. **OR** CMB 1630 + *(gap M 1812-14, B 1812-17)* (Inc). **BT** 1614-1848 (L **Cop** CMB 1630-1812 (SPRS 4). *M 1630-1812 in Boyd.*

TREFLACH WOOD. (Wes). *f 1833. Prob. in* **Shrewsbury Circuit** *before 1837 Now in* **Llanymynech Circuit.** *No regs known.*

TREFONEN. *formed 1842 from Oswestry.* **OR** CB 1821 +, M 1848 + (Inc).

TRELYSTAN. *– see Woolstonmynd.*

TUGFORD. **OR** CMB 1787 + (Inc). **BT** 1638, 1660 + (HX). **Cop** CMB 1755-1812 Ms (SBL).

UFFINGTON. **OR** CMB 1578 + *(gap M 1813)* (Inc). **BT** 1631-1868 (L). **Cop** CMB 1578-1812 (SPRS 5), C 1813-1944, M 1813-37 Ms (SRO). *M 1581-1812 in Boyd.*

UPPINGTON. **OR** CMB 1650 + *(gap M 1830-40)*, Banns 1754-1812 (Inc). **BT** 1813-1874 (L). *Earlier B T 's perhaps bundled in error with Uffington.* **Cop** CMB 1650-1812 (SPRS 4), Extracts CMB 1651-1823 Ptd (Shrop Arch Soc Ser I, Vol V). *M 1676-1812 in Boyd.*

UPTON CRESSETT. **OR** CB 1813 +, M 1814 + *(gap M 1835-40)* (Inc). **BT** 1637 1638, 1660 + (HX). **Cop** CMB 1765-1812 Ms (SBL).

UPTON MAGNA. **OR** CMB 1563 +, Banns 1824 + (Inc). **BT** 1630-1877 (L). **Cop** Extracts CMB 1567-1792 (Shrop Arch Soc Ser I, Vol 5), CB 1563-1812, M 1563-1753 Ms (SBL).

UPTON PARVA. *– see Waters Upton.*

ATERS UPTON or UPTON PARVA. OR CMB 1547 + (gap M 1811-1815), Banns 1765-1811, 1823 + (Inc), B 1679-84, 1686-8 in High Ercall regs (separate lists) (Inc High Ercall). BT 1674-1865 (L). Cop CMB 1547-1815 (SPRS 13). M 1547-1815 in Boyd.

ELCH HAMPTON. – see Welshampton.

ELLINGTON. All Saints. OR CMB 1626 + (gaps C 1806-13, M 1674-1701, B 1677-1701, 1807-12), Banns 1754-1805, 1897 + (Inc), Banns 1823-1888 believed destroyed. BT 1659-1884 (L). Cop C 1628-1700, M 1626-1679, B 1626-1677 I (SPRS 21), C 1628-1812, M 1626-1674, 1712-1812, B 1626-1667, 1701-1812 Ts (SBL).

ELLINGTON. Christchurch. OR CMB 1839 + (Inc).

ELLINGTON. St Patrick, King St (RC). f 1830. OR ZCMDB 1853 +, Confirm. 1858 + (Inc).

ELLINGTON. Constitution Hill (Free Bapt). f 1807. No regs known. Not at PRO or Ch. Sec.

ELLINGTON. Tanbank Chapel (Ind). OR ZC 1829-37 (PRO).

ELLINGTON CIRCUIT. (Wes). – see Wellington, Wrockwardine Wood, Wombridge, St George's,Oakengates.

ELLINGTON. (Wes). OR ZC 1827-35 (PRO). Perhaps a Circuit register.

ELSHAMPTON. OR CMB 1713 + (gap CMB 1766-1772) (Inc). BT 1636-1856 (L). Cop C 1772-1843, M 1772-1836, B 1772-1864 Mf (SBL Mf No 6).

EM. OR CMB 1583-1693, 1695 + (gap M 1746-1754), Banns 1754 + (Inc). BT 1659-1810, 1813-1881 (L). Cop CMB 1583-1812 (SPRS 9 and 10). M 1576-1812 in Boyd.

EM. Cripple St (now Market St) (Bapt). f 1815. OR Z 1823-36 (PRO).

EM. Chapel St (Ind). f 1775. OR C 1785-1836 (PRO). Cop C 1785-1836 (SPRS Nonc Vol).

EM. Noble St (Pres). f 1662. Closed 1874 and congregation united with Chapel St Ind. OR C 1755-1836 (PRO). Cop 1755-1814 (SPRS Nonc Vol). Some C in Shrewsbury High St regs.

WENLOCK, LITTLE. OR CMB 1689 +, Banns 1754-88, 1823 + (Inc). BT 1638, 1660 + (HXX). Cop CB 1689-1812, M 1689-1837 Ms (SBL).

ENLOCK, MUCH. – see Much Wenlock.

WENTNOR. OR C 1662-1915, M 1662-1837, B 1662-1878, Banns 1754-1812 (SRO), Banns 1824-1878 (Inc). BT 1638, 1660 + (HX). Cop CMB 1662-1812 Ms (SBL), CMB 1662-1837 Mf (SRO and SLC).

WESTANSWICK. (Ind). f 1805. Not at PRO. No information.

WESTBURY. OR CMB 1637 +, Banns 1754-1813 (Inc). BT 1638, 1660 + (HXX). Cop CMB 1637-1812 (SPRS 12). M 1637-1812 in Boyd.

WESTBURY. Minsterley Chapel (Ind). f 1795. OR ZC 1806-1837 (PRO). Cop ZC 1806-1837 (SPRS Nonc. Vol).

WEST FELTON. – see Felton, West.

WESTON UNDER RED CASTLE. (Weston and Whixill). **OR** CMB 1565 + (Inc).
BT 1679-1810, 1813-1880 (L). **Cop** CMB 1565-1813 (SPRS 11). *M 1574-1754 in Boyd.*

WHEATHILL. **OR** CMB 1573 + (*gap CB 1758-60, 1811-13*), Banns 1754-1812 (Inc). **BT** 1622, 30, 34, 37, 38, 1661 + (*gaps 1672, 1736, 1738, 1754*) (H). **Cop** CMB 1573-1812 Ms (SBL).

WHITCHURCH with TILSTOCK. **OR** C 1635+ M 1627+ (*gap 1744-54*) B 1630+ (Tilstock CB listed separately 1797-1812) Banns 1754-1782, 1798-1811, 1813-1820, 1845+ (Inc). **BT** 1674-1858 (*gap 1692-1701*) (L) **Cop** C 1635-1797, M 1627-1776, B 1630-1797 (SBL and Ms SG). See also Tilstock.

WHITCHURCH. Dodington Chapel (Ind). *f 1789.* **OR** ZC 1807-1837 (PRO).

WHITCHURCH. Broughall Chapel (Ind). – *see Broughall.*

WHITCHURCH. Dodington Chapel (Pres). *f 1672.* **OR** C 1708-24, 1743-1836, B 1746-77, 1823-36 (PRO). **Cop** CB 1708-1812 (SPRS Nonc. Vol).

WHITCHURCH (Wes). **OR** ZC 1813-37 (PRO). *Probably a Circuit register including Dudleston Heath and other churches. No other register known.*

WHITE LADIES (RC). **OR** B 1816-1844 (Inc St Mary's Brewood). **Cop** B 1816-1844 (SPRS 3). *M.I's from 1669.* (Inc St Mary's Brewood).

WHITTINGTON. **OR** CMB 1591 + (Inc), *Z 1808-64 in Halston Register 1686-1889.* **BT** 1682-3 (St A-NLW), 1662-1840 (L). **Cop** CMB 1591-1812 (SPRS 2). *M 1591-1800 in Boyd.*

WHITTINGTON. Preeshenlle Chapel (Ind). *f 1831.* **OR** ZC 1832-36 (PRO).

WHITTINGTON, Frankton (Ind). **OR** C 1835-37 (PRO).

WHITTON. **OR** C 1825 +, M 1840 +, B 1856 + (Inc).

WHIXHALL. **Peculiar** *of Prees. Chapelry of Prees.* **OR** CB 1758 +, M 1847 + Banns 1847 + (Inc). **BT** 1756-1812 (*no gaps*) (LCL) 1813-1881 (L). **Cop** CB 1758-1812 Mf (SBL Mf No 18).

WHIXHALL. (Ind). *f 1790.* **OR** ZC 1805-37 (*PRO cat. under Prees, Whixhall Chapel*). **Cop** ZC 1805-23 (SPRS Nonc. Vol).

WILCOT. (Ind). *f 1834. No regs known. Not at PRO or Ch. Sec.*

WILLEY. **OR** C 1644 +, M 1665 +, B 1666 + (*gap MB 1812*) (Inc). **BT** 1600, 1605, 08, 14, 20, 22, 26, 38, 40, 1660 + (HXX). **Cop** CMB 1644-1812 (SPRS 11). *M 1665-1812 in Boyd.*

WISTANSTOW. **OR** CMB 1687 + (*gap C 1800-1813*), Banns 1754-1809, 1823 + (Inc). **BT** 1660 + (HXX). **Cop** CMB 1638, CB 1661-1812, M 1661-1831 (SPRS 17). *M 1638-1837 in Boyd.*

WITHINGTON. **OR** C 1591 +, MB 1592 + (*gap B 1712*) (Inc). **BT** 1631-1868 (L). **Cop** CMB 1591-1812 (SPRS 5). *M 1591-1812 in Boyd.*

WOLLASTON, GREAT. *Chapel to Alberbury.* **OR** 1829 + (Inc).

WOLLERTON. (Ind). *f 1800. – see Hodnet.*

WOMBRIDGE. **OR** CB 1721 $^+$, M 1802 $^+$ *(gap C 1775-82, B 1775-1793)*,
Banns 1855 $^+$ (Inc). **BT** 1809-1836, 1856-1868 (L). *No earlier BT's
known.* **Cop** CB 1721-1812, M 1802-1812 Ms (SBL).

WOMBRIDGE . Coal Pit Bank Chapel (Wes). **OR** ZC 1817-37 (PRO).

WOOLSTASTON. **OR** CMB 1601 $^+$ *(gap M 1835-38)*, Banns 1755-1812 (Inc).
BT 1598, 1605, 20, 22, 30, 40, 1660 $^+$ (HXX). **Cop** CMB 1601-1811
(SPRS 1). *M 1607-1812 in Boyd.*

WOOLSTONMYND (or TRELYSTAN). *Chapelry in parish of Worthen.* **OR** – *see
Worthen.* **BT** 1638, 1660 $^+$, (HXX).

WOORE. *(formerly in parish of Mucklestone, Staffs).* **OR** C 1831 $^+$,
MB 1842 $^+$ (Inc). *No BT's. See Mucklestone, Staffs.*

WORFIELD. **OR** CMB 1562-1894 *(gap M 1725-33)*.Z 1794-1812, Banns 1898-
1924 (SRO). **BT** 1655-1871 (L). **Cop** CMB 1562-1812 I Ts (SG) Ms (SBL).

WORTHEN. **OR** CMB 1558 $^+$ *(gap CMB 1642-59)*, Banns 1823-38 (Inc).
BT 1660 $^+$ (HXX). **Cop** CMB 1558-1812 (SPRS 11). *M 1558-1812 in Boyd.*
See also Woolstonmynd.

WROCKWARDINE. **OR** CMB 1591 $^+$ *(gap CMB 1742-45, CB 1758-60)* (Inc).
BT 1630-1805, 1810-1895 (L). **Cop** CMB 1591-1812 (SPRS 8). *M 1592-
1812 in Boyd.*

WROCKWARDINE. The French Chapel (Wes). **OR** ZC 1827-37 (PRO).

WROCKWARDINE WOOD. **OR** CB 1833 $^+$, Banns 1847 $^+$ (Inc). **BT** 1833-1856 (L).
See also St George's Oakengates.

WROCKWARDINE WOOD. Nabb Chapel (Wes). **(Wrockwardine Wood Circuit.** *Now*
Wellington Circuit). **OR** ZC 1818-37 (PRO), ZC 1818 $^+$ (Wellington
Circuit Supt.)

WROCKWARDINE WOOD. (Prim Meth). **OR** ZC 1822-37 (PRO). *(Almost certainly
a circuit register.)*

WROXETER. **OR** CMB 1613 $^+$ *(gap CMB 1680-1700, C 1747-1772, M 1747-54,
B 1747-1813)* (Inc). **BT** 1631-1810, 1813-1868 (L). **Cop** CMB 1613-1812
(SPRS 11). *M 1613-1812 in Boyd.*

WARWICKSHIRE

ACKNOWLEDGMENTS

The editor gratefully acknowledges the assistance of the following in compiling this section:-

Mr. A.C. Wood, County Archivist of Warwickshire and his staff for supplying considerable information on parish registers and other records at the County and Diocesan Record Offices and for giving facilities for the examination of them, for supplying details of Catholic registers in Church hands and for offering useful comments and suggestions for the Warwickshire parish list and for the County preface; Revd. H.G. Holbeche for assistance with the County preface; Messrs V.H. Woods and W.A. Taylor successive Librarians of Birmingham Reference Library for supplying information and dealing with queries, and the latter for reading through the County preface and offering useful criticism; Mr. C.M. Turner for, over a prolonged period, examining and listing the original deposited registers and for dealing with numerous queries; Dr. Levi Fox, Director, Shakespeare's Birthplace Trust for supplying detailed information and for reading through the County preface, offering useful comments and suggestions; Mrs. D. Bramwell for listing details of registers still in ecclesiastical hands which have been surveyed; Mr. E.H. Sargeant County Archivist of Worcestershire for lending a copy of the detailed lists of Bishop's transcripts and for dealing with numerous queries; Mr. A.J. Coker for listing the Lichfield Bishop's transcripts, for dealing with queries and for offering comments and suggestions for the preface; Mr. F.M. Barrell for checking the copies at the Society of Genealogists; Mr. F.L. Leeson for listing surrendered Nonconformist registers; Revd. J.D. McEvilly, Archivist of the Catholic Archdiocese of Birmingham for supplying information on Catholic Registers and for reading the draft of the Catholic section of the preface and offering useful comments and suggestions; Mr. M.B.S. Exham, Diocesan Registrar of Lichfield for supplying information on Marriage Licences and dealing with various queries; Mr. D.W. Parkes and Mr. A.E. Marshall for making useful comments and suggestions for the preface, and the former for examining some Methodist records; Mr. J.R. Cunningham of the Church of Jesus Christ of Latter Day Saints and Edward Milligan, Archivist at Friends' House, Euston, for granting access to their records; numerous Librarians, Catholic Parish Priests, Methodist Circuit Superintendents, Baptist and Congregationalist Ministers and Secretaries, and the Secretaries of Nonconformist Unions, Associations and Districts for supplying information.

GENERAL INFORMATION

Record Repositories (*See also list on page xx*)

A.   – *Warwick County Record Office, Shire Hall, Warwick.*
(*Hours Mon-Fri 9 - 1, 2 - 5.30, Sat 9 - 12.30*)
This holds microfilms of the Bishop's Transcripts for the
Diocese of Worcester, of a number of Parish Registers and of
all Roman Catholic Registers.

A. B.   – *Birmingham Diocesan Record Office, Shire Hall, Warwick.*
(*Hours as Warwick County Record Office above*)
Set up at the Shire Hall, Warwick, 1st April, 1957, by agreement between The Lord Bishop of Birmingham and the Warwickshire County Council, for those parishes within the Diocese
of Birmingham which are also within the present Administrative County of Warwick (i.e., excluding all those in the
County Borough of Birmingham). Thirty-two parishes have deposited records on loan for safekeeping and in twenty-eight
cases they include the parish registers.

A. C.   – *Coventry Diocesan Record Office, Shire Hall, Warwick.*
(*Hours as Warwick County Record Office above*)
Set up at the Shire Hall, Warwick, 1st January, 1934, by
agreement between the Lord Bishop of Coventry and the
Warwickshire County Council. It covers all parishes within
the diocese. One hundred and sixty-eight parishes have deposited records on loan for safekeeping and in one hundred
and fifty-seven cases they include parish registers.

   The Staff of the above two diocesan record offices will deal with
simple enquiries, but the enquirer desiring a search covering many
years is referred to a list of searchers drawn up by the Midland Region
of the Society of Archivists. Persons making the searches themselves
are charged the diocesan scale of fees with the exception of:-

(1) Students working on a Thesis or persons doing research purely for
the advancement of learning, who need make no payment.
(2) Persons studying family histories or other concerns as a matter of
private interest, who are asked to make a voluntary contribution.
   All fees paid are immediately forwarded to the incumbents.

.R.O. – *Worcestershire Record Office, Shirehall, Worcester.*
(Hours Mon-Fri 9 - 12.45; 2 - 5, Sat closed).
This is the official Diocesan Record Office for the Diocese
of Worcester and holds the Bishop's Transcripts and Marriage
Licences for the parishes in that Diocese. These are kept
(together with Wills and all other Diocesan material) at
St Helen's Church, Fish Street, Worcester, which has its own
search room.

.H.B. – *Archbishop's House, Bath Street, Birmingham 4.*
This holds the Archives of the Roman Catholic Archdiocese of
Birmingham including a number of Warwickshire registers.

.R.O. – *The Public Record Office, Chancery Lane, London, W.C.2.*
(Hours 9.30 - 5; Sat 9.30 - 1).
This holds the vast majority of the Nonconformist Registers,
and one Catholic Register.

.R.L. – *Birmingham Reference Library, Ratcliff Place, Birmingham 1.*
(Hours Mon-Fri 9 - 9, Sat 8 - 5)
This is the official diocesan repository for parishes within
the present City of Birmingham. It holds the original
Bishop's Transcripts for two Birmingham Parishes, a number of
original registers and many copies. Amongst much other
material of Genealogical interest, it holds a microfilm copy
of the 1851 Census covering Birmingham and nearby parishes.
The microfilm of the 1841 Census has also been ordered.

.LX. – *Joint Record Office, Bird St., Lichfield, Staffs.*
(Hours 10 - 1, 2.15 - 5; Sat 10 - 12.30 by special arrangement)
This holds most original Bishop's Transcripts for the Diocese
of Lichfield. *No searches are permitted during August unless
arrangements are made not later than 15th July preceding.*
Fees are charged for the examination of Bishop's Transcripts
and Marriage Licences.

.C.L. – *Lichfield Cathedral Library.* This holds some pre-1813 Bishop's
Transcripts and Marriage Licences for Lichfield Peculiars.
This is not open for searchers, but on written application
to the Diocesan Registrar, arrangements may be made for
documents to be inspected at the Diocesan Registry.

.L.G. – *City Library, Brunswick Rd., Gloucester.*
(Hours Mon-Fri 9 - 8.30, Sat 9 - 7).
This holds the Bishop's Transcripts and Marriage Licences
for 6 Warwickshire parishes in the diocese of Gloucester and
the post-1813 Bishop's Transcripts of Sutton-under-Brailes.

– *Kent Archives Office, County Hall, Maidstone, Kent.*
(Hours 9 - 5.15, Sat by arrangement).
This holds Marriage Bonds for the Peculiar of Stratford-upon-Avon 1613-1621.

Leamington Spa Library, Art Gallery and Museum, Avenue Rd.
(Hours Mon., Tues., Thurs., Fri 10 - 8, Wed., Sat 10 - 6)
This holds one parish register.

S.O.A. – *Shakespeare's Birthplace Trust Library, Henley St,*
Stratford-on-Avon.
(Hours 10 - 1, 2 - 5, Sat 10 - 12.30)
This holds a large number of copies of parish registers.

S.L.C. – *The Genealogical Society of the Church of Jesus Christ of Latter Day Saints, Salt Lake City.*
This holds microfilms of the entire Bishop's Transcripts for the Diocese of Worcester and a number of Parish Registers.

Coventry City Record Office, 9 Hay Lane, Coventry.
(Hours 9 - 5.30, Sat closed)
This holds the Archives of the City of Coventry but these do not include any parish register material.

The Birmingham Library, Margaret Street, Birmingham 3.
This is a private library attached to the Birmingham and Midland Institute and holds a good collection of printed registers and printed genealogical material.

Birmingham University Library. The University, Edgbaston, Birmingham 15.
This holds no Parish Register material other than printed copies.

Parishes

Ancient Parishes 208, of which four are in Birmingham, three in Coventry and two in Warwick.

Changes in County Boundaries. In 1842, Sutton-under-Brailes and Little Compton were transferred to Warws. from Glos., and Tutnal and Cobley from Warws. to Worcs.

Since 1888 the following areas have been transferred *from* Warws: part of Tamworth borough and parts of adjoining parishes to Staffs., part of Mollington to Oxon., part of Batsford to Glos., Ipsley and part of Bickmarsh to Worcs., parts of Monks Kirby etc. to Leics.

190

Since 1888 the following areas have been transferred *to* Warws. from other counties: 1895, Stoneton from Northants., 1896 Oldberrow from Worcs., 1931, Clifford Chambers, Dorsington, Long Marston, Preston-on-Stour, Welford-on-Avon and Weston-on-Avon from Glos., and Alderminster, Shipston-on-Stour, Tidmington and Tredington from Worcs., 1935, Admington, Clopton and Quinton from Glos. and parts of Higham-on-the-Hill etc. from Leics.

With these parishes it has not been possible to preserve perfect consistency; some are listed under Warwickshire and others under other counties. However, cross references have been made in all cases.

A number of parishes have been transferred from Warwickshire and Worcestershire to the City of Birmingham. From Warwickshire, Saltley, Little Bromwich and Balsall Heath in 1891, Aston Manor and Erdington in 1911 and Castle Bromwich and Sheldon in 1929. From Worcestershire, Kings Norton, Northfield and Yardley in 1911, all of which are listed under Worcestershire.

Ecclesiastical Divisions

The County was covered by the Archdeaconry of Worcester in the Diocese of Worcester, and the Archdeaconry of Coventry in the Diocese of Lichfield until by a statute of 1836 and an Order in Council 24 January 1837, the Archdeaconry of Birmingham was transferred to the Diocese of Worcester.

By Order in Council 12 January 1905 this Archdeaconry, together with parts of Staffordshire and Worcestershire, became the diocese of Birmingham. By Order in Council 7 August 1905 the new diocese was divided into the archdeaconries of Aston and Birmingham.

By Order in Council 4 September 1918 the present diocese of Coventry was constituted, which comprised most of the rest of the then County of Warwick as well as Coventry itself. The diocese was divided into a smaller archdeaconry of Coventry and an archdeaconry of Warwick.

A further adjustment was made by Order in Council 29 October 1919 when Stretton-on-Fosse was transferred from the diocese of Worcester to that of Coventry, Barston from the diocese of Coventry to that of Birmingham, and Sutton-under-Brailes (in Warwickshire since 1842) from the diocese of Gloucester to that of Coventry.

Diocese of Gloucester.

Six Warwickshire parishes are in this diocese. By authority of the Bishop the records, including registers, of three are deposited at the Shire Hall, Warwick. They are Clifford Chambers, Marston Sicca and Quinton. The other parishes are Dorsington, Welford-on-Avon and Weston-on-Avon.

Parishes, chapelries and hamlets in other dioceses.

Diocese of Leicester: Hydes Pastures is a Warwickshire hamlet in the parish of Hinckley, Leicestershire; the chapel once there disappeared many centuries ago. Wibtoft is a Warwickshire parochial chapelry annexed to the parish of Claybrooke, Leicestershire; the registers date from 1705.

Diocese of Lichfield: There were two 'new parishes' in Warwickshire which were in this diocese but in 1964 one of these was transferred to Staffordshire. Of these, No Man's Heath was formerly an extra parochial liberty; a church was built in 1863, under trustees, and district chapelry was assigned in 1873; the registers date from 1863; for civil purposes it was amalgamated with Newton Regis, Warwickshire, in 1887. The other, Wilnecote, was a Warwickshire township in the parish of Tamworth, which was partly in Warwickshire and partly in Staffordshire; the chapel at Wilnecote was rebuilt in 1821 and a consolidated chapelry was assigned in 1856; the registers date from 1837; Wilnecote and Castle Liberty were constituted a civil parish 1894, which was transferred to Staffordshire 1 August 1964.

Diocese of Oxford: Little Compton is a Warwickshire parish in this diocese, to which it was transferred from the diocese of Gloucester by Order in Council 1919; the registers date from 1588.

Diocese of Peterborough: Stoneton, which was formerly extra parochial was constituted a civil parish; it was transferred from Northamptonshire to Warwickshire in 1895; the chapel once there disappeared many centuries ago.

Original Parish Registers

For about six years an intensive survey of the parish records of Warwickshire has been in progress, undertaken by the County Council, in connection with the work of the Birmingham Diocesan Record Office and the Coventry Diocesan Record Office and, at the time of writing, is about two-thirds complete. The survey has revealed that, of the parish registers deposited in the Diocesan Record Offices at the Shire Hall, Warwick, from one hundred and eighty-eight parishes, half (ninety-three exactly) date back to the sixteenth century, thirty-four to the reign of Henry VIII and thirteen start in 1538.

Warwickshire registers do not reveal any particular local disturbances which have caused gaps in the registers, except, as is usual, for the Commonwealth period. As is to be expected, a new register frequently begins in 1653, either in connection with a former register sometimes after a gap from 1649, or as the first surviving register, the earlier one or more having been lost or destroyed.

Parishes with an abnormal number of Marriages

A number of Warwickshire rural parishes, often very small, were popular' for marriages. An example, in the present diocese of Birmingham, is Curdworth. Another, in the present diocese of Coventry, is Kinwarton. In the Kinwarton register covering 1723 to 1812 marriages to 1753), there are each year in the period 1723 to 1753 only one or two baptisms and two or three burials; the maximum is five, and this in one year only in each case, and some years are marked none'. On the other hand, marriages increase from twelve at the beginning of this period to fifty-one in 1731, then decrease to twelve in 1737, twenty-one in 1738, two in 1739 and keep around that small, and probably normal number for the parish, through the remaining years up to the Marriage Act of 1753. The marriages are entered in detail, stating, with a few exceptions, that they are by licence and giving the parish of the parties, who come from all over Warwickshire and well over the borders of Worcestershire and Gloucestershire. This large yearly number of marriages begins in the previous register, from about 1708. Kinwarton was a very small, but quite important parish. Another small parish with many marriages was Wormleighton. It is interesting to note that there exists among the parish records a notebook kept by the vicar, as surrogate, 1747-1754. In this he lists the full details of the licence (the marriages in the notebook agree with the register proper) and also, in a few cases, details of a licence granted for a marriage elsewhere.

Family Reconstitution

Seven Warwickshire registers have been broken down on to Family Reconstitution forms for the purpose of demographic analysis, and two more up to 1699. Work on a further 23 is in progress.

Diocesan Record Offices, Shire Hall, Warwick

There has been a very strong policy of centralisation in Warwickshire, and as indicated under *Record Repositories*, above, the majority of registers have been deposited at the two diocesan record offices, *For fees and arrangements for searchers see under "Record Repositories" above.*

Birmingham Reference Library (BRL). This is the Diocesan Record Office for the City of Birmingham and at present (1966) holds registers of six parishes beginning before 1837 and registers of a further twelve parishes beginning after 1837. The latter are not listed in the index, and consist of:-

All Saints, Oscott   Christchurch, Sparkbrook
Christchurch, Perry Bar   Immanuel (Later united with St Thomas)

St Asaph	St Matthias
St Edward	St Nicholas
St Gabriel, Deritend	St Stephen, Selly Hill
St Luke	St Thomas and Immanuel

Further deposits are likely in the near future.

Leamington Spa Public Library holds a 17th century parish register of Leamington Priors.

Dates given in this Index.

The deposited registers have been examined and the starting dates and gaps taken from the actual volumes. The dates of other registers have been taken from the Warwick County Council Survey. The figures obtained from both of these sources have been compared parish by parish with the registers listed in the 1899 *A Digest of the Parish Registers within the Diocese of Worcester previous to 1812* and with *Parish Registers of Warwickshire* by William B. Bickley[1]. Discrepancies have been followed up and missing registers confirmed. The comparatively recent losses come from the parishes of Barford (CB 1800-1812), Hampton Lucy (C 1813-1884, M 1813-1837, B 1813-1932) and Moreton Morrell (CMB 1538-1678).

Modern Copies of Parish Registers

Printed

Compared with some counties few Warwickshire Parish Registers have been printed.

Phillimore's Warwickshire Marriages. Three volumes only were printed.

Parish Register Society printed the registers of Rowington and Solihull Weddington and Stratford-on-Avon.

Dugdale Society printed the registers of Edgbaston.

The following parish registers have also been printed in whole or in part: Aston-Juxta-Birmingham, St Martin's Birmingham, Beaudesert, Fillongley, Knowle, Southam, Stratford-on-Avon, Tanworth-in-Arden, Wolfhamcote, Wootton, Wawen and Wroxall. Many of these, however, cover the first register only.

Memorials of a Warwickshire Parish by Robert Hudson 1904.
Appendix II pp 287-306 consists of "An index to the Names contained within the registers of the parish of Lapworth for three hundred years – 1561-1860 – showing the successive decades of each Century in which such names occur and thereby indicating the relative continuance of families in the parish".

---

[1] See Bibliography at the end of this 'General Information' section.

Typescript and Manuscript

The Shakespeare Birthplace Trust, Stratford-upon-Avon (SOA).

This holds a large collection of typescript and manuscript copies, though many of these extend only to dates in the 18th Century and very few go beyond 1812. Apart from those listed there are also a great number of partial copies or extracts made for various purposes such as notes relating to particular families or when a single series contains a full transcript down to a particular date and notes thereafter. All these are excluded from the list. Also excluded are a few cases where the intention, or performance of the transcriber is uncertain. With one or two exceptions, therefore (as e.g. the Luddington fragment, included for its special local interest), the list contains only substantial portions of registers or transcripts copied as far as is known in full; though they have not been checked with the originals.

Society of Genealogists (SG).

This holds a number of typescript and manuscript copies, but many fewer than the Birthplace Library.

Warwick County Record Office and the two Diocesan Record Offices (A, AB, AC).

These hold many typescript and manuscript copies. Some are duplicates of those in one or other of the two collections above, although others have been only recently located.

Birmingham Reference Library (BRL).

This holds a few typescript copies.

College of Arms (C of A).

This holds about 11 copies, the majority being typescript duplicates of those at Stratford-upon-Avon, though some are manuscript copies ending at 1812 or at various dates in the 18th Century.

Microfilms

The Church of Jesus Christ of Latter Day Saints have microfilmed the entire Bishop's Transcripts for the Diocese of Worcester, and a large number of parish registers deposited at the two Diocesan Record Offices at Shire Hall, Warwick. Copies of these are at the Genealogical Society, Salt Lake City (SLC) and at the Warwick County Record Office. (A) Microfilming of all the Bishop's Transcripts at Lichfield Diocesan Registry commenced in 1965, and is now (1966) nearing completion.

195

Photostats

Birmingham Reference Library (BRL) holds photostat copies of Baptisms, Marriages and Burials for a number of parishes up to 1812.

Boyd's Marriage Index

There is no Warwickshire Section of the Index but marriages from a number of parishes have been included in Boyd's Miscellaneous Volumes. The dates are indicated in the text under the parishes concerned with the abbreviation *Boyd Misc.*

Bishop's Transcripts

Diocese of Worcester. At Worcestershire Record Office.

Summary

Pre-1700 transcripts in parish order. Post-1700 transcripts arranged by year and then by Deanery.

The original arrangement, as with most other Dioceses was by year and then by Deanery. In 1878, Mr. J. Amphlett, Revd. T.P. Wadley and Mr. H. Wickham King began sorting and listing the transcripts. However, their efforts, though well-meaning were misguided, and they thoroughly disrupted the original order, re-arranging the transcripts by parishes. Not only did this have the effect of making the consultation of the transcripts for the whole diocese or a whole deanery for a particular year virtually impossible, but also certain transcripts with no clear place names were not easily identifiable.

The Worcestershire Record Office holds an index which is to be incorporated in the printed *Guide to Worcestershire Records* which is in course of preparation.

While the Record Office index was in progress, the Church of Jesus Christ of Latter Day Saints was given permission by the Bishop of Worcester to microfilm the transcripts. [2] The filming had the effect of " freezing " the order (or rather lack of order) of the transcripts. For the microfilm to be effective, and the place index to apply equally to the film as well as to the originals, the originals must remain as they stood when filmed. The transcripts have therefore been serially numbered in that order. For those dated before 1701 the serial number reflects the 19th Century re-arrangement by parish; for those dated between 1700 and 1838 the order is basically by deanery, but misplacements had occurred before the Record Office took over the documents.

---

[2] See Microfilms above under *"Modern Copies"*.

The majority of the transcripts start about 1610, and on the whole, in spite of past mis-handling the collection is fairly comprehensive, and large gaps are rare. Nevertheless, a number of odd years are not infrequently missing. In this section of the National Index, therefore, which has been compiled from the detailed lists to be published in the "Guide to Worcestershire Records", it has been possible to list all gaps of four years or more, but smaller gaps have been ignored unless they are frequent, in which case the transcripts have been described as "irregular" between certain dates.

Further information on the transcripts will be found in the Worcestershire preface.

Worcester Peculiars in Warwickshire

Stratford-upon-Avon – Stratford and Hamlets of Bishopton, Bridgtown, Clopton, Dodwell, Drayton, Luddington, Shottery and Welcombe. Though not strictly speaking a Peculiar of the Diocese of Worcester, returns were normally made to the Bishop of Worcester, though there is a 28 year gap (except for two isolated years) in the 18th Century. Bishopton sent in separate transcripts until 1738 and Luddington a few in the early 17th Century. Otherwise, these and the other hamlets were on Stratford returns.

Hampton Lucy – (Hampton Lucy, Alveston, Charlecote, Wasperton). Normal returns. A few transcripts have been located in a Miscellaneous Bundle at Lichfield Diocesan Registry. (*see below*).

Tredington – Normal Transcripts.

Diocese of Lichfield

At Diocesan Registry, Lichfield, except for some for the Peculiars, which are at Lichfield Cathedral Library. This included about half the parishes in the County.

The dates given are overall dates only and must not be taken as an indication that the series is complete, though gaps of ten years or more have been noted. In general, they begin in the 1660's and continue to dates between 1855 and 1880. The transcripts have not been fully sorted and fresh transcripts may come to light, which may alter the gaps in some cases.

Unlike most other dioceses, the returns were made not annually but every three years. Consequently many of the transcripts are very bulky, particularly with the large industrial parishes where three years of CMB cover up to a dozen skins each about three feet square.

Four parishes have Bishop's Transcripts with 16th Century commencing dates. They are Baxterley (1542), Bubbenhall (1558),

Coleshill (1538) and Sutton Coldfield (1565). Baxterley and Bubbenhall, however, have the commencing dates only; Sutton Coldfield is complete except for a gap from 1600-1675 and Coleshill has a complete series with only minor gaps, but the period 1538-1600 includes Baptisms only.

The transcripts are on parchment and have been made by the incumbent. The skins are roughly sewn into book form. All are nearly perfect and are completely legible.

There are other parishes with more than three years written up together on one transcript. The probable reason for both these peculiarities – the first as far as is known unique in the country – is that about 1693 the Bishop instructed incumbents to make good gaps in the transcripts as apparently returns had become irregular. Many of these portmanteau transcripts start at 1660 and include all the years up to 1693 except for the years where separate transcripts already exist, which indicates that the clergymen knew which years were missing and only completed the returns accordingly. The reason for the 16th Century transcripts is most probably that these four incumbents misunderstood the instructions and completed the transcripts back to the beginning of the registers.

LX For about 30 parishes no details are given in the volume of the Index of Bishop's Transcripts at Lichfield Diocesan Registry covering the pre-1812 transcripts. The bundles have been examined and the first and last dates for each parish noted. It has not been possible, however, in the case of these parishes to note any gaps and the abbreviation *LX* has been used to indicate this. Furthermore many odd sheets belonging to other parishes were found in these bundles and a thorough sorting of the transcripts is necessary before any difinitive list can possibly be made.

A few transcripts from other parishes are to be found in a Miscellaneous Bundle of Transcripts. The Warwickshire parishes, each with transcripts for a few years are:- Hampton Lucy, Honiley, Shilton and Weddington.

Transcripts for a number of parishes appeared on Terriers and have been deposited at the Coventry Diocesan Record Office. They are:- Whitnash (1662-1809 with gaps) and Withybrook (1662-1809 with only one gap, 1802-4). In addition there are others with short runs, usually only three years. These include Leamington Hastings and Wolfhampcote (both 1682-1684), Weston-under-Wetherley (1682-1685), Warmington (1775-1779), Exhall near Coventry (1801-5) and Upper and Lower Shuckburgh (1801-5).

Lichfield Peculiars in Warwickshire

Post-1813 transcripts for all the Peculiars are at the Lichfield Diocesan Registry.

Pre-1813 Transcripts. For the following Peculiars they are in the Lichfield Cathedral Library. On written application to the Diocesan Registrar, transcripts will be brought to the Diocesan Registry for searchers to consult there.

Peculiar of Dean and Chapter. This included *Arley* and *Edgbaston* in Warwickshire. Fairly complete series for both parishes.

Bishop's Itchington. Two isolated transcripts 1614 and 1633. Fairly complete series from 1662.

Bishop's Tachbrook. Complete series from 1666 except for a ten year and a three year gap in the 18th Century.

For the following Peculiars, no pre-1813 transcripts have been located (pre-1809 in the case of Temple Balsall)

Baddesley Clinton	Knowle
Barston	Packwood
	Temple Balsall

Diocese of Gloucester

Sutton-Under-Brailes was in Gloucestershire until 1842 and in the Diocese of Gloucester until 1919 when it was transferred to that of Coventry. The Bishop's Transcripts 1605-1812 are held by the Coventry Diocesan Record Office. The post-1813 transcripts are at the City Library, Gloucester.

All transcripts for the six Warwickshire parishes still in the Diocese of Gloucester (Clifford Chambers, Marston Sicca, Quinton, Dorsington, Welford-on-Avon and Weston-on-Avon) are at the City Library Gloucester. *For details see General Information Section of Gloucestershire.*

Marriage Licences

Diocese of Worcester

Originals — Worcestershire Record Office (kept at St Helen's Church — *See Record Repositories above*).

About 134,000 Bonds, Affidavits and Allegations (in one series) on single sheets for the period 1582-1965. Canon J. Davenport made an index of the 16th-17th Century papers. There are also registers of Marriage Licences for the 18th and 19th Centuries. A few others are mentioned in the Calendar of Wills and Admons.

Copies

Some 1446-1662, 1676-1698, 1712-1717, 1720-1722 were printed in " The Genealogist " Old Series Vols 6, 7: New Series Vols 1 and 2.

Extracts 1446, 1532-4, 1541, 1579-84, 1600-11, 1641-45, 1661-1725 are
in *Marriage Licences in the Diocese of Worcester* by T.P. Wadley
(*copies in Guildhall Library, London and Worcestershire Record Office
no copy at S.G.*). The Marriage Licence of William Shakespeare is included.

<u>Worcester Peculiars</u> (*for parishes covered see Bishop's Transcripts
above*)

Peculiar of Stratford-on-Avon. Marriage Bonds 1618-1621 are in Kent
Archives Office.

<u>Diocese of Lichfield</u> — *At Lichfield Diocesan Registry.*

The Marriage Bonds and Allegations and (after 1824) the Affidavits
for Marriage Licences in the Registry are arranged by years for the
whole Diocese: either a year is divided alphabetically (e.g. A-K, L-Z)
into two bundles or there is one bundle for the year. The Bonds available are as follows:-

Prior to 1660: only a few bonds are extant.
1660-1670: a number of Bonds extant, but probably not complete.
1670 onwards: nearly all the Bonds sworn during this period are believed to be extant.

In each bundle the Bonds etc. for the whole Diocese (except
peculiars) are arranged in quasi-alphabetical order, i.e. the initial
letters of the surname of the male party to the proposed marriage is
the governing factor, and all Bonds and Allegations with the same
initial are placed together: thus to search for a marriage of
"William Smith and Hannah Brown in the year 1794", the bundle L-Z
1794 would first be located, and the "S" would be found all together
in the bundle. It would be necessary to search all the "S"s but not
outside the "S"s in normal circumstances. If a Bond which was
practically certain to exist was not discovered in its correct place,
a search could then be made through the whole bundle, but it is believed that such misplacements are rare. The bundles have not been
kept in good order of recent years, and the task of reorganising their
storage is at present being undertaken but may take some time. The
work of sorting the documents in the Registry has shown that a fairly
large number of Bonds etc. have become separated from their bundles.
The task of replacing these will take a considerable time, and therefore failure to locate a Bond and Allegation does not necessarily
mean that it is not in existence or that it is not deposited in the
Registry. About 10% of the Allegations have not yet been sorted. If a
particular Bond and Allegation is required, at least three weeks'
notice should be given to the Registrar of the year and surname of
the male party to the Marriage. Bonds, Allegations and Affidavits may

be inspected at the Registry by approved searchers by appointment, at least 14 days' notice having previously been given.

ichfield Peculiars. (for parishes covered see Bishop's Transcripts above).

The Bonds etc. sworn in respect of Licences issued out of the former Peculiar Courts are not included in the Diocesan Bonds, but some are in the Registry under separate storage. Those for the Peculiars of the Dean and Chapter are kept in the Cathedral Library, but there is no catalogue or list. The Cathedral Library is not open to searchers, and applications to inspect the Bonds should be made to the Diocesan Registrar.

Roman Catholics

Warwickshire lies within the Catholic Archdiocese of Birmingham. The whole of the Warwickshire parishes have had their archives listed by the County Record Office, and all parish registers before 1837 have been microfilmed by the same office. The registers of _St Peter's Franciscan Mission, Birmingham_, which start in 1657 are the earliest Catholic Registers known in the whole country. The originals are in the care of the Diocesan Archivist and they have been printed in Phillimore's Parish Register Series. The Mission served a wide area ranging from Wolverhampton in the North to Alcester and Studley in the South. A large number of the entries came from Tanworth, Solihull, Lowington, Coleshill, Alvechurch and Fillongley. After 1800 most of the entries are local. Irish families begin to appear from 1785. There are also a large number of Warwickshire entries in the registers of the Jesuit House in Worcester (1685-1837).

Warwickshire is especially rich in 18th Century registers. The Diocesan Archivist holds the registers of Wappenbury (1747), Abbotts Salford (1763), Wootton Wawen (1765), Baddesley Clinton (1765), Ilmington (1767) and Solihull (1776). In addition to these, the Parish Priest of Brailes, as well as holding the registers of his parish beginning in 1778, also holds the registers of its predecessor Weston in the parish of Long Compton, a chapel of the Sheldon Family. These begin in 1763 and were privately printed in 1898. The Parish Priests of Coughton and Coventry hold registers beginning in 1744, and 1769 respectively. A noteworthy feature of these early registers is that the majority include marriages as well as baptisms.

Of the early 19th Century registers, two, Hampton-on-the-Hill (1808) and Kenilworth (1831) are held by the Diocesan Archivist, and one other, the earliest register of Leamington starting 1822 was surrendered to the Registrar-General and is now in the Public Record

Office. The Parish Priest of St Chad's, Birmingham holds registers beginning in 1807 (which include both marriages and deaths) and the parish Priest of Nuneaton a Confirmation Register beginning in 1834. The Church of Sutton Coldfield too, dates from 1834.

There is also at Archbishop's House a Confirmation register of Vicars Apostolic 1768-1816 covering the whole Midland district.

Nonconformists

There are some noteworthy topographical features in the development of Nonconformity in Warwickshire between 1660 and 1750: the confinement of the Baptists and Presbyterians to, apart from the towns, the North and East and especially the North-East of the County, the catastrophic extinction of the General Baptists in the rural East, the more even spread of the Quakers over the whole of the County and their ability to endure longer than the General Baptists in rural areas, the presence of all denominations in the larger towns of Alcester, Birmingham, Coventry, Stratford (except for the Baptists) and Warwick and the almost complete confinement of the Particular Baptists to, and their survival in the towns[3].

The period after 1750 saw the majority of the Presbyterian Churches becoming Unitarian and the gradual decline of the Quakers. On the other hand, particularly after 1800 there were many new Independent and Baptist foundations, and the Methodists were strong in the larger towns.

Baptists

Particular Baptists

In 1690, there were only two churches, Alcester and Warwick. By 1750 there were four main churches – Alcester, Birmingham, Coventry and Warwick, with a number of others such as Henley-in-Arden subsiduary to them. Registers exist for Cannon St Birmingham, and Cow Lane Coventry. Alcester entries are in the Henley-in-Arden register and though no registers are known for Warwick, the Minute Book contains records of Baptisms from 1796 to 1818. Bond St Birmingham surrendered registers beginning in 1750.

General Baptists

In 1669 there were certainly 5 conventicles, probably 3 more and possibly a further 4. Only 3 Churches survived into the period of

---

[3] The above paragraph is taken from J.G. Hodson "Survey of Nonconformist Meetings and Meeting Houses in Warwickshire between 1660 and 1750. Warw. County Records 8 1953. Supplement to Introduction from which much of the Nonconformist information included in the Warwickshire list has also been taken.

oleration – Coventry, Napton and Priors Marston. 6 and perhaps one or
wo more small meetings were formed between 1689 and 1750, but the last
arwickshire General Baptist Church of the old Connexion died out
bout 1762. No registers are known for any of these churches. Churches
f the New Connexion of General Baptists were subsequently founded at
ombard St, Birmingham and Longford Coventry, both of which surrendered
egisters beginning in the late 18th Century.

ther 18th Century Baptist Churches were at Shipston-on-Stour and
olvey, the former of which surrendered registers.

9th Century Foundations

13 Churches founded between 1800 and 1837 have been listed. 4 (New
all Street, Birmingham; Whitefriars Lane, Coventry; Draycott and
olston) surrendered registers. Stratford-on-Avon has baptisms in the
linute Books from 1832. For 3, no registers exist and no information
as been received from the remaining 5.

No registers are held by the Secretary of the West Midland Area.
useful work of reference is *"Records of an old Association"* a
emorial Volume of the 250th Anniversary of the Midland, now the
'est Midland Baptist Association, formed in Warwick May 3rd 1655 (1905),
dited by J.M. Gwynne Owen. [4]

Presbyterians and Unitarians

In 1669 there were 31 Presbyterian Meetings, including Alcester,
therstone, Birmingham Old Meeting, Kenilworth, Nuneaton, Stratford
nd Stretton-under-Fosse. All have been listed. A few others such as
3edworth (1686), Warwick (1688) and Birmingham New Meeting (c.1689)
vere founded before Toleration, but the decline of Presbyterianism had
lready begun. By 1772 there were only 11 surviving Meeting Houses,
early all urban, and of these, Bedworth, Nuneaton, Stratford and
3tretton-under-Fosse had become Independent. The remaining 7 – Alcester,
therstone, Birmingham Old and New Meetings, Coventry, Kenilworth and
Varwick – became Unitarian as was also the new foundation in Paradise
3treet, Birmingham. All the Unitarian Churches surrendered registers,
the description in the Catalogue varying between "Presbyterian" (5),
"Unitarian" (2), and "Presbyterian or Unitarian" (1). A Presbyterian
Church was founded at Broad Street, Birmingham in 1824, but no
registers are known. A post-1837 register of Alcester is deposited at
the Warwickshire Record Office.

A useful work of reference is *"Midland Churches, a History of the
Congregations on the Roll of the Midland Christian Union"* by
George Eyre Evans (1899).

---

4   Part I and General editing by J.M. Gwynne Owen, Part II by James Ford.
    Part III by six others.

Independents (Congregationalists)

There were relatively few 17th Century Conventicles described as Independent. Only Warwick dated before the Civil War and the Church had died out by 1688. Coventry was founded in 1662, but was merged with Bedworth Presbyterian Church from 1707 to 1720 becoming Independent again in 1720. The registers which were surrendered date from 1757. In 1704 churches existed at Pailton (a hamlet of Monk's Kirby) and Willey, and there were later churches at Bretford and Churchover. No registers are known for these. In the 18th Century the Independents were strengthened by the secession of Bedworth, Nuneaton, Stratford and Stretton-under-Fosse from the Presbyterians. Registers were surrendered from all of these and also from the new Independent foundations of Atherstone, Coventry (West Orchard Chapel), Foleshill and Warwick. Hartshill surrendered a register beginning in 1799 which includes Ansley. Another register beginning in 1801 and doubtless a duplicate is held by the Church Secretary. 24 19th Century foundations have been listed of which 12 surrendered registers.

No registers are held in the Warwickshire Congregational Union safe or by the secretaries of the Birmingham, Coventry or Leamington districts.

Society of Friends (Quakers)

Warwickshire Quarterly Meeting was established in 1668 and by 1715 comprised the following Monthly Meetings:-[5]

Warwickshire Middle (1668-1837) listed under Coventry. United to Warwickshire North Monthly Meeting 1837.

Fulford Heath (1668-1716) United to Birmingham Monthly Meeting 1716.

Wishaw afterwards Baddesley (1668-1710) united to Birmingham Monthly Meeting 1710.

Brailes afterwards Warwickshire South (1668-1936).

Birmingham afterwards Warwickshire North (1668-1936).

Wigginshill (c.1690-1710) united to Birmingham Monthly Meeting 1710.

Between 1654 and 1750 there were 30 Meetings in the County: 15 founded before 1669, 7 founded between 1669 and 1689.

In 1790 the *Warwickshire* Quarterly Meeting was united to the *Leicestershire* Quarterly Meeting as the *Warwick, Leicester and Rutland* Quarterly Meeting.

---

[5] The details given here and in the text are taken mainly from the records at Friends' House Euston London, and differ on points of detail from those given by J.H. Hodson *"Survey of Nonconformist Meetings and Meeting Houses in Warwickshire between 1660 and 1750"* (Warwick County Records viii 1953).

Registers. Warwickshire Quarterly Meeting Z 1776-1792, M 1777-1790,
B 1776-1790 (PRO 1160, 1165, 1167).
Warwick, Leicester and Rutland Quarterly Meeting ZB 1792-
1837, M 1794-1837 (PRO 1161-4, 1166, 1168-71).

Other registers are listed under the respective Monthly Meetings.

Birth and Burial Notes held in 1837 by the Warwick, Leicester and
Rutland Quarterly Meeting are in the catalogue as Nos. 1500-1501 and
cover Z 1777-1794, B 1749-1794.

The majority of Warwickshire registers were surrendered and are at
the PRO. All these appear in the consolidated "Digest" [6] at Friends'
House, Euston Rd, London, N.W.1.

Methodists

Wesleyans

In 1837, Warwickshire was covered by 4 Circuits in the *Birmingham
and Shrewsbury* District viz; Birmingham East; Birmingham West;
Coventry; Leamington and Stratford-on-Avon, though until 1837,
Leamington was in the Coventry Circuit and Stratford was yoked to
Evesham, Worcestershire. Parts of Warwickshire were also covered by
the Banbury (Oxon) Circuit, and by the Redditch (Worcestershire)
Circuit, which at present includes Alcester, Studley and Mappleborough
Green. In Warwickshire, the tendency seems to have been for registers
to have been kept by individual Churches rather than by Circuit
Churches only. Thus, registers were surrendered by four Birmingham
Churches and registers of another, New John Street are in the Circuit
safe at Somerset Road Church. From the Coventry Circuit, registers
were surrendered by two Coventry Churches and by Rugby. From the
Leamington and Stratford Circuit, registers were surrendered by both
Leamington and Harbury, both formerly, of course in the Coventry
Circuit. Warwick and Kenilworth were in the Banbury Circuit up to
between 1810 and 1816, and Tysoe, Oxhill and Northend were still in
the Banbury Circuit in 1837. A register for Tysoe, beginning in 1805
is in the Kineton Circuit safe.

The Story of Methodism in Stratford-on-Avon by J.S.M. Hooper gives
much useful information on the History of Methodism in the whole
Stratford Area.

Primitive Methodists

In 1837 there were three Circuits, Birmingham East, Birmingham
West and Coventry. One register, presumably a Circuit register, was
surrendered by the Bordesley Street Chapel. No registers are known for

6   See General Article on Quaker Registers in Vol 1.

the Coventry Circuit, but some Baptisms, particularly in the Coventry Area are in the register of the Banbury (formerly Welton) Circuit held by Banbury Methodist Church.

Methodist New Connexion

There was one Warwickshire Circuit, that of Birmingham. No registers are known.

Present Methodist Circuits

The following Circuits are in the Area covered by the Warwickshire Section in this Index. Circuits in the part of Birmingham formerly in Staffordshire and Worcestershire have not been included:-

Birmingham. Moseley Road and Sparkhill – no pre-1837 registers held.
Birmingham Mission, Birmingham Central Hall – no pre-1837 registers held.
Birmingham, Elmdon[7] – no information.
Birmingham, Wesley. Registers of New John Street from 1804 in Circuit safe. Post-1837 registers for Wesley Chapel and Aston Villa.
Birmingham, Islington – no information.
Birmingham, South-West – no pre-1837 registers held.
Nuneaton and Atherstone – no registers held.
Coventry – no information.
Coventry Mission – no information.
Leamington – no registers held.
Stratford-on-Avon – no pre-1837 registers held.
Kineton – holds register for Tysoe 1805-13.
Blackwell – no pre-1837 registers held.

Calvinistic Methodists

One Chapel, Leamington, surrendered registers beginning in 1831.

New Jerusalemites

The Birmingham Chapel surrendered registers beginning in 1791.

Regimental Registers

These cover Births, Baptisms, Marriages and Deaths for the period 1790-1924 and are at Somerset House, London. They are the original registers kept by the various regiments. They are indexed and to

---

[7] The circuit is so designated although Elmdon is in the Administrative County of Warwick not in the County Borough of Birmingham.

search this index, one does not need to know the regiment. For
Marriages, Deaths and Burials, it is preferable, though not essential
to know the regiment. The most likely regiment for Infantry were the
6th Regiment of Foot (1st Royal Warwickshire) or 24th Regiment of
Foot (Warwickshire). Search should also be made of the Guards'
Regiments, the Royal Artillery, the Royal Engineers and the Royal
Marines.

Monumental Inscriptions

The only published book devoted solely to Monumental inscriptions
is C.H. Beale's *"Memorials of the Old Meeting House and Burial
Ground, Birmingham"* (1882). There is also a useful list of re-inter-
ments and inscriptions in *"A History of the Church of England
Cemetery together with the History of Christ Church, Birmingham now
demolished"*, by Wright Wilson (1900). Dugdale's *"Antiquities of
Warwickshire"* (1730) prints selections of Monumental Inscriptions
and his example has been followed by subsequent county histories and
by parish or church histories such as *Aston Parish Church* by
Rev. W. Eliot (1889) which lists some inscriptions inside the Church
of Aston-juxta-Birmingham.

There is a composite volume of Warwickshire Monumental Inscriptions in the Library of the Society of Genealogists and the
Shakespeare Birthplace Trust Library has manuscript lists of monumental inscriptions in Warwickshire parish churches and churchyards.

Newspapers

Birmingham

The Warwickshire and Staffordshire Journal 1737-1743. Sept 1737 –
   Oct 1741 complete in BRL.
Aris's Birmingham Gazette or the *General Correspondent* afterwards as
   Birmingham Daily Gazette and later, *Birmingham Gazette* 1741-1956.
   In 1956 absorbed by *Birmingham Post*. BRL 1741-1956 almost complete.
Birmingham Journal 1825-1869.
Birmingham Advertiser 1833-1848
Birmingham Herald (afterwards *Midland Counties Herald*) 1836-1933.

Warwick

Warwick and Warwickshire Advertiser 1806- present. Copies from the
   first number are held by the Warwick County Record Office.
Warwickshire Chronicle 1826-7.

Coventry

Jopson's Coventry Mercury, continued as *Jopson's Coventry and Northampton Mercury* or the *Weekly County Journal*, as *Jopson's Coventry and Warwick Mercury* or the *Weekly County Journal*, as *Jopson's Coventry Mercury* or the *Weekly County Journal*. 1741 onwards. Bod 1758-9.

Coventry Observer 1827-30 (incorporated with *Coventry Herald*).

Coventry Herald.

Leamington Spa

Leamington Press, afterwards *Royal Leamington Spa Chronicle* 1834-1859.

Publishing Societies

Dugdale Society. Secretary: Dr Levi Fox, Shakespeare's Birthplace Trust, Stratford-upon-Avon.
   Publications 1921- date. Occasional papers 1924 onwards.
   The Dugdale Society publishes Warwickshire records generally but only two volumes (VIII and XIX of the Society's series) have been concerned with parish registers and both are for Edgbaston. The first volume (1928) covers baptisms and burials, 1636-1812, and marriages, 1630-1854, while the second (1936) brings the marriages to 1812.

Warwickshire County Council Records and Museum Committee. Records 1935 date (mostly Quarter Sessions Records).

Birmingham Archaeological Society. Secretary: Mrs. M.G. Saunders, Birmingham and Midland Institute, Margaret Street, Birmingham 3. Transactions and Proceedings 1870 onwards.

Other Local Societies

Birmingham and Midland Society for Genealogy and Heraldry. Secretary: J.C. Sharp, Reference Library, Birmingham 1. Members are making transcripts of local registers.

Historical Association (Birmingham Branch). Secretary: Mr. W.J. Fowler 20 Donegal Road, Sutton Coldfield.

Historical Association (Coventry Branch). Secretary: Mr. J.E. Short. 7 Orchard Crescent, Coventry.

Warwickshire Local History Society. Secretary: Mrs. J. Lane, 47 Newbold Terrace, Leamington Spa.

ormer Publishing Societies and Magazines

arwickshire Natural History and Archaeological Society. Annual
Report Vols 1-50. 1837-1892.

arwickshire Antiquarian Magazine. ed. J. Fetherston. 8 Vols. 1859-
1877. Supplementary volume 1859 – Heraldic and Genealogical
Memoranda Relating to the County of Warwick.

arwickshire Naturalists and Archaeologists Field Club. Proceedings
1860-1910.

irmingham Historical Society. Transactions Vols. I-III. 1881-1883.

arwickshire Village History Society. 8 Vols. published 1927-39.

he Midland Antiquary. ed. W.F. Carter. Vols. I-V (pt. 1) 1882-91.
The transcript of the parish register of Aston 1600-1639 first
appeared in this publication.

idland Record Society. Transactions 1896/7-1902. Vol. V. 1901 includes the index to Vol. IV and also contains, in a supplement,
pages 23-44 of a transcript of the 1327 Subsidy Roll of
Warwickshire.

seful Works of Reference

*illiam B. Bickley *The Parish Registers of Warwickshire* (Birmingham
and Midland Institute, Archaeological Section – Transactions for
1893 Vol. XIX, pp 71-104, 1894).

*Digest of the Parish Registers within the Diocese of Worcester
Previous to 1812* (1899).

*udrey H. Higgs A.LA, and Donald Wright F.LA. *West Midland Genealogy*
(published 1966 under the auspices of the West Midland Branch of
the Library Association).[8] This is a survey of local genealogical
material which is available in the public libraries of Herefordshire, Shropshire, Staffordshire, Warwickshire and Worcestershire.

*.B. Wilson *Handlist of Books relating to the County of Warwick* (1955).

*ir William Dugdale *The Antiquities of Warwickshire* 2 Vols. (2nd
edition revised 1730).

Victoria County History of Warwick 7 Vols. 1904-64.

*.W. Kittermaster *Warwickshire Arms and Lineages compiled from
Heralds' Visitations etc.* (1866).

*.L. Colvile *The Worthies of Warwickshire 1500-1800* (1869).

*. Hobart Bird *Old Warwickshire Churches* (1936).

The works of J. Burman, viz. *Old Warwickshire Families and Houses*
(1934), *Gleanings from Warwickshire History* (1933), *Warwickshire
People and Places* (1936), *The Burman Chronicle* (1940), *The Story
of Tanworth in Arden* (1930), *Solihull and its School* (1939).

---

8 Copies available from A.T. Fox Esq., F.L.A., Birchfield Library,
Birmingham 20. Price 10/- (11/- Post paid).

W. P. Carter *Birmingham and Aston-juxta-Birmingham.* Reprint of
Dugdale's Warwickshire with notices and additions (1891).

J. T. Smith *Memorials of Old Birmingham, 13th-16th Century* (1864).

W. L. Smith *Historical Notices and recollections relating to Southam*
(with Parish Registers and Churchwardens' Accounts) (2 parts
1894-5).

Wills from Shakespeare's Town and Times. ed. E. V. Hall (2 series 1931-
1933).

ABBOTS SALFORD (RC). – *see Salford Priors.*

ALCESTER. **OR** C 1560-1943 *(gap 1746)*, M 1561-1959 *(gap 1660-62)*,
B 1560-1959 (AC). **BT** 1612 + *(gaps 1617-21, 1641-60)* (WRO).
Cop CMB (BT) 1612 + Mf (A, WRO and SLC).

ALCESTER (S of F). **Redditch (Worcs) Monthly Meeting** *(1668-1706)*,
Evesham (Worcs) Monthly Meeting *(1706-1810)*, **Worcestershire Monthly
Meeting** *(1810-1835) closed 1835.* Regs. *The Redditch Monthly
Meeting regs were eventually used as registers for* **Alcester Meeting.**
See **Redditch Monthly Meeting,** (Worcs) *note on registers.* B 1706-
1784 (FMH Worcester). *For* **Worcestershire Monthly Meeting** *see Worcs
preface.*

ALCESTER. (Partic. Bapt). *f before 1669. Meeting House before 1737. –
see Feckenham, Worcs. and Henley in Arden.*

ALCESTER. (Pres). *f.c. 1633. Meeting House and 3 smaller meetings in
1721. Became Unitarian in 18th century, demolished 1901.* **OR** C 1749-
1773 (PRO non auth.), ZCD 1774-1836 (PRO), C 1837-1874 (A).

ALCESTER. (Wes). *In* **Redditch (Worcs) Circuit** *q.v.*

ALDERMINSTER. (In Worcester until 1931). **OR** C 1628-89 *(gap 1638-54)*,
1691-1936, M 1641-88, 1698-1791, 1793-1842, B 1650-1687, 1691 +
(CMB defective to 1654), Banns 1823-1954 (AC). **BT** 1612 + *(gaps
1619-28* (except 1622-25), *1642-67* (except 1660, 1663) (WRO).
Cop C (BT) 1610-23, 1632-88, M 1613-1700, B 1611-88 Ms (WRO),
M 1613-1812 (Phil 1), CB 1611-1700 (BRL), C 1628-1812, M 1651-
1812, B 1650-1812 (SOA), CMB (BT) 1612 + Mf (A, WRO and SLC).
M 1651-1675 in Boyd Misc.

ALLESLEY. **OR** C 1569-1936, M 1562-1946, Banns 1813-1901, B 1562-1678,
1686-1855 (AC). **BT** 1673-1854 (L).

ALLESLEY. (Pres). *Conventicle in 1669. No regs.*

ALNE, GREAT or ROUND ALNE. **OR** C 1605-56, 1670-92, 1707-1962, M 1613-
56, 1697-1706, 1726-1962, B 1612-56, 1668-1702, 1708-47 (AC).
BT 1616, 1621, 1638-9, 1662 + (WRO). **Cop** CB (BT) 1704-11, 1748-50,
M 1704-11, 1748-53 Ms (SG), CMB (BT) 1616 + Mf (A, WRO and SLC).

ALVECOTE. (Pres). *f.c. 1689, disc. before 1750. No regs.*

ALVESTON. **Peculiar** *of Hampton Lucy.* **OR** CB 1539-1812, M 1539-1769,
1790-1814, Banns 1754-90 (AC). **BT** 1608 + *(gaps 1642-70* (except
1660, 61, 67) *1733-6, 1740-44)* (WRO). **Cop** C 1529-1764, M 1539-1769,
B 1539-1751 (SOA), CMB (BT) 1608 + Mf (A, WRO and SLC).

ANSLEY. **OR** C 1637-1947, M 1637-1938, B 1637-1941, Banns 1754-1953 (AC).
BT 1667-1809, 1813-1847 (L).

ANSLEY. (Ind). *f 1824*. OR ZC 1824-37 *in Hartshill register* (PRO).

ANSTY. OR CMB 1589-1812 (AC). BT 1662-1846 (L). Cop M 1591-1812 (Phil 1). *M 1651-1675 in Boyd Misc.*

ANSTY. (Pres). *Conventicle c. 1672.*

ARLEY. Peculiar *of Dean and Chapter of Lichfield.* OR CB 1557-1641, 1663-1929 (AC). BT 1673-1812 *(gaps 1687-9, 1675, 1682, 1696-8, 1702-5, 1707-13, 1717-18, 1732-5, 1741-4, 1768-71)* (LCL), 1813-1846 (L). Cop (PR) C 1564-1947, M 1564-1963, B 1564-1963, Banns 1754-1812 Mf (SLC).

ARROW. OR C 1592-1648, 1653-1938, M 1591-1641, 1654-1754, 1761-1837, B 1588-1894, Banns 1701-50, 1784-1793, 1823-1879 (AC). BT 1623 + *(gap 1641-62)* (WRO). Cop CMB (BT) 1623 + Mf (A, WRO and SLC).

ASHOW. *(Transferred from Lichfield to Worcester Dio 1836).* OR CB 1733-1812, M 1733-1837, Banns 1780-1812 (AC), CB 1813 + (Inc). BT 1663-1809, 1813-1832 (L) BT 1833 + (WRO). Cop CMB (BT) 1833 + Mf (A, WRO and SLC).

ASHOW. (Pres). *Conventicle 1669. No regs.*

ASHTED, now St James the Less, Birmingham. *Chapel of Aston.* OR C 1810-1924, M 1853-1945, B 1810-1935 (B). BT 1813-32 (L).

ASTLEY. OR C 1670-1905, M 1676-1836, B 1671-1953, Banns 1755-1942 (AC). BT 1676-1864 (L). Cop M 1675-1818 (SOA).

ASTON-JUXTA-BIRMINGHAM. OR C 1563 +, M 1561 +, B 1544 + *(gaps CMB 1586-91, 1603-4, 1646-51, CB 1741-44, C 1566-78, B 1552-60, 1571-82, 1776-83)*, Banns 1769-71, 1802-3 (Inc). BT 1677-1835 *(gaps CMB 1679-82, 1742-5, 1779-87, 1792-7, M 1772-5, 1805-9)* (L). Cop C 1563-1639, M 1561-1639, B 1544-1639 ("Regs of the Parish Church of Aston-juxta-Birmingham" by W.F. Carter, 1900 Ptd I Vol 1), CMB 1600-1637 (Ptd Midland Antiquary), CMB 1664-1695 (SOA). *See also Ashted, Erdington, Saltley, Water Orton, Castle Bromwich, Deritend.*

ASTON-JUXTA-BIRMINGHAM. (Pres). *3 conventicles in 1669 and 1672. 2 meetings in 1689. No regs.*

ASTON CANTLOW. OR C 1578-1838, M 1560-1837, B 1567-1864 *(gap M 1671-3)*, Banns 1823-1895 (AC). BT 1612 + *(gap 1641-1662)* (WRO). Cop CMB (BT) 1612 + Mf (A, WRO and SLC).

ATHERSTONE. *Formerly chapelry of Mancetter.* OR CMB 1825-1928 (AC). BT 1825-1829 (L). *From 1830 included in Mancetter.*

ATHERSTONE (S of F). Warwickshire North Monthly Meeting *(see* Birmingham Monthly Meeting*). Established 1729, closed 1836. No regs known except Monthly Meeting regs.*

ATHERSTONE. (Pres). *Old Meeting f.c. 1662. Meeting House 1728. Became Unitarian. Closed c. 1794.* OR C 1765-1794 (PRO). *Earlier C in Elder Yard Chapel, Chesterfield, Derbyshire.*

THERSTONE. (Ind). *f 1794.* OR ZC 1796-1837, DB 1827-1836 (PRO).

THERSTONE. (Genl Bapt). *Conventicle 1669-1679 became defunct. No regs known.*

THERSTONE-ON-STOUR. OR C 1661-1927, M 1664-1928, B 1661-1916, Banns 1920-1962 (AC). BT 1611 + *(gaps 1619-28, 1633-67, 1677-86)* (WRO). Cop M 1611-1812 (Phil 1), C 1654-1812, M 1664-1810, B 1661-1812 (SOA), CMB (BT) 1611 + Mf (A, WRO and SLC). *M 1651-1675 in Boyd.*

TTLEBOROUGH. *Not separate parish until after 1837. CB start 1842, M in 1854.*

TTLEBOROUGH. (Ind). *f.c. 1722. Probably short lived. No regs known.*

USTREY. OR CMB 1558 + *(Incomplete 1665-70)* (Inc). BT 1674-1832 (L). Cop CMB 1558-1947 Ms (BRL Cat. 661189), (PR) C 1558-1900, M 1558-1900, B 1558-1900, Banns 1824-1900 Mf (SLC).

USTREY. (Pres). *Conventicles c. 1669 and 1672.*

USTREY. (Bapt). *f 1808. Not at PRO. No information.*

VON DASSETT or DASSET PARVA. OR C 1559-1812, M 1559-1832, B 1559-1811, Banns 1758-1811 (AC), CB 1812 + (Inc). BT 1664-1843 (L).

VON DASSETT. (Gen Bapt). *Conventicle in 1669. No regs.*

BADDESLEY CLINTON. *Lichfield* Peculiar. OR CMB 1633-1747, C 1813-1962, B 1813-1927 (AC). BT 1813-35 (L). *No earlier BT's traced.* Cop (PR) C 1633-1812, M 1633-1849, B 1633-1927 Mf (SLC).

BADDESLEY CLINTON, St Francis of Assisi (RC). OR C 1765-1853, M 1827-1870, D 1755, 1760-1811, 1826-29, 1855-1870 (AHB). Cop C 1765-1837, M 1827-37, D 1755-1829 Mf (A). *See also Budbrooke (RC).*

BADDESLEY ENSOR. OR CMB 1688 + B of Quakers 1695-1709 (Inc). BT 1676-1846 (L). Cop (PR) CM 1688-1899, B 1688-1875, Banns 1823-1899 Mf (SLC).

BADDESLEY ENSOR. (Ind). *f 1801.* OR ZC 1801-36 (PRO).

BADDESLEY MONTHLY MEETING (S of F). − see Wishaw Monthly Meeting.

BADDESLEY ENSOR (S of F). Wishaw Monthly Meeting *(1668-1710)*, Warwickshire North Monthly Meeting *(see* Birmingham Monthly Meeting*)* *(1710-1836) closed 1836.* Wishaw Monthly Meeting Registers *continued in use for Baddesley and Hartshill after Monthly Meeting was dissolved.*

BADGLEY. − see *Baddesley.*

BAGINTON. OR 1628-1949, M 1628-1837, B 1628-1812, Banns 1824-32, 1888-1957 (AC), B 1813 + (Inc). BT 1634, 1662-1852 (L).

BALSALL. − see *Temple Balsall.*

BALSALL COMMON. *Formerly parish of Temple Balsall. Now Anglican "statutory district".*

BALSALL COMMON. (Wes). **Coventry Circuit.** *f 1825 demolished 1965. Not at PRO. No information.*

BARCHESTON. **OR** C 1559-1837, M 1561-1697, 1701-1837, B 1559-1837, Banns 1823-1935 (AC), CMB 1813 + (Inc). **BT** 1612 + (*gaps 1618-22, 1640-60*) (WRO). **Cop** C 1659-1812, M 1561-1754, B 1559-1812 (SOA), CMB (BT) 1612 + Mf (A, WRO and SLC). *M 1561-1754 in Boyd Misc.*

BARFORD. **OR** C 1538-1629, 1634-1799, 1845-53, M 1539-1628, 1634-1960, B 1538-1629, 1634-1799, 1813-1867 (*gap CB 1800-1812*), Banns 1899-1956 (AC). **BT** 1616, 1622 + (*gaps 1628-33, 1642-60, 1816-23*) (WRO). **Cop** C 1538-1629, 1634-1641, M 1539-1628, 1634-7, B 1539-1628, 1634-1641 Ms (A), Extracts CMB 1539-1721 (SOA), CMB 1538-1812 (C of A), CMB (BT) 1616 + Mf (A, WRO and SLC). *M 1539-1812 in Boyd Misc.*

BARSTON. *Lichfield (Manorial).* **Peculiar** *Transferred from Lichfield to Worcester Diocese 1837, Coventry 1918, Birmingham 1919.* **OR** CMB 1598 (Inc). **BT** 1813-41 (L), 1836 only (WRO).

BARTON ON THE HEATH. **OR** C 1575-1812, M 1577-1753, 1755-1804, 1807-10, 1813-36, B 1580-1757, 1760-1812 (AC), CB 1813 +, M 1837 + (Inc). **BT** 1612 + (*gaps 1616-21, 1641-61*) (WRO). **Cop** M 1577-1810 (Phil 3), CB 1575-1782 (SOA) CB 1575-1812 (C of A), CMB (BT) 1612 + Mf (A, WRO and SLC). *M 1651-1675 in Boyd Misc.*

BARTON ON THE HEATH (RC). *Entries in Brailes regs.*

BAXTERLEY. **OR** C 1654-1899, M 1654-1836, B 1654-1812, Banns 1825-1941 (*CMB defective 1654-73*) (AB). **BT** 1542-1846 (*gap 1598-1674*) (L). **Cop** MB 1662-1674 Ts (A and SG), (PR) C 1654-1899, M 1654-1836, B 1654-1812, Banns 1829-1940 Mf (SLC).

BEARLEY. *Formerly a parochial chapelry annexed to Wootton Wawen.* **OR** C 1546-1648, 1653-1724, 1730-1940, M 1546-1630, 1667-1721, 1732-1748, 1756-1836, B 1546-1621, 1653-1724, 1729-1812 (AC), M 1837 +, B 1813 + (Inc). **BT** 1616 + (*gaps 1626-30, 1641-60*) (WRO). **Cop** CMB 1546-1835 (SOA), CMB (BT) 1616 + Mf (A, WRO and SLC).

BEAUDESERT. **OR** C 1661-1929, M 1664-1917, B 1662-1920 (AC). **BT** 1607, 1612 + (*gap 1641-60*) (WRO). **Cop** (BT and PR) CMB 1607-1837 (SG), CMB (BT) 1607-1773 (WRO), CB 1607-1812, M 1609-1837 ("Records of Beaudesert" Ptd 1931), CMB (PR) 1539-1658 Mf (SLC), CMB (BT) 1607 Mf (A, WRO and SLC).

BEAUSALE. *Hamlet in parish of Hatton. See Hatton.*

BEDWORTH. **OR** C 1653-1910, M 1653-1907, B 1653-1920 (AC). **BT** 1662-1847 (L). **Cop** CMB 1652 only ("A Short History of Bedworth" – 1st page of oldest register Ptd) (WRO).

BEDWORTH (S of F). **Warwickshire Middle Monthly Meeting** *(see Coventry)*
*established 1702 closed late 18th century. No regs known apart
from Monthly Meeting regs.*

BEDWORTH. Old Meeting. (Pres. afterwards Ind). *f 1686. 1707 Coventry
Ind Ch ended and merged with Bedworth, but became Ind again 1720.
1727 Old Meeting founded. Defunct c. 1938.* **OR** ZC 1688-1837, B 1820-
1837 (PRO).

BENTLEY. *Chapel formerly in parish of Shustoke. Now with parish of
Merevale.* **OR** CMB 1837 + *(gap M 1872-1947)* (Inc). *No BT's.*
Cop CMB 1837-1943 Ts (A).

BERKESWELL. **OR** CMB 1653 + (Inc). **BT** 1665-1836 (L).

BERKESWELL. (Pres). *Existed in 1702. 3 meetings c. 1725. Disc. before
1772.*

BERKESWELL (S of F). *— see Meriden.*

BICKENHILL. **OR** C 1558-1859, M 1559-1593, 1682-1896, B 1558-1812,
Banns 1758-1812, 1886-1923 (AB), B 1813 + (Inc). **BT** 1671-1844 (L).
Cop (PR) C 1558-1859, M 1558-1812, 1818-1896, B 1558-1890, Banns
1886-1923 Mf (SLC).

BICKENHILL (RC). *Some entries in St Peter's Franciscan Mission,
Birmingham.*

BIDFORD-ON-AVON. **OR** CMB 1644-1801 (AC), CMB 1802 + (Inc). **BT** 1612 +
(gaps 1618-33, 1639-62) (WRO). **Cop** M (BT) 1614-85 (SOA),
CMB (BT) 1612 + Mf (A, WRO and SLC).

BILLESLEY. **OR** CMB 1817 +, **BT** 1816 + *(gap 1823-30,* except 1828). (WRO).

BILTON. **OR** C 1655-1942, M 1655-1752, 1754-1960, B 1655-1931, Banns
1823-1949 (AC). **BT** 1662-1809, 1813-1884 (L).

BINLEY. **OR** C 1660-1940, M 1660-1754, 1756-1946, B 1660-1809, 1813-94,
Banns 1757-77, 1805-17, 1824-49, 1907-31 (AC). **BT** 1665-1841 (L).

BINTON. **OR** C 1580-1812, M 1539-1725, 1729-1949, B 1540-1812, Banns
1824-1924 (AC), B 1813 + (Inc). **BT** 1608 + *(gap 1641-60)* (WRO).
Cop CMB (BT) 1608 + Mf (A, WRO and SLC).

BIRBURY. *— see Birdingbury.*

BIRDINGBURY or BIRBURY. **OR** CB 1559-1812, M 1559-1836, CMB defective
1570-8, 1584-7, (AC), CB 1813 + (Inc). **BT** 1665-1862 (L).

BIRMINGHAM, St Martin *— Parish Ch.* **OR** C 1555-1647, 1653 +, M 1554-
1641, 1653 + *(Index to M 1766-1822),* B 1554-1630, 1653-1704, 1708 +,
Banns 1754-72 (Inc). **BT** 1662, 1681-1831 (L). **Cop** C 1554-1647,
1653-1708, M 1554-1641, 1653-1707, B 1554-1630, 1653-1704 ("Regs
of St Martin, Birmingham " Vols 1 and 2, 1889 and 1903 Ptd).

BIRMINGHAM, All Saints. **OR** CB 1833 +, M 1835 + (Inc).

BIRMINGHAM, (St Bartholomew, Edgbaston). *— see Edgbaston.*

BIRMINGHAM, Christ Church, *Chapel of St Philip.* OR CM 1865 +, B 1817 +
BT 1817-1831 (L).

BIRMINGHAM, St George. OR C 1823-1955, M 1830-1956, B 1822-1916 (BRL).
BT 1822-1847 (L).

BIRMINGHAM, St James the Less, Ashted. - *see Ashted.*

BIRMINGHAM, St John the Baptist, Deritend. - *see Deritend.*

BIRMINGHAM, St Mary, *Chapelry of St Martin.* OR CB 1779 +, M 1842 +
(Inc St Martins), CB 1774-9 (duplicate in St Martin's regs).
BT 1774-1847 (L).

BIRMINGHAM, St Mary, Handsworth. OR CMB 1558-1627, 1669 + (Inc).
BT CMB 1660-1776, CB 1776-1805, M 1786-1809 (BRL), 1805 + (L).

BIRMINGHAM, St Paul. OR CB 1779 +, M 1841 + (Inc St Martin's),
CB 1779-1812 entries also recorded in St Martin's regs. BT CB 1779-
1832 *(C 1822 and C 1823 missing)* (BRL). Cop CB 1779-1812 (Inc).

BIRMINGHAM, St Peter. OR CMB 1827 + (Inc). *No BT's.*

BIRMINGHAM, St Philip. OR CMB 1715 + (Inc). BT 1715-1832 (L).

BIRMINGHAM, St Thomas. OR C 1829-1948, M 1835-1940, B 1830-1908 (BRL).
BT 1829 + (L).

BIRMINGHAM, St Peter's Franciscan Mission, Broad St (RC). OR C 1657-
1814 *(gaps C 1699-1708, 1713-15, 1717-22, 1726-35, 1735-40, 1747-
1762)*, M 1657-1804 *(gaps 1699-1710, 1725-40, 1749-1803)*, D 1657-
1699, 1711, 1722-6, 1740-9, 1766, 1774, 1790, 1792 (AHB).
Cop CMD 1657-1830 (Phil 2 and 3), CMD 1657-1830 Mf (A). *M 1657-
1675 in Boyd Misc.*

BIRMINGHAM, St Chad (RC). *f 1808.* OR C 1807-26, 1835 +, M 1807-1850,
1856 +, D 1807-1849 (St Chad's Cathedral House). Cop CMD 1807-1837
Mf (A).

BIRMINGHAM, Old Meeting House (Pres) now Bristol St Unit. Ch. *In 1669
5 Pres. conventicles in Birmingham and Aston. In 1672 9 Pres.
meetings and 1 Ind.; 3 Pres. in Aston 1689. Old Meeting House,
Phillip St. became Unit. 18th century; destroyed 1791, rebuilt 179.*
Moved to Bristol St 1885. OR ZC 1774-1838, B 1784-1858 (PRO).

BIRMINGHAM, New Meeting House (Pres). *Now Unitarian Church of the
Messiah, Broad St. f at Deritend 1692. 1732 Moore St. Became Unit.
18th century, destroyed 1792, rebuilt 1802. Moved to Broad St 1861.*
OR Z 1719, C 1735-1840, some D (PRO).

BIRMINGHAM, Broad St, Oozells St N. (Pres). *f 1824. Not at PRO. No
information.*

BIRMINGHAM, Paradise St. (Unit). OR C 1791-1813 (PRO).

BIRMINGHAM, Carr's Lane. (Ind). *f 1747 break away from Old Meeting
House.* OR C 1806-1837 (PRO).

BIRMINGHAM, Old Cannon St. (Ind). Cop CMB 1837-58 (SG - D. Mss).

BIRMINGHAM, Ebenezer Chapel, Steel House Lane. (Ind). OR ZC 1817-1837
(PRO).

BIRMINGHAM, Elmwood Chapel. (Ind). *f 1818. Not at PRO. No information.*

BIRMINGHAM. (Ind). *- see also Erdington, Handsworth (Staffs), Saltby.*

BIRMINGHAM, Cannon St. (Particular Bapt). *f 1737. Now Cannon St Memorial Church, Soho Rd, Handsworth.* OR Z 1785-1837, B 1792-1837 (PRO). *See also next entry.*

BIRMINGHAM, Needless Alley, later Bond St. (Particular Bapt). *f 1785.* OR Z 1750-1837, B 1794-1834 (PRO), *probably earlier part in register of Cannon St, above.*

BIRMINGHAM, Freeman St. (Gen Bapt). *f early 18th century. At Freeman St 1729. Meeting became defunct between 1747 and 1770. No regs known.*

BIRMINGHAM, Lombard St. (Gen Bapt). *f 1775.* OR Z 1786-1808, 1813-36 (PRO).

BIRMINGHAM, Zion Chapel, New Hall St. (Bapt). OR Z 1821-37 (PRO).

BIRMINGHAM, Hagley Rd. (Bapt). *f 1828. No information. Not at PRO.*

BIRMINGHAM, High St, King's Heath. (Bapt). *f 1835.* OR *Not at PRO. Church holds only M from 1918.*

BIRMINGHAM MONTHLY MEETING (S of F). *Afterwards* **Warwickshire North Monthly Meeting** *(1668-1936).* **Constituent Meetings.** *Birmingham (1668-1936), Wigginshill (1668-1690, 1710-c.1800), Baddesley Ensor (1710-1836), Hartshill (1710-1838), Tamworth, Staffs (1710-1852), Fulford Heath (1716-c.1727), Lapworth (1716-c.1727), Henley-in-Arden (1716-c.1800), Grendon and Polesworth (1721-1821), Nuneaton (c.1721-6), Atherstone (1729-1836), Lichfield, Staffs (1816-1829), Dudley, Worcs (1819 +), Stourbridge (1819 +), Coventry (1837 +), Warwick (1837 +).* **Registers:** Z 1682-1726, 1744-1775, M 1678-1777, B 1686-1756, 1749-1776 (PRO 1172, 1174), Z 1712-1726 (1173), ZB 1777-1837, M 1777-1792, 1794-1837 (1187-1192), Z 1838-1886, B 1838-1884 (FMH Bull St Birmingham), Marriage Intention notices 1702-1820 (FMH Bull St). *Separate regs were not kept by the Constituent Meetings, except for Dudley and Stourbridge. (See Worcestershire).*

BIRMINGHAM, Bull St. (S of F). **Birmingham Monthly Meeting.** *No separate regs.*

BIRMINGHAM, (Wes). *2 pre-1837 Circuits.* **Birmingham West** *(Circuit Church Cherry St),* **Birmingham East** *(Circuit Church Belmont Row). Separate registers appear to have been kept by most churches. No regs held by the Birmingham Central Hall or the present* **Blackheath Circuit.**

BIRMINGHAM, Cherry St. (Wes). *(Forerunner of present Birmingham Central Hall). f 1782.* OR ZC 1802-1837 (PRO). *Perhaps register of* **Birmingham West Circuit,** *though separate registers seem to have been kept.*

BIRMINGHAM, Belmont Row. (Wes). *f 1789.* OR ZC 1830-1837 (PRO). *Perhaps register of* **Birmingham East Circuit,** *though separate registers seem to have been kept.*

BIRMINGHAM, Bradford St. (Wes). *f 1786.* OR ZC 1829-1837 (PRO).

BIRMINGHAM, New John St. (Wes). OR C 1804-1896 (Circuit Safe, Somerset Rd Church).

BIRMINGHAM, Wesley Chapel. (Wes). *f 1828, closed 1917.* OR C 1868-1917, M 1869-1896 (Circuit Safe, Somerset Rd Church).

BIRMINGHAM, Islington. (Wes). OR ZC 1831-37 (PRO).

BIRMINGHAM. (Prim Meth). *2 pre-1837 Circuits,* **Birmingham West** *and* **Birmingham East.** *At present only one register is known which is presumably a Circuit register. (See next entry).*

BIRMINGHAM, Bordesley St. (Prim Meth). OR ZC 1831-37 (PRO). *Presumably a Circuit register.*

BIRMINGHAM. (Methodist New Conn). *There was one pre-1837 Circuit, but no register is at present known.*

BIRMINGHAM, King St. (Calv. Meth. *formerly Lady Hunt Conn.*). OR ZC 179 1837 (PRO).

BIRMINGHAM, Summer Lane *(formerly New Hall St).* (New Jerusalemite). OR ZC 1791-1838 (PRO).

BISHOP'S ITCHINGTON. *Lichfield* Peculiar. OR C 1559-1922, M 1559-1947, Banns 1824-1879, B 1559-1905 (AC). BT 1614, 1633, 1662-1812 *(gaps 1667-71, 1693-5, 1725-7)* (LCL), 1813 + (L).

BISHOP'S ITCHINGTON. (Ind). *f 1834. Not at PRO.* OR C 1842, Z 1843 to 1943 (393 entries) (Ch. Sec.).

BISHOP'S ITCHINGTON. (Gen Bapt). *Conventicle in 1689. Became defunct. No regs.*

BISHOPS TACHBROOK. *Lichfield* Peculiar. OR C 1538-1732, M 1538-1812, B 1538-1811 (AC), CMB 1813 + (Inc). BT 1666-1810 *(gaps 1718-28, 1786-9)* (LCL), 1813-1847 (L). Cop M 1538-1812 (Phil 3). *M 1651-1675 in Boyd Misc.*

BISHOPTON. Peculiar *of Stratford-on-Avon.* OR C 1591-1749, M 1591-1728, B 1590-1728 (WRO), CMB 1813 + (Inc). BT 1609-1738 *(gaps 1617-25, 1634-78 except 1666)* (WRO). *Later entries probably on Stratford-on-Avon returns.* Cop C 1595-1752, M 1591-1701, B 1590-1634, CMB 1635-1689 (SOA), (PR) C 1591-1751, M 1591-1728, B 1590-1728 Mf (SLC), CMB (BT) 1609-1738 Mf (A, WRO and SLC). *See also Stratford-on-Avon.*

BORDESLEY. Holy Trinity, *Previously Hamlet of Aston-juxta-Birmingham q.* OR C 1823-1950, M 1864-1946, B 1823-1925 (BRL). *No BT's.*

BOURTON-ON-DUNSMORE. OR C 1560-1893, M 1560-1836, B 1560-1813, Banns 1829-1905 (AC). *(Small gaps in CMB between 1600-1641 and 1661-1680* B 1814 + (Inc). BT 1662 + (L). Cop M 1560-1813 (Phil 1). *M 1651-1675 in Boyd Misc.*

BOURTON-ON-DUNSMORE. (Gen Bapt). *Conventicle c. 1669-72. No regs.*

BOURTON. (Bapt). − *see Draycott.*

BRAILES. OR C 1570-1859, M 1570-1753, 1760-1924, B 1570-1954,(*CMB 1570-1582 fragmentary*) (*gaps C 1653-1660*) (AC). BT 1608, 1611, 1614 + (*gap 1641-60*) (WRO). Cop CMB 1653-1701 (SOA), CMB 1570-1653 (C of A), CMB (BT) 1608 + Mf (A, WRO and SLC).

BRAILES, St Peter and St Paul (RC). OR C 1778 +, M 1785-92, 1820 +, B 1785-89, 1820-1912, 1944-1963, Confms 1779 + (Inc). Cop C 1778-1844, M 1785-1792, 1821-1865, B 1786-1789, 1820-1912, Confms 1779-1888 p/s (A), CMB 1786-1912 p/s (BRL). *For earlier regs see Weston, (Sheldon Chapel).*

BRAILES MONTHLY MEETING. (*Afterwards* Warwickshire South Monthly Meeting) *1668-1936.* Constituent Meetings: *Long Compton (1673-c.1830), Radway (1668-1850), Ettington (1668-1936), Brailes (1668-1936), Campden, Glos (1790 +), Shipston, Worcs (1790 +), Stow, Glos (1790 +).* Monthly Meeting Registers: ZMB (family list) 1650-1836 (PRO 1581), Z 1777-1793 (1591), M 1778-88 (1588), B 1776-1795 (1593), ZB 1795-1837, M 1797-1835 (1202-4). *Also Constituent Meeting registers (see separate meetings).*

BRAILES (S of F). Brailes Monthly Meeting. OR Z 1636-1808, M 1662-1765, B 1676-1788 (PRO 1586).

BRANDON (Gen Bapt). *Conventicle in 1672. No regs.*

BRETFORD. (Ind). *Existing 1747. No regs known.*

BRIDGTOWN. *Hamlet of Stratford-on-Avon q.v.*

BRINKLOW. OR CB 1558-1930, M 1574-1632, 1748-1930, Banns 1754-1812, 1824-1915 (AC). BT 1673-1841 (L).

BRINKLOW. (Ind). *f 1827.* OR *Not at PRO only* Z 1908 +, CMD 1909 + (Ch. Sec).

BROADWELL. (Pres). *Meeting in 1689. No regs.*

BROWNSOVER. OR CB 1593-1812, M 1593-1837 (AC), CB 1813 +, M 1837 + (Inc). BT 1663-1845 (L).

BUBBENHALL. OR C 1698-1914, M 1698-1836, B 1698-1762, 1764-1812, Banns 1754-1863 (AC), B 1813 + (Inc). BT 1558-1854 (L).

BUDBROOKE. OR C 1539-1883, M 1539-1836, B 1539-1964, Banns 1823-1925 (AC). BT 1625 + (*gaps 1628-36, 1640-60*) (WRO).

BUDBROOKE. Chapel at Grove Park (RC). OR C 1780-1805 (AHB).

BULKINGTON. OR C 1606-1801, M 1606-1957, B 1606-1869 (AC), C 1813 + (Inc). BT 1660-1809, 1813-1840 (L).

BULKINGTON. (Ind). *f 1811.* OR ZC 1812-1836 (PRO). *See also Ryton.*

BULKINGTON. (Gen Bapt). *Conventicle c. 1663-72. No regs known.*

BURMINGTON. **OR** C 1583-1601, M 1585-1601, B 1582-1601, CMB 1616-25, 1676-1685 (surviving fragments of 1st reg), C 1703-1812, M 1711-1812, 1816-34, B 1711-1812, Banns 1754-1822 (AC), CB 1813 + (Inc). **BT** 1612 + (*gaps 1615-19, 1640-62*) (WRO). **Cop** CMB 1582-1812 (SOA), CMB (BT) 1612 + Mf (A, WRO and SLC). *M 1585-1812 in Boyd Misc.*

BURTON DASSETT (GREAT DASSETT or DASSETT MAGNA). **OR** C 1565-1575, 1580-1623, 1626-36, 1647-1931, M 1564-75, 1581-1623, 1647-1837, B 1564-1575, 1579-1623, 1647-1871, Banns 1824-1948 (AC), C 1660 + , MB 1663 + (Inc). **BT** 1714-1845 (L). **Cop** CMB 1564-1623 Ms (A).

BURTON DASSETT. (Pres). *Conventicle 1669. No regs.*

BURTON DASSETT. (Gen Bapt). *Conventicle 1685. Congregation in 1745. Became defunct. No regs.*

BURTON DASSETT, Northend. (Wes). *f 1832.* **Banbury Circuit.** *Now* **Kineton Circuit.** *No regs known. Not at PRO or Circuit Safe.*

BURTON HASTINGS. **OR** CMB 1574 + (Inc). **BT** 1662-1862 (L).

BUTLERS MARSTON. **OR** CMB 1538-1788 (Inc), C 1789-1834, M 1754-1836, Banns 1754-82, 1792-1814, B 1789-1812, 1829-34 (AC). **BT** 1612 + (*gap 1641-65* except 1660) (WRO). **Cop** M 1538-1812 (Phil 1), CB 1538-1812 (SOA), CMB (BT) 1612 + Mf (A, WRO and SLC). *M 1651-1675 in Boyd Misc.*

CALDECOTE. **OR** CB 1725-1961, M 1725-1752, 1758-1954, Banns 1823-1960 (AC). **BT** 1674-1805, 1813-1840 (*gap 1701-11*) (L).

CASTLE BROMWICH. *Previously hamlet of Aston-juxta-Birmingham.* **OR** C 1619 + , M 1630-1749 (*CM after 1749 at Aston*), B (*at Aston*) 1659-1728, 1763-81, B (*at Castle Bromwich*) 1810 + . (*All B before 1810 in Aston regs*). (Inc). **BT** 1810-1846 (L). **Cop** (PR) C 1619-1899, M 1630-1725, B 1639-1781, 1810-1891 Mf (SLC).

CHADSHUNT and GAYDON. *– see Gaydon.*

CHARLECOTE. **Peculiar** *of Hampton Lucy.* **OR** C 1543-1911, M 1543-1752, 1755-1836, Banns 1827-1924, B 1539-1812 (AC), B 1813 + (Inc). **BT** 1616 + (*gap 1639-60*) (WRO). **Cop** M 1543-1812 (Phil 3), CM 1543-1812, B 1539-1812 (SOA), CMB (BT) 1616 + Mf (A, WRO and SLC). *M 1651-1675 in Boyd Misc.*

CHERINGTON. **OR** 1540-1662, 1664-1747, 1750-1894, M 1540-1589, 1665-1714, 1716-23, 1750-1837, B 1538-1653, 1664-1747, 1750-1802, 1813-1959, Banns 1824-1902 (AC), B 1862 + (Inc). **BT** 1608 + (*gaps 1615-21, 1641-67*) (WRO). **Cop** Extracts CMB 1540-1812 (SOA), CMB 1540-1812 (C of A). *M 1540-1588, 1665-1812 in Boyd Misc.*

CHERINGTON (RC). *Entries in Brailes regs.*

CHESTERTON. **OR** C 1538-1949, M 1538-1960, B 1538-1961, Banns 1824-1961 (AC). **BT** 1662-1805, 1813-1850 (*gap 1684-93*) (L). **Cop** CMB 1538-1738 Ms (B'ham Arch Society), M 1538-1731 (SOA).

CHILVERS COTON. **OR** CMB 1654-1915 (AC). **BT** 1674-1846 (L).

CHILVERS COTON (Ind). *Existed 1720, 1738. Probably short-lived. No regs known.*

CHURCH LAWFORD with KING'S NEWNHAM (NEWNHAM REGIS). **OR** C 1575-1879, M 1575-1948 *(gap 1640-65)*, B 1575-1916 *(gap 1643-56)*, Banns 1823-1925 (AC). **BT** 1662-1809, 1813-1838 (L).

CHURCH LAWFORD. (Pres). *– see King's Newnham.*

CHURCHOVER. **OR** C 1658-1913, M 1658-1929, B 1658-1812 *(gaps CMB 1670-1721, C 1767-71)* (AC), B 1813 + (Inc). **BT** 1660-1840 (L). **Cop** M 1658-1668, 1722-1812 (Phil Ms and Mf SLC). *M 1658-1812 in Boyd Misc.*

CHURCHOVER. (Ind). *f before 1743.* **OR** ZC 1822-1836 (PRO).

CLAVERDON. **OR** 2 loose sheets, C 1593-6, B 1596-7, C 1629-1949, M 1637-1960, B 1629-1961 *(gap CMB 1700-6)* (AC), **BT** 1611 + *(gap 1641-60)* (WRO). **Cop** CB 1629-1812, M 1637-1812 Ms (AC), C 1594-7, 1629-1700, M 1637-94, B 1596-97, 1629-1700 (SOA), CMB (BT) 1611 + Mf (A, WRO and SLC).

CLIFFORD CHAMBERS. *Formerly in Glos. Still in Dio. of Gloucester.* **OR** C 1538-1948, M 1538-1836 *(gaps 1541-50, 1681-92, 1738-41, 1753-5, 1808-16)*, B 1538-1889 *(gaps 1543-5, 1566-70, 1592-1600)*, Banns 1824-1828, 1895-1938 (A). **BT** 1623 + (CLG). **Cop** M 1538-1812 (Phil Glos 5), M 1538-1753, CB 1538-1812 (SOA), CMB 1538-1662 (CLG), CB 1538-1837, M 1617-1837 Ts (SG). *M 1538-1812 in Roe's Glos. Marr. Index. See also Marston Sicca, Quinton, Welford-on-Avon and Weston-on-Avon all listed under Gloucestershire.*

CLIFTON-UPON-DUNSMORE. **OR** C 1594-1897, M 1594-1837, B 1594-1882 (AC). **BT** 1662-1837 (L). **Cop** CMB 1594-1786 (C of A).

CLOPTON. *Hamlet of Stratford-on-Avon q.v.*

COLESHILL. **OR** CMB 1538 + *(gap B 1700-4)* (Inc). **BT** C 1538-1600, CMB 1600-1809, 1813-1846 (L). **Cop** (PR) C 1538-1700, 1704-1888, M 1538-1700, 1704-1898, B 1538-1700, 1704-1855 Mf (SLC).

COLESHILL. (Pres). *Conventicles c. 1669-90. No regs.*

COLESHILL. (Ind). *f 1835.* **OR** C 1835-36 (PRO).

COLESHILL (RC). *Numerous entries in regs of St Peter's Franciscan Mission, Birmingham.*

COLESHILL (S of F). **Wishaw Monthly Meeting.** *f.c. 1668, disc. c.1700. No regs known apart from Monthly Meeting regs.*

COMBROKE. **OR** C 1715-1803, M 1716-1786, B 1701-3, 1716-1803 (AC), CMB 1813 + (Inc). **BT** 1608, 1613 + *(sometimes with Kineton)* *(gap 1641-63)* (WRO). **Cop** (PR) M 1716-1786 and CMB (BT) 1608-1640, 1663-1700 (SOA), (PR and BT) M 1608-1786 (Phil Ms, Mf SLC), CMB (BT) 1608 + Mf (A, WRO and SLC). *M 1608-1786 in Boyd Misc.*

COMPTON, FENNY. *– see Fenny Compton.*

COMPTON, LITTLE. *In diocese of Oxford since 1919.* OR CB 1588 +,
   M 1589 + *(gaps CB 1650-8, M 1644-1758)*, Banns 1824 + (Inc).
   BT 1605 + (CLG). Cop M 1608-1812 (Ptd). *No copy SG.*

COMPTON, LONG. OR C 1670-81, 1683-1898, M 1685-1763, 1772-1837,
   B 1683-1866, Banns 1873-1952 (AC). BT 1608 + *(gaps 1641-1660, 1662-
   1666)* (WRO). Cop M 1608-1812 (Phil 1), CMB 1608-1812, CMB (BT) 1608
   1640, 1660-1700 (SOA), CMB (BT) 1608 + Mf (A, WRO and SLC).
   M (BT) 1651-1675 in Boyd Misc.

COMPTON, LONG (RC). *– see Weston. Also entries in Brailes regs.*

COMPTON, LONG (S of F). **Brailes Monthly Meeting.** *Established 1673,
   closed c. 1830. No regs known other than Monthly Meeting regs.*

COMPTON, LONG. Ebenezer Chapel. (Ind). *f 1820.* OR ZC 1820-1836 (PRO).

COMPTON VERNEY. OR B 1852-1923 (AC). Cop M 1747-1852 (SOA). *No BT's
   known.*

COMPTON WYNYATES. OR C 1683-1812, M 1713-1774 *(gap 1774-1812)*, B 1698-
   1812 (AC), CMB 1813 + (Inc). BT 1826 + (WRO). *Whereabouts of earlie
   BT's not known.* Cop CMB 1683-1812 (C of A), CMB (BT) 1826 + Mf
   (A, WRO and SLC). *M 1713-1774 in Boyd Misc.*

COPSTON. (Pres). *f before 1672. Existing 1672 and 1689. No regs.*

CORLEY. OR CB 1540-1638 *(gaps between 1607 and 1619)*, 1654-80, 1686-
   1942 (B 1932), M 1540-1638, 1654-80, 1704-1954 (AC). BT 1660-1809,
   1813-1844 (L). Cop MB 1662-1674 Ts (A and SG).

COUGHTON. OR C 1673-1886, M 1754-1952, B 1673-1736, 1755-1934, Banns
   1769-1896 (AC), CB 1737 +, M 1737-1754, 1769 + (Inc). BT 1616,
   1624 + *(gap 1642-60)* (WRO). Cop CMB (BT) 1615-1641, 1660-1685 (SOA)
   CMB (BT) 1616 + Mf (WRO, A, SLC).

COUGHTON, St Peter and Paul and St Elizabeth (RC). OR C 1744-1843,
   M 1758-98, B 1758-1800 (also a few MB 1744-1754) (A awaiting trans-
   fer to Douai Abbey), C 1843 +, MB 1856 +, Confirmations 1836-50,
   1856 + (Inc). Cop C 1744-1843, M 1758-1798, B 1758-1800 (alph)
   (A awaiting transfer to Douai Abbey), C 1744-1837, M 1758-1798,
   B 1758-1800 Mf (A).

COUGHTON. (Pres). *Conventicle 1672. No regs.*

COVENTRY, St Michael. OR *Surviving regs badly burned – fragments
   remaining* C 1770-72, 1794-99, 1813-1924, M 1714, 1715, 1716/7,
   1827-1927, B 1723, 1724/5, 1760-1778, 1815-1945 (AC). BT 1640-
   1846 *(gap 1641-1662)* (L). Cop CMB (BT) 1640-1726 Ts (SG and A,
   Mf SLC).

COVENTRY, Holy Trinity. OR CMB 1561 + (Inc). BT 1662-1848 (L).

COVENTRY, St John the Baptist. OR CMB 1734 + (Inc). Registers severely
   damaged by flooding. BT 1752-1841 *(gap 1801-9)* (L).

COVENTRY, St Osburg (RC). *f 1766.* **OR** ZC 1769-1853, M 1770-1855, DB 1795-1855, Confirmations 1771, 1779, 1807-1849 (A, pending transfer to Douai Abbey, Woolhampton, Berks). **Cop** ZC 1769-1853, M 1770-1855, DB 1795-1855 Mf (A).

COVENTRY, Great Meeting, Smithford St. (Pres). *f.c. 1669. Became Unitarian c. 1725, demolished 1935 and replaced by Unitarian Church, Holyhead Rd.* **OR** C 1777-1819, 1821-1837 (PRO).

COVENTRY, St Nicholas or Leather Hall. (Pres). *f.c. 1669. 1687 at Leather Hall. 1700 larger meeting house. Disc. before 1735. No regs known.*

COVENTRY, Bayley Lane. (Pres). *f before 1724, disc. before 1735. Subsid. meeting of above. No regs known.*

COVENTRY, New Park St. (Pres). *f before 1724, disc. before 1735. Subsid. meeting of Leather Hall. No regs known.*

COVENTRY, Vicar Lane. (Ind). *f 1662, Much Park St. reconstructed 1687. Absorbed by Bedworth 1707 but separate congregation served from Bedworth continued to meet in Coventry. 1720 became independent of Bedworth. 1725 joined by secessionists from Great Meeting. New church built in Vicar Lane. 1891 moved to present church in Warwick Rd.* **OR** ZC 1757-1837 (PRO). *Entries 1707-1720 probably in Bedworth register.*

COVENTRY, West Orchard Chapel. (Ind). *f 1775.* **OR** ZC 1766-1836, B 1799-1837 (PRO).

COVENTRY, Foleshill Rd. (Ind). *f 1795. Not at PRO. No information. Perhaps same ch. as Foleshill q.v.*

COVENTRY, Well St. (Ind). *f 1827. Not at PRO. No information.*

COVENTRY. (Ind). *– see also Potters Green.*

COVENTRY, Jordans Well. (Particular Bapt). *Alleged f. 1626, but probably not separate congregation before c. 1684. Jordans Well ch. built 1723. 1793 at Cow Lane. Queen's Rd since 1884.* **OR** Z 1761-1836 I (PRO).

COVENTRY. (Gen Bapt). *f early 17th century, existing 1718, defunct c. 1762. No regs known.*

COVENTRY, Salem Chapel, Longford. (Gen Bapt New Connexion). *f 1770.* **OR** Z 1785-1837, B 1801-1837 (PRO).

COVENTRY, Union Place, Longford. (Gen Bapt). *f 1826. Not at PRO. No information. Probably in regs of above.*

COVENTRY, Lenton's Lane. Hawkesbury. (Gen Bapt). *Formerly Wyken Baptist Church. f. 1816.* **OR** *Not at PRO.* DB 1845 + (Ch. Sec.). *No earlier regs known.*

COVENTRY, Whitefriars Lane. (Gen Bapt). *f 1822. Later Gosford St and now Meredith Rd.* **OR** Z 1826-1837 (PRO).

COVENTRY. **WARWICKSHIRE MIDDLE MONTHLY MEETING** (S of F). *Established 1668. United to* **Warwickshire North Monthly Meeting** *1837.*
Constituent Meetings: *Coventry (1668-1837), Kenilworth (1668-1689), Warwick (1668-1837), Harbury (1668-c.1795), Radford Semele (1668-late 18th century), Bedworth (1668-late 18th century), Meriden, afterwards Berkeswell or Balsall St (1668-1783), Pailton (1688-1694), Southam (c.1680-1711).* **Monthly Meeting Registers:** ZMB 1623-1833 (PRO 1193), Z 1655-1835, M 1695-1772, 1780-94, 1796-1837, B 1696-1837 (1194-1201), Coventry and Warwick B 1837-1858 (FMH Bull St, Birmingham). *No constituent meeting registers known.*

COVENTRY (S of F). **Warwickshire Middle Monthly Meeting** *(1668-1837) see above. No registers known apart from Monthly Meeting registers.*

COVENTRY CIRCUIT. (Wes). *See Coventry, Gosford St and Warwick Lane; Rugby, Leamington and Harbury. Harbury, also included Wellesbourne.*

COVENTRY, Gosford St. (Wes). **Coventry Circuit.** OR ZC 1807-1828 (PRO).

COVENTRY, Warwick Lane. (Wes). **Coventry Circuit.** OR ZC 1820-1837 (PRO).

COVENTRY CIRCUIT. (Prim Meth). *No regs known. Not at PRO. Many Coventry entries in Banbury Circuit register. See Oxfordshire, Banbury.*

CUBBINGTON. **OR** C 1606-45, 1707 +, M 1590-1643, 1731-52, 1784-1812, B 1559-1622, 1731 + (Inc) *(CMB to 1645 defective).* **BT** 1662-1809, 1813-1845 (L).

CURDWORTH. **OR** C 1653-1844, M 1653-1836, B 1653-1918 (AB). **BT** 1673-1809, 1813-1840 *(gap 1787-97)* (L). **Cop** Index to PR 1653-1721, (PR) C 1653-1844, M 1653-1836, B 1653-1918, Marr. Lic. 1818-1836 Ts (A), Mf (SLC).

DASSETT MAGNA. *– see Burton Dassett.*

DASSETT PARVA. *– see Avon Dassett.*

DERITEND, St John Baptist. *Previously Hamlet of Aston-juxta-Birmingham.* **OR** 1699-1922, M 1700-1753, 1890-1919, B 1791-1812 (BRL). **BT** 1813-1842 (L).

DERITEND. (Pres). *– see Birmingham, New Meeting House.*

DITCHFORD FRARY. *Parish united with Stretton-on-Fosse 1642. See Stretton-on-Fosse.*

DODWELL. *Hamlet of Stratford-on-Avon q.v.*

DORSINGTON. *Formerly in Glos. Transferred to Warws. 1931. Still in Dio of Gloucester. See Gloucestershire.*

DRAYCOTE, Parish of Bourton. (Bapt). **OR** Z 1812-37 (PRO).

DRAYTON. *Hamlet of Stratford on Avon q.v.*

DUDDESTON. *Hamlet of Aston-juxta-Birmingham q.v.*

DUNCHURCH. **OR** CMB 1538-1655, 1658-93, 1695-1748 (AC), CB 1813 +, M 1754 + (Inc). **BT** 1662-1809, 1813-1843 (L).

DUNNINGTON. (Bapt). *f 1825.* **OR** *Not at PRO.* M 1901 + (Ch. Sec). *No earlier regs known.*

EATINGTON. *– see Ettington.*

EDGBASTON, St Bartholomew. **Peculiar** *of Dean and Chapter of Lichfield.* **OR** CM 1636 +, B 1635 + (Inc). **BT** 1678-1812 *(gaps 1681-4, 1686-90, 1700-3, 1721-4)* (LCL), 1813-1838 (L). **Cop** CMB 1636-1812 Ptd (Dugdale Society).

EDGBASTON (RC). *Entries in regs of St Peter's Franciscan Mission, Birmingham.*

ELMDON. **OR** CMB 1538-1665, 1671-1725, M 1754-1810, 1813 +, Banns 1754-1822, 1827-1944 (AB), CMB 1726-1812, CB 1813 + (Inc). **BT** 1676-1847 (L). **Cop** (PR) CB 1538-1725, M 1538-1725, 1754-1942, Banns 1827-1944 Mf (SLC).

ELMWOOD. *– see Birmingham, Elmwood Chapel (Ind).*

ERDINGTON. *Chapel of Aston.* **OR** CB 1824 +, M 1856 +. **BT** 1824-31 (L).

ERDINGTON. (Ind). *f 1814.* **OR** C 1822-36, 1838-56 (PRO).

ETTINGTON (EATINGTON). **OR** C 1661-1857, M 1670-1945, B 1669-1877, Banns 1782-1827 (AC). **BT** 1612, 1621 + *(gap 1641-66* except 1661) (WRO). **Cop** M 1623-1812 (Phil 1) (SLC), CMB (BT) 1621-1668, C 1661-1782, M 1670-1754, B 1669-1783, CMB (BT) 1621 + Mf (A, WRO and SLC). *M 1651-1675 in Boyd Misc.*

ETTINGTON (S of F). **Brailes Monthly Meeting. OR** Z 1673-1774, M 1664-1774, B 1668-1774 (PRO 1587). **Cop** P 1866-1896 (WRO).

EXHALL, Near Coventry. **OR** CB 1540-1802, M 1540-1801 (AC), CB 1802 +, M 1801 + (Inc). **BT** 1663-1809, 1813-1852 (L), 1801-5 on Terriers (A).

EXHALL, Near Alcester.
Exhall. **OR** C 1605-86, M 1606-83, B 1605-87 (AC).
Wixford. **OR** C 1540-1691, M 1541-8, 1559-63, 1606-27, 1641, 1665-88, B 1542-1691 (AC).
Exhall and Wixford. **OR** C 1687-1926, M 1687-1836, B 1687-1812, 1823-1912 (AC). **BT** 1612, 1616 + *(gap 1641-59)* (WRO) *– also on Wixford returns 1616-37, 1688-1700* (WRO). **Cop** M 1539-48, 1559-63, 1606-1627, 1641, 1665-1812 (SOA), CMB 1612 + Mf (A, WRO and SLC).

FARNBOROUGH. **OR** C 1558-1883, M 1558-1841, B 1558-1947 (AC), (Inc). **BT** 1663-1846 *(gap 1665-75)* (*M missing in many years*) (L).

FARNBOROUGH. (RC). *Entries in Brailes regs.*

FENNY COMPTON. **OR** C 1627-1927, M 1628-1810, 1813-1949, B 1627-1882 (AC). **BT** 1662-1809, 1813-1847 (L). **Cop** M 1627-1812 (Phil 1) (SLC). *M 1651-1675 in Boyd Misc.*

FENNY COMPTON. (Gen Bapt). *Coventicle in 1669. No regs.*

FILLONGLEY. **OR** CMB 1538 + *(gap M 1715-54)* (Inc). **BT** 1675-1809, 1813-1847 (L). **Cop** CMB 1538-1653 (Ptd 1893) (SG, A, SLC).

FILLONGLEY (RC). *Numerous entries in regs of St Peter's Franciscan Mission, Birmingham.*

FILLONGLEY. (Pres). *Conventicle 1669, 1672. Existed 1703.*

FLECKNOE. (Pres). *Meeting in 1691. No regs.*

FOLESHILL, St Laurence. OR C 1564 + (1680-91 defective), M 1565 + (*gap 1677-1692*), B 1565-1829 (*gap 1679-91*) (Inc), B 1830-1955 (AC). BT 1662-1836 (L).

FOLESHILL. (Ind). OR ZC 1788-1837 (PRO).

FOXCOTE (RC). *Ilmington since 1935.* OR C 1767-1868, M 1818-41, B 1768-80, 1815-37, 1867-1869 (AHB), C 1867-73, 1882 + (Inc). Cop C 1767-1812 (SOA), C 1767-1848, M 1818-41, D 1768-80, 1815-1837 Mf (A).

FRANKTON. OR C 1559-1949, M 1559-1836, B 1559-1812, Banns 1824-1963 (AC), B 1813 + (Inc). BT 1677-1859 (L).

FULBROOK. *– see Sherborne.*

FULFORD HEATH MONTHLY MEETING (S of F). *Established 1668, dissolved 1716 and joined to* Birmingham Monthly Meeting. Constituent Meetings: *Fulford Heath, Henley-in-Arden (both 1668-1716), Lapworth (c.1700-1716).* OR ZB 1669-1754 (PRO 1186), M 1697-1763 (1185).

FULFORD HEATH (S of F). Fulford Heath Monthly Meeting (*1668-1716*), Birmingham Monthly Meeting (*1716-c.1727*) *disc. c.1727. No regs known apart from Monthly Meeting registers.*

GAYDON and CHADSHUNT. Peculiar *of Bishop's Itchington.* OR C 1701-1930, M 1701-49, B 1701-1812, Banns 1909-1953 *– Listed under Gaydon in RO catalogue,* M 1754-1930, Banns 1754-1812, 1823-30 (AC) *listed under Chadshunt in RO catalogue,* B 1813 + (Inc). BT (*listed under Chadshunt*) 1660, 1670-4, 1685-1723, 1736-40, 1745-1812 (LCL), 1813-21 (L). *Sep BT for Gaydon 1813-21* (L).

GRANDBOROUGH. OR CMB 1581-1812, M to 1837, Banns 1895-1959 (AC), CB 1813 + (Inc). BT 1662-1809, 1813-1844 (L).

GREAT ALNE. *– see Alne Great.*

GREAT BARR. *– see Barr, Great.*

GREAT DASSETT. *– see Burton Dassett.*

GREAT HARBOROUGH. *– see Harborough Magna.*

GRENDON. OR CB 1570-1812, M 1570-1837, Banns 1754-90, 1802-4, 1821-1898 (*gaps CB 1666-1766, M 1666-1754*) (AB). BT 1674-1840, (*no M 1788-1804*) (L). Cop CMB 1570-1812 Ts (BRL cat. no 661288), (PR) CMB 1567-1653, 1655-1666, CB 1766-1812, M 1754-1837, Mf (SLC).

GRENDON AND POLESWORTH (S of F). Warwickshire North Monthly Meeting (*see* Birmingham Monthly Meeting) *established 1721, disc. 1821. No regs known except Monthly Meeting registers.*

ALFORD. OR C 1545-1912 (*gap 1720-48*), M 1545-1812 (*gap 1718-1750*),
B 1545-1812 (*gaps 1677-95, 1720-48*) (AC), Banns 1750-4 (Inc).
BT 1608 + (*gap 1641-62 except 1651*) (WRO). Cop M 1552-1812 (Phil 3)
(SLC), M 1545-51 (C of A), C 1545-1720, 1748-1812, M 1552-1718,
1748-1812, B 1545-1677, 1695-1720, 1748-1812 (SOA), CMB (BT) 1608 +
Mf (A, WRO and SLC). *M 1651-1675 in Boyd Misc.*

HALL GREEN, *Chapel of Yardley, Worcs.* OR CB 1705 +, M 1704-1753, 1863 +.
BT *with Yardley to 1812.* Cop C 1705-1840, M 1704-1746, B 1705-1839
(SG).

HAMPTON-IN-ARDEN. OR CM 1599 +, B 1608 + (Inc). BT 1665-1846 (L).
Cop C 1590-1732, MB 1599-1732 Ts I (SG and SLC), CMB 1599-1732
Ts (A and BRL cat. No. 547526).

HAMPTON-IN-ARDEN (Pres). *Conventicles c. 1669-90. No regs.*

HAMPTON-ON-THE-HILL, St Charles Borromeo (RC). OR C 1808-1843, B (*in
Dormer Vault*) 1835-1883 (AHB), C 1808 +, M 1853 +, B 1854 + (Inc).
Cop C 1808-1843, B (*in Dormer Vault*) 1835-83 Mf (A).

HAMPTON LUCY. Peculiar. OR CMB 1556-1812, M 1556-1960 (AC), CB post-1813
lost. BT 1603, 1611 + (*gaps 1640-60, 1662-9 except 1666, irregular
1704-12, 1734-42*) (WRO), 1683-86 (*L — in Misc. bundle*).
Cop CMB 1569-1800 (SOA), CMB 1556-1812 (C of A), CMB (BT) 1603 +,
Mf (A, WRO and SLC). *M 1553-1812 in Boyd Misc.*

HANDSWORTH. — *see Staffs.*

HARBERBURY. — *see Harbury.*

HARBORNE. *Formerly in Staffs. Became part of Birmingham 1891. See
Staffs.*

HARBOROUGH MAGNA. OR CB 1540-1696, C 1737-1877, B 1737-1938, M 1540-
1696, 1737-52, 1755-1957, Banns 1760-1823 (AC). BT 1662-1838 (L).

HARBURY or HARBERBURY. OR C 1564-1931, M 1565-1630, 1653-1666, 1670-
1750, 1754-1942, B 1565-1914, Banns 1754-1770, 1772-1805, 1807,
1852-1921 (AC). BT 1662-1851 (L).

HARBURY. (Pres). *f before 1730. Became defunct. No regs known.*

HARBURY (S of F). **Warwickshire Middle Monthly Meeting** (*see Coventry*).
*Established 1668, disc. 1795. No regs known other than Monthly
Meeting regs.*

HARBURY. (Wes Meth) or HARBERBURY. **Leamington and Stratford Circuit.**
OR CB 1811-1878 (PRO *non auth.*).

HARDWICK PRIORS. — *see Priors Hardwick.*

HARTSHILL. — *see Mancetter.*

HARTSHILL (S of F). *Established 1704.* **Wishaw Monthly Meeting** (*1704-
1710*), **Warwickshire North Monthly Meeting** (*see Birmingham*) (*1710-
1838*). *Wishaw Monthly Meeting registers continued in use for
Baddesley and Hartshill after dissolution of Monthly Meeting.*

HARTSHILL. (Pres). *Conventicle c.1672. No regs.*

HARTSHILL, Chapel End. (Ind). **OR** ZC 1799-1837 *includes Ansley* (PRO), ZC 1801-1837 (Ch. Sec).

HASELEY. **OR** CB 1588-1633, 1716-1806, 1813 +, M 1588-1625, 1716-1806, 1808 + (Inc Hatton). **BT** 1612 + *(gap 1640-60)* (WRO). **Cop** CMB 1588-1633 Ms (SG), M 1588-1806 (SOA), CMB (BT) 1612 + Mf (A, WRO and SLC)

HASELEY. (Pres). *Meeting 1696. No regs.*

HASELOR. **OR** C 1594-1959, MB 1589-1959 *(gaps C 1631-79, 1736-1809, M 1630-79, 1736-54, B 1619-79, 1736-1809)* (AC). **BT** 1615, 1621, 1625, 1639, 1641, 1661, 1663, 1666 + (WRO). **Cop** 1594-1620, 1681-1705, M 1589-1620, 1679-1703, B 1589-1618, 1679-1704 (SOA), CMB (BT) 1615 + Mf (A, WRO and SLC).

HATTON. **OR** C 1538-1666, 1716 +, M 1538-1640, 1716 +, B 1538-1689, 1716 + (Inc). **BT** 1613 + *(gap 1639-1665,* irregular 1667-1678) (WRO). **Cop** CMB 1538-1663, Ms (SG), M 1558-1812 (Phil 3), CMB (BT) 1613 + Mf (A, WRO and SLC). *M (BT) 1651-1675 in Boyd Misc.*

HAWKESBURY. *– see Coventry.*

HENLEY-IN-ARDEN. **OR** CMB 1679-81, 1695-1762, C 1772-1921, M 1772-1812, 1816, Banns 1840-1921, B 1772-1812, 1824, 1831, 1861 (AC), MB 1813 (Inc). *CB 1700-1812, M 1700-54 in Wootton Wawen regs.* **BT** 1662-3, 1697 – *no post-1700 BT's exist.–* (WRO). **Cop** CMB 1546-1700 (Ptd in " Wootton Wawen, its History and Records ").

HENLEY-IN-ARDEN, High Street. (Particular Bapt). *f 1688, dependent on Alcester until 1803.* **OR** Z 1791-1830 (PRO). *Includes entries from a wide area, extending as far as Evesham.*

HENLEY-IN-ARDEN (S of F). **Fulford Heath Monthly Meeting** *(1668-1716),* **Birmingham Monthly Meeting** *(1716-1800) disc. c.1800. No regs known other than Monthly Meeting registers.*

HILL. **OR** CB 1836 +, M 1842 + (Inc).

HILLMORTON. **OR** C 1564-1959 *(gap 1651-3)*, M 1564-1940 *(gap 1692-4)*, B 1564-1901, Banns 1823-1960 (AC). **BT** 1662-1852, odd years to 1873 (L).

HONILEY. **OR** CB 1745-1812, M 1745-1835, 1842-1951 (AC). **BT** 1805-1812 (Misc. bundle) 1813-35 (L).

HONINGTON. **OR** C 1571-1653 *(many gaps)*, 1657-1927, M 1573-1701, 1714-1837 *(many gaps 1591-1653)*, B 1573-1812 *(many gaps 1573-1654)*, Banns 1824-1902 (AC), B 1813 + (Inc). **BT** 1612 + *(gap 1641-60)* (WRO) **Cop** M 1571-1812 (Phil 1), C 1571-1812, M 1571-1754, B 1573-1812 (SOA and A), CMB (BT) 1612 + Mf (A, WRO and SLC). *M 1651-1675 in Boyd Misc.*

HUNNINGHAM. **OR** CM 1718-1951, B 1718-1812 (AC), B 1813 + (Inc). **BT** 1662-1845 (L).

HYDES PASTURES. *Warwickshire hamlet in parish of Hinckley, Leics. q.v.*

DLICOTE. **OR** CB 1556-1812, M 1556-1662, 1670-1709, 1721-1837 (AC),
CB 1813 + (Inc). **BT** 1611 + *(gap 1639-1661)* (WRO). **Cop** M 1557-1812
(Phil 1), C 1556-1812, M 1557-1612, 1625, 1661-1708, 1722-1812,
B 1557-1615, (BT) 1617-1637, 1662-1812 (SOA), CMB (BT) 1611 + Mf
(A, WRO and SLC). *M 1651-1675 in Boyd Misc.*

LMINGTON. **OR** C 1588-1847, M 1588-1837, B 1588-1925, Banns 1824-1906
(AC). **BT** 1611 + *(gap 1638-63)* (WRO). **Cop** CMB 1588-1812 (SOA),
CMB (BT) 1611 + Mf (A, WRO and SLC).

LMINGTON, St Philip the Apostle (RC). *– see Foxcote.*

PSLEY. *Transferred to Worcs 1931.* **OR** CMB 1615 + (Inc). **BT** 1612 +
(gap 1641-60) (WRO). **Cop** CMB (BT) 1612 + Mf (A, WRO and SLC).

TCHINGTON, LONG. **OR** C 1653-1892, M 1658-1942, B 1653-1950, Banns 1754-
1782, 1794-1818, 1823-1931 (AC). **BT** 1653-1809, 1813-1846 (L).

ITCHINGTON, LONG. (Ind). *f 1828. Not at PRO. No information.*

KENILWORTH, St Nicholas. **OR** CB 1630-1943, M 1630-1945 (AC). **BT** 1676-
1847 (L).

KENILWORTH, St Augustine (RC). **OR** C 1831-1890, B 1844-1890 (AHB),
CB 1890 +, M 1860 + (Inc). **Cop** C 1831-7 Mf (A).

KENILWORTH (S of F). **Warwickshire Middle Monthly Meeting** *(see Coventry).*
f 1668, disc. c.1689. No regs known other than Monthly Meeting
registers.

KENILWORTH, Rosemary Hill. (Pres). *f.c. 1662. 2 conventicles in 1670's*
(estimated a quarter of population Pres. in 1676). 1706 Rosemary
Hill Meeting House built. Now Kenilworth Unitarian Church.
OR ZC 1819-1832 (PRO).

KENILWORTH, Abbey Hill. (Ind). *f 1787 by breakaway from Rosemary Hill*
Meeting, partial return 1804, 2nd exodus 1816, new Meeting House
built 1828-9. Present church built 1872. **OR** C 1831-6 (PRO).

KINETON. **OR** C 1538-1952 *(1538-47 defective)*, M 1538-1932 *(1546-1581*
defective), B 1577-1635, 1638-1906, Banns 1854-1939 (AC). **BT** 1611 +
(gaps 1641-61, 1711-16, 1737-1760 (except 1745, 51, 54), 1766-1770:
very irregular 1700-1781). Sometimes Kineton entries on Combroke
returns) (WRO). **Cop** CMB 1538-1794, CMB (BT) 1661-99 (SOA),
CMB 1795-1812 (C of A), CMB (BT) 1611 + Mf (A, WRO and SLC).

KINETON. (Gen Bapt). *Probably conventicle in 1669 – became defunct.*
No regs.

KINGSBURY. **OR** C 1537-1875, M 1537-1837, B 1537-1898 *(gap CMB 1676-9)*,
Banns 1816-77 (AB). **BT** 1668-1852 (L). **Cop** CMB 1537-1812, p/s (BRL
cat. No. 606851), CMB 1539-1676, C 1679-1875, M 1679-1837, B 1679-
1918, Banns 1816-1877 Mf (SLC).

KINGSBURY. (Pres). *Conventicle c. 1672. No regs.*

KINGS HEATH. *– see Birmingham.*

KINGS NEWNHAM. – see Church Lawford.

KINGS NEWNHAM. (Pres). Conventicle c. 1669-1672. No regs.

KINGS NORTON. Parish in Birmingham formerly in Worcs (see Worcs).

KINWARTON. OR C 1556-1832, M 1571-1695, 1706-1812, B 1596-1703, 1706-1812 (AC), C 1833 +, MB 1813 + (Inc). BT 1634, 1639, 1660 + (WRO).

KNIGHTCOTE. (Gen Bapt). Congregation in 1745. No regs.

KNOWLE. Lichfield Peculiar. OR CMB 1682 + (Inc). BT 1813 + (L). No earlier BT's traced. Cop CMB 1682-1812 (Ptd and I as "Records of Knowle").

KNOWLE (RC). Entries in St Peter's Franciscan Mission, Birmingham.

KNOWLE. (Pres). f.c. 1669, disc. c.1735. No regs known.

LADBROKE. OR C 1559-1812, M 1560-1837, B 1558-1812 (AC), CB 1813 + (Inc) BT 1662-1836 (L), 1837 + (WRO). Cop CB 1538-1762, M 1538-1754 (C of A).

LAPWORTH. OR CMB 1561 + (Inc). BT 1613 + (gap 1641-61, irregular 1661-1684) (WRO). Cop CMB 1561-1812 (SOA). Index to surnames 1561-1860 in "Memorials in a Warwickshire Parish" – Hudson 1904, (PR) C 1561-1853, M 1561-1812, 1814-1913, B 1561-1870, Banns 1754-1794 Mf (SLC), CMB (BT) 1613 + Mf (A, WRO and SLC).

LAPWORTH. (Pres). Conventicle in 1669. No regs.

LAPWORTH (S of F). Fulford Heath Monthly Meeting (c. 1700-1716), Warwickshire North Monthly Meeting (see Birmingham) (1716-c.1727). No regs known except for Monthly Meeting registers.

LAWFORD, LONG. (Gen Bapt). Conventicle c.1663-1672. No regs.

LEA MARSTON. OR C 1570-1894, M 1570-1936, B 1570-1952, Banns 1755-1812 (AB). BT 1673-1805, 1813-1843 (L). Cop MB 1662-1674 Ts (SG and A), (PR) C 1570-1894, M 1570-1936, B 1570-1952 Mf (SLC).

LEAMINGTON HASTINGS. OR CMB 1559-1812, Banns 1823-1956 (AC), CMB 1813 + (Inc). BT 1662-1846 (L), 1682-84 on Terriers at (A).

LEAMINGTON PRIORS (SPA), All Saints. OR CMB 1618-1710 with small gaps, 1717, 1718-23, 1725-39 (Leamington Spa P/Lib.), CMB 1702 + (Inc). BT 1662-1842 (L). Cop M 1704-1812 (Phil 1). Surnames index 1618-1723 (Leamington P/Lib.).

LEAMINGTON, St Mary. OR 1839 + (Inc). BT 1839-1844 (L).

LEAMINGTON PRIORS (SPA), St Peters Chapel, Dormer Place (RC). OR C 1822-40, M 1839-40 (PRO) – contains extracts from Wappenbury regs. C 1842 +, MB 1876 + (Inc).

LEAMINGTON PRIORS, Mill St Chapel. (Calv Meth). OR ZCB 1831-37 (PRO).

LEAMINGTON PRIORS. (Pres). Conventicle in 1664. No regs.

LEAMINGTON PRIORS, Spencer St. (Ind). f 1816. OR ZC 1830-37 (PRO).

LEAMINGTON PRIORS, Warwick St. (Particular Bapt). *f 1830 branch of Castle Hill, Warwick. Not at PRO. No information.*

LEAMINGTON PRIORS. (Wes). **Coventry Circuit.** *From 1837* **Leamington and Stratford Circuit.** OR ZC 1832-37 (PRO).

LEAMINGTON SPA. *– see Leamington Priors.*

LEEK WOOTTON. OR C 1581-1883, M 1581-1837, B 1581-1916, Banns 1754-1938 (*gaps C 1641-1685, B 1641-88, M 1641-89*) (AC). BT 1662-1852 (*gaps 1668-77, 1685-93, 1742-55*) (L). **Cop** CMB 1581-1710 p/s (BRL cat. No. 370441), CMB 1685-1745 (Guildhall Lib.), CMB 1581-1742 (Ptd Crisp 1887). (No copy SG).

LEEK WOOTTON (RC). *Some entries in registers of St Peter's Franciscan Mission, Birmingham.*

LEEK WOOTTON. (Gen Bapt). *Conventicle c.1669. No regs.*

LIGHTHORNE. OR C 1538-1885, M 1539-1932, B 1538-1942 (*gap CB 1734-6, M 1733-6*) (AC). BT 1611 + (*gap 1640-62*) (WRO). **Cop** CB 1538-1812, M 1539-1753 (SOA), CMB (BT) 1611 + Mf (A, WRO and SLC).

LILLINGTON. OR CMB 1539-1643, CB 1653 +, M 1654 + (Inc). BT 1662-1845 (L).

LONG COMPTON. *– see Compton, Long.*

LONG ITCHINGTON. *– see Itchington, Long.*

LONGFORD. *– see Coventry.*

LOWER SHUCKBURGH. *– see Shuckburgh, Lower.*

LOXLEY. OR C 1601-1888, M 1540-99, 1613-41, 1662-1945, B 1540-1577, 1627-58, 1703-91, 1803-12 (AC), B 1813 + (Inc). BT 1612 + (*gaps 1631-6, 1640-60*) (WRO). **Cop** C 1601-1812, M 1540-99, 1613-41, 1662-1812, B 1540-77, 1627-58, 1703-91, 1803-12 (SOA), M 1540-1812 (SLC), CMB (BT) 1612 + (A, WRO and SLC). *M 1539-1812 in Boyd Misc.*

LOZELLS. *Hamlet of Aston-juxta-Birmingham q.v.*

LUDDINGTON. OR CMB 1850 + (Inc Stratford-on-Avon). BT *Sometimes on Stratford-on-Avon returns – separate irregular returns 1617-1639*) (WRO). **Cop** C 1617-1638, M 1621-38, B 1628-32 (SOA), CMB (BT) 1617-1639 Mf (A, WRO and SLC).

MANCETTER. OR C 1576-1899, M 1576-1958, B 1576-1869, Banns 1845-1958 (AC). BT 1660-1855 (L). *See also Atherstone.*

MANCETTER. (Pres). *Conventicle c.1672. No regs.*

MARSTON SICCA. *– see Gloucestershire and also Cliford Chambers.*

MARTON. OR C 1660-1876, M 1660-1835, B 1660-1928 (AC). BT 1662-1847 (LX).

MARTON. (Ind). *f 1833. Not at PRO.* OR C 1872 + (Ch. Sec.).

MAXSTOKE. **OR** C 1647, 1653 +, M 1654-63, 1700-52, 1755-1809, 1816 +
B 1653-1667, 1699 + (Inc). **BT** 1676-1843 (*M missing 1772-1805*) (L).
Cop (PR) C 1653-1705, 1770-1899, M 1654-1752, 1755-1812, 1815-
1835, B 1653-1734, 1771-1899, Banns 1755-1825 Mf (SLC).

MEREVALE. *Lichfield* **Peculiar. OR** C 1727-1899, M 1728-1837 (*gap 1751-4*),
B 1727-1812, Banns 1824-1956 (AB), B 1813 + (Inc). **BT** 1813-1846 (L).
No earlier B T's known. **Cop** (PR) C 1727-1898, M 1727-1837, B 1727-
1812 Mf (SLC).

MEREVALE, Our Lady of the Assumption (RC). *f 1679. No information.*

MEREVALE. (Pres). *Conventicle c.1672. Existing 1689, disc. before 1750.
No regs.*

MERIDEN. **OR** C 1646-1907, M 1647-1939, B 1646-1902, Banns 1823-1960
(AC). **BT** 1673-1844 (L).

MERIDEN (S of F). *Afterwards Berkeswell or Balsall St.* **Warwickshire
Middle Monthly Meeting** (*see Coventry*) *established 1668, disc. 1783.
No regs known other than Monthly Meeting regs.*

MIDDLETON. **OR** C 1671 +, M 1681 +, B 1675 + (Inc). **BT** 1655-1812, 1845-
46 (L). **Cop** (PR) CM 1675-1899, B 1675-1894, Banns 1824-1899 Mf (SLC'

MILVERTON. **OR** CMB 1742-1812, Banns 1794-99 (AC). **BT** 1664-1842 (L).

MONKS KIRBY. **OR** C 1647 +, MB 1649 + (Inc), Banns 1824-42, 1847-1948 (AC).
BT 1677-1835 (L). *See also Withybrook.*

MONKS KIRBY. (Ind). – *see Stretton-under-Fosse.*

MONKS KIRBY. (Bapt). **OR** Z 1805-37 (PRO).

MORETON MORRELL. **OR** C 1689-1821, M 1692-1750, 1774-1836, B 1678-1812
(AC), C 1822 +, M 1837 +, B 1813 + (Inc). **BT** 1608 + (*gap 1639-66*
except 1660, 1665) (WRO). **Cop** C 1689-1840, M 1692-1750, 1773-1837,
B 1678-1837 (SG), CMB 1539-1812 (C of A), CMB (BT) 1608 + Mf (A,
WRO and SLC).

MORETON MORRELL. (Wes). *f.c. 1827. Church built 1843. No regs known.
Not at PRO or Circuit Superintendent. Now* **Stratford-on-Avon
Circuit.**

MORTON BAGOT. **OR** C 1663-1812, M 1664-1811, 1813-1836, B 1664-1812,
Banns 1813-24 (AC). **BT** 1614-15, 1621, 1634, 1663 + (irregular 1663-
1683) (WRO). **Cop** CMB (BT) 1614 + Mf (A, WRO and SLC).

NAPTON-ON-THE-HILL. **OR** C 1604-1871, M 1604-1960, B 1604-1950 (AC).
BT 1662-1809, 1813-1847 (L).

NAPTON-ON-THE-HILL. (Gen Bapt). *Conventicle c.1663-5. Congregation
in 1689 and 1723. Defunct before 1770. No regs.*

NETHER WHITACRE. – *see Whitacre Nether.*

NEWBOLD-ON-AVON. **OR** C 1559-1930, M 1559-1935, B 1559-1935, Banns 1808-
1822, 1839-1950 (*gap CMB 1652-9*) (AC). **BT** 1663-1809, 1813-1844 (L).

NEWBOLD-ON-STOUR. **OR** C 1838 +, M 1839 +, B 1836 + (Inc).

NEWBOLD PACEY. **OR** C 1554-1890, M 1554-1964, B 1555-1812, Banns 1827-1937 (AC). **BT** 1613 + *(gap 1640-66*, except 1643, 1660, 1663) (WRO). **Cop** CB 1554-1812, M 1554-1753 (C of A), CMB (BT) 1613 + Mf (A, WRO and SLC).

NEWNHAM, KINGS or REGIS. – *see Church Lawford.*

NEWTON REGIS. **OR** (*CMB defective 1591-1608*), C 1591-1875, M 1591-1836, B 1591-1949 (*gap CMB 1644-55, CB 1752-62*), Banns 1824-95 (AB). **BT** 1663-1809, 1813-1851 (L). **Cop** CMB 1591-1812 Ts and Ms (BRL cat. No. 661290). (PR) CMB 1591-1644, C 1655-1875, M 1655-1836, B 1655-1900, Banns 1824-1895 Mf (SLC).

NEWTON REGIS. (Pres). *Conventicle c. 1669. No regs.*

NORTHEND. (Wes). *f 1832.* **Banbury Circuit** *now* **Kineton Circuit.** *No registers known.*

NORTHFIELD. *Formerly in Worcestershire. Became part of Birmingham 1912. See Worcestershire.*

NORTON LINDSEY. **OR** C 1742-1812, M 1744-1810, 1815-36, B 1743-1812 (AC), CB 1813 +, M 1837 + (Inc). **BT** 1607, 1613 + *(gap 1640-63)* (WRO). **Cop** CMB (BT) 1607-1700 (SOA), CMB (BT) 1607 + Mf (A, WRO and SLC).

NUNEATON, St Nicholas. **OR** C 1577-1632, 1653-59, 1662-1913, M 1587-1632, 1653-59, 1662-1960, B 1585-1632, 1653-59, 1662-1913, Banns 1775-1857 (AC). **BT** 1674-1852 (L).

NUNEATON, Our Lady of the Angels (RC). *f 1829.* **OR** C 1855 +, M 1860 +, DB 1880 +, Confirmations 1834 + (Parish Priest).

NUNEATON, Zion Chapel, Coton Rd. (Ind). *f.c. 1693 as Pres. Became Ind during 18th century. 1719 building erected in Coton Rd. Subsidiary meetings 1722 Attleborough; 1738 Chilvers Coton. 1793 New church erected. Present church built 1903.* **OR** ZC 1818-1836 (PRO).

NUNEATON, Bond St. (Ind). *f 1815 by secession from above. 1902 reunited with above. No regs known. Not at PRO.*

NUNEATON. (Ind). – *see also Hartshill.*

NUNEATON. (Gen Bapt). *Conventicle c. 1669-72. No regs.*

NUNEATON (S of F). **Warwickshire North Monthly Meeting** *(see Birmingham) c. 1721-6. No registers known except for Monthly Meeting registers.*

NUTHURST cum HOCKLEY HEATH. **OR** C 1835-1920, M 1879-1926 (AB). **BT** 1835-1846, 1859-1862 (L).

OFFCHURCH. **OR** C 1669-1918 (*1669-95 fragmentary*), Z 1721-34, 1740-1764, 1805-12, M 1689-1754, 1777-1811, 1813-37, B 1680-1812, Banns 1824-1895 (AC), B 1813 + (Inc).. **BT** 1662-1809, 1813-43 (LX).

OLDBERROW. *Transferred from Worcestershire 1896.* **OR** C 1649-1812, M 1649, 1659-1785, 1788-1810, 1813-35, B 1649, 1659-1812, Banns 1754-1784 (AC), CB 1813 + (Inc). **BT** 1613 + *(gap 1641-1659)* (WRO).

OVER WHITACRE. – *see Whitacre, Over.*

OXHILL. **OR** CB 1568-1926 (*gap B 1617-32*), M 1569-1837 (M defective 1748-54), B 1617-32 (AC). **BT** 1605-10, 1618, 1628, 1630, 1633-5, 1638-40, 1660 + (WRO). **Cop** C 1568-1618, M 1569-1747 (SOA), CMB 1568-1812 (C of A), CMB (BT) 1605 + Mf (A, WRO and SLC).

OXHILL. (Wes). *f 1814.* **Banbury Circuit.** *Now* **Kineton Circuit.** *No regs known. Not at PRO or Kineton Circuit safe.*

PACKINGTON, GREAT or PACKINGTON MAGNA. **OR** CMB 1538 + (*small gaps CMB 1664-70, gap CMB 1682-1703*) (Inc), Banns 1824-1959 (AC). **BT** 1667-1847 (LX).

PACKINGTON, LITTLE or PACKINGTON PARVA. **OR** CMB 1628-72, 1694 + (*gap M 1772-4*) (Inc). **BT** 1676-1847 (LX).

PACKINGTON (RC). *Some entries in regs of St Peter's Franciscan Mission Birmingham.*

PACKWOOD. *Parochial chapelry or perpetual curacy with Wasperton until 1850.* **Peculiar. OR** C 1668-1880, M 1668-1761, 1777-1890, B 1668-1927, Banns 1784-99, 1851-1936 (AB). **BT** 1813-35 (L). *No earlier BT's known. Perhaps on Wasperton returns.* **Cop** (PR) C 1668-1880, M 1668-1890, B 1668-1927, Banns 1899-1936 Mf (SLC).

PAILTON. (Ind). *Existed in 1704. No regs.*

PAILTON. (Gen Bapt). *Congregation in 1743. No regs.*

PAILTON (S of F). **Warwickshire Middle Monthly Meeting** (*see Coventry*) *f 1688, disc. 1694. No regs known other than Monthly Meeting regs.*

PILLERTON HERSEY. **OR** C 1539-1811, M 1543-1579, 1602-1729, 1732-9, 1746, B 1539-70, 1586-87, 1596-1731, 1738-1812 (AC) (*M 1754-1812 in Pillerton Priors register*) (AC), CMB 1813 + (Inc). **BT** 1611 + (*gap 1640-60*) (WRO). **Cop** CB 1539-1812, M 1543-1786 Ts (A), CB 1539-1812, M 1749-1811 (SOA), CMB (BT) 1611 + Mf (A, WRO and SLC).

PILLERTON PRIORS. **OR** C 1604-1812, M 1594-1649, 1670-71, 1714, 1749, 1751 (M 1754-1812 Pillerton Hersey), B 1594-1729, 1731-9, 1751-1812 (AC), CMB 1813 + (Inc). **BT** 1613-1667 (*gap 1639-66*) (WRO). **Cop** C 1604-1812, M 1594-1786, B 1595-1812 Ts (A), C 1604-1728, M 1594-1649, 1670-71, B 1594-1729 (SOA), CMB (BT) 1613 + Mf (A, WRO and SLC).

PILLERTON PRIORS. (Gen Bapt). *Conventicle c. 1683-5. No regs.*

POLESWORTH. **OR** CMB 1631 + (Inc). **BT** 1669-1844 (L). **Cop** M 1631-1741 (SOA), CMB 1631-1759 Ts (BRL cat. No. 661287), (PR) C 1631-1895, M 1631-1902, B 1631-1947 Mf (SLC).

POLESWORTH (S of F). – *see Grendon.*

POLESWORTH. (Ind). *f 1832.* **OR** ZC 1832-36 (PRO).

POLESWORTH. The Gullett. (Bapt). *f 1828. Not at PRO. No information.*

OTTERS GREEN. *Parish of Walsgrave-on-Sowe.* (Ind). *f 1816. Not at PRO. No information.*

OULTON. (Gen Bapt). *Congregation in 1743. Became defunct. No regs.*

RESTON BAGOT. OR CB 1677-1812, M 1677-1959 (*gap M 1836-39*), CB 1813 + (Inc). BT 1612-14, 1620, 1634, 1638-40, 1662 + (WRO). Cop Warwick Advertiser 1891 (Ptd), CMB (BT) 1612 + Mf (A, WRO and SLC).

RESTON-ON-STOUR. *Formerly in Glos. Transferred from Glos. Dio to Coventry in 1918.* OR C 1540-76, 1593-1644, 1666-1928, M 1542-76, 1593-1643, 1661-4, 1689-1928, B 1540-1576, 1594-1641, 1653, 1684-1928 (AC). BT 1606 + (CLG). Cop M 1541-1812 (Phil 4, Glos), CMB 1540-1610 (CLG), CMB 1540-1812 (SOA). *M 1541-1812 in Roe's Glos Marriage Index.*

RESTON-ON-STOUR. (Bapt). *f date not known. Not at PRO. No information.*

RIORS HARDWICK. OR C 1661-1887, M 1662-1834, Banns 1823-1895, B 1662-1812 (AC), B 1813 + (Inc). BT 1662-1809, 1813-1846 (L). Cop M 1662-1812 (Phil 1). *M 1662-1675 in Boyd Misc.*

RIORS MARSTON. OR C 1689-1854, M 1700-1837, B 1695-1877, Banns 1873-1932 (AC). BT 1662-1809, 1813-1847 (L).

RIORS MARSTON (Gen Bapt). *Conventicle in 1669. Congregation in 1689, 1708, 1733. Defunct before 1770. No regs.*

QUINTON. *– see Clifford Chambers.*

RADFORD SEMELE. OR C 1565-1919, M 1565-1634, 1652-1680, 1690-1778, 1780-1836, B 1565-1636, 1652-1682, 1743-1891, Banns 1754-1778, 1823-1929 (AC). BT 1662-1846 (LX).

RADFORD SEMELE. (Bapt). *f date not known. Not at PRO. No information.*

RADFORD SEMELE. (Ind). *f 1825. Not at PRO. No information.*

RADFORD SEMELE (S of F). Warwickshire Middle Monthly Meeting (*see Coventry*). *Established 1668, disc. late 18th century. No regs known other than Monthly Meeting regs.*

RADWAY. OR C 1608-1904, M 1605-1837 (*gaps 1638-68, 1674-97, 1699*), B 1605-1963 (*gap 1672-97*), Banns 1824-1948 (AC), CMB 1813 + (Inc). BT 1663-1836 (LX). Cop CMB 1605-1701 Ts I (SG).

RADWAY (S of F). *Established 1668, disc. 1850.* Brailes Monthly Meeting. OR ZM 1660-1815, B 1660-1827 (PRO 1585).

RATLEY. OR C 1701-1868, M 1701-1837, B 1701-1924 (AC). BT 1662-1805, 1813-1836 (LX).

ROUND ALNE. *– see Alne, Great.*

ROWINGTON. OR C 1638-1916, M 1638-1956, B 1638-1859 (*gap CMB 1655-62*) (AC). BT 1612, 1616 + (*gap 1640-62*) (WRO). Cop CMB 1612-1812 (PRS 21), CMB (BT) 1612 + Mf (A, WRO and SLC).

ROWINGTON (RC). *Numerous entries in regs of St Peter's Franciscan Mission, Birmingham.*

RUGBY. **OR** C 1620-1920, M 1620-1921, B 1620-1947 (B 1754-1814 in M reg) (AC). **BT** 1665-1847 (L).

RUGBY. (Pres). *Conventicle c. 1669-72. No regs.*

RUGBY. (Gen Bapt). *Congregation in 1729. Became defunct. No regs.*

RUGBY, Regent Place. (Bapt). *f 1808. Not at PRO.* **OR** M 1906 + (Ch. Sec. *No earlier regs known.*

RUGBY. (Wes). **Coventry Circuit. OR** ZC 1815-1837 (PRO).

RYTON-ON-DUNSMORE. **OR** C 1538-1655, 1662-1931, M 1539-1648, 1662-1739, 1755-1837, B 1560-1879, Banns 1823-1911 (AC). **BT** 1671-1809, 1813-1840 (LX).

RYTON. *Parish of Bulkington* (Ind). *Meeting existed in 1739. No regs.*

SALFORD PRIORS. **OR** CMB 1568 +. **BT** 1614 + (irregular to 1641, *gap 1641-1660,* irregular 1660-70) (WRO). **Cop** CMB (BT) 1614 + Mf (A, WRO and SLC).

SALFORD PRIORS (RC). Our Lady and St Anthony, Salford Abbots. **OR** C 1763-1837 (AHB), Confirmations 1830-71 (Inc). **Cop** C 1763-1835 (Inc), C 1763-1835 Mf (A).

SALTLEY. *Hamlet of Aston-juxta-Birmingham q.v.*

SALTLEY. (Ind). *f 1825. Not at PRO.* **OR** M 1870 + (Ch. Sec). *Earlier records destroyed.*

SECKINGTON. **OR** CB 1612-1813, M 1612-1754, 1756-1837, Banns 1827-1959 (AB), CB 1813 + (Inc). **BT** 1679-1845 (L). **Cop** CMB 1612-1813 Ts (BRL Cat. No. 661289), (PR) CB 1612-1813, M 1612-1837, Banns 1827-1899 Mf (SLC).

SHELDON. *Now in Birmingham.* **OR** CMB 1558 + (Inc). **BT** 1676-1844 (*gaps 1772-1775, 1841-2*)(L). **Cop** (PR) CM 1558-1899, B 1558-1900, Banns 1823-1900 Mf (SLC).

SHERBORNE (including Fulbrook). **OR** C 1587-1939, M 1587-1722, 1754-1821, B 1587-1812 (*many regs in poor condition*) (AC), M 1822 +, B 1813 + (Inc). **BT** 1615 + (*gap 1620-63,* except 1635) (WRO).

SHILTON. **OR** CMB 1695-1812 (*gap M 1749-54*) (AC), CMB 1813 + (Inc). **BT** 1668-92 (*in misc. bundle*) 1809-1846 (L).

SHILTON. (Gen Bapt). *Conventicle c. 1672. No regs.*

SHIPSTON-ON-STOUR. **OR** C 1603 +, MB 1572 + (Inc). **BT** 1608 + (*gap 1641-1660*) (WRO). **Cop** M 1571-1812 (Phil Worcs 1), C 1572-1669, M 1572-1746, B 1572-1625, 1650-6 (SOA), CMB (BT) 1608 + Mf (A, WRO and SLC). *M 1651-1675 in Boyd Misc.*

SHIPSTON-ON-STOUR (S of F). **OR** Z 1657-1776, M 1662-1776, B 1673-1775 (PRO *Cat. under Worcs.*).

SHIPSTON ON STOUR, Church Street. (Bapt). *f 1781.* **OR** Z 1783-1836
(PRO cat. *under Worcs*).

SHIRLEY. **OR** CMB 1832 +. **BT** 1839-40 (L).

SHOTTERY. *Hamlet of Stratford on Avon q.v.*

SHOTTERY. (Ind). *f 1833. Not at PRO. No information.*

SHOTTESWELL. **OR** C 1564-1927, M 1566-1738, 1741-1749, 1755-1836,
B 1564-1812 (AC), B 1813 + (Inc). **BT** 1670-1809, 1813-1846 (LX).
Cop CMB 1565-1673 (SOA).

SHUCKBURGH, LOWER. **OR** CMB 1678-1801 (AC), CMB 1800 + (Inc). **BT** 1662-
1847 (L), 1801-1805 on Terriers (A).

SHUCKBURGH, UPPER. **OR** C 1781-1809, 1816 +, M 1757-87, 1812, 1818 +,
B 1781 + (Shuckburgh Hall). **BT** 1672-1839 (LX).

SHUSTOKE. **OR** CMB 1538 + *(gap 1659-61)* (Inc). **BT** 1674-1843 (L).
Cop M 1539-1812 (Phil Ms and Mf SLC), CMB 1538-1722 p/s (BRL Cat.
No. 487570-72), (PR) C 1538-1885, M 1563-1837, B 1562-1899, Banns
1754-1812, 1824-1899 Mf (SLC). *M 1538-1812 in Boyd Misc. See also
Bentley.*

SHUTTINGTON. **OR** CB 1557-1812, M 1557-1783, 1813-37, Banns 1754-1812
(CMB defective 1653-79) (AB), CB 1813 + (Inc). **BT** 1676-1805, 1813-
1838 (LX). **Cop** (PR) CMB 1557-1899 Mf (SLC).

SHUTTINGTON (S of F). **Wishaw Monthly Meeting** *disc. c. 1679. No regs
other than Monthly Meeting regs.*

SHUTTINGTON. (Pres). *Conventicle c. 1669-1672. No regs.*

SMALL HEATH. (Pres). *f.c. 1700, disc. before 1715. No regs known.*

SNITTERFIELD. **OR** C 1561-1682, 1689-1802, 1805-1923, M 1561-1677,
1689-1736, 1740-1953, B 1562-1682, 1689-1802, 1805-1930, Banns
1754-97 (AC). **BT** 1611 + *(gap 1640-63)* (WRO). **Cop** M 1561-1812 (Phil
3), CMB 1561-1682 (SOA), CMB (BT) 1611 + Mf (A, WRO and SLC).
M 1651-1675 in Boyd Misc.

SNITTERFIELD. (Wes). *f.c. 1830. Church built 1839. Now* **Stratford-on-
Avon Circuit.** *No regs known. Not at PRO or Circuit Superintendent.*

SOLIHULL. **OR** CMB 1538 + *(Regs kept at Lloyds Bank, Solihull* – key
with Churchwarden). **BT** 1673-1809, 1813-1846 (L). **Cop** CMB 1538-
1668 Ptd (PRS 53) (SLC), (PR) C 1538-1921, M 1538-1914, B 1538-
1909 Mf (SLC).

SOLIHULL, St Augustine of England (RC). **OR** C 1776-1864, M 1824-43,
B 1821-57, Confirmations 1823-65 (AHB). **Cop** C 1776-1837, M 1824-37,
B 1821-37 Mf (A). *A large number of earlier Solihull entries in
regs of St Peter's Franciscan Mission, Birmingham.*

SOLIHULL, Bethesda Chapel. (Ind). *f 1825.* **OR** ZC 1836-37 (PRO).

SOUTHAM. **OR** CB 1539-1809, M 1539-1812 (*gap CMB 1675-78*) (AC), CB 1810 [+] M 1813 [+] (Inc). **BT** 1662-1840 (LX). **Cop** C 1539-1606, M 1539-1630, B 1539-1601 (Ptd as "Historical Notes and Recollections relating to the Parish of Southam in the County of Warwick " 1894), C 1539-1633, M 1539-1657, B 1539-1647 (SG), CMB 1633-1812 Ts I (SG).

SOUTHAM. (Pres). *Conventicle c. 1669-1672. Meeting existed 1639, 1727. No regs.*

SOUTHAM. (Ind). *f 1832. Not at PRO. No information.*

SOUTHAM. (Gen Bapt). *Conventicle c. 1669. No regs.*

SOUTHAM (S of F). **Warwickshire Middle Monthly Meeting** (*see Coventry*) *f.c. 1680, disc. 1711. No regs known other than Monthly Meeting regs.*

SOWE (or WALSGRAVE-ON-SOWE). **OR** C 1538-1961, M 1538-1929, B 1538-1881, Banns 1754-1816 (AC). **BT** 1677-1837 (LX).

SPERNALL. **OR** CB 1562-1812, M 1562-1751, 1754-1761, 1763-1812, 1815-1836 (AC). **BT** 1612 [+] (*irregular to 1623, gap 1623-63 except 1639*) (WRO). **Cop** M 1622-1796 (SOA), CMB (BT) 1612 [+] Mf (A, WRO and SLC).

STIVICHALL or STYVECHALE. (*Civil parish Stivichall, ecclesiastical parish Styvechale*). **OR** C 1648-1942 (*gap 1798-1813*) M 1648-1944 (*gaps 1740-54, 1799-1804*) B 1648-1797 (*gap B 1797-1813*), Banns 1824-1956 (AC). **BT** 1662-1809, 1813-1844 (LX).

STOCKINGFORD. **OR** C 1824-1942, M 1824-1951, B 1824-1909 (AC). **BT** 1824-1844 (L).

STOCKTON. **OR** CMB 1567-1954 (*CMB defective 1567-1717*), Banns 1824-1953 (AC). **BT** 1670-1865 (LX).

STOKE. **OR** CMB 1574-1649, 1672 [+] (Inc). **BT** 1664-1845 (L).

STOKE, Harefield Rd. (Ind). *f 1813. Not at PRO. No information.*

STONELEIGH. **OR** C 1634-1958, M 1634-1953, B 1634-1894, Banns 1823-1953 (Inc). **BT** 1662-1845 (LX). **Cop** Extracts CMB 1633-1728 Ptd (Northampton P/Lib).

STRATFORD-UPON-AVON. **Peculiar** *of Stratford-upon-Avon.* **OR** CMB 1574 [+] (*gap 1649-1672*) (Inc). **BT** 1600, 1615 [+] (*gaps 1640-66, except 1660; 1743-1771, except 1757, 1767*) (WRO). **Cop** CB 1558-1652, M 1558-1812 Ptd I (PRS 6, 16, 55), C 1653-1700, B 1653-1686, Ms (SOA), CMB (BT) 1600 [+] Mf (A, WRO and SLC). *See also Bishopton and Luddington.*

STRATFORD-UPON-AVON. Rother Market. (Ind). *f before 1689 as Pres. 1714 New Meeting House, Rother Market. Pres. until 1785. 1880 moved to Rother St.* **OR** ZCB 1786-1836 (PRO).

STRATFORD-UPON-AVON. (Ind). *– see also Shottery, Wilmcote.*

STRATFORD-UPON-AVON, Payton St. (Bapt). *f 1832.* **OR** *Not at PRO.* C 1832 [+] (in Minute Books), M 1912 [+], B 1841 [+] (Ch. Sec.).

TRATFORD-UPON-AVON. (S of F). **Warwickshire Middle Monthly Meeting** *(see Coventry) established 1668, disc. 1751. No regs known other than Monthly Meeting registers.*

TRATFORD-UPON-AVON, Birmingham Road. (Wes). *f 1819. Chapel built 1834.* **Evesham Circuit** *1825.* **Redditch Circuit** *1825-7.* **Coventry and Stratford Circuit** *1828.* **Evesham Circuit** *1829-1834.* **Evesham and Stratford Circuit** *1835-6.* **Leamington and Stratford Circuit** *1837-1846. No registers known. Not at PRO or Circuit Superintendent.*

STRATFORD-UPON-AVON. (Prim Meth). *f.c. 1830.* **Birmingham Circuit.** *No regs known. Not at PRO or Circuit Superintendent.*

STRETTON-ON-DUNSMORE. **OR** C 1681-1842, M 1681-1739, 1742-1837, B 1682-1740, 1742-1863 (AC). **BT** 1670-1809, 1813-1847 (LX).

STRETTON-ON-FOSSE. *(with Ditchford Frary from 1642 and Ilmington since 1956).* **OR** C 1538-1862, M 1538-1836, B 1538-1921 (AC). **BT** 1611 + *(gap 1641-60)* (WRO). **Cop** CB 1538-1733, M 1541-1754 (SOA).

STRETTON-UNDER-FOSSE. *Parish of Monk's Kirby.* (Ind). *f 1662 as Pres. from congregations of Brinklow, Copston, Monk's Kirby and Withybrook. Became Ind. in 18th century. Present meeting house built 1780-1.* **OR** ZC 1787-1794, 1797-1836, B 1788-1790 (PRO).

STUDLEY. **OR** CMB 1663 +. **BT** 1613, 1619 + *(gap 1639-63)* (WRO). **Cop** CMB (BT) 1663 + Mf (A, WRO and SLC).

STUDLEY (RC). *Some entries in regs of St Peter's Franciscan Mission, Birmingham.*

STUDLEY. (Wes). *In* **Redditch (Worcs) Circuit.** *q.v.*

STYVECHALE. – *see Stivichall.*

SUTTON COLDFIELD. **OR** C 1603-1892, M 1603-1837 *(gap 1649-54)*, B 1603-1869 (AB). **BT** 1565-1809, 1813-1844 *(gap 1600-75)* (L). **Cop** CMB 1603-1747 p/s (BRL Cat. No. 406912), (PR) C 1603-1892, M 1603-1649, 1653-1837, B 1603-1869 Mf (SLC).

SUTTON COLDFIELD, Holy Trinity (RC). *f 1834. No information.*

SUTTON COLDFIELD. (Pres). *f.c. 1669. Still existed in 1772. No regs known. Not at PRO.*

SUTTON COLDFIELD (S of F). **Wishaw Monthly Meeting** *disc. c. 1676. No regs known other than Monthly Meeting regs. See also Wiggins Hill.*

SUTTON-UNDER-BRAILES. *Transferred from Gloucestershire 1842. Transferred from Gloucester Diocese to Coventry 1919.* **OR** CB 1715-1812, M 1718-1837 (AC). **BT** 1605-1812 (AC), 1813 + (City Library, Gloucester). **Cop** M 1578-1812 (Phil 4 Glos), CB 1577-98, M 1578-98 (SOA), CMB 1715-1837 (A). *M 1578-1812 in Roe's Glos. M Index.*

TACHBROOK. – *see Bishop's Tachbrook.*

TAMWORTH. – *see Staffs.*

TANWORTH-IN-ARDEN. **OR** C 1558-1651, 1653-79, 1681 +, M 1558-1646, 1654 +
B 1558 + (Inc). **BT** 1608, 1613 + *(gap 1640-1662,* except 1654-6) (WRO)
Cop C 1558-1864, MB 1558-1924 (Ptd 1930 – "Parish Registers of
St Mary Magdalen, Tanworth-in-Arden"), (PR) C 1559-1809, 1813-1899,
M 1559-1899, B 1559-1837, Banns 1754-1768 Mf (SLC), CMB (BT) 1608 +
Mf (A, WRO and SLC).

TANWORTH-IN-ARDEN (RC). *Numerous entries in St Peter's Franciscan*
Mission, Birmingham.

TARDEBIGG. – *see Worcestershire.*

TEMPLE BALSALL. *Lichfield* **Peculiar. OR** CMB 1736-1812 (Inc), C 1813-
1906, M 1823-1948, B 1813-1875, Banns 1863-1954 (AB). **BT** 1809-34
(L). *No earlier BT's known.* **Cop** C 1828-1833 Ts (A), C 1828-33 (SG),
C 1813-1899, M 1823-1899, B 1813-1876, Banns 1863-1899 Mf (SLC).

TEMPLE BALSALL (RC). *Some entries in regs of St Peter's Franciscan*
Mission, Birmingham.

TEMPLE GRAFTON. **OR** CB 1757-1950, M 1754-1950, Banns 1824-1927 (AC).
BT 1612 + *(gaps 1623-8* (except 1625), *1630-34, 1641-68* (except
1663) (WRO). **Cop** (BT and OR) M 1612-1812 (Phil 1), CMB (BT) 1612-
1640, 1663-1700 (SOA), CMB (BT) 1612-1700 Ms (A), CMB (BT) 1612 +
Mf (A, WRO and SLC). *M 1651-1675 in Boyd Misc.*

THURLASTON (Gen Bapt). *Congregation in 1705. Became defunct. No regs.*

TIDDINGTON. *Parish of Alveston.* **Cop** CMB 1691-1871 (SOA).

TIDMINGTON. **OR** C 1691-1811 *(gap 1800),* M 1693-1833 *(gap 1774-81),*
B 1691-1801 *(gap 1802-3)* (AC), CB 1813 +, M 1837 + (Inc). **BT** 1611 +
(gap 1640-62, irregular 1670-77) (WRO). **Cop** M 1693-1812 (Phil 1),
CMB (BT) 1611-1691, (PR) CB 1691-1812, M 1754-1812 (SOA),
CMB (BT) 1611 + (A, WRO and SLC).

TREDINGTON. **Peculiar** *of Tredington.* **OR** C 1541-1838, M 1560-1837,
B 1560-1861, Banns 1823-62 (AC). **BT** 1608 + *(gap 1642-62)* (WRO).
Cop C 1541-1650, M 1560-1749, B 1560-1566, 1578-1660 (SOA),
CB 1660-1812 (C of A), CMB (BT) 1608 + Mf (A, WRO and SLC).

TYSOE. **OR** C 1575-1698, 1700-1900, M 1575-1947, B 1575-1898,
Banns 1754-1813, 1824-1948 (AC). **BT** 1620 + *(gap 1643-63)* (WRO).
Cop CMB 1577-1801 (SOA), CMB 1802-12 (C of A), CMB (BT) 1620 +
Mf (A, WRO and SLC).

TYSOE (RC). *Entries in Brailes regs.*

TYSOE. (Wes). *f. c. 1805.* **Banbury Circuit.** *Now* **Kineton Circuit.**
OR *Not at PRO.* C 1805-1813 (Manse, Kineton).

UFTON. **OR** C 1671 (1 entry), 1709-1918, M 1709-50, 1807-9, 1814-36,
Banns 1754-1826, B 1709-1816 (AC), B 1813 + (Inc). **BT** 1660-1836 (L).
Cop CB 1660-1703, M 1661-1698 Ms (A), CMB 1660-1709 Ms (SG).

ULLENHALL. **OR** C 1855 +, M 1862 +, B 1836 + (Inc). *For earlier regs see Wootton Wawen.* **Cop** CMB 1546-1700 (" Wootton Wawen, its History and Records ").

ULLENHALL. (**Pres**). *Meeting in 1690. No regs.*

UPPER SHUCKBURGH. – *see Shuckburgh, Upper.*

WALSGRAVE-ON-SOWE. – *see Sowe.*

WALTON D'EIVILE. *Parish incorporated with Wellesbourne c. 1633 – disunited 1842.* **OR** CM 1843 +, B 1844 + (Inc).

WAPPENBURY. **OR** CB 1753-84, 1788-1812, M 1754-1837 (AC), CB 1813 + (Inc). **BT** 1653-1847 (LX).

WAPPENBURY, St Annes (**RC**). **OR** C 1747-95, 1857-1910, M 1769-1798 (*gap to 1857*) (AHB). **Cop** C 1747-58 (AHB), C 1747-95, M 1769-1798 Mf (A). *Wappenbury entries also in regs of St Peter's Franciscan Mission, Birmingham and of Leamington Spa.*

WARD END. *Hamlet of Aston-juxta-Birmingham q.v.*

WARMINGTON. **OR** C 1636-1876, M 1636-1837, B 1636-1919, Banns 1802-13, 1824-29 (AC). **BT** 1662-1809, 1813-1847 (LX), 1775-1779 (*on Terriers*) (A).

WARWICK, St Mary. **OR** CMB 1651 + (Inc). **BT** 1611 + (*gaps 1641-61, 1664-8*) (WRO). **Cop** CB (BT) 1611-39, M 1614-39 Ms (SG), CMB (BT) 1611 + Mf (A, WRO and SLC).

WARWICK, St Nicholas. **OR** C 1539-1907, M 1539-1910 (*gap 1761-1786*), B 1539-1889 (AC). **BT** 1612 + (*gap 1641-62*) (WRO). **Cop** C 1539-1589, B 1578-99 Ms (A), CMB (BT) 1612 + Mf (A, WRO and SLC).

WARWICK, High St. (**Pres**). *f before 1648 as Ind, died out c. 1688. Refounded by Pres c. 1691. 1780 new church in High St. Now Warwick Unitarian Church.* **OR** ZC 1790-1837 (PRO).

WARWICK, Brook St. (**Ind**). *f. c. 1758 in Cow Lane as secession from High St. Pres. Church built 1826.* **OR** ZC 1784-1837, B 1806-1837 (PRO).

WARWICK, Castle Hill. (**Particular Bapt**). *Alleged f 1640 c. 1670-80 worshipped with Independents. 1681 Castle St. Still on same site. No regs exist. Not at PRO or Ch. Sec. C.1796-1818 in Minute Book* (A).

WARWICK (**S of F**). **Warwickshire Middle Monthly Meeting** (*see Coventry*) *1668-1837, No regs known other than Monthly Meeting registers.*

WASPERTON. **Peculiar** *of Hampton Lucy.* **OR** CB 1538-1926, M 1538-1837, B 1538-1926 (AC). **BT** 1611 + (*gap 1641-60*) (WRO). **Cop** CMB 1538-1812 (C of A), CMB (BT) 1611 + Mf (WRO, A and SLC). *See also Packwood.*

WATER ORTON. *Hamlet of Aston-juxta-Birmingham.* **OR** CB 1813 +, M 1872 + (Inc). **BT** 1813-31 (L). *See also Aston-juxta-Birmingham.*

WEDDINGTON. **OR** C 1663-1743, 1800-1950, M 1663-1743, 1814-64, B 1663-1743, 1814-1956 (AC). **BT** 1772-5, 1809-13 (*in misc. bundle*), 1813-1847 (L). **Cop** CMB 1663-1812 Ptd I (Warwick PRS 51).

WEDDINGTON. (Pres). *Conventicle 1872. No regs.*

WEETHLEY. **OR** C 1613-1703, 1784-5, 1792-1812, M 1605-1678, 1793-1811, 1814-35, B 1572-1685, 1797-1811, 1826-1928 (AC). **BT** 1612, 1638-41, 1665, 1669-72, 1675 + (WRO). **Cop** CMB (BT) 1612 + Mf (A, WRO and SLC).

WEETHLEY. (RC). *Entries in regs of St Peter's Franciscan Mission, Birmingham.*

WELCOMBE. *Hamlet of Stratford-on-Avon q.v.*

WELFORD-ON-AVON. (*Transferred from Glos. 1931*). *– see Gloucestershire and also Clifford Chambers.*

WELLESBOURNE. **OR** C 1560-1765, 1767-1942, M 1560-1954, B 1560-1765, 1767-1931 (AC). **BT** 1611 + (*gaps 1641-64, except 1660, 1735-1740*) (WRO). **Cop** CMB 1560-1812 (SOA), CMB (BT) 1611 + Mf (A, WRO and SLC).

WELLESBOURNE. (Wes). *f 1835* **Coventry Circuit.** *No information.*

WESTON. *Parish of Long Compton.* Chapel of Sheldon Family (RC). **OR** C 1763-84, Confirmations 1763-1780 (Inc Brailes). **Cop** C 1763-1784, Confirmations 1763-1780 I (Ptd Crisp 1898), C 1763-84 Mf (A). *For later regs see Brailes.*

WESTON-ON-AVON (*formerly in Glos*). *See Gloucestershire and also Clifford Chambers.*

WESTON-UNDER-WETHERLEY. **OR** C 1661-1723, 1733-1812, M 1715, 1719-24, 1727-42, 1754-1836, B 1662-1724, 1727-54, 1772-1812 (AC), CB 1813-1837 (Inc). **BT** 1676-1809, 1813-1847 (*gap 1768-96*) (L).

WETHERLEY. *– see Weethley.*

WHATCOTE. **OR** C 1572-1743, 1754-1812, M 1571-1643, 1671-3, 1684-1743, 1754-1837, B 1579-1743, 1746-1812 (AC), CB 1813 + (Inc). **BT** 1611 + (*gap 1641-1666 except 1662*) (WRO). **Cop** CB 1572-1812, M 1572-1644, 1671-1801 (SOA), CMB (BT) 1611 + Mf (A, WRO and SLC).

WHICHFORD. **OR** CM 1540 +, B 1542 + (*many gaps in 1st reg, especially Commonwealth*) (Inc). **BT** 1613 + (*gap 1641-1670 except 1662, 1667*) (WRO). **Cop** CMB (BT) 1613 + Mf (A, WRO and SLC).

WHICHFORD. (Particular Bapt). *f before 1669, defunct before 1715. No regs known.*

WHITACRE, NETHER. **OR** C 1539-1642, 1653 +, M 1539-1633, 1653-1747, 1756 +, B 1564-1638, 1653-1747, 1767 + (Inc). **BT** 1673-1845 (LX). **Cop** (PR) C 1539-1642, 1653-1869, M 1539-1633, 1653-1746, 1756-1840 B 1564-1644, 1653-1747, 1767-1894 Mf (SLC).

WHITACRE, NETHER. (Pres). *Conventicle c. 1672. No regs.*

WHITACRE, NETHER (S of F). **Wishaw Monthly Meeting.** *f 1668, disc. c. 1700. No regs known apart from Monthly Meeting regs.*

WHITACRE, OVER. OR C 1653-1910, M 1653-1836 (gap 1753-1815), B 1653-1953, Banns 1824-1916 (AB). BT 1673-1848 (LX). **Cop** (PR) C 1653-1910, M 1653-1787, 1815-1836, B 1653-1953, Banns 1824-1916 Mf (SLC).

WHITCHURCH. OR CB 1561-1812 (gap 1646-58), M 1562-1845, Banns 1756-1795, 1806-1808, 1824-1964 (AC). BT 1611+ (gap 1640-62) (WRO). **Cop** M 1562-1812 (Phil 1) (SLC), CMB 1561-1812 (SOA), CMB (BT) 1611+ Mf (A, WRO and SLC). *M 1651-1675 in Boyd Misc.*

WHITNASH. OR CMB 1679-1959 (gaps M 1755-60, B 1757-9), Banns 1823-1958 (AC). BT 1809-1844 (L), 1662-1809 (with gaps) on terriers (AC).

WHITTINGTON. (General Bapt). *Conventicle c. 1672. No regs.*

WIBTOFT. *Warwickshire chapelry of Claybrooke, Leicestershire.* OR CMB 1705+ (Inc). BT *See Claybrooke, Leicestershire.*

WIGGINS HILL MONTHLY MEETING (S of F). *Established 1687, dissolved 1710 and joined to* **Birmingham Monthly Meeting. Constituent Meetings:** *Wiggins Hill (c.1690-1710), Wishaw (c.1690-1710).* **Registers:** ZMB 1687-1774 (PRO 1186).

WIGGINS HILL, *parish of Sutton Coldfield* (S of F). **Birmingham Monthly Meeting** (1668-1687 and 1710-c.1800). **Wiggins Hill Monthly Meeting** (c.1690-1710), *disc. c.1800. Regs — see above.*

WILLEY. OR CMB 1660+ (Inc). BT 1664-1844 (L).

WILLEY. (Ind). *Existed 1704. No regs.*

WILLEY. (Pres). *Existed 1744. No regs.*

WILLOUGHBY. OR CB 1625-1941 (AC). BT 1665-1847 (LX), 1837 (WRO).

WILMCOTE. (Ind). *f 1802. Not at PRO. No information.*

WILNECOTE. *Transferred to Staffs 1964.* OR 1837+ (Inc).

WISHAW. OR C 1685+, B 1688+, M 1690+ (Inc). BT 1662-1832 (LX). **Cop** CB 1685-1899, M 1685-1898 Mf (SLC).

WISHAW (*afterwards Baddesley*) **MONTHLY MEETING** (S of F). *Dissolved 1710 and joined to* **Birmingham Monthly Meeting. Constituent Meetings:** *Baddesley Ensor, Tamworth (Staffs) (both 1668-1710), Wishaw (1668-c.1690), Coleshill, Nether Whitacre (both 1668-c.1700), Shuttington (1668-before 1679), Sutton Coldfield (1668-c.1676), Hartshill (1704-1710).* **Monthly Meeting Registers:** Z 1660-1796, M 1660-1773, B 1660-1789 (PRO 1181, 1182 cat. as "Badgley and Hartshill").

WISHAW (S of F). **Wishaw Monthly Meeting** (1668-c.1690), **Wigginshill Monthly Meeting** (c.1690-before 1710), *discontinued before 1710. No regs known other than Monthly Meeting registers.*

WITHALL. – *see Wythall, Worcestershire.*

WITHYBROOK, with MONKS KIRBY. OR CB 1653-1837, M 1654-1837 (gap 1753) (Inc). BT 1809-36 (L), 1662-1809 (gap 1802-4) on terriers (AC). *See also Monks Kirby.*

WITHYBROOK. (Pres). *Conventicle 1672. No regs.*

WIXFORD. – *see Exhall, near Alcester.* **OR** C 1540-1691, M 1541-1688, B 1542-1691 (AC) *with Exhall regs. Parish combined with Exhall 1691.* **BT** 1612 + *(gap 1640-60)* (WRO) *(with Wixford 1616-37, 1688-1700).* **Cop** CMB 1539-1688 (C of A), CMB (BT) 1612 + Mf (A, WRO and SLC).

WOLFHAMPCOTE. **OR** CMB 1558-1929, Banns 1823-1919 (AC). **BT** 1670-1839 (LX) 1682-1684 on Terriers (A). **Cop** CB 1558-1768, M 1558-1754 Ts (A), CMB 1558-1768 Ts I (SG).

WOLFORD. **OR** C 1654-84, 1687-1855, M 1656-76, 1688-1837, B 1655-1684, 1687-1897 (AC). **BT** 1612, 1621 + *(gap 1641-62)* (WRO). **Cop** CMB 1656-1812 (C of A), M 1626-1812 (Phil Ms) (SLC), CMB (BT) 1612-1700 (SOA) CMB (BT) 1612 + Mf (WRO, A and SLC). *M 1626-1812 in Boyd Misc.*

WOLSTON CUM BRANDON. **OR** CMB 1558-1734 (AC), CMB 1735 + (Inc). **BT** 1665-1809, 1813-1845 (LX). **Cop** CMB 1558-1811 I ("Genealogist" NS 6).

WOLSTON. (General Bapt). *Conventicle c. 1669. No regs.*

WOLSTON, Main Street. (Bapt). *f 1816.* **OR** Z 1811-1837 (PRO).

WOLVERTON. *(Formerly Woolverdington).* **OR** CB 1680-1836, M 1680-1796, 1801-36 (AC). **BT** 1614 + *(gaps 1618-22, 1633-38, 1640-60)* (WRO). **Cop** M 1684-1796 (SOA), CMB (BT) 1614 + Mf (A, WRO and SLC).

WOLVEY. **OR** Z 1653-65, C 1667 +, M 1654-1753, 1755 +, B 1654 +. **BT** 1661-1882 (L).

WOLVEY. (Pres). *Conventicle 1672. No regs.*

WOLVEY, Wolds Lane. (Bapt). *f 1789. Not at PRO. No information.*

WOOTTON WAWEN. **OR** C 1546-1620, 1631-43, 1654-1896, M 1550-1625, 1643-1662, 1700-1952, B 1552-1625, 1630, 1654-1869, Banns 1823-44 (AC). *CB 1700-1812, M 1700-54 include Henley and Ullenhall.* **BT** 1608 + *(gap 1640-60)* (WRO). **Cop** CMB 1546-1700 ("Wootton Wawen – its History and Records " 1936), C 1545-1641, 1653-99, M 1545-1601, 1654-99, B 1545-1621, 1654-99 Ms (A), CMB (BT) 1608 + Mf (A, WRO and SLC). *See also Ullenhall and Henley-in-Arden.*

WOOTTON WAWEN, Our Lady and St Benedict. (RC). **OR** 1765-1843, M 1786-1808 (AHB). **Cop** C 1765-1819, M 1786-1819 I (Ptd Cath. RS 2), C 1765-1843, M 1786-1808 Mf (A).

WORMLEIGHTON. **OR** C 1586-1640, 1646, 1657, 1661-1665, 1675-1812, M 1587-1639, 1661-2, 1690-1751, 1756-1837, B 1586-1648, 1660, 1678, 1680-88, 1690-1812 (AC – entries up to 1688 may be in only one of the two registers covering this period), CB 1813 + (Inc). **BT** 1660-1846 (L).

WROXALL. **OR** C 1586-1810, M 1586-1659, 1664-1752, 1756-1962, B 1587-1812 (AC), CB 1813 + (Inc). **BT** 1634, 1664 + (irregular 1666-1685, 1831-7) (WRO). **Cop** CMB 1586-1604, 1641-1732, 1744-1812 (A), 1586-1812 in supp. to "Records of Wroxall" Ryland 1903 (Ptd), CMB (BT) 1634 + Mf (A, WRO and SLC).

WYKEN. **OR** C 1600-1937, M 1611-71, 1677-1752, 1756-1833, 1842-1942, B 1600-1942, Banns 1923-1930 (AC). **BT** 1662-1847 (LX).

WYKEN. (Bapt). – *see Coventry, Lentons Lane, Hawkesbury.*

WYTHALL. – *Parish near Birmingham formerly in Worcs. – see Worcestershire.*

YARDLEY. *Parish in Birmingham formerly in Worcestershire. – see Worcestershire.*

WORCESTERSHIRE

ACKNOWLEDGMENTS

The editor gratefully acknowledges the assistance of the follow-
ng persons in compiling this section.

Mr. E.H. Sargeant F.L.A., County Archivist of Worcestershire for
upplying information, for lending a copy of the detailed lists of
ishop's Transcripts, for dealing with a very considerable number of
ueries over a prolonged period, for permitting the inclusion in the
reface of information on Bishop's transcripts from the forthcoming
'Guide to Worcestershire Records" and for reading through the pre-
ace and offering numerous comments and suggestions:
rs. A.M. Hodgson for obtaining details on Worcestershire Catholic
egisters still in church hands and for writing the Catholic section
f the preface;
r. Levi Fox, Director Shakespeare's Birthplace Trust for supplying in-
ormation and offering numerous suggestions for the preface;
evd. J.D. McEvilly, Archivist of the Catholic Archdiocese of
irmingham for supplying information on Catholic Registers;
r. A.D. Francis for listing and compressing information on original
egisters from the detailed returns at the National Register of
rchives;
r. F.M. Barrell for checking the holdings of the Society of Genealo-
ists and checking starting dates of original registers;
r. D.W. Parkes for assisting with queries and for making useful com-
ents and suggestions for the preface;
r. F.L. Leeson for listing surrendered Nonconformist registers and
hecking at the British Museum; Messrs. A.E. Marshall and A.J. Coker
for reading through the preface and offering suggestions, particularly
for the bibliography;
r. J.R. Cunningham of the Church of Jesus Christ of Latter Day Saints
for granting access to their records;
dward Milligan Archivist at Friends' House, Euston for allowing ac-
ess to their records and for helping with various queries;
r. P. Gwynne James, Registrar of the Diocese of Hereford for facilities to examine the Bishop's transcripts;
numerous Librarians, Anglican Clergy, Catholic Parish Priests,
Methodist Circuit superintendents, Baptist and Congregationalist
Ministers and Secretaries and the Secretaries of Nonconformist Unions,
Associations and Districts for supplying information.

251

GENERAL INFORMATION

Record Repositories (*see also list on page xx*)

W. R. O.   — *Worcestershire Record Office, Shirehall, Worcester.*
             (*Hours 9 - 12.45, 2 - 5; Saturdays closed*)
             This holds almost all records of the County, and is the
             diocesan record office for the diocese of Worcester.
             The Bishop's Transcripts, Marriage Bonds, Wills and all
             other diocesen material are kept at St. Helen's Church,
             Fish Street, Worcester, which has its own search room.
             The Record Office has a large number of original
             Registers, some Nonconformist records and many typescript,
             manuscript and microfilm copies. These are all kept at
             Shirehall, but both places have microfilm copies of all
             the registers that have been filmed. Amongst much other
             material of genealogical interest, the Record office also
             holds a microfilm copy of the 1851 Census covering the
             whole of the County. The Worcestershire Record Office
             maintains a Handlist which includes Parish Registers,
             Bishop's Transcripts and Copies and details of newspapers.

A. H. B.   — *Archbishop's House, Birmingham.*
             This holds a number of Worcestershire Catholic Registers.

H, HX, HXX   — *The Hereford Diocesan Registry, 5 St. Peter's Street,*
             Hereford. (Searches by appointment)
             This holds the Bishop's Transcripts for a few parishes in
             the Diocese of Hereford. *See Bishop's Transcripts.*

C. L. G.   — *City Library, Brunswick Rd., Gloucester.*
             (*Hours 9 - 8.30 Sat 9 - 7*)
             This is the Diocesan Record office for the diocese of
             Gloucester and holds the Bishop's Transcripts for a few
             Worcestershire parishes. *See Bishop's Transcripts.*

LX   — *Joint Record Office, Bird St., Lichfield, Staffs.*
             This holds the Bishop's Transcripts for one Worcestershire
             parish. *See Bishop's Transcripts.*

A.   — *Warwickshire R.O., Shire Hall, Warwick.*
             (*Hours 9.15 - 1, 2 - 5.30, Sat 9.15 - 12.30*)
             This holds microfilm copies of the Bishop's Transcripts
             of the Diocese of Worcester.

G.L.C. – *The Genealogical Society of the Church of Jesus Christ of*
the Latter Day Saints, Salt Lake City.
This holds Microfilms of the entire Bishop's Transcripts
for the Diocese of Worcester, and of numerous parish registers.

S.O.A. – *Shakespeare's Birthplace Trust Library, Henley St.,*
Stratford-on-Avon.
(Hours 10 - 1, 2 - 5, Sat 10 - 12.30)
This holds many copies.

B.L. – *The Birmingham Library, Margaret Street, Birmingham 1.*
This is a private Library attached to the Birmingham and
Midland Institute, and holds a large collection of printed
registers and printed genealogical material.

B.R.L. – *Birmingham Reference Library, Ratcliff Place, Birmingham 1.*
(Hours Mon-Fri 9 - 9, Sat 9 - 5)
This holds many copies and amongst much other material a microfilm copy of the 1851 census covering Birmingham and nearby
parishes. A microfilm of the 1841 census has also been ordered.

G.L. – *Guildhall Library, Basinghall St., London, EC2.*
(Hours Mon-Sat 9.30 - 5)
This holds a few copies.

Dudley Public Library, St James's Rd., Dudley.
(Hours 9 - 7, Sat 9 - 5)
This is a Diocesan Record Office for the Deanery of Dudley,
and holds the parish registers of St Thomas, Dudley.

Parishes

Ancient Parishes – 209 including 10 in the City of Worcester.

Changes in County Boundaries. Kings Norton, Northfield and Yardley,
parishes formerly in Worcestershire, transferred to the City of
Birmingham in 1911 have been included on the Worcestershire list.
There have been some other adjustments chiefly with regard to
the boundary with Gloucestershire, but a few also with Warwickshire, Herefordshire and Shropshire. Most of the parishes affected by these adjustments have been included on the Worcestershire list and cross references included for the remainder.

Original Parish Registers

Although most registers are still held by the Incumbents, more and
more are being deposited at the Worcestershire Record Office. The
Dudley registers are in Dudley Public Library. The dates given for
those still in ecclesiastical hands have been largely compiled from
returns made for the National Register of Archives. These have been

compared with the details given in the "Digest of Parish Registers in the Diocese of Worcester" published in 1899, and all doubtful cases and discrepancies followed up by circularisation of the incumbents. The Worcestershire Record Office maintains a Handlist of Parish Registers, Bishop's Transcripts and Copies. Worcestershire is remarkable in that no less than 55 parishes – well over a quarter of the total – have registers beginning in 1538 – 1540, and of the remainder most begin in the 16th Century.

Elusive Worcestershire marriages particularly those by licence may possibly be found among the Worcester City parishes.

One Worcestershire register has been broken down on Family Reconstitution forms for the purpose of demographic analysis. Work on a further 6 is in progress and a further 13 projected.

Modern Copies Of Parish Registers.

Printed

Phillimore's Worcestershire Marriages.
These cover 28 parishes in two volumes.

Worcestershire Parish Register Society.
The Society printed 5 volumes of registers 1913-16. A second series was begun in 1950, but has stopped because the sale of copies did not provide enough money to continue.

Other registers have been printed including the Harvington Hall Registers by the Catholic Record Society, and the Nonconformist Registers of Dudley in "The Non-Parochial Registers of Dudley". Some are in very limited editions.

Typescript and Manuscript

The Society of Genealogists.
This holds a number of typescript and manuscript copies. Most of the latter are bound into volumes indicated in the text by "Worcs Pink" and the Vol. number.

Worcestershire Record Office.
This holds a considerable number of copies.

Shakespeare's Birthplace Trust Library, Stratford-on-Avon.
This holds copies of parts of registers for about 20 parishes. In most cases, although Baptisms, Marriages and Burials have been copied, the transcripts cease during the 18th Century or even earlier.

Birmingham Reference Library.
This holds copies of a number of parishes, the majority up to 1812.

College of Arms.

This holds copies of parts or all the registers of 11 parishes.

Guildhall Library, London.

This holds a number of copies, especially of the parishes in the City of Worcester.

Phillimore Manuscript.

This is a manuscript copy of the marriages of Chaceley in the possession of Phillimore & Co., 18 Market Place, Henley-on-Thames, Oxon. A search will be made on payment of a fee.

Microfilms.

Extensive microfilming has been done at the Worcestershire Record Office by the Church of Jesus Christ of Latter Day Saints.

The microfilming of the entire Bishop's Transcripts for the Diocese of Worcester, which started on 4th November 1960 took two operators, working every day, nearly four years, the work not being completed until 16th April 1964. In addition to the copies at Salt Lake City, copies of all films were given to the Worcestershire Record Office where they are stored at the Shirehall, well away from the original documents, providing a useful second copy for consultation as well as a security duplicate. The Bishop of Worcester was presented with a second positive copy of every film which he has sent for storage at the Warwickshire Record Office.

In addition to the Bishop's Transcripts, the Church of Jesus Christ of Latter Day Saints have also microfilmed nearly all the parish registers deposited at the Worcestershire Record Office and many others still in the hands of incumbents. This work is still in progress and will be for some years. Copies of the microfilms are at both Shirehall and the St. Helen's Record Office.

Boyd's Marriage Index

There are no Worcestershire volumes in the Index, but most of the marriages printed by Phillimore and some other copies are included in Boyd's Miscellaneous Volumes. The dates covered are given in the text with the abbreviation *Boyd Misc.*

Bishop's Transcripts.

Diocese of Worcester. At Worcestershire Record Office.

Pre-1701 Transcripts in parish order. Post-1701 transcripts arranged by year and then by Deanery.

Throughout the period for which the Bishop's transcripts were returned, there were frequent alterations to the boundaries of both the Diocese and the County of Worcester; four bishoprics have taken part of their area from the See of Worcester; and the Diocese itself should not be thought conterminous with the County since it included parishes within the counties of Gloucester, Warwick and Hereford. Bishop's Transcripts are therefore held in the Worcester Diocesan Archives for many parishes outside both the Diocese and County of Worcester. Those for parishes in the dioceses of Gloucester and Bristol do not fall into this category as these sees were created in 1541 and 1542 respectively. Those for parishes in the dioceses of Birmingham and Coventry are affected, however, as these sees were not established until 1905 and 1918.

The Bishop's Transcripts of Worcester Dioceses, after long storage in the roof of the Cathedral, were moved in the nineteenth Century to the Edgar Tower, where their damp and dilapidated state became apparent; some of the larger transcripts, such as those of Old Swinford had been used to wrap other bundles.

The original arrangement as with most other dioceses was by year and then by Deanery. In 1878, Mr. J. Amphlett, Revd. T.P. Wadley and Mr. H. Wickham King began sorting and listing the transcripts. However, their efforts, though well-meaning were misguided, and they thoroughly disrupted the original order, re-arranging the transcripts by parishes. This not only had the effect of making the consultation of the transcripts in the whole diocese or a whole deanery for a particular year virtually impossible, but also left unidentified certain transcripts with no clear place names. Efforts are being made however to identify these by elimination.

When the Record Office first became interested in the Diocesan Archives, two things became immediately apparent; the first was that to restore the natural accumulation order or even to sort the parish bundles of Transcripts into exact date order was a task greater than the Record Office resources would allow at the time of deposit, and the second that the steady flow of enquiries, even while negotiations for the deposit were still in progress, demonstrated that the transcripts would be in constant demand. Furthermore, the state of near-chaos in which these 67,000 records were found obviously required immediate remedial action if the time of the staff was not to be wasted in fruitless searching.

In consequence a place index on slips was started even before the transfer to the Office had been effected, first for use by enquirers and then for boxing and indexing. While official negotiations dragged on to 1956 this index and the transfer and boxing of transcripts continued. All kinds of staff were put on to this work, and its quality therefore varies considerably. Not until 25th February 1964, 11 years later, was this slip index finally completed. It consists of 16 boxes containing over 40,000 entries alphabetically arranged and covering all identified transcripts up to the year 1838.

The slip index was then written in sheet form to be incorporated in the printed *Guide to Worcestershire Records* which is in course of preparation.

While the Record Office index was in progress, the Church of Jesus Christ of Latter Day Saints was given permission by the Bishop of Worcester to microfilm the transcripts. [1]

The filming had the effect of "freezing" the order (or rather lack of order) of the transcripts. For the microfilm to be effective, and the place index to apply equally to the film as well as to the originals, the originals must remain as they stood when filmed. The transcripts have therefore been serially numbered in that order. For those dated before 1701 the serial number reflects the nineteenth century re-arrangements by parish; for those dated between 1700 and 1838 the order is basically by deanery, but misplacements had occurred before the Record Office took over the documents.

Much physical work was also done on the actual transcripts. Gradually they were flattened and placed in folders between stiff card. To obviate the danger of disarrangement not more than one box of transcripts at a time will normally be produced for any one user, and the practice of two persons with a box each working side by side on the same problem is discouraged.

The majority of the transcripts start about 1610, and on the whole, in spite of past mis-handling the collection is fairly comprehensive, and large gaps are rare. Nevertheless, some odd years are not infrequently missing. The Bishop's Transcripts dates given in this section of the National Index have been taken from the detailed lists to be published in the *Guide to Worcestershire Records*, and it has been possible to list all gaps of four years or more. Smaller gaps have been ignored unless they are frequent, in which case the transcripts have been described as *irregular* between certain dates.

Peculiars in Worcestershire.

Peculiars of Dean and Chapter of Worcester.
Worcester Cathedral, Berrow, Kempsey, Norton-juxta-Kempsey, St. Michael in Bedwardine (Worcester), Stoulton, Tibberton, Wolverley.

Peculiar of Rector of Alvechurch.

Peculiar of Rector of Bredon.

Peculiar of Rector of Fladbury.
Fladbury and the chapelries of Wyre Piddle, Throckmorton, Stock and Bradley.

---

[1] *See* Microfilms, above under *Modern Copies.*

Peculiar of Hanbury.

Peculiar of Hartlebury.

Peculiar of Rector of Ripple.
Ripple, Queenhill, and Holdfast.

Compared with other dioceses, Worcester has a good series of transcripts for the Peculiars. In most cases they are not markedly more irregular than for other parishes. The Peculiars of Bredon and Fladbury are slightly fewer in number than for the majority of parishes, but there is still a reasonably good series. Ripple has a fair series except for one long gap from 1783 to 1801. The solitary exception is Worcester Cathedral for which there are no transcripts before 1702 and transcripts only for less than half the years of the eighteenth Century

Diocese of Hereford.

A number of parishes near the Herefordshire and Shropshire borders were formerly, and in some cases still are, in the Diocese of Hereford. The Transcripts are kept in the Muniment Room of Hereford Cathedral and applications to examine them should be made to the Diocesan Registrar. *(See Record Repositories above)* A fee is usually charged. They have been sorted into parish bundles to 1812. The majority start about 1660 and continue to 1812 with only minor gaps which have been noted in full. The Diocesan Registrar has a detailed list describing the condition of the transcripts and other details. A few, though sorted into approximate order of year have not been fully listed. HX indicates that the period 1754-1812 has been checked and missing years noted, but not the period 1660-1753. HXX indicates that both periods are unchecked. In all cases any transcripts dating before 1660 are noted. The post-1813 transcripts are arranged by deaneries, but not sorted into parishes, listed or checked to discover missing transcripts.

Diocese of Gloucester *(At Gloucester City Library)*.

17 parishes, some of them transferred from Gloucestershire were in the Diocese of Gloucester. The pre-1813 transcripts are in parish order. Transcripts 1813-1868 are in bound volumes year by year.

Pre-1813 Transcripts.

The bundles of transcripts, mostly on vellum, are assembled in parishes, and some of them, on paper, are dated as early as 1569. The general pattern, however, is that few early pre-1600 documents are followed by c.1607, then a few in the mid 1610's, a fair number in the 1620's and very few in the 1630's. There is invariably a gap for the period 1640-1660 or so. From then the transcripts continue, often with only a few, if any, years missing.

For the most part the transcripts at Gloucester are in good condition. Formerly in paper bundles, the transcripts have now been put into boxes.

Post-1813 Transcripts.

Considerable work has been carried out on the re-binding of these volumes from 1813. Having suffered from damp and rough handling, they are now in excellent condition and much easier to handle, though very bulky. Most years have about four volumes to cover all parishes. The repair work is proceeding. The transcripts continue in these volumes up to about the year 1868 and then in bundles.

Further information on all the Gloucester transcripts will be found in the Gloucestershire preface.

Diocese of Lichfield (At Lichfield Diocesan Registry).

This included the Worcestershire Parish of Over or Upper Arley. As with about 30 other Lichfield parishes, no details are given in the volume of the Index at Lichfield Diocesan Registry covering the pre 1812 transcripts. The bundle has been examined and the commencing date noted, but search has not been made for gaps and the abbreviation LX has been used to indicate this.

Marriage Licences.

Diocese of Worcester.

Originals are in Worcestershire Record Office. *(Kept at St. Helen's Church — See Record Repositories above).*

About 134,000 bonds, affidavits and allegations (in one series) in single sheets for the period 1582-1965. Canon J. Davenport made an index of the 16th-17th Century papers.

Registers of Marriage Licences 18th-19th Century exist. A few others are mentioned in the Calendar of Wills and Admons, and the Index Library, Vols. 31 and 39 also contain references.

Copies.

The Marriage Bonds and Allegations have been microfilmed by the Church of Jesus Christ of Latter Day Saints and copies are at Salt Lake City.

Extracts 1446-1662, 1676-1698, 1712-1717, 1720-1722 were printed in *The Genealogist* (Old Series vols 6,7, New Series vols 1 and 2) and Extracts 1446, 1532-4, 1541, 1579-84, 1600-11, 1641-45, 1661-1725 are in *Marriage Licences in the Diocese of Worcester* by T.P. Wadley. *(copies in Guildhall Library, London and Worcestershire Record Office –*

– no copy at SG). The Marriage Licence of William Shakespeare is included.

Diocese of Gloucester

Originals – City Library, Gloucester.

A list of Marriage Ponds and Allegations appears in the City Library's Supplementary catalogue 1928-1955.

Allegations.

Marriage Licence Allegations in single sheets survive for the period 1747-1837 with very few gaps. There are also 94 volumes of Allegations 1637-1823 which relate to affidavits sworn at Gloucester.

Bonds.

Varying numbers have survived for the period 1730-1823 except for years 1731, 1733, 1735, 1745, 1791. The numbers of documents per year range from 1 to 508.

Licences.

The only considerable numbers of Marriage Licences surviving is for 1822 (84 items)

There are Marriage Licence indexes for the periods 1830-54 and 1876-1906.

Copies

Gloucestershire Marriage Allegations 1637-1680. Surrogate Allegations 1637-1694 (printed). Published by Bristol and Gloucestershire Archaeological Society (Records section No. 2). The *Allegations up to 1705* have been copied in Manuscript by Mr. B. Frith for future publication.

Gloucester Marriage Allegations and Grants of Marriage Licences. 1637, 1638, 1660-1733. Copied and indexed by C.V. Appleton Ms. (SG).

Diocese of Hereford.

At Muniment Room, Hereford Cathedral. Apply Dicoesan Registrar.

The Marriage Bonds (1660-1831) are on files in boxes; Licence Books (1603-1787) are bound and indexed but need repair. The Licence Allegations (1834-1909) with Affidavits are bound and indexed. Later Allegations are in parcels.

Diocese of Lichfield at Lichfield Diocesan Registry.

One Worcestershire Parish, Over or Upper Arley was in the Lichfiel Diocese. The Marriage Bonds and Allegations and (after 1824) the

Affidavits for Marriage Licences in the Registry are arranged by years for the whole Diocese. The Bonds available are as follows:-

Prior to 1660: only a few bonds are extant.

1660-1670: a number of bonds extant, but probably not complete.

1670 onwards: nearly all the bonds sworn during this period are believed to be extant.

About 10% of the Allegations have not yet been sorted.

Further information concerning the arrangement and state of the Licences will be found in the Shropshire and Warwickshire prefaces. For those requiring a particular allegation, at least three weeks' notice should be given to the Registrar of the year and surname of the male party to the Marriage. Bonds, Allegations and Affidavits may be inspected at the Registry by approved searchers by appointment (at least 14 days' notice having previously been given).

Roman Catholics.

The Jesuit house in *Worcester*, known as the "Residence of St. George" served the counties of Worcestershire and Warwickshire. The Registers run from 1685-1837. They contain mostly baptisms, a few 'reconciliations', some obiits, but only four marriages and those in the early 19th century. Up to 1718 names are included from places in Monmouthshire, Gloucestershire, Warwickshire, Staffordshire and North Wales, – after 1718 places are seldom mentioned. The Registers were printed privately (50 copies only), a copy being at Worcester Record Office and another at Archbishop's House Birmingham.

In 1791 when the Second Catholic Relief Act was passed five chapels in private houses were registered for Catholic worship at the Worcester Quarter Sessions, i.e. those at Spetchlev Park, Purshall Hall, Heath Green, Blackmore Park, Little Malvern Court.[2] Those at Harvington Hall and Grafton Manor were registered in 1796.

The baptismal registers of only three of these seven chapels have survived, i.e. those of Harvington, Spetchley, and Little Malvern. The Blackmore Park records were lost when the house was burnt down in the 19th century – those of Heath Green, Purshall and Grafton have not yet been traced.

A number of Worcestershire entries are also to be found in the Register of the Franciscan Mission of *St. Peter's, Birmingham*. The original is at Archbishop's House, Birmingham, and it has been Printed by the Warwickshire Parish Register Society, Phillimore's and Whitfield and Bloom.

One of the most interesting of the extant registers is that of *Harvington Hall* near Kidderminster. Belonging successively to the

---

[2] The full text of the legal recognition of these chapels is quoted in the General Article on Catholic Registers in Vol.I.

Pakingtons, Lady Mary Yate, and the Throckmortons, the domestic
chapel served a large area including Kidderminster until 1831 and
Stourbridge until 1816.[3] It was registered for Roman Catholic
worship in 1796 by Father Richard Cornthwaite, a secular priest.
Early registers were lost in a fire, but baptisms are recorded from
1752, marriages from 1804, obituaries from 1792 (a few), and are
printed by the Catholic Record Society in their Volume 17,
Miscellanea. Registers after 1823 are preserved in the present
church which was opened in 1825.

At *Little Malvern Court*, although Mass was said there during
the whole of the Penal Period, no registers have survived before
1783 when Father John Williams, S.J. was acting as Chaplain to
his niece Miss Mary Williams, the Lady of the Manor. He began
to record the baptisms in a small note book made of odd pieces of
paper sewn together. After his death in 1801 a series of Benedictine
Chaplains took over and they continued to keep records until the
Chapel was moved out of the Court into the new church of St. Wulstans
built in 1866. The registers after 1826 are in a larger book bound
in boards. Early entries include names from Birtsmorton; Bosbury;
Colwall; Castlemorton; Dymock; Housell; Great, West and North Malvern;
Malvern Link, and Malvern Wells; Ledbury; Mathon; Leigh Sinton;
Newent; and Welland. Besides the baptisms there are a few obiits,
no marriages. St. Wulstan's Church, Little Malvern where the registers
are now kept is still under the care of the Benedictines of Downside.

Spetchley has a set of registers in good preservation kept by
the Jesuits who served this chapel for the Berkeley family. Baptisms
from 1750, marriages from 1760. They are now in the possession of
the Jesuit Church, Sansome St. Worcester.

The Registers of the domestic chapel at *Blackmore Park* having
been lost, the registers at the present church built by J.V. Hornyold
in 1846 commence only from that date.

Heath Green was originally a domestic chapel of the Sheldon
family of Beoley. When the last of the Catholic Sheldons left Beoley.
in the late 18th cent. the chapel was moved to a house at Heath Green,
now (1964) called Chapel Farm. The modern Catholic Church at *Redditch*,
successor to Heath Green was built in 1833/4.

Grafton Manor, a house belonging to the Talbots (Earls of
Shrewsbury) had a chapel registered in 1796 by Father Andrew Robinson
S.J. St. Peter's Bromsgrove, built in 1858, is the successor to
the Grafton Mission.

The Mission at *Purshall Hall* was moved from Badge Court in 1750.
After 1796 it was merged with that at Grafton.

Other Catholic houses in the County where there were certainly

---

[3]   Cross references have been supplied under Anglican parishes mentioned.

chapels and chaplains or visiting priests were: *Hindlip Hall* belonging to the Habingtons (probably too early for registers): *Hill End, Castlemorton*, the home of the Bartletts: *Woolershall*, where the Handford family lived. At *Soddington* there were Blounts, at *Huddington* the Winters. The latter family also owned *Cooksey* and *Badge Court*. Unfortunately no trace of registers of any of these places have been found to date.

Churches founded after 1791 were Stourbridge, Dudley, Kidderminster, Broadway and Redditch.

Stourbridge was founded in a room over a shop as early as 1816 by a Father Martyn from Oscott. Father J.T. Brownlow became first resident priest in 1823. The registers before 1842 are not at present to hand.

Dudley was founded from West Bromwich in 1835. Before that date the nearest Mass Centre for Dudley Catholics was at Sedgley in Staffordshire.

Kidderminster was opened in 1831.

Broadway was founded by Benedictines. Abbot Birdsall from Cheltenham began the registers in 1830.

Redditch successor to Heath Green. *See above.*

Nonconformists

The standard work of reference on this subject is *Nonconformity in Worcester* by William Urwick (London 1897), which gives a comprehensive survey of the activities of all the main denominations.

Baptists
21 churches have been listed, viz:-

6 17th Century foundations; Bewdley, Bromsgrove and Worcester surrendered registers beginning in 1776, 1788 and 1793 respectively. Bromsgrove is described in the catalogue of surrendered registers as "Independent and Baptist". Netherton did not surrender registers, but the Church Roll 1654-1697, preserved in Dudley Library contains Adult Baptisms and some Deaths. Entries after 1820 are also found in Minute Books. An excellent account of Baptist activity in the area is to be found in *Three Hundred Years of Baptist Witness in Netherton and Thereabouts* by Revd. Idris Williams, Minister of Cradley Heath Baptist Church. No information has been received from the Church Secretaries of the remaining two – Pershore and Upton on Severn.

4 18th Century foundations. Three – Feckenham and Alcester, Dudley and Cradley surrendered registers beginning in 1788, 1816 and 1809 respectively. No information has been received concerning Westmancote.

11 founded between 1800 and 1837 – 4, Catshill, Clent, Kidderminster and Tenbury surrendered registers. Atch Lench has a few burials recorded in the Church Book. For Redditch and Alvechurch,

no registers exist and no information has been received concerning
the remaining 4 – Blockley; St. Giles Street, Dudley; Moseley; and
Stourbridge. No registers are held by the Secretary of the
Worcestershire Association. A useful work of reference is *"Records
of an old Association", being a Memorial Volume of the 250th
Anniversary of the Midland, now the West Midland Baptist Association,
formed in Warwick May 3rd 1655* (1905) Edited by Owen and others.[4]

Presbyterians and Unitarians.
    The following chapels surrendered registers beginning in the 18th
Century viz:- Bewdley; Cradley; Dudley; Evesham; Kidderminster and
Oldbury. All are now Unitarian Churches except Bewdley. Other meeting
houses existed at Stourbridge (1698) Kingswood (1708) and Lye (1790)
also all now Unitarian. A useful work of references is *Midland
Churches. A History of the Congregations on the Roll of the Midland
Christian Union* by George Eyre Evans (1899).

Independents.
10 Churches have been listed.
 5 17th Century foundations – 2 at Bromsgrove (Worcester St. and
    Chapel Lane – the former in the Catalogue of surrendered registers
    as "Independent and Baptist") Kidderminster; Stourbridge and
    Worcester. All surrendered registers which, except for those of
    Worcester commencing in 1699, begin in the 18th Century. A duplicate
    copy of Angel St, Worcester is at the Worcestershire Record Office.
 1 18th Century foundation – Dudley. Registers begin in 1803.
 4 founded between 1800 and 1837 – Halesowen and Redditch surrendered
    registers. No registers exist for Lye. No information has been
    received concerning Ombersley.

Society of Friends (Quakers).
    The Worcestershire Quarterly Meeting (1668-1791) covered the
following Monthly Meetings:-
    Chadwick (1668-1810)
    Evesham (1668-1810)
    Broadway (– c 1698) united to Evesham M.M. 1698
    Pershore (– c 1699)   "   "   "   "   1699
    Redditch or Rudgeway (1668-1706) United to Evesham M.M. 1706
    Worcester (1668-1810)
    Shipston (1668-1790) United to Warwickshire South M.M 1790
    In 1791 the Worcestershire Quarterly Metting was merged with the
Herefordshire Quarterly to form the Herefordshire and Worcestershire
Quarterly Meeting, and in 1832 with the Wales Half Yearly Meeting to

---
4   Part I and general editing by J.M. Gwynne Owen, Part II by James Ford,
    Part III by six others.

form the Herefordshire, Worcestershire and Wales Quarterly Meeting.
The three surviving Worcestershire Monthly Meetings were merged in
1810 to form the Worcestershire Monthly Meeting.

Registers Worcestershire Quarterly Meeting ZMB 1776-1791 (PRO 633,
634).

Hereford and Worcester Quarterly Meeting Z 1791-1800, MB 1791-
1799 (PRO 633,634).

The Worcestershire Quarterly Meeting registers continued in use
for the enlarged jurisdiction Z 1800-1837, M 1800-1836, B 1799-1837
(PRO 635-637).

Other registers are listed under the respective monthly meetings
with the exception of
Worcestershire Monthly Meeting Z 1812-1837 (PRO 674)
B 1812-1837 (PRO 672)

Birth and Burial Notes and Marriage Certificates held in 1837 by
the Herefordshire, Worcestershire and Wales Meeting are in the
catalogue as No.1472 and cover Z 1774-1800, M 1795-1799, B 1777-1797.

Birth Notes 1880-1909, Burial Notes 1872-1933 and Marriages
1936-1952 for Shropshire and Worcestershire are at the Worcestershire
Record Office.

The majority of the Worcestershire registers were surrendered
and are at the PRO. All these appear in the consolidated *Digest* of
the Herefordshire, Worcestershire and Wales General Meeting at
Friends' House, Euston Rd, London, N.W. of which there is a copy at
the Worcestershire R.O.[5] Some registers, however, are at Friends'
Meeting House Worcester and were not included in the "Digest", though
they probably largely duplicate surrendered registers (*See under
relevant Monthly Meetings and also constituent Meetings of Chadwick,
Bewdley and Evesham.*) A register of the Shipston Monthly Meeting is at
Friends' Meeting House, Birmingham.

The inaccuracy of the catalogue of surrendered registers mentioned
in the General Article is particularly applicable to Worcestershire.
The following list of Worcestershire registers may serve as a partial
corrective though there may be inaccuracies:-

664 Worcester M.M. Z 1660-1793, M 1663-1792, B 1663-1793	)	
665 Evesham M.M. Z 1648-1778, M 1687-1774, B 1650-1776	)All bound	
Redditch M.M. Z 1660-1775, M 1666-1681, B 1675-1757	) together	
(former meetings of Redditch M.M. after 1706	) in same	
Alcester alone after 1766)	) volume.	
? Evesham M.M. M 1671-1808	)	

666 Bewdley Constit. Meeting M 1679-1758
667 Worcester M.M. M 1776-1800
668 Worcester M.M. M 1801-1836

---

[5] For an explanation of these *Digests* see General Article on Quaker
Registers in Vol.I.

669 Evesham M.M. Z 1792-1813, M 1796-1810, B 1796-1814
670 Worcester M.M. B 1776-1801
671 Evesham M.M.   B 1776-1794
672 Worcestershire M.M. B 1812-1837
673 Worcester M.M. B 1801-1837
674 Worcestershire M.M. Z 1812-1837
675 Worcester Z 1801-1837
676 Worcester M.M. Z 1776-1800

Wesleyan Methodists.

The following circuits existed in 1837 – all in the Birmingham and Shrewsbury District – Worcester, Bromsgrove and Evesham, Dudley, Stourbridge and Stourport.

The Circuit Churches of all of these surrendered registers and in addition, registers were surrendered from Kidderminster; Bloomfield and Oldbury.

Primitive Methodists.

There were two Primitive Methodist Circuits in Worcestershire in 1837 – Kidderminster and Dudley. The former surrendered a register but no register has been located for the latter.

Methodist New Connexion.

There was only one Worcestershire Circuit, that of Dudley whose register was surrendered.

Modern Methodist Circuits.

Worcester   Records are deposited in the Worcestershire Record Office.
Malvern   No pre-1837 registers
Bromsgrove   No information
Evesham   No information
Redditch   No information
Dudley   No information
Oldbury   No pre-1837 registers known
Hasbury and Halesowen   No pre-1837 registers held
Blackheath   No pre-1837 registers
Blackheath and Langley Green   No information
Stourbridge and Brierley Hill   No information
Kidderminster and Stourport   No pre-1837 registers held.

Lady Huntingdon's Connexion

Five Churches have been listed, Leigh Sinton, Suckley and Cradley kept a joint register.

Registers were also surrendered by Kidderminster; Malvern Link and Worcester.

Regimental Registers.

These cover Births, Baptisms Marriages and Deaths for the period
1790-1924 and are at Somerset House, London. They are the original
registers kept by the various regiments. They are indexed, and to
search this index one does not need to know the regiment. For
Marriages, Deaths and Burials, it is preferable, though not essential
to know the regiment. The most likely regiment for infantrymen was the
29th regiment of Foot. Search should also be made of the Guards'
Regiments, the Royal Artillery, the Royal Engineers and the Royal
Marines.

Monumental Inscriptions.

The Monumental Inscriptions of Worcester Cathedral are published
in *The Cathedral Church of Worcester, Its Monuments and their Stories*
(W.M.Ede 1925).

Bromsgrove Church: Its History and Antiquities by Cotton contains
some M.I.'s. The Shakespeare's Birthplace Trust Library, Stratford-on-
Avon has manuscript lists of monumental inscriptions in about a dozen
Worcestershire parishes.

Newspapers.

Only pre-1837 newspapers for which there is a reasonably connected series available have been included.

The Worcester Post Man 1709-1721 afterwards the *Worcester Post* or
Western Journal 1722-4; then the *Weekly Worcester Journal* 1725-
1748; then the *Worcester Journal* and *Berrows Worcester Journal*
from 1753.

The Public Library, Worcester holds an incomplete series from
1712 to 1760. Berrows Newspapers Ltd., Worcester hold copies from
1733 onwards.

Worcester Herald 1808 onwards.
Worcestershire Miscellany 1829-31.
Worcestershire Guardian 1834-1848.
Kidderminster Messenger 1836-1849.

To this list may be added the Birmingham newspapers listed in the
Warwickshire preface.

Publishing Societies.

Worcestershire Historical Society – Secretary J. Harrison B.A. City of
Worcester College of Education, Henwick Grove, Worcester. Publica-
tions 1893 onwards.
Worcestershire Archaeological Society. Transactions 1854 onwards.

Former Publishing Society

Worcestershire Parish Register Society. See Modern Copies above.

Other Local Societies.

Stourbridge Historical and Archaeological Society, 34 Hagley Road,
    Stourbridge.
Vale of Evesham Historical Society Almonry Museum, Evesham.
Historical Association, Worcester Branch, City of Worcester
    College of Education, Henwick Grove, Worcester.

Useful Works of Reference.

Audrey H. Higgs A.L.A. and Donald Wright F.L.A. *West Midland
    Genealogy* (Published 1966 under the auspices of the West Midland
    Branch of the Library Association) This is a survey of Local
    Genealogical material which is available in the public libraries
    of Herefordshire, Shropshire, Staffordshire, Warwickshire and
    Worcestershire. Copies available from A.J. Fox esq. F.L.A.,
    Birchfield Library, Birmingham 20. Price 10/- (11/- post paid).

Burton and Pearson. *Bibliography of Worcestershire* (Oxford 1898, 1903).

A Digest of the Parish Registers of the Diocese of Worcester 1899.

The Victoria County History of the County of Worcester 4 Vols 1901-
    1924.

G. Miller. *The Parishes of the Diocese of Worcester.* Vol.II. The
    parishes of Worcestershire (Birmingham Hall and English 1890).

H.S. Grazebrook *Heraldry of Worcestershire* 2 Vols. (London. J.
    Russell Smith 1873).

E.A.B. Barnard *The Prattinton Collections of Worcestershire History*
    (Evesham. Journal Press 1931).

T.R. Nash *Collections for the History of Worcestershire.* 2 Vols.
    1781-2. Supplement 1799 Index (1895).

J. Chambers *Biographical Illustrations of Worcestershire* (1820).

Notes and Queries for Bromsgrove and Central Worcestershire. Vols.
    1-5 1909-14 and 1927.

J. Amphlett *Index to Worcestershire Fines* 1649-1714. Worcestershire
    Historical Society 1896.

W.H. Price and E.A. **Barnard** *Churchwardens' Accounts of the Parish
    of Badsey* 1525-1571 (1913).

J.R. Burton *History of Bewdley.* (1883).

J.R. Burton *History of Kidderminster.* (1890).

*Calendar of Wills and Administrations in the Consistory Court of the
    Bishop of Worcester.* Vols. I and II 1451-1652. ed. E.A. Fry
    (1904-10).

ABBERLEY. *(In Hereford Dio till 1920)*. OR CMB 1558 +, Banns 1759-1812, 1823 + (Inc). BT 1638, 1662 + *(gaps 1663, 77, 81, 85, 94, 1706, 32, 34, 45)* (H).

ABBERTON. OR C 1661-1722, 1730-1812, M 1661-1701, 1730-1753, 1759-1835, B 1661-1812 (WRO), CB 1813 +, M 1837 + (Inc). BT 1608-1882 *(gap 1641-62)*. Cop C 1661-1963, M 1661-1954, B 1661-1962 Mf (WRO and SLC), CMB (BT) 1608-1875 Mf (WRO and SLC).

ABBOTS MORTON. OR CB 1728 +, M 1728-1811, 1813 +, Banns 1754-1811, 1826 + (Inc Inkberrow). BT 1611-1861 *(gap 1642-60)*. Cop C 1728-1965, M 1729-1963, B 1728-1964, Banns 1754-1811, 1826-1924 Mf (WRO and SLC), CMB (BT) 1611-1861 Mf (WRO and SLC).

ACTON BEAUCHAMP. *(Now in Herefordshire)*. OR CB 1577-1803, 1813 +, M 1577-1695, 1700 + (Inc). BT 1613-1867 *(gaps 1642-61, 1791-6 except 1793)*. Cop CMB (BT) 1613-1867 Mf (WRO and SLC).

ALCESTER (S of F). – *see Warwickshire*.

ALDERMINSTER. *Transferred to Warwickshire 1931. See Warwickshire*.

ALDINGTON. – *see Badsey*.

ALFRICK. OR CB 1656 +, M 1655-1809, 1813 +, Banns 1754-1809 (Inc). *Some CB 1695-1808, M 1695-1754 in Suckley Reg*. Mar. Lic. 18th and 19th century (Inc). *The CMB 1655-1812 register includes Lulsley*. BT 1622, 1642, 1701-9, 1727-91, 1797-1870. Cop CB 1656-1964, M 1655-1837, 1841-1963, Banns 1754-1809, 1882-1964 Mf (WRO and SLC), CMB (BT) 1622-1875 (WRO and SLC).

ALLCHURCH. – *see Alvechurch*.

ALSTON (ALSTONE) with LITTLE WASHBOURNE. *Chapelry of Overbury in parish of Teddington*. OR CM 1550 +, B 1546 + *(gaps CMB 1804-12, C 1749-88, M 1732-55, B 1736-81)* (Inc). BT 1619 + *(gaps 1641-63, 1734-47 (except 1737, 39, 42, 44) 1772-1800 (except 1774, 77, 88, 1789))*. *The Transcripts are described as Alston with Washbourne for the years 1621-31, 1634-40, 1672-92. There are separate BT's for Washbourne 1632-3, 1663-70, 1674-91, 1693-1700, 1820-1874*.

The pre-1701 separate Washbourne returns appear to relate only to Great Washbourne. Little Washbourne *entries before 1701 should therefore be sought on* Alston *returns*.

"Washbourne" (i.e. Great Washbourne*) entries are presumably on the* Alston *returns for the remaining years 1619, 1620, 1671, but other Great Washbourne transcripts from 1600 are at City Library, Gloucester*.

Little Washbourne *has separate returns 1701-1874 (gaps 1733-44, (except 1737, 39, 42) and 1772-1800 (except 1774, 76, 88, 89), 1830-37 (except 1834))*. Cop C 1550-1748, M 1550-1731, 1756-1805, B 1546-1735 (SOA and Inc), M 1550-1805 (Phil 1), CMB 1806-1812 (C of A), CB 1550-1805 (SOA), CMB (BT) 1619-1874 (WRO and SLC). *M 1651-1675 in Boyd Misc*.

ALVECHURCH (ALLCHURCH). **Peculiar** *of Rector of Alvechurch.* **OR** CMB 1545 +
(*gap 1548-1754*) (Inc). **BT** 1609 + (*gaps 1627-35, 1640-61, 1800-13*).
Cop CB 1545-1690, M 1545-1699 (C of A), CMB (BT) 1609-1875 (WRO and
SLC).

ALVECHURCH (RC). *Many entries in regs of St Peter's Franciscan Mission*
Birmingham.

ALVECHURCH, Red Lion St. (Bapt). *f 1826. No regs known. Not at PRO or*
Ch. Sec. A branch of Cannon St, Birmingham; Alvechurch entries may
be in their regs. See Warwickshire.

AMBLECOAT. *Chapel in Old Swinford. – see Swinford, Old.*

ARLEY KINGS. **OR** C 1539-1702, 1783 +, M 1539-1664, 1669-1702, 1754-
1780, 1783 +, B 1539-1694, 1784 + (Early regs at Midland Bank,
Stourport, remainder Inc). **BT** 1608-1932 (*gaps 1641-63, 1792-1813*).
Cop CMB (BT) 1608-1875 Mf (WRO and SLC).

ARLEY OVER (or UPPER ARLEY). *Worcs. Dio since 1920.* **OR** CMB 1564 + (Inc)
BT 1606 + (LX). **Cop** CMB 1564-1812 (Worcs PRS), C 1564-1947,
MB 1564-1963 Mf (SLC).

ASHTON UNDER HILL. (*Transferred from Glos 1931*). **OR** C 1596-1886, M 159
1837, B 1596-1945 (WRO). **BT** 1618 + (CLG). **Cop** Extracts CB 1606-1700
(Ptd), Extracts CMB 1598-1754 (SOA), CB 1586-1812, M 1586-1777 (C
of A), C 1586-1886, M 1586-1837, B 1586-1945 (SLC). *M 1586-1778*
in Roe's Glos. M Index.

ASTLEY (near Stourport). **OR** CB 1539 +, M 1539-1768, 1784 + (*gap CMB 1630*
1670), Banns 1824 + (Inc). **BT** 1609-1890 (*gaps 1642-60, 1717-23*).
Cop CM 1539-1630, B 1539-1581 (C of A), CMB (BT) 1609-1875 Mf (WRO and
SLC), Mar. Lic. 1855-1932 Mf (WRO and SLC). *M 1539-1630 in Boyd Misc.*

ASTON SOMERVILLE. (*Transferred from Glos. 1931*). – *see Glos.*

ASTON, WHITE LADIES. **OR** CMB 1558 +. **BT** 1604, 1609-1869 (*gap 1643-60,*
1788-92, irregular 1783-1800). **Cop** CMB 1558-1840 Ms (SG),
CMB (BT) 1669-1869 Mf (WRO and SLC).

ASTWOOD BANK. (Bapt). – *see Redditch.*

ATCH LENCH. (Bapt). – *see Church Lench.*

BADSEY WITH ALDINGTON. **OR** CMB 1539 + (Inc). **BT** 1614-1875 (*gap 1641-61,*
1776-83). **Cop** CMB (BT) 1614-1875 Mf (WRO and SLC). *M 1539-1733 in*
Boyd Misc.

BAYTON. *In Hereford Dio till 1920.* **OR** CMB 1564 + (*gap M 1740-1754*),
Banns 1824 + (Inc). *Early entries include Mamble.* **BT** 1638, 1660 +
(HX). **Cop** CMB 1564-1964, Banns 1756-1964 Mf (WRO and SLC).

BECKFORD. (*Transferred from Glos. 1931*). **OR** C 1549-1882, M 1573-1836,
B 1538-1925, Banns 1799-1891 (WRO). **BT** 1607 + (CLG). **Cop** Extracts
CB 1600-1697 (Ptd), C 1549-1882, M 1573-1836, B 1538-1925 Mf (SLC).
M (BT) 1607-1700 (X) in Boyd Misc.

BECKFORD (RC). **OR** C 1817 + (Inc). **Cop** C 1817-1850 (Cath RS on loan to SG).

BEDWARDINE, St Michael. — *see Worcester.*

BELBROUGHTON (with FAIRFIELD). **OR** CMB 1539 + *(gap CMB 1631-33)* (Inc). **BT** 1615, 18, 1624-1871 *(gap 1643-60, 1805-9).* **Cop** CMB 1540-1837 (BRL), CMB (BT) 1615-1871 Mf (WRO) and SLC).

BELBROUGHTON (RC). *Some entries in Harrington regs.*

BENGEWORTH. **OR** CMB 1538 + *(gaps C 1783-1808, M 1732-4, 1750-4, 1802-1813, B 1783-1811)* (Inc). **BT** 1615, 1620-1867 *(gap 1632-68,* except 1637, 39; *1671-5, 1830-37* except 1835). **Cop** C 1538-1783, ZC 1808-1812, C 1813-1963, M 1538-1802, 1813-1963, Banns 1754-1802, 1824-1950, B 1538-1783, 1811-1963 Mf (WRO and SLC), CMB (BT) 1611-1867 Mf (WRO and SLC). *Notes on Registers* (SOA).

BEOLEY. **OR** CMB 1558 +, Mar. Lic. 1800 + (Inc). **BT** 1622 + *(gap 1642-1663).* **Cop** CMB (BT) 1622-1875 Mf (WRO and SLC).

BEOLEY (RC). *Entries in regs of St Peter's Franciscan Mission, Birmingham.*

BERROW. **Peculiar** *of Dean and Chapter of Worcester.* **OR** C 1698-1871, M 1698-1952, B 1698-1812, Banns 1754-1812, 1823-1930 (WRO), B 1813 + (Inc). **BT** 1611-1893 *(gap 1642-60) (1626 transcript dated 1526 in error).* **Cop** C 1698-1871, M 1698-1948, B 1698-1812, Banns 1754-1812, 1823-1930 Mf (WRO and SLC), CMB (BT) 1611-1875 Mf (WRO and SLC).

BESFORD. **OR** C 1539-1650, 1697-1742, 1751 +, M 1539-1650, 1697-1742, 1754 +, B 1539-1642, 1697-1742, 1751 +, Banns 1824 + (Inc Defford). **BT** 1611-1907 *(gap 1641-60,* irregular 1660-80). **Cop** CMB (BT) 1611-1875 Mf (WRO and SLC).

BEWDLEY. — *see Ribbesford, Hill Croome, Earls Croome and Ripple.*

BEWDLEY, High St. (Bapt). *f 1649.* **OR** Z 1776-1836, DB 1756-1836 (PRO).

BEWDLEY, High St. (Pres). **OR** ZC 1744-1823, B 1812-1815 (PRO).

BEWDLEY. (Wes). — *see* **Stourport Circuit.**

BEWDLEY (S of F). *Constituent Meeting of* **Chadwick Monthly Meeting** *(1668-1807) q.v., disc. 1807.* **OR** Z 1683-1767, M 1682-1759, B 1669-1774 (FMH Worcester — *not in Digest),* M 1679-1758 (PRO 666). *Refounded 1816 as Constituent Meeting of* **Worcestershire Monthly Meeting** *(1816 +). See Preface. No constituent meeting regs known.*

BIRLINGHAM with NAFFORD. **OR** 1566-1633, 1638-1746, 1751 +, M 1566-1636, 1663 +, B 1566-1633, 1638 +, Banns 1754-1789 (Inc). **BT** 1611-1867 *(gap 1642-62* except 1654) (WRO). *See also Nafford.* **Cop** CMB (BT) 1610-1875 Mf (WRO and SLC).

BIRTSMORTON. (with HOLLYBUSH). **OR** CB 1539-1812, M 1539-1754, 1763-1809, 1815-37 (WRO). **BT** 1609-1874 *(gap 1642-60, 1805-10)*. **Cop** M 1539-1812 (Phil 2), C 1539-1812, M 1539-1809, 1815-1837, B 1539-1812 Mf (WRO and SLC), CMB (BT) 1609-1875 Mf (WRO and SLC). *M 1651-1675 in Boyd Misc.*

BISHAMPTON. **OR** C 1599-1962, M 1629-1962, B 1600 – 1963 (WRO), Banns 1825 + (Inc). **BT** 1616-1889 *(gap 1642-62)*. **Cop** C 1599-1949, M 1603-1948, B 1600-1949 Ms (SG), CMB (BT) 1599-1962, M 1629-1962, B 1600-1963 Mf (WRO and SLC), CMB (BT) 1616-1875 Mf (WRO and SLC).

BISHAMPTON (S of F). *Constituent Meeting of* **Redditch Monthly Meeting** *(1668-1706) q.v.,* **Evesham Monthly Meeting** *(1706- before 1748) q.v. 1729 moved to Naunton Beauchamp. Disc. before 1748.* **OR** *No constituent meeting regs as such, but see note on Redditch Monthly Meeting regs.*

BLACKMORE PARK (RC). **OR** CD 1846 + (Inc). *Earlier regs destroyed in 19th century.*

BLAKEDOWN. – *see Churchill in Halfshire.*

BLOCKLEY. **OR** CB 1538 +, M 1539 + (Inc). **BT** 1613-1875 *(gap 1647-60)*. **Cop** Extracts CMB 1583-1660, CMB (BT) 1612-1699 (SOA), CMB (BT) 1613-1875 Mf (WRO and SLC).

BLOCKLEY, High St. (Bapt). *f 1820. Not at PRO. No information.*

BLOOMFIELD. (Wes). **OR** ZC 1823-1837 (PRO).

BOCKLETON. *(Dio of Hereford).* **OR** C 1574-1885, M 1574-1850, B 1574-1963 (WRO). **BT** 1660 + *(gap 1791, 2)* (HX). **Cop** CMB 1558-1812 (Inc), C 1574-1885, M 1574-1850, B 1574-1963 Mf (WRO and SLC).

BORDESLEY CHAPEL, *parish of Tardebigg.* **OR** C 1704-70, M 1722-69, B 1713-69 (Inc Tardebigg), C 1823 +, M 1864 +, B 1823 + (Inc). **BT** 1823-1835 (Lichfield). *Previously on Tardebigg returns.*

BRADLEY (or BRADLEY GREEN) with STOCK. *Chapelry in Fladbury Parish.* **Peculiar** *of Fladbury.* **OR** CMB 1562 + *(gap B 1697-1719)*, Banns 1756-1794 (Inc Feckenham). **BT** 1612-1885 *(gap 1641-60, irregular 1660-1676, gaps 1785-1799, 1809-1814)*. **Cop** CMB 1614-1812 Ms Alpha (SG), C 1562-1963, M 1565-1962, B 1564-1963 Mf (WRO and SLC), CMB (BT) 1612-1875 Mf (WRO and SLC), CMB (BT) Stock 1685-1686 Mf (WRO and SLC). *See also Fladbury.*

BRANSFORD. *(Chapel in Leigh).* **OR** CB 1767-1944, M 1767-1838, B 1813-1872, Banns 1767-1809 (WRO). *Earlier CMB and some later B in Leigh regs.* **BT** *on Leigh returns.* **Cop** C 1767-1944, M 1767-1809, 1813-1838, B 1813-1872 Mf (WRO and SLC).

BREDICOT. **OR** C 1702-1752, 1813-1964, M 1702-1752, 1813-1924 *(gap 1836-1840)* 1951-62, B 1702-1752, 1813-1944 (WRO). **BT** 1609-1912 *(gap 1619-1623, 1642-62, 1792-99, 1801-13, 1821-4)*. **Cop** C 1702-1752, 1813-1964, M 1702-1752, 1813-1836, 1840-1924, 1951-1962, B 1702-1752, 1813-1944 Mf (WRO and SLC), CMB (BT) 1609-1875 Mf (WRO and SLC).

BREDON. **Peculiar** *of Rector of Bredon.* **OR** C 1563 $^+$, M 1562 $^+$, B 1559 $^+$(Inc).
  BT 1622-1914 *(gaps 1641-60, 1663-68, 1673-78, 1782-89, 1793-7,*
  1801-5), 1675-92 on Bredons Norton returns. **Cop** Extracts C 1559-
  1649, M 1562-1662, B 1559-1662 Ts (SG), C 1563-1963, M 1562-1963,
  B 1559-1963 Mf (WRO and SLC), CMB (BT) 1622-1875 Mf (WRO and SLC).

BREDONS NORTON. **Peculiar** *of Rector of Bredon.* **OR** CB 1813 $^+$, M 1754 $^+$
  (gap 1835-38) (Inc). *Early M in Bredon regs.* **BT** 1612-1912 *(gaps*
  1616-22, 1641-79 except 1675, *1732-57, 1785-9, 1793-7, 1801-8,*
  1812-19, 1831-34). Throughout the whole period there are also a
  large number of small gaps (WRO). *With Bredon 1675-92* (WRO).
  Cop C 1813-1962, MB 1813-1963, Banns 1824-1963 Mf (WRO and SLC),
  CMB (BT) 1612-1875 Mf (WRO and SLC).

BRETFORTON. **OR** CB 1538-1703, 1783 $^+$, M 1538-1777, 1784 $^+$, Banns 1755-
  1777, 1825 $^+$ (Inc). **BT** 1613-1868 *(gap 1642-61).* **Cop** CMB 1538-1837
  I (Ptd), C 1538-1782, M 1538-1772, B 1538-1783 (SOA), C 1538-1900,
  M 1538-1964, B 1538-1895, Banns 1755-1777, 1825-1939 Mf (WRO and
  SLC), CMB (BT) 1613-1875 Mf (WRO and SLC).

BRICKLEHAMPTON. *Chapel in Pershore St Andrew.*
  B 1813 $^+$ (Inc). **BT** 1611 $^+$ *(gap 1641-62* except for 1651, *1788-97).*
  Cop CMB (BT) 1611-1875 Mf (WRO and SLC).

BROADWAS. **OR** CMB 1676 $^+$, Banns 1754-1811, 1824 $^+$ (Inc). **BT** 1612-1909
  (gap 1643-60 (except 1648), *1788-92, 1804-8).* **Cop** CM 1676-1963,
  B 1676-1812, Banns 1754-1811, 1824-1964 Mf (WRO and SLC),
  CMB (BT) 1612-1875 Mf (WRO and SLC).

BROADWAY. **OR** C 1541 $^+$, M 1539-1753, 1813 $^+$, B 1539 $^+$, (Inc).
  BT 1608-1900 *(gap 1641-65).* **Cop** C 1562-1704, M 1539-1812, B 1539-
  1704, M 1539-1812 (SOA and GL), CMB (BT) 1608-1875 Mf (WRO and SLC).

BROADWAY, St Saviour's Retreat (RC). **OR** C 1830-38, M 1833-37, B 1834-
  1837 (Inc).

BROADWAY. (Ind). *f 1808.* **OR** ZC 1801-1837 (PRO).

BROADWAY MONTHLY MEETING (S of F). *(1668-c.1698). United with*
  Evesham Monthly Meeting *c.1698.* **Constituent Meeting:** Broadway.
  No Monthly Meeting regs known.

BROADWAY (S of F). **Broadway Monthly Meeting** *(1668-c.1698),* **Evesham**
  Monthly Meeting *(c.1698-before 1750) disc. before 1750. No*
  meeting regs known.

BROMSGROVE. **OR** CB 1774 $^+$, M 1773 $^+$ (Inc). **BT** 1613 $^+$ *(gap 1642-62).*
  Cop Extracts CMB 1590-1712 p/s, M 1719-1812 Ts (SG), CMB 1590-
  1719 (Inc and BM Add. Mss 41310, 41311, 42850, 44876), C 1774-
  1946, M 1773-1962, B 1774-1954 Mf (WRO and SLC), CMB (BT) 1613-
  1875 Mf (WRO and SLC). *See also Catshill.*

BROMSGROVE, Little Cat's Hill. (Bapt). – *see Catshill.*

BROMSGROVE, Worcester St. (Ind and Bapt). *f 1666.* OR C 1788-1804, Z 1804-1836 (PRO).

BROMSGROVE. (Wes). OR ZC 1815-1837, B 1835-1837 (PRO). *Register for the* **Bromsgrove Circuit.**

BROMSGROVE, Chapel Lane, formerly Upper Meeting. (Ind). OR ZC 1739-1767, 1770-1837, B 1772-1837 (PRO).

BROMSGROVE (S of F). *Constituent Meeting of* **Chadwick Monthly Meeting** *(1668-1802) q.v. disc. 1802.* OR *PRO reg 1183 cat. as "Chadwick and Bromsgrove" is probably Bromsgrove Constituent Meeting register* Z 1655-1794, M 1667-1778, B 1669-1797.

BROOME. OR CMB 1666 +, Banns 1824 + (Inc). BT 1613, 1616, 1619, 1625-1873 *(gap 1641-60).* Cop CMB (BT) 1616-1873 Mf (WRO and SLC).

BROUGHTON HACKETT. OR CB 1761 +, M 1759 +, Banns 1759 + (Inc Upton Snodsbury). BT 1610-1873 *(gap 1642-61, 1790-6).* Cop CB 1761-1965, M 1759-1962, Banns 1759-1901 Mf (WRO and SLC), CMB (BT) 1609-1873 Mf (WRO and SLC).

BUSHLEY. OR CMB 1538 + (Inc). BT 1611-1868 *(gap 1641-61).* Cop M 1539-1837 (Phil 2), CB 1538-1812 I (Worcs PRS), C 1538-1812, M 1539-1812, B 1538-1678, 1696-1812, B (BT) 1679-1695 (SOA), CMB (BT) 1611-1875 Mf (WRO and SLC). *M 1651-1675 in Boyd Misc.*

CASTLEMORTON. OR C 1558 +, M 1651 +, B 1558-1629, 1648 + (Inc). BT 1612-1870 *(gap 1641-60).* Cop M (BT) 1609-1641 Ts (SG, GL and Bod), CMB (BT) 1609-1870 Mf (WRO and SLC). *M 1609-1641 in Boyd Misc.*

CASTLEMORTON, Hill End (RC). *No regs traced. Some entries in regs of Little Malvern Court. See Malvern, Little.*

CATSHILL. OR CMB 1838 + (Inc). *No BT's.*

CATSHILL. (Bapt). *f 1830.* OR Z 1837 (PRO *Cat. as Bromsgrove, Little Cat's Hill).*

CHACELEY. *(Transferred to Glos 1931).* OR C 1538 +, M 1540-1714, 1755 +, B 1539 + (Inc). BT 1613-1873 *(gap 1642-60).* Cop M 1540-1837 (Phil Ms and SG), CMB (BT) 1613-1873 Mf (WRO and SLC). *M 1540-1837 in Boyd Misc.*

CHADDESLEY CORBETT, OR CMB 1538 +, Banns 1823 +. (Inc). BT 1613, 1618-1871 *(gap 1646-60).* Cop M 1601-1625 Ms (SG), CMB 1538-1964, Banns 1823-1931 Mf (WRO and SLC), CMB (BT) 1613-1871, 1871 Mf (WRO and SLC).

CHADDESLEY CORBETT (RC). – *see Harvington Hall.*

CHADWICK (RC). *Some entries in Harvington regs.*

CHADWICK MONTHLY MEETING (S of F). *(1668-1810)*. *1810 united with* Evesham Monthly Meeting *and* Worcester Monthly Meeting *to form* Worcestershire Monthly Meeting *(see preface).*
Constituent Meetings:- *Chadwick (1668-before 1819), Dudley (1668-1810), Stourbridge (1668-1810), Bewdley (1668-1807), Bromsgrove (1698-1802).*
Monthly Meeting Registers:- Z 1635-1813, M 1658-1776, 1781-1808, B 1689-1813 (PRO 1175-1180).
Each Constituent Meeting would also seem to have kept registers, though none are known for Stourbridge. Register 1183 cat. as "Chadwick and Bromsgrove" was probably Bromsgrove Constituent Meeting register – see Bromsgrove.

CHADWICK (S of F). *Constituent Meeting of* **Chadwick Monthly Meeting** *1668-before 1810. Disc. before 1810.* **Registers** Z 1668-1777, M 1682-1759, B 1683-1786 (FMH Worcester).

CHILD'S WICKHAM. **Peculiar** *of Rector of Child's Wickham.* **OR** CMB 1552 + (Inc). **BT** 1639 + (CLG). **Cop** M 1560-1812 (Phil Glos 4).

CHURCH HONEYBOURNE. **OR** CB 1673 +, M 1673-1735, 1744 +, Banns 1824 + (Inc Honeybourne). *Originally a Civil parish – now combined with Honeybourne.* **BT** 1614-1883 *(gap 1641-1674 except for 1660).* **Cop** CB 1673-1812, M 1673-1758 (SOA), CMB (BT) 1614-1837 Mf (WRO and SLC).

CHURCH ICOMBE. *– see Icombe, Glos.*

CHURCHILL IN HALFSHIRE, St James (near KIDDERMINSTER and BLAKEDOWN). **OR** 1540 + (Inc). **BT** 1612 + *(gaps 1641-60, 1788-1811, irregular 1660-1682).* **Cop** M 1601-1625 Ms (SG), CMB 1540-1712 ps (WRO), CM 1540-1964, B 1540-1965, Banns 1754-1924 Mf (WRO and SLC). *M 1601-1625, 1651-1675 in Boyd Misc. The two Churchills have been confused in the 1899 Digest and the information given there is incorrect.*

CHURCHILL IN OSWALDSLOW, near WORCESTER. **OR** C 1565-1794, 1813 +, M 1564-1750, 1761 +, B 1566-1792, 1813 +, Banns 1762-92, 1824 + (Inc, White Ladies Aston). **BT** 1609 + *(gap 1641-60)* (WRO – Pershore Deanery). **Cop** CMB 1564-1839 (Worcs PRS), M 1564-1812 (Phil 2), CB 1795-1840, M 1751-1761 Ms (SG), CMB (BT) 1609-1875 Mf (WRO and SLC). *See note under Churchill in Halfshire.*

CHURCH LENCH. **OR** C 1666 +, M 1702-1750, 1755 +, B 1702 +, Banns 1755-1812, 1823 + (Inc). **BT** 1615, 1620-1888 *(gaps 1641-60, except 1657, 1800-1808, except 1803).* **Cop** M 1702-1812 (Phil 1), C 1692-1965, M 1702-1964, B 1702-1965, Banns 1756-1812, 1824-1903 Mf (WRO and SLC), CMB (BT) 1615-1875 Mf (WRO and SLC).

CHURCH LENCH, Atch Lench Chapel. (Bapt). *f 1825.* **OR** *Not at PRO.* B 1827-1837 (5 entries) in Church Book (Church Sec.).

CLAINES. **OR** C 1538 +, M 1540 + *(gap CMB 1656-61, B 1784-1828)* (Inc). **BT** 1615-1908 *(gaps 1637-63, 1735-9, 1786-1800)*. **Cop** Banns 1841-1951 p/s (WRO), C 1538-1937, M 1540-1955, B 1540- 1948 Mf (WRO and SLC), CMB (BT) 1615-1875 Mf (WRO and SLC).

CLEEVE PRIOR. **OR** C 1598 +, M 1599-1748, 1754 +, B 1599 + *(gap CMB 1641-61)*, Banns 1823 + (Inc). **BT** 1612, 1615, 1620-1892 *(gaps 1641-1661* (except 1644), *1673-80* (except 1675))*. **Cop** M 1599-1837 (Phil 2), C 1598-1793, M 1599-1640, 1662-1748, B 1598-1812 (SOA), Extracts CMB 1598-1717 (BRL), C 1598-1965, M 1599-1965, B 1599-1964, Banns 1754-1812 Mf (WRO and SLC), CMB (BT) 1612-1875 Mf (WRO and SLC). *M 1651-1675 in Boyd Misc.*

CLENT. **OR** CMB 1561-1625, 1637 +, Banns 1754-89 (Inc). **BT** 1612-1916 *(gaps 1615-26* (except 1621), *1641-60* (except 1644))* M only 1774-1785. **Cop** CMB (BT) 1612-1916 Mf (SLC).

CLENT, Holy Cross. (Bapt). **OR** Z 1807-30 (PRO *cat. under Staffs*).

CLIFTON UPON TEME. *(Hereford Dio until 1920).* **OR** 1598 + (Inc). **BT** 1638, 1660 + (HXX).

COBLEY. – *see Tardebigg.*

COFTON HACKETT. **OR** CMB 1550-1651, 1654-83, 1702-54, CB 1785 +, M 1755 + (Inc). **BT** 1611-1899 *(gap 1642-63)*. **Cop** C 1550-1554, 1601-1627, M 1580, 1600-1619, B 1582, 1597-1626 (SOA), CMB (BT) 1611-1875 Mf (WRO and SLC).

COMBERTON, GREAT. **OR** C 1540-1705, 1721 +, M 1558-1705, 1721 +, B 1541-1704, 1721-1908 (Inc Little Comberton). **BT** 1612, 1615, 1621 + *(gap 1640-61)*. **Cop** CMB 1540-1705, C 1721-1963, MB 1721-1964 Mf (WRO and SLC), CMB (BT) 1612-1875 Mf (WRO and SLC).

COMBERTON, LITTLE. **OR** C 1542-1687, 1695 +, M 1540-1693, 1695 +, B 1586 +, Banns 1824 + (Inc). **BT** 1612-1888 *(gap 1642-60, 1730-34,* irregular 1738-47). **Cop** M 1540-1812 (Phil 2), M 1540-1627 (SOA), CMB 1543-1964, Banns 1755-1809 Mf (WRO and SLC), CMB (BT) 1612-1875 Mf (WRO and SLC). *M 1651-1675 in Boyd Misc.*

COOKLEY. (Wes). *f 1814.* – *see* **Stourport Circuit.**

COTHERIDGE. **OR** CMB 1653-1672, 1690 + (Inc). **BT** 1611-1890 *(gap 1637-1660)*. **Cop** CMB 1611-1875 Mf (WRO and SLC).

COW HONEYBOURNE. – *see Honeybourne.*

CRADLEY. *Formed from Parish of Halesowen 1799).* **OR** CB 1798 +, M 1802 + (Inc). **BT** 1799-1820 (WRO).

CRADLEY, High St. (Bapt). *f 1798.* **OR** Z 1809-1836, B 1805-1837 (PRO).

CRADLEY, Park Lane Chapel. (Pres). *f 1796.* **OR** ZC 1789-1837, B 1761-1826 (PRO).

CROOME. – *see Earls Croome, Hill Croome, Ripple, Strensham.*

CROOME D'ABITOT. **OR** C 1560-1733, 1741 [+], M 1560-91, 1593-1729, 1741 [+], B 1560 [+] (Inc). **BT** 1608-1893 (*gap 1640-62*). **Cop** (BT) CMB 1608-1875 Mf (WRO and SLC).

CROPTHORNE. **OR** CM 1557 [+], B 1718 [+] (Inc Croome d'Abitot). **BT** 1611-1866 (*gap 1640-63*). **Cop** CMB 1557-1717 (Ptd 1896), CB 1718-1812, M 1718-1746 (C of A), C 1557-1852, M 1557-1837, 1937-1954, B 1718-1873 Mf (WRO and SLC), CMB (BT) 1612-1866 Mf (WRO and SLC), *M 1557-1751 in Boyd Misc.*

CROWLE. **OR** C 1539-1649, 1662 [+], M 1539 [+], B 1539-1640, 1662 [+] (Inc). **BT** 1611-1882 (*gap 1642-61*). **Cop** C 1539-1649, 1662-1963, M 1539-1962, B 1539-1640, 1662-1963, Banns 1911-1963 Mf (WRO and SLC), CMB (BT) 1611-1875 Mf (WRO and SLC).

CUTSDEAN. – *Chapelry in Bredon.* **OR** CMB 1696 [+] (Inc). **BT** 1634, 37, 70, 1675, 1709-1850, 1872 (*gap 1785-9*). **Cop** CMB (BT) 1634-1850, 1872 Mf (WRO and SLC).

DAYLESFORD. **OR** C 1674 [+], M 1684-1748, 1755 [+], B 1679 [+] (*gap B 1789-1816*), Banns 1823 [+] (Inc). **BT** 1624, 1660 [+]. **Cop** CMB (BT) 1624 [+] Mf (WRO and SLC).

DEFFORD. **OR** C 1540 [+], M 1679-1683, 1687 [+], B 1540-1683, 1687 [+], Banns 1754 [+] (Inc). **BT** 1611-1908 (*gap 1641-60*). **Cop** CMB 1540-1682, 1687-1812 (WRO and BM), CMB (BT) 1611-1875 Mf (WRO and SLC).

DITCHFORD. – *see Stretton-under-Fosse, Warwickshire.*

DODDENHAM with KNIGHTWICK. **OR** C 1538-1779, 1813 [+], M 1538-1695, 1698-1751, 1760-1809, 1813 [+], B 1538-1695, 1813 [+] (*CMB 1649-74 defective*), Banns 1813-1855 (Inc Broadwas). **BT** 1612-1864 (*gaps 1625-9, 1641-62, 1667-72 [except 1669], 1676-82, 1786-1799*. **Cop** CMB 1538-1812 I (Ptd 1891); C 1538-1779, 1813-1963, M 1538-1695, 1698-1751, 1760-1809, 1813-1855, B 1538-1695, Banns 1813-1855 Mf (WRO and SLC), CMB (BT) 1612-1864 Mf (WRO and SLC).

DODDERHILL. **OR** CMB 1651 [+], Banns 1789-1823 (Inc). **BT** 1613-1862 (*gaps 1642-1661, 1735-59 [except 1744, 1745], (irreg 1723-33) – Also on Elmbridge Returns 1676-1700.* **Cop** CMB 1613-1641 (Inc), Index to CMB 1651-1812 (Inc), CB 1651-1963, M 1651-1837, 1857-1963, Banns 1789-1942 (WRO and SLC), CMB (BT) 1613-1862 Mf (WRO and SLC).

DORMSTON. **OR** C 1756-1788, 1813 [+], MB 1761-1811 (Inc Kington). *Some B are in regs of Inkberrow – earlier CMB in Kington regs.* **BT** 1607, 1612-1870 (*gaps 1636-63 [except 1639] 1669-75*). **Cop** (BT and PR) CMB 1612-1736 Ms (SG). *See Kington for Mf with Dormston,* CMB (BT) 1612-1870 Mf (WRO and SLC). *M 1612-1736 in Boyd Misc.*

DOVERDALE. **OR** CB 1704-1812, M 1704-1837, Banns 1755-1812 (WRO), CB 1813 [+] (Inc Ombersley). **BT** 1612-1896 (*gaps 1629-34, 1642-63, 1788-1813 [except 1793], CMB (BT) 1612-1875 Mf (WRO and SLC), (PR) M 1813-1837 Mf (WRO and SLC).

DOWLES. *Formerly in Shropshire. – see Shropshire.*

DROITWICH, St Nicholas. **OR** C 1870-1903 (WRO), *pre 1837 regs destroyed by fire.* **BT** 1611-1641 (WRO). *No separate returns appear to have been made after 1641. (See Droitwich St Andrew and St Peter).* **Cop** C 1870-1927, M 1870-1961, B 1872-1944, Banns 1925-1961 Mf (WRO and SLC), CMB (BT) 1611-1641 Mf (WRO and SLC).

DROITWICH, St Andrew and St Mary de Witton. **OR** C 1571-1769, 1771 [+], M 1571 [+], B 1572-1769, 1771 [+] (Inc). **BT** 1608-1865 (*gaps 1642-61, 1735-39, 1788-92*). **Cop** CMB 1571-1963 Mf (WRO and SLC), CMB (BT) 1608-1865 Mf (WRO and SLC).

DROITWICH, St Peter. **OR** CB 1544 [+], M 1544-1760, 1792 [+] (Inc). **BT** 1613 [+] (*gap 1642-60*). **Cop** CMB 1544-1792 (BRL), CMB (BT) 1613-1875 Mf (WRO and SLC).

DROITWICH (S of F). *Constituent Meeting of* **Worcester Monthly Meeting** (*1668-before 1791*), *disc. before 1791. No meeting regs known other than Monthly Meeting registers.*

DUDLEY, St Edmund. (*Church demolished 1646 and parish united with St Thomas in 1650 – see St Thomas and St Edmund below*). **OR** CMB 1540-1646 (Dudley Pub Lib). **BT** 1607, 1613-42, 1648, 1682 (WRO). **Cop** CMB 1540-1646 (Dudley Pub Lib), CMB 1540-1611 Ptd 1961, CMB 1540-1611 Ts (WRO), CMB 1540-1646 Mf (WRO and SLC), CMB (BT) 1615-1642 (WRO and SLC).

DUDLEY, St Thomas. (*United with St Edmund 1650 – see St Thomas and St Edmund below*). **OR** CMB 1541-1649 (Dudley Pub Lib). **BT** 1613, 1618-1643 (WRO). **Cop** CMB 1541-1649 Ms (Dudley Pub Lib), CMB 1541-1649 Mf (WRO and SLC), CMB (BT) 1613-1642 (WRO and SLC).

DUDLEY, St Thomas and St Edmund. C 1646-1948, M 1646-1954, B 1646-1926, B at Queen's Cross Cemetery 1919-1937. (*122 volumes in all. Index to Baptisms 1794-1812. Some volumes have draft indexes inside*), Banns 1815-1840, 1848-1854, 1902-1961 (all Dudley Pub Lib). **BT** 1660-1851. **Cop** CM 1650-1691, B 1650-1677 (Dudley Lib), CB 1650-1964, M 1650-1954 Mf (WRO and SLC), CMB (BT) 1828-1851 Mf (WRO and SLC).

DUDLEY. Our Lady and St Thomas of Canterbury (RC). **OR** CMB 1835 [+] (Inc) *Earlier C possibly at West Bromwich and Sedgeley.*

DUDLEY, New St Chapel, now Priory Rd. (Bapt). *f 1772.* **OR** Z 1816-1837, B 1814-1837 (PRO). **Cop** Z 1816-1837, B 1814-1837 I (Ptd. Non-Parochial Regs of Dudley 1899).

DUDLEY, Netherton Baptist Chapel, *now Messiah Chapel, Cinder Bank.* (Bapt). *f 1654. See Netherton.*

DUDLEY, Sweet Turf, St Giles St. (Bapt). *f 1810. Not at PRO. No information.*

DUDLEY, Wolverhampton St, Old Meeting House. (Pres). *f 1704.* **OR** C 1743-1772, ZC 1775-1837, DB 1811-1837 (PRO). **Cop** C 1743-1772, ZC 1775-1837, DB 1811-1837 I (Ptd as above).

DUDLEY, King St (Ind). *f 1792.* **OR** ZC 1803-1837 (PRO). **Cop** ZC 1803-1837 I (Ptd as above). 280

DUDLEY, King St. (Wes Meth). *f 1788.* OR ZC 1804-1837 (PRO). Cop ZC 1804-1837 I (Ptd as above). *A Circuit register for the Dudley Circuit.*

DUDLEY CIRCUIT. (Prim Meth). No registers known. Not at PRO.

DUDLEY, Wolverhampton St (Meth New Connexion). *f 1829.* OR B 1829-1837 (PRO). *A Circuit register.* Cop B 1829-1837 I (Ptd as above).

DUDLEY (S of F). *Constituent Meeting of* Chadwick Monthly Meeting *(1668-1810) q.v.* Worcestershire Monthly Meeting *(1810-1819). See* Worcs Preface. Warwickshire North Monthly Meeting *(1819-1837). See* Warwickshire Preface. OR Z 1656-1801, M 1662-1694, B 1662-1827 (PRO 1184), B 1839-1848 (FMH, Bull St, Birmingham). Cop Z 1656-1801, M 1662-1772, B 1662-1827 (Ptd. Non Parochial Regs of Dudley 1899 I).

DUDLEY, Netherton (S of F). *– See Netherton.*

EARL'S CROOME. OR C 1647 [+], M 1659 [+], B 1658 [+], Banns 1812 [+] (Inc). BT 1612-1877 *(gaps 1617-21, 1640-60, 1802-11, 1817-25).* Cop CMB (BT) 1612-1837 Mf (WRO and SLC).

EASTHAM with ORLETON and HANLEY CHILD. *(Hereford Dio till 1920).* OR CMB 1571 [+], Banns 1755-1812 (BRL) (Inc). *Separate M for Orleton 1760-80. (See also Hanley Child and Hanley William).* BT 1660 [+] (HXX). Cop CMB 1571-1812 (BRL), CB 1572-1812, M 1571-1837 (Phil 2), CMB 1572-1812 Ptd (Worcs PRS), C 1572-1963, M 1571-1962, B 1571-1964, Banns 1755-1812, 1918-1962 Mf (WRO and SLC), *M 1651-1675 in Boyd Misc.*

ECKINGTON. OR CMB 1678 [+] *(CMB 1678-1756 defective).* BT 1612-1900 *(gaps 1640-60, 1675-9).* Cop CMB 1678-1756 Ms (WRO), C 1678-1965, M 1678-1964, B 1678-1965, Banns 1754-1826, 1886-1963 Mf (WRO and SLC), CMB (BT) 1612-1875 Mf (WRO and SLC).

EDWIN LOACH. *– see Herefordshire.*

EDWIN RALPH. *– see Herefordshire.*

ELDERSFIELD. OR CMB 1718 [+] (Inc). BT 1611, 1614, 1622-1889 *(gaps 1641-60, 1791-98* (except 1795) *1804-11).* Cop CMB (BT) 1611-1875 Mf (WRO and SLC).

ELMBRIDGE. OR CMB 1570 [+] (Inc Dodderhill). BT 1613-1890. *With Dodderhill 1676-1700 (gap 1641-1676* (except 1665, 1667)). Cop CB 1570-1892 (Inc), M 1570-1812 (Phil 1), CMB (BT) 1613-1862 Mf (WRO and SLC). *M 1651-1675 in Boyd Misc.*

ELMLEY CASTLE. OR. A few entries CMB 1612-40. Then 1665 [+] *(gaps CMB 1729-1734, M 1740-1754, 1836-1839)* (Inc). *Many small gaps. The registers up to 1812 are in fact transcripts.* BT 1612-1900 *(gaps 1641-65, 1730-34)* (WRO). Cop M 1705-1740 Ms (SG Worcs Pink 6), CMB 1665-1812 Mf (WRO and SLC), CMB (BT) 1612-1875 Mf (WRO and SLC).

ELMLEY LOVETT. OR CMB 1539-1802, 1805 + (Inc). BT 1608-10, 1613, 1615,
1622-1894 *(gaps 1641-60, 1812-15, irreg 1791-8)*. Cop CMB 1539-1730
(Inc), CMB (BT) 1608-1875 Mf (WRO and SLC).

EVENLODE. OR C 1604 + *(gap 1720, 1721)*, M 1687 +, B 1561 + (Inc).
BT 1613, 1621 + *(gap 1641-61)*. Cop CMB 1561-1722 (Royce Mss B and
G Arch Socy C L G), CMB (BT) 1613-1699 Mf (WRO and SLC).

EVESHAM, All Saints. **Peculiar** *of Evesham*. OR C 1539-1701, 1703 +,
M 1538-1701, 1703 +, B 1538-1701, 1703-84, 1798 + *(gap CMB 1640-
1646)* (Inc). BT 1613-1894 *(irreg to 1628, gap 1641-62)*. Cop M 1539-
1775, 1797-1812 (SOA), CMB 1539-1812 (C of A), CMB (BT) 1613-1837,
1838-1875 Mf (WRO and SLC). *M 1538-1812 in Boyd Misc.*

EVESHAM, St Lawrence. **Peculiar** *of Evesham*. OR CB 1599 +, M 1599-1745.
No M were solemnized after 1745. BT 1612, 1615, 1622-1894 *(gaps
1627-31, 1640-60)*. Cop C 1625-1650, M 1556-1725, B 1556-1567, 1585-
1669 (SOA), CMB (BT) 1612-1875 Mf (WRO and SLC), CMB 1556-1812
(C of A). *M 1556-1725 in Boyd Misc.*

EVESHAM, Oat St (Pres). *f 1720.* OR ZC 1778-1837, B 1822-1836 (PRO).

EVESHAM (Wes). *f 1813.* OR ZC 1813-1837 (PRO). *Register for the Evesham
Circuit.*

EVESHAM MONTHLY MEETING (S of F). *(1668-1810). 1810 united with*
Evesham Monthly Meeting *and* **Worcester Monthly Meeting** *to form*
Worcestershire Monthly Meeting *(see preface)*. **Constituent
Meetings.** *Evesham (1668-1810), Netherton (1668-1803), Broadway
(1698-before 1750), Pershore (1699-1803), Redditch (1706-1766),
Keinton (1706-before 1754), Rudgeway (1706-1737), Alcester (1706-
1810), Bishampton (after 1729 Naunton Beauchamp) (1706-before 1748)*.
Monthly Meeting Registers. Z 1648-1778, M 1687-1774, B 1650-1776;
Z 1660-1775, M 1666-1681, B 1675-1757; M 1671-1808 (PRO all in 665.
*prob 2 separate regs bound together, the second having been
Redditch Monthly Meeting register until 1706)*, B 1777-1794 (PRO 671),
Z 1792-1813, M 1796-1810, B 1796-1814 (PRO 669), Z 1648-1775,
B 1660-1776 (FMH Worcester). *No constituent meeting registers known
except Alcester. (See note on regs of Redditch Monthly Meeting)*.

EVESHAM (S of F). *Constituent Meeting of* **Evesham Monthly Meeting**
(1668-1810) q.v. **Worcestershire Monthly Meeting** *(1810 +), see
Preface.* OR *No pre-1837 constituent meeting regs known.* B notes
1839-1862 (FMH Worcester).

FAIRFIELD. − *see Belbroughton.*

FECKENHAM. OR CMB 1538 +, Banns 1754-86, 1809 + (Inc). BT 1609-1858
(gaps 1641-60, 1790-96). Cop C 1538-1940, M 1538-1950, B 1538-1957,
Banns 1754-1786, 1809-1912 Mf (WRO and SLC), CMB (BT) 1609-1875
Mf (WRO and SLC).

FECKENHAM and ALCESTER. (Bapt). *f 1793.* OR Z 1788-1837, B 1800-36
(PRO).

FLADBURY. **Peculiar** *of Rector of Fladbury.* **OR** CB 1560-1861, M 1560-1837, Banns 1755-1834 *(gaps CMB 1640-60, CB 1713-1804, M 1713-1754)* (WRO). **BT** 1612-1884 *(gaps 1617-22, 1641-59, 1807-13, irreg 1660-72, 1788-96. Transcripts for 1692-5, 1698 include Throckmorton and Wyre Piddle.* **Cop** C 1560-1713, 1804-50, M 1560-1713, M with Banns 1754-1834, 1813-37, B 1560-1713, 1804-1861 Mf (WRO and SLC), CMB (BT) 1612-1875 Mf (WRO and SLC). *See also Bradley, Throckmorton and Wyre Piddle.*

FLYFORD FLAVELL. **OR** CB 1671 [+], M 1676-1809, 1813 [+], Banns 1759-1809 (Inc). **BT** 1613-1869 *(gaps 1640-60, 1790-1804 (except 1801)).* **Cop** CMB (BT) 1613-1869 Mf (WRO and SLC).

FRANKLEY. **OR** C 1598-1697, 1701 [+], M 1604-95, 1701-45, 1748 [+], B 1642-1695, 1701 [+] (Inc), CB 1813-19 in Romsley Regs. **BT** 1612, 1624-1868 *(gaps 1642-60, 1665-71, 1747-54, irreg 1624-1633).* **Cop** M 1604-1812 (Phil 2), CMB (BT) 1612-1875 Mf (WRO and SLC). *M 1651-1675 in Boyd Misc.*

FRITH COMMON (Wes). *f 1810. – see* **Stourport Circuit**

GRAFTON FLYFORD. **OR** CB 1676 [+], M 1678-1777, 1813 [+] (Inc). **BT** 1612-1879 *(gaps 1642-62, 1670-75).* **Cop** CMB (BT) 1612-1871 Mf (WRO and SLC).

GRAFTON MANOR (RC). No registers traced.

GREAT COMBERTON. *– see Comberton, Great.*

GREAT HAMPTON. *– see Hampton, Great.*

GREAT KYRE. *– see Kyre Wyard.*

GREAT MALVERN. *– see Malvern, Great.*

GREAT SHELSLEY. *– see Shelsley, Great.*

GREAT WASHBOURNE. *– see Alston.*

GREAT WITLEY. *– see Witley, Great.*

GRIMLEY. **OR** CB 1573 [+], Banns 1754-1812, 1824 [+] (Inc). **BT** 1611-1883 *(gap 1642-62).* **Cop** Extracts CMB 1587-1744 (SOA), CB 1573-1963, M 1575-1963, Banns 1824-1933 Mf (WRO and SLC), CMB (BT) 1611-1875 Mf (WRO and SLC).

HADZOR. **OR** C 1554-1746, 1750-1962, M 1554-1746, 1750-1834, 1838-1956, B 1554-1746, 1750-1947 (WRO). **BT** 1611-1888 *(gap 1640-60 (except 1646), 1831-6 (except 1834)).* **Cop** (PR) C 1554-1746, 1750-1962, M 1554-1746, 1750-1834, 1838-1956, B 1554-1746, 1750-1947 Mf (WRO and SLC), CMB (BT) 1611-1875 Mf (WRO and SLC).

HAGLEY. **OR** CM 1538-1631, 1731 [+], B 1538-1630, 1731 [+] (Inc). **BT** 1613-1863 *(gap 1643-60).* **Cop** CMB 1538-1899 Ms I Alpha (SG Worcs Pink 1), CMB (BT) 1613-1863 Mf (WRO and SLC).

HALESOWEN. (*formerly part Worcs, part Salop. All in Worcs since 1844*).
OR C 1559-1643, Z 1653-60, C 1661 $^+$, MB 1559-1643, 1653 $^+$ (CMB 1601
1609 defective, gap CB 1754-61 (Inc Registers kept at Lloyd's Bank,
Halesowen). BT 1613-1842 (*gap 1627-32 (except 1629), 1641-60, illeg
1663-78*). Cop CMB 1559-1643 (PRS – 66), CMB (BT) 1613-1842 Mf (WRO
and SLC).

HALESOWEN (RC). *Entries in regs of St Peter's Franciscan Mission,
Birmingham.*

HALESOWEN. (Ind). *f 1807.* OR ZC 1805-1837 (PRO. *Cat under Shropshire*).

HALL GREEN. *Chapel to Yardley. – see Warwickshire.*

HALLOW. OR C 1583 $^+$, M 1584-1647, 1652-1751, 1754 $^+$, B 1596 $^+$, Banns
1754-1812, 1853 $^+$ (Inc). BT 1609-1918 (*gaps 1641-63, 1807-13*).
Cop C 1645-1650, B 1647 Ms (SG), Extracts CMB 1583-1651 (SOA),
CMB 1583-1963, Banns 1754-1812, 1853-1936 Mf (WRO and SLC),
CMB (BT) 1609-1875 Mf (WRO and SLC).

HAMPTON, GREAT and LITTLE. OR CB 1539 $^+$, M 1539-1753, 1756 $^+$ (Inc).
BT 1620-1874 (*gap 1643-61*). Cop CMB 1538 $^+$ (Inc), CB 1538-1965,
M 1538-1961, Banns 1756-1785, 1902-1933 Mf (WRO and SLC), CMB (BT)
1620-1874 Mf (WRO and SLC).

HAMPTON LOVETT. OR CMB 1666 $^+$ (Inc). BT 1615 $^+$ (*gap 1641-60*).
Cop CMB (BT) 1615-1875 Mf (WRO and SLC).

HANBURY. Peculiar. OR CMB 1577 $^+$, Banns 1826 $^+$ (Inc). BT 1612-1855
(*gaps 1618-23, 1632-38, 1640-60, 1788-92*). Cop CMB 1716-1837
ps (WRO), CMB 1716-37 Ts (SG), C 1577-1958, M 1577-1810, 1813-1958,
B 1577-1897 Mf (WRO and SLC), CMB (BT) 1612-1855 Mf (WRO and SLC).

HANLEY (S of F). *Constituent Meeting of* **Worcester Monthly Meeting**
(*1700-before 1791*), *disc. before 1791. No meeting regs known apart
from Monthly Meeting Registers.*

HANLEY CASTLE and ST MARY. OR CB 1538-1636, 1653 $^+$, M 1539-1632, 1653-
1773, 1813 $^+$ (Inc). BT 1613-1904 (*gaps 1617-21, 1631-38, 1642-60*).
Cop CMB 1538-1812 Ms (WRO), CMB (BT) 1613-1875 Mf (WRO and SLC).

HANLEY CHILD with EASTHAM and ORLETON. *– see also Eastham.* OR M 1816-
1926 (WRO). BT 1660-1753. *Period 1754-1812 may be with unchecked
earlier period* (HXX). Cop C 1813-1964, M 1927-1949, B 1901-1963 Mf
(WRO and SLC).

HANLEY WILLIAM. (*Hereford Dio till 1920*). OR CB 1586-1812, M 1586-1954,
Banns 1754-1815 (*gap M 1835-6*) (WRO), CB 1813 $^+$ (Inc). BT 1614,
1623, 24, 28, 30, 38, 1660 $^+$ (HXX). Cop M 1586-1837 (Phil 2),
CMB 1586-1800 (Gen 2), CB 1586-1812, M 1586-1954, Banns 1754-1815
Mf (WRO and SLC). *M 1651-1675 in Boyd Misc.*

HARTLEBURY. Peculiar. OR CMB 1540 $^+$, (*gaps CMB 1553-60, 1672-3*), Banns
1803 $^+$ (Inc). BT 1614, 1623-1920 (*gaps 1641-60, 1788-98*).
Cop CMB 1614-1875 Mf (WRO and SLC).

HARVINGTON. OR C 1573 $^+$, M 1570-1729, 1734-52, 1755 $^+$, B 1570-1731, 1734 $^+$ (gap CMB 1633-1660), Banns 1755-1812 (Inc). BT 1614-1923 (gaps 1635-60, 1779-83, 1794-99, 1805-9). Cop CMB (BT) 1614-1875 Mf (WRO and SLC).

HARVINGTON HALL (RC). OR C 1752-1827, M 1804-1827, D 1792-1823, (Inc St Martins, Harvington). Cop C 1752-1823, M 1804-23, D 1792-1823 Ptd (CRS 17).

HARVINGTON, St Mary (RC). OR CMB 1823 $^+$ (Inc).

HEATH GREEN (RC). Registers untraced.

HIGHLEY. (Wes). f 1816. — see Stourport Circuit.

HILL and MOOR. OR C 1670-1812, M 1688-1852, B 1670-1812 (WRO), CB 1813 $^+$ (Inc).

HILL CROOME. OR CB 1721 $^+$, M 1721-1807, 1813 $^+$ (Inc). Also register containing B 1591, 1702-1802 with Inc Ripple is probably Hill Croome. BT 1607-1837 (gap 1641-61) (WRO). Cop CMB (BT) 1611-1837 Mf (WRO and SLC).

HIMBLETON. OR CMB 1713 $^+$ (gap M 1753-8) (Inc). BT 1611-1866 (gaps 1640-1660, 1784-1813 (except 1800)). Cop M 1711-1812 Ms (SG), M 1713-1812 (Phil 2), CMB 1713-1963, Banns 1824-1874, 1900-1963 Mf (WRO and SLC), CMB (BT) 1611-1866 Mf (WRO and SLC). M 1713-1812 in Boyd Misc.

HINDLIP. OR CMB 1736 $^+$ (Inc). BT 1612-1893 (gaps 1641-67 (except 1660, 1664), 1742-7 (except 1744), 1814-23). Cop (BT) CMB 1612-1737 (Inc), CMB (BT) 1612-1875 Mf (WRO and SLC).

HINDLIP HALL (RC). No registers traced.

HINTON-ON-THE-GREEN. (formerly in Glos). OR CB 1735 $^+$, M 1755 $^+$, Banns 1824 $^+$ (Inc). BT 1618 $^+$ (CLG). Cop M 1735-1812 (Phil Glos 4). M 1735-1812 in Roe's Glos M Index.

HOLDFAST. — see Queenhill.

HOLLYBUSH. — see Birtsmorton.

HOLT. OR CB 1538 $^+$, M 1539 $^+$, Banns 1754-1812, 1823 $^+$ (Inc). BT 1609-1875 (gap 1643-60 (except for 1651-3)). Normally returns also include Little Witley. For Little Witley separate returns see Little Witley. Cop CB 1538-1963, M 1539-1963, Banns 1754-1962 Mf (WRO and SLC), CMB (BT) 1611-1875 Mf (WRO and SLC).

HONEYBOURNE (or COW HONEYBOURNE). Now combined with Church Honeybourne. Transferred to Glos Dio in 1920 — Transferred from Glos to Worcs in 1931. OR 1673 $^+$ (Inc). BT 1614-1838 (WRO — Church Honeybourne). Cop Extracts CMB 1673-1785 (Misc Gen 2 NS), (BT) C 1611-1639, M 1624-1639, B 1625-6 Ms (SG on Warwickshire shelves).

HUDDINGTON. **OR** CMB 1695 [+] (*gaps M 1810-17, 1835-38*) (Inc Himbleton).
BT 1612-14, 1660-1882 (*gap 1785-1813*). **Cop** CB 1695-1812, M 1695-
1752 I Ms (SG), M 1695-1835 (Phil 2), C 1695-1963, M 1695-1955,
B 1695-1964, Banns 1767-1791 Mf (WRO and SLC), CMB (BT) 1612-1875
Mf (WRO and SLC).

HUDDINGTON (RC). *No registers traced.*

ICOMBE. – *see Gloucestershire.*

INKBERROW. **OR** CMB 1675 [+], Banns 1793 [+] (Inc). BT 1612-1880 (*gaps 1616-
1622, 1641-61, 1673-77, 1789-1808*). **Cop** CMB 1613-1674, 1675-1779
I Ms (SG Worcs Pink 2), CM 1675-1964, B 1675-1911, Banns 1793-1938
Mf (WRO and SLC), CMB (BT) 1613-1875 Mf (WRO and SLC).

IPSLEY. – *see Warwickshire.*

KEINTON (or LEIGHT GREEN) (S of F). *Constituent Meeting of* **Redditch
Monthly Meeting** (*1668-1706*) *q.v., then* **Evesham Monthly Meeting** *q.v.
Disc. before 1754. No constituent meeting regs known but see note
on Redditch Monthly Meeting registers.*

KEMERTON. (*formerly in Glos*). **OR** CB 1572 [+], M 1575 [+] (Inc).
BT 1602 [+] (CLG). **Cop** M 1575-1812 (Phil Glos 4), CMB 1572-1948 Ts
(SG Glos shelf). *M 1575-1812 in Roe's Glos M Index.*

KEMPSEY. **Peculiar** *of Dean and Chapter of Worcester.* **OR** C 1688-1857,
M 1690-1852, B 1688-1873, Banns 1754-1812 (WRO). BT 1608, 1614-1916
(*gaps 1641-60, 1799-1804* (except 1802)). *Some Kempsey entries on
Norton returns.* **Cop** M 1690-1812 (Phil 1), C 1688-1857, M 1690-1852,
B 1688-1873, Banns 1754-1812 Mf (WRO and SLC), CMB (BT) 1608-1875
Mf (WRO and SLC).

KIDDERMINSTER, St Mary. **OR** CMB 1539-1672, 1674 [+] (*defective 1553-63*)
(Inc). BT 1612-1914 (*gaps 1614-19, 1640-60*). **Cop** Extracts CMB 1539-
1690 I (Ptd – Burtons "History of Kidderminster"), CMB 1539-1626
Ms (SG), CMB 1539-1586, 1631-36 I Ms (SG Worcs Pink 6), CMB 1539-
1930 Ts (Kidderminster Lib), C 1539-1965, M 1539-1964, B 1539-1941,
Banns 1906-1934 Mf (WRO and SLC), CMB (BT) 1612-1875 (WRO and SLC).

KIDDERMINSTER, St George. **OR** 1824 [+] (Inc).

KIDDERMINSTER, St Ambrose (RC). **OR** C 1831 [+], M 1831-1833, 1836, 1838 [+].
Some earlier entries in Harvington regs.

KIDDERMINSTER, Union St Chapel, now Church St. (Bapt). *f 1808.*
OR Z 1814-1837 (PRO).

KIDDERMINSTER, New Meeting House (Pres). *f 1782.* **OR** ZC 1783-1836 (PRO).

KIDDERMINSTER, Old Meeting House, now Baxter (Ind). *f 1660.* **OR** C 1727-
1837 (PRO).

KIDDERMINSTER, Mill St (now Central Church). (Wes). *f 1788.* **Stourport
Circuit. OR** ZC 1788-1837 (PRO). *Reg perhaps includes other churches.
See* **Stourport Circuit.**

KIDDERMINSTER, Sion Field (Prim Meth). *f 1823.* **OR** ZC 1833-1837 (PRO).

KIDDERMINSTER, Ebenezer Chapel (Lady Hunt Conn). *f1820.* **OR** ZC 1790-1798, 1820-1837 (PRO).

KING'S ARELEY. – *see Areley Kings.*

KING'S NORTON. **OR** CB 1546 ⁺, M 1547 ⁺ (Inc). **BT** 1613-1855 (*irreg to 1633, gaps 1641-60*). **Cop** CB 1546-1791, M 1546-1754 Ts – Sep I (SG), CMB (BT) 1613-1855 Mf (WRO and SLC). *M 1546-1754 in Boyd Misc. See also Wythall.*

KING'S NORTON (RC). *Entries in regs of St Peter's Franciscan Mission, Birmingham.*

KINGTON. (*including Dormston to 1716*). **OR** CMB 1587 ⁺ (*gaps CMB 1645-1653, M 1754-1813*), Banns 1825 ⁺ (Inc). **BT** 1600-1873 (*gaps 1617-26, 1641-60*). **Cop** CMB 1587-1812 Ms (SG), M 1588-1836 (Phil 1), CMB 1587-1836 Mf (WRO and SLC), CMB (BT) 1600-1873 Mf (WRO and SLC). *M 1651-1675 in Boyd Misc.*

KNIGHTON-ON-TEME. (*Hereford Dio till 1920*). **OR** CMB 1559 ⁺ (*gaps CMB 1638-1654, M 1697-1706*), Banns 1756-1812 (Inc). **BT** 1630, 31, 38, 1660 ⁺ (HX). **Cop** C 1559-1638, 1654-1963, M 1559-1638, 1654-1963, M with Banns 1756-1812, B 1559-1638, 1654-1963 Mf (WRO and SLC).

KNIGHTWICK. **OR** C 1539-1812 (*gap 1687-95*), M 1542-1837 (*gaps 1684-95, 1753-6, 1811-14*), B 1617-1927 (*gap 1687-1702*), Banns 1756-1811, 1825-1963 (WRO). **BT** 1612-1864 (*gaps 1641-60, 1708-13, 1786-93*). **Cop** CMB 1539-1812 I (Ptd), CB 1539-1963, M 1542-1962, Banns 1756-1811, 1825-1963 Mf (WRO and SLC), CMB (BT) 1612-1864 Mf (WRO and SLC). *See also Doddenham.*

KYRE, GREAT. – *see Kyre Wyard.*

KYRE WYARD or GREAT KYRE. (*Hereford Dio till 1920*). **OR** CMB 1694 ⁺ (*gaps M 1779-1812, B 1761-1812*) (Inc Stoke Bliss). **BT** 1599, 1600, 1614, 30, 38, 1660 ⁺ (HX). **Cop** CM 1694-1964, B 1694-1965, Banns 1784-1866 Mf (WRO and SLC).

LEIGH with BRANSFORD. **OR** CMB 1538-1945 (*gaps C 1678-1689, M 1672-1689, 1754-1807, B 1673-1689*) (WRO). **BT** 1612-1885 (*gap 1641-60*). **Cop** C 1538-1678, 1689-1914, M 1538-1672, 1689-1754, 1807-1945, B 1538-1673, 1689-1812 Mf (WRO and SLC), CMB (BT) 1612-1875 (WRO and SLC).

LEIGH SINTON, SUCKLEY and CRADLEY. (Lady Hunt Conn). *f 1818.* **OR** ZC 1818-1837 (PRO).

LEIGH SINTON (RC). *Entries in regs of Little Malvern Court. See Malvern, Little.*

LEIGHT GREEN (S of F). – *see Keinton.*

LENCH. – *see Church Lench and Rous Lench.*

LENCHWICK and NORTON. **OR** CMB 1538 ⁺, Banns 1824 ⁺ (Inc). **BT** 1611 ⁺ (*gaps 1630-38 (except 1635), 1641-60, 1827-35*), *cat under Norton.* **Cop** CMB 1538-1745, Extracts C 1813-1868, M 1745-1835, B 1758-1866 Ms. (Evesham Lib and SG), CMB (BT) 1611-1875 Mf (WRO and SLC).

LINDRIDGE. *(Hereford Dio till 1920)*. **OR** CMB 1574 [+] *(gap M 1641-1648)*, Banns 1754-1812, 1828 (Inc). **BT** 1638, 1660 [+] (H). **Cop** CMB 1574-1728 (BRL and GL), Banns 1828-1951 ps (WRO), CMB 1574-1963, M and Banns 1754-1812, Banns 1828-1951 Mf (WRO and SLC). *M 1574-1727 in Boyd Misc.*

LITTLE COMBERTON. – *see Comberton, Little.*

LITTLE HAMPTON. – *see Hampton, Little.*

LITTLE MALVERN. – *see Malvern, Little.*

LITTLE WITLEY. – *see Witley, Little.*

LITTLE WASHBOURNE. – *see Alston.*

LITTLETON, NORTH and MIDDLE. **OR** C 1661 [+], M 1662-1752, 1755 [+], B 1661-1786, 1789 [+], Banns 1824 [+] (Inc S Littleton). **BT** 1611-1922 *(gaps 1619-25, 1641-60)*. **Cop** M 1662-1812 (Phil 2), CB 1661-1788, M 1662-1750 (SOA). Extracts from lost reg 1595-1719 (BM – Lansdowne Ms 1233), CMB (BT) 1611-1875 Mf (WRO and SLC). *M 1662-1675 in Boyd Misc.*

LITTLETON, SOUTH. **OR** CMB 1538 [+] *(gap 1654-61)*, Banns 1824 [+] (Inc). **BT** 1611-1922 *(gap 1642-60)*. **Cop** M 1539-1812 (Phil 2), C 1538-1812, 1539-1647, 1661-1755, B 1538-1644, 1661-1812 (SOA and BM), CMB 1538-1654 (WRO), CMB 1538-1654 Mf (WRO and SLC), CMB (BT) 1611-1875 Mf (WRO and SLC). *M 1651-1675 in Boyd Misc.*

LONGDON. **OR** CMB 1538-1737 (WRO), CMB 1653 [+] (Inc), Banns 1828-1951 (WRO). **BT** 1612-1924 *(gap 1643-66* (except 1660, 1662)). **Cop** CMB 1538-1737 ps (WRO), M 1538-1836 (Phil Ms), Banns 1828-1951 Mf (WRO and SLC), CMB (BT) 1612-1875 Mf (WRO and SLC). *M 1538-1837 in Boyd Misc.*

LOWER MITTON. – *see Mitton or Mytton, Lower.*

LOWER SAPEY. – *see Sapey, Lower.*

LULSLEY. **OR** CB 1783 +, M 1762 [+] *(gaps M 1808-1819, B 1812-1819)*. *Earlier entries in Alfrick regs. Some CB 1695-1808, M 1695-1754 in Suckley regs.* **BT** 1622-1641 *(Later BT's on Suckley or Alfrick returns)*. **Cop** CB 1783-1964, M 1762-1963 Mf (WRO and SLC), CMB (BT) 1622-1641 Mf (WRO and SLC). *See also Alfrick and Suckley.*

LYE, Mount Lion Chapel (Ind). *f 1809. Not at PRO. No records known before 1840. Some CMB in Minute Book beginning 1869* (Ch Sec).

MADRESFIELD. **OR** C 1742 [+], M 1742-1810, 1813 [+], B 1742-1763, 1813 [+] (Inc) **BT** 1611-1883 *(gaps 1640-61, 1788-1803)*. **Cop** CMB (BT) 1611-1875 Mf (WRO and SLC).

MALVERN, GREAT. **OR** CB 1556-1701, 1709 [+], M 1556-1701, 1709-1803, 1813 [+] (Inc). **BT** 1612-1875 *(gap 1641-60)*. **Cop** CMB 1556-1708 (Malvern Lib). **Cop** CMB (BT) 1612-1875 Mf (WRO and SLC).

MALVERN, GREAT (RC). *Entries in regs of Little Malvern Court. See Malvern, Little.*

MALVERN, GREAT – MALVERN LINK. (Lady Hunt now Ind). *f 1835.* **OR** ZC 1828-1837 (PRO).

MALVERN. (Wes). *Societies existed, meeting in homes. 1st Chapel built 1840. No regs known. Not at PRO or Malvern Circuit Superintendent.*

MALVERN, LITTLE. **OR** CMB 1691[+] (Inc). **BT** 1615, 1622-1928 (*gaps 1640-1660, 1793-1820* (except 1805)),(*irreg 1735-44*). **Cop** CMB (BT) 1615-1875 Mf (WRO and SLC). *Copy 1691-1837 in progress.*

MALVERN, LITTLE, LITTLE MALVERN COURT (RC). **OR** C 1783-1864, M none, D 1826-1875 (Inc – St Wulstan's, Ledbury Rd). *Early entries include names from a large number of Anglican parishes (see list in preface).*

MALVERN WELLS. **OR** 1836[+] (Inc).

MALVERN WELLS (RC). *Entries in regs of Little Malvern Court above.*

MAMBLE. (*In Hereford Dio till 1920*). **OR** CMB 1737[+], Banns 1755-1812, 1824[+] (Inc Bayton). *Mamble entries in early Bayton registers.* **BT** 1638, 1660[+] (HX). **Cop** C 1691-1963, MB 1691-1964, Banns 1755-1812 Mf (WRO and SLC).

MARSTON. (*Chapelry of Yardley*). **OR** CB 1767-1781, M 1754-85 (*entered separately in Yardley regs*).

MARTIN HUSSINGTREE. **OR** C 1539-1708, 1725[+], M 1538-1708, 1725-54, 1756[+], B 1540-1708, 1725[+] (Inc). **BT** 1612-1855 (*gap 1643-60*). **Cop** CMB 1539-1904 (Inc), CMB 1539-1725 Mf (WRO and SLC), CMB (BT) 1612-1855 Mf (WRO and SLC).

MARTLEY. **OR** C 1625-1926, M 1625-1923 (*gap 1762-1810*), B 1625-1953 (*gap 1784-1813*), Banns 1754-1810, 1824-1908 (WRO). **BT** 1628-1920 (*gap 1639-68* (except 1660, 1662), *1670-74* (except 1672), *1820-1823*). **Cop** C 1625-1926, M 1625-1762, 1810-1923, Banns 1754-1810, 1824-1908, B 1625-1953 Mf (WRO and SLC), CMB (BT) 1628-1875 Mf (WRO and SLC).

MATHON. (*now in Herefordshire*). **OR** CMB 1631[+] (Inc). **BT** 1613[+] (*gaps 1641-60, 1676-81* (except 1677)). **Cop** CMB (BT) 1613-1875 Mf (WRO and SLC)./

MATHON (RC). *Entries in regs of Little Malvern Court. See Malvern, Little.*

MIDDLE LITTLETON. – *see Littleton, North and Middle.*

MITTON or MYTTON, LOWER. **OR** CMB 1693[+] (Inc). **BT** 1603-1893 (*gaps 1642-1663* (except 1651), *1666-71* (except 1667), *1676-9, irreg 1614-42*). **Cop** CMB 1693-1731 I Ms (SG – Worcs Pink 6), CMB (BT) 1603-1893 Mf (WRO and SLC).

MOSELEY, St Mary. *Chapel in Kings Norton.* **OR** CB 1761[+], M 1853[+] (Inc). *Separate parish from Kings Norton 1853.* **BT** 1795[+] (*gaps 1807-25* (except 1816)). **Cop** CMB (BT) 1838-1875 Mf (WRO and SLC).

MOSELEY, Oxford St. (Bapt). *f 1835. Not at PRO.*

MOSELEY COURT (RC). **OR** 1773-1825 (AHB).

NAFFORD. **OR** – *see Birlingham.* **BT** 1610-1641, 1662 ⁺ (WRO).

NAUNTON BEAUCHAMP. **OR** CMB 1559 ⁺ (Inc), Banns 1755-1797 (WRO).
  BT 1611-1892 *(gaps 1616-21, 1641-61)*. **Cop** CMB 1559-1812, Banns 1755-1797 Mf (WRO and SLC), CMB (BT) 1611-1837 Mf (WRO and SLC).

NETHERTON, Baptist Chapel. *Now Messiah Chapel, Cinder Bank, Netherton.*
  OR (Adult) C and some D 1654-1697 and 1820 ⁺ Minute Books (Dudley Lib). See "A sketch of Three Hundred Years of Baptist Witness in Netherton and Thereabouts" (by Rev Idris Williams, Minister of Cradley Heath Baptist Church).

NETHERTON (S of F). *Constituent Meeting of* **Evesham Monthly Meeting** *(1668-1803) q.v. disc. 1803. No regs known other than Monthly Meeting registers.*

NEWLAND. **OR** C 1596 ⁺ *(gap 1740-2)*, M 1562 ⁺ *(gaps 1641-1742, 1751-4)*, B 1732 ⁺ *(gaps 1741-58, 1804-8)*, Banns 1754-1812, 1824 ⁺ (Inc).
  BT 1612-1867 *(gaps 1616-23, 1641-72, 1775-9, 1782-7* (except 1784)).
  Cop CMB (BT) 1612-1867 Mf (WRO and SLC).

NORTHFIELD. **OR** CMB 1560 ⁺ (BRL). **BT** 1612-1855 *(gap 1643-60)*.
  Cop CMB 1560-1812 p/s (BRL Cat No 465134-39), CMB (BT) 1612-1855 Mf (WRO and SLC).

NORTH LITTLETON. – *see Littleton, North and Middle.*

NORTH PIDDLE. – *see Piddle, North.*

NORTON JUXTA KEMPSEY. **Peculiar** *of Dean and Chapter of Worcester.*
  OR C 1540-1811, 1813 ⁺, M 1572 ⁺, B 1538-1709, 1711 ⁺ (Inc).
  BT 1613-1910 *(gap 1641-60)*. **Cop** CB 1538-1965, M 1572-1965, Banns 1911-1959 Mf (WRO and SLC), CMB (BT) 1613-1875 Mf (WRO and SLC).

NORTON and LENCHWICK. – *see Lenchwick.*

ODDINGLEY. **OR** C 1661-1962, MB 1661-1963 *(gaps CMB 1745-8, C 1754-1813, M 1754-6, 1812-14, 1835-9, B 1754-1814)* (WRO). **BT** 1611-1876 *(gaps 1642-60, 1782-93)*. **Cop** C 1661-1962, MB 1661-1963 *(with gaps above)*, Mf (WRO and SLC), CMB (BT) 1611-1875 Mf (WRO and SLC).

OFFENHAM. **OR** C 1538-1720, 1724 ⁺, M 1538-1714, 1754 ⁺, B 1538-1724, 1812 ⁺ *(gap CMB 1644-52)* (Inc). **BT** 1613-1897 *(gap 1643-60)*.
  Cop M 1543-1812 (Phil 1), M 1538-1542 (C of A), C 1538-1617, M 1543-1640, 1654-1721, B 1538-1626 (SOA), CMB (BT) 1613-1875 Mf (WRO and SLC). *M 1651-1675 in Boyd Misc.*

OLDBERROW. *Transferred to Warwickshire 1896. See Warwickshire.*

OLDBURY. *Formerly in Shropshire. Made separate parish 1841; previously chapelry to Halesowen. Now Birmingham diocese.* **OR** CB 1714 ⁺, M 1838 ⁺ (Inc). **BT** 1725-9, 1730, 1734, 1736, 1741-61 (irreg 1750-56) 1770, 1774, 1780, 1782, 1800-20, 1834 ⁺. *Other years on Halesowen transcripts.*

OLDBURY. (Wes). *f 1801*. **OR** ZC 1832-1837, B 1823-1837 (PRO).

OLDBURY, Old Dissenting Chapel. (Pres). *f pre-1662*. **OR** ZC 1715-1745, 1759-1837 (PRO *cat under Salop*). **Cop** ZC 1715-1813 (Shropshire PRS Nonc Vol).

OLD SWINFORD. — *see Swinford, Old.*

OMBERSLEY. **OR** C 1574-1674, 1676 [+], M 1574-1752, 1754 [+], B 1574 [+] (Inc). **BT** 1608 [+] (*gap 1648-1660*). **Cop** CMB 1704-1812 Mf (WRO and SLC), CMB (BT) 1608-1875 Mf (WRO and SLC).

OMBERSLEY. (Ind). *f 1823. Not at PRO.*

ORLETON. **OR** CB 1813 [+], M 1760-1780 (Inc). *Other entries in regs of Eastham and Hanley Child.* **Cop** M 1760-1780 (Phil 2), C 1813-1947, B 1813-1964 Mf (WRO and SLC).

OVERBURY. **OR** C 1557 [+], M 1563-1681, 1686 [+], B 1563 [+] (*including Teddington entries 1726-1730*). **BT** 1611-1875 (*gaps 1642-60, 1664-80* (except 1666, 1670, 1673, 1675), *1794-1800*). **Cop** C 1557-1603, M 1563-1658, B 1563-1603 (SOA), CMB (BT) 1612-1875 Mf (WRO and SLC).

PEBWORTH. (*formerly in Glos*). **OR** CMB 1594 [+] (Inc). **BT** 1613 [+] (CLG). **Cop** M 1595-1700 Ptd (Glos N and Q 1 1881), CMB 1727-1733 (C of A), CMB 1595-1613, Extracts M 1613-1700 (CLG), C 1595-1679, M 1595-1640, 1654-1726, B 1595-1683 (SOA). *M 1612-1726 in Roe's Glos M Index.*

PEDMORE, St Peter. **OR** CMB 1539 [+] (*gap M 1752-4*) (Inc). **BT** 1612, 1615, 1619, 1623-1861 (*gap 1642-60*). **Cop** CMB 1540-1886 Ms (Alpha SG — Worcs Pink 3), C 1539-1898, M 1539-1960, B 1539-1963, Banns 1824-1962 Mf (WRO and SLC), CMB (BT) 1612-1861 Mf (WRO and SLC).

PENDOCK. **OR** C 1558-1928, M 1558-1836 (*gap 1753-5*), B 1558-1813, Banns 1828-1948 (WRO), B 1813 [+] (Inc). **BT** 1611-1882 (*gap 1641-1660*). **Cop** C 1558-1928, M 1558-1836, B 1558-1813, Banns 1823-1948 Mf (WRO and SLC), CMB (BT) 1611-1875 Mf (WRO and SLC).

PENSAX. (*In Hereford Dio until 1920*). **OR** CMB 1563 [+], Banns 1825 [+] (Inc). **BT** 1620, 30, 38, 1660 [+] (*gap 1790*) (HX). **Cop** C 1791-1963, M 1838-1961, B 1791-1963, Banns 1825-1887 Mf (WRO and SLC), CMB 1560-1812 (SG).

PEOPLETON. **OR** CB 1632-1646, 1662-1812, M 1632-1646, 1662-1812 (WRO), CMB 1813 [+] (Inc). **BT** 1612-1889 (*gap 1618-20, 1642-64*). **Cop** CMB 1632-1965, Banns 1912-1965 Mf (WRO and SLC), CMB (BT) 1612-1815 Mf (WRO and SLC).

PERSHORE, St Andrew. (*See also Bricklehampton and Pinvin*). **OR** CMB 1641 [+] (Inc). **BT** 1608-1895 (*gap 1643-60*). **Cop** CMB (BT) 1609-1641 Ms (WRO), CM 1641-1812, B 1641-1696 Mf (WRO and SLC), CMB (BT) 1609-1875 Mf (WRO and SLC), CMB 1609-1641 Mf of BT copy (WRO and SLC).

PERSHORE, Holy Cross. (*Now combined with St Andrew*). **OR** CMB 1540-1641, 1682 + (Inc St Andrew). **BT** 1616 + (*gap 1640-60*). **Cop** CMB 1540-1875 Mf (WRO and SLC), CMB (BT) 1616-1837 Mf (WRO and SLC).

PERSHORE, Broad St. (Bapt). *f 1658. Not at PRO.*

PERSHORE MONTHLY MEETING (S of F). (*1668-1699*). *United with Evesham 1699.* **Constituent Meeting:** *Pershore. No Monthly Meeting Registers known.*

PERSHORE (S of F). *Constituent Meeting of* **Pershore Monthly Meeting** (*c.1668-1699*) *q.v.* **Evesham Monthly Meeting** (*1699-1803*) *disc. 1803. No Meeting regs known apart from Evesham Monthly Meeting regs.*

PIDDLE, NORTH. **OR** C 1565 +, M 1571-1749, 1754 +, B 1572 +, Banns 1754-1810 (Inc Grafton Flyford). **BT** 1612-1870 (*gap 1641-60*). **Cop** CMB 1565-1803 I Ms (SG), C 1582-1641, 1660-1774, M 1571-1641, 1665-1759, B 1571-1640, 1660-1727 (SOA), CB 1804-1812 (C of A), M 1571-1810 (Phil 2), CMB (BT) 1612-1837 Mf (WRO and SLC). *M 1571-1810 in Boyd Misc.*

PIDDLE WYRE. – *see Wyre Piddle.*

PINVIN. **OR** C 1552-1799, 1813 +, M 1552-1796, 1813 +, B 1552-1779, 1813 + (Inc). **BT** 1612-1916 (*gaps 1622-6, 1642-60, 1667-71, 1791-5*). **Cop** CMB (BT) 1612-1875 Mf (WRO and SLC).

PIRTON. **OR** CB 1538 +, M 1538-1750, 1754 + (Inc). **BT** 1612-1892 (irreg to 1622, *gaps 1622-35, 1639-60*). **Cop** CMB (BT) 1612-1875 Mf (WRO and SLC).

POWICK. **OR** CB 1662 +, M 1664 + (Inc). **BT** 1611-1866 (*gap 1632-62* (except 1634)). **Cop** CB 1662-1962. M 1664-1957 Mf (WRO and SLC), CMB (BT) 1611-1866 Mf (WRO and SLC).

PURSHALL (RC). *Registers untraced.*

QUEENHILL and HOLDFAST. **Peculiar** *of Ripple.* **OR** CB 1733-1789, 1813 +, M 1733-54, 1837 + (Inc Longdon). *Some CB from 1580 in Ripple regs.* **BT** 1608-1867 (*gaps 1640-60, 1754-8, 1783-89*). **Cop** CMB (BT) 1608-1867 Mf (WRO and SLC). *See also Ripple.*

REDDITCH. **OR** CB 1770 +, M 1808 + (Inc). *M before 1808 in registers of Tardebigg.* **BT** 1791, 1795, 1797, 1807, 1809, 1811, 1814-1886. **Cop** M 1808-1812 (Phil 1), CMB (BT) 1791-1875 Mf (WRO and SLC).

REDDITCH. (Ind). *f 1818.* **OR** C 1824-1837, B 1827-1837 (PRO).

REDDITCH. Our Lady of Mount Carmel (RC). **OR** C 1832 +, MB none (Inc). *Earlier C may be at Coughton (Warwickshire). Some Redditch entries in regs of St Peter's Franciscan Mission, Birmingham.*

REDDITCH. (Wes). *f 1807.* **OR** ZC 1810-1837 (PRO).

REDDITCH, Chapel Lane, Astwood Bank. (Bapt). *f 1813. No regs known. Not at PRO or Church Sec.*

REDDITCH MONTHLY MEETING (S of F). *1668-1706. United with* **Evesham** **Monthly Meeting** *1706.*
Constituent Meetings:- *Redditch, Keinton, Rudgeway, Bishampton, and Alcester in Warwickshire (all 1668-1706).*
Monthly Meeting Registers. Z 1660-1775, M 1666-1681, B 1675-1757. *The first part of this register to 1706, is probably Redditch Monthly Meeting Register, the latter part containing entries for the meetings formerly in Redditch Monthly Meeting until finally, only Alcester remained. (Bound in with Evesham Monthly Meeting register, PRO 665). B 1675-1706, continuing with B for Alcester until 1784* (FMH Worcester).

REDDITCH (S of F). *Constituent Meeting of* **Redditch Monthly Meeting** *(1668-1706).* **Evesham Monthly Meeting** *(1706-1766) disc. 1766. No constituent meeting regs known, other than the continued Monthly Meeting registers. (See Redditch Monthly Meeting above).*

REDMARLEY D'ABITOT. *(Now in Glos).* **OR** C 1542 [+], MB 1539 [+] *(gap M 1752-1754 (Inc).* **BT** 1613-1878 *(gap 1642-60).* **Cop** CMB (BT) 1613-1875 Mf (WRO and SLC).

RIBBESFORD (RIBSFORD) *with Bewdley.* **OR** 1574 [+] *(Inc).* **BT** 1660 [+] (HX). **Cop** Extracts CMB 1574-1720 (Ptd — *Burton's History of Bewdley).*

RIPPLE. **Peculiar** *of Rector of Ripple.* **OR** CMB 1558 [+] *(Inc).* **BT** 1608-1870 *(irreg to 1618, gaps 1618-22, 1638-60, 1783-1801).* **Cop** CMB (BT) 1838-1870 (WRO and SLC). *See also Queenhill.*

ROCHFORD. *Formerly in Herefordshire. In Hereford Dio until 1920.* **OR** CMB 1561 [+], Banns 1755-1812 (Inc St Helen's, Worcester). **BT** 1638, 1660 [+] (HX). **Cop** C 1561-1964, M 1562-1963, B 1561-1963 Mf (WRO and SLC), CMB (BT) 1608-1700, 1820-1837 Mf (WRO and SLC).

ROCK. *In Hereford Dio until 1920.* **OR** CMB 1548 [+] *(gaps MB 1641-53, CMB 1654-78),* Banns 1754-1812 (Inc). **BT** 1638, 1660 [+] (HX). **Cop** C 1548-1654, 1678-1964, M 1548-1641, 1653, 1678-1963, B 1548-1641, 1653, 1678-1964, Banns 1754-1812 Mf (WRO and SLC).

ROMSLEY. *In Hereford Dio until 1920.* **OR** CMB 1736-1820, C 1820 [+] (with Frankley CB 1813-19) (Inc). *No BT's traced.*

ROUS LENCH. **OR** C 1539-1772, 1779 [+], M 1539-1752, 1754-1811, 1813 [+], B 1538 [+], Banns 1754-1811 (Inc). *Includes notes on the Rous family from 1513.* **BT** 1615-1884 *(gap 1640-60).* **Cop** 1539-1811 (Phil 1), C 1539-1965, M 1539-1964, B 1538-1965, Banns 1754-1811, 1824-1965 Mf (WRO and SLC), CMB (BT) 1615-1875 (WRO and SLC). *M 1651-1675 in Boyd Misc.*

ROWLEY REGIS. **OR** CMB 1539-1558, 1599-1632, 1639 [+] (Inc). **BT** 1606, 1619-1871 *(gap 1641-60).* **Cop** CMB (BT) 1606-1871 Mf (WRO and SLC).

ROWLEY REGIS (RC). *Entries in regs of St Peter's Franciscan Mission, Birmingham.*

RUDGEWAY (S of F). *Constituent Meeting of* **Reddi tch Monthly Meeting**
   (1668-1706) *q.v.* **Evesham Monthly Meeting** *(1706-1737)* *disc. 1737.*
   No constituent meeting regs known, but see note on Redditch Monthly
   Meeting registers.

RUSHOCK. **OR** CMB 1661-1681, 1685 $^+$ (Inc). **BT** 1608 $^+$ *(gap 1642-60)*.
   Cop M 1667-1837 (Phil 2), CB 1685-1812 (Inc), CMB (BT) 1608-1921
   Mf (WRO and SLC). *M 1667-1675 in Boyd Misc.*

SALWARPE. **OR** CMB 1666 $^+$, Banns 1754 $^+$ (Inc). **BT** 1608, 1613-1862
   (gap 1643-60 (except 1645) *1793-1807)*. **Cop** CMB (BT) 1613-1837 Mf
   (WRO and SLC).

SAPEY LOWER or SAPEY PRITCHARD. *Formerly chapelry to Clifton upon Teme.*
   Transferred from Hereford Dio in 1920. **OR** CM 1674 $^+$, Banns 1824 $^+$
   (Inc Clifton upon Teme). **BT** CM 1614, 1630, 1638, 1660 $^+$ (H). *No B*
   as no Burial Ground.

SEDGEBERROW. **OR** C 1566 $^+$, M 1566-1751, 1756-1782, 1785 $^+$, B 1567 $^+$.
   BT 1612, 1622-1899 *(gaps 1641-63, 1668-75, irreg 1675-82)*.
   Cop C 1566-1783, M 1566-1782, B 1567-1783 (SOA), CB 1559-1739,
   CMB 1783-1812 (C of A). CMB (BT) 1612-1837 Mf (WRO and SLC),
   CB 1559-1570 (SLC).

SEVERN STOKE. **OR** CMB 1538 $^+$, Banns 1824 $^+$ (Inc). **BT** 1614-1914 *(gaps*
   1619-23, 1629-33, 1641-62). **Cop** CB 1538-1600, M 1538-1621 Ts (SG),
   CMB 1538-1930 Mf (WRO and SLC), CMB (BT) 1611-1837 Mf (WRO and SLC).

SHELSLEY BEAUCHAMP or GREAT SHELSLEY. **OR** CMB 1538 $^+$ (Inc). **BT** 1613-
   1886 *(gaps 1642-60, 1789-1800)*. **Cop** CMB (BT) 1613-1886 Mf (WRO and
   SLC).

SHELSLEY WALSH or LITTLE SHELSLEY. *Transferred from Hereford in 1905.*
   OR CB 1729 $^+$ *(gap B 1812-14)*, M 1729-1812 (Inc). **BT** 1598, 99, 1600,
   1614, 23, 25, 30, 38, 1660 $^+$ (HX).

SHIPSTON-ON-STOUR. − *see Warwickshire.*

SHIPSTON-ON-STOUR (S of F). − *see Warwickshire.*

SHIPSTON-ON-STOUR. (Bapt). − *see Warwickshire.*

SHRAWLEY. **OR** CMB 1539 $^+$, Banns 1813 $^+$ (Inc). **BT** 1612-1921 *(gaps 1645-*
   1660, 1785-1801 (except 1791))*. **Cop** CMB (BT) 1611-1837 Mf (WRO and
   SLC).

SODDINGTON (RC). − *No registers traced.*

SOUTH LITTLETON. − *see Littleton, South.*

SPETCHLEY. **OR** CB 1539 $^+$, M 1539-1745, 1748-53, 1764-1806, 1813 $^+$,
   Banns 1764-86, 1831 $^+$ (Inc Aston White Ladies). **BT** 1610-1864
   (gap 1642-60). **Cop** CMB 1539-1840 Ms (SG Worcs Pink 4 and 6),
   CMB (BT) 1610-1837 Mf (WRO and SLC).

SPETCHLEY PARK, Worcester, St John Baptist, Round Hill (RC). **OR** C 1750-
   1840, M 1760-1821, D 1840 $^+$ (Inc St George's, Sensome Place, Worcester)
   Cop C 1750-1840, M 1760-1821 (Ptd. − Copies at WRO and AHB).

STANFORD-ON-TEME. *In Dio of Hereford until 1920.* **OR** CMB 1594 [+],
   Banns 1754-1809 *(gap M 1812-15)*, (Inc Stockton-on-Teme).
   BT 1630, 31, 38, 1660 [+] (H). **Cop** (PR) C 1594-1963, M 1594-1812,
   1815-1964, B 1594-1812 Mf (WRO and SLC).

STAUNTON. **OR** CMB 1559 [+] (Inc). **BT** 1604, 1611 [+] *(gap 1641-60)*.
   Cop CMB 1604-1875 Mf (WRO and SLC).

STOCK and BRADLEY. — *see Bradley.*

STOCKTON-ON-TEME. *In Dio of Hereford until 1920.* **OR** C 1541 [+], MB 1539 [+]
   (gaps CMB 1772-4, CM 1812-14), Banns 1755-1778 (Inc). **BT** 1625,
   1637, 38, 1660 [+] (HX). **Cop** C 1741-1963, M 1539-1963, B 1539-1959,
   Banns 1755-1778 *(with above gaps)* Mf (WRO and SLC).

STOKE BLISS. *In Hereford Dio until 1920.* **OR** CMB 1571 [+], Banns
   1823 [+] (Inc). **BT** 1660 [+] *(gaps 1694, 1705, 1711, 1727* (H).
   Cop CMB 1571-1964 Mf (WRO and SLC).

STOKE PRIOR. **OR** C 1557-1903, M 1574-1710, 1712-1896, B 1564-1886,
   Banns 1754-1812, 1851-79, 1896-1927 (WRO). **BT** 1615-1888 *(gap 1641-
   1660)*. **Cop** CMB 1557-1710 (C of A), C 1557-1944, M 1557-1953,
   Banns 1754-1812, 1851-1879, 1896-1927, B 1557-1929 Mf (WRO and SLC),
   CMB (BT) 1615-1888 Mf (WRO and SLC).

STOKE SEVERN. — *see Severn Stoke.*

STONE. **OR** CB 1601-1709, 1785 [+], M 1601-1709, 1754 [+] (Inc). **BT** 1614-
   1814 *(irreg to 1624, gap 1644-60)*. **Cop** CMB (BT) 1613-1837 Mf (WRO
   and SLC).

STOULTON. **Peculiar** *of Dean and Chapter of Worcester.* **OR** C 1542-1663,
   1677 [+], M 1542-1652, 1677 [+], B 1542-1651, 1677 [+], Banns 1823 [+] (Inc).
   BT 1614 [+] *(gap 1645-60)*. **Cop** CMB (BT) 1614-1875 Mf (WRO and SLC).

STOURBRIDGE. *Eccles Parish formed 1862 — formerly served from Old
   Swinford. — See Swinford Old.*

STOURBRIDGE, High St. (Ind). *f 1672.* **OR** ZC 1792-1837 (PRO).

STOURBRIDGE. Our Lady and All Saints (RC). **OR** *CB 1816-41 at present
   missing,* 1842 [+] (Inc).

STOURBRIDGE, Hanbury Hill. (Bapt). *f 1837.* **OR** *Not at PRO. No information.*

STOURBRIDGE. (Wes). *f 1800.* **OR** ZC 1809-1837 (PRO). *A register for the*
   Stourbridge Circuit.

STOURBRIDGE (S of F). *Constituent Meeting of* **Chadwick Monthly Meeting**
   (1668-1810) q.v. **Worcestershire Monthly Meeting** *(1810-1819). See
   Preface. Warwickshire North (1819-1837). See Warwickshire Preface.*
   OR *No pre-1837 Constituent Meeting Registers known.* B 1839-1876
   (FMH Bull St, Birmingham).

STOURPORT (RC). *Some entires in Harvington registers.*

STOURPORT CIRCUIT. (Wes). *Included Stourport (1788), Bewdley (1794), Kidderminster, Mill St. (1803), Frith Common (1810), Cookley (1814), Highley (1816). Regs known only for Kidderminster and Stourport. The latter is perhaps a Circuit register. See below.*

STOURPORT. (Wes). *f 1785.* OR ZC 1788-1837 (PRO). *Probably the Circuit register for the Stourport Circuit.*

STRENSHAM. OR C 1569-1694, 1700 +, M 1573-1694, 1704 +, B 1573-1695, 1703-1729, 1732 +, Banns 1812 + (Inc Earl's Croome). BT 1608 + (*gaps 1641-60, 1802-1813*). Cop CMB (BT) 1608-1837 Mf (WRO and SLC).

SUCKLEY. OR CMB 1695 + (*CB 1695-1808, M 1695-1754 include entries from Alfrick and Lulsley*) (WRO). BT 1612, 1619-1872 (*gaps 1642-1661, 1793-1801*). Cop CMB (BT) 1613-1837 Mf (WRO and SLC).

SUCKLEY. (Lady Hunt Conn). *– see Leigh Sinton.*

SWINFORD, OLD. OR CMB 1602 + (Inc). *Registers include Amblecoat.* BT 1613, 1619-1873 (*gap 1643-60, irreg 1666-1679*). Cop CMB 1602 + (Inc), CMB (BT) 1613-1875 Mf (WRO and SLC).

TARDEBIGG. OR CMB 1566 + (*gaps 1648-53, M 1648-52, M 1751-4*), Banns 1823 + (Inc). BT (with Bordesley) 1613 + (*gaps 1616-24, 1643-1661 (except 1646, 1657), 1735-1744*). Cop CMB 1566-1647 (C of A), CMB (BT) 1613-1875 Mf (WRO and SLC). *See also Bordesley.*

TEDDINGTON. *Chapel in Overbury. Transferred from Worcs to Glos 1931. Since 1935 includes Alstone, Tithing Chapelry and Ease of Overbury, transferred to Glos 1844.* OR C 1560-1781, M 1560-1753 (*gap 1656-1736*), B 1692-1781 (Inc), *CMB 1726-30 in Overbury regs.* BT 1611 + (*gaps 1641-70, 1789-1800*). Cop C 1550-1749, M 1550-1731, 1756-1805, B 1546-1735 (SOA), M 1550-1805 (Phil 1), CMB 1806-12 (C of A), CMB (BT) 1611-1874 Mf (WRO and SLC).

TENBURY. *Hereford Dio.* OR 1653 + (Inc). BT 1662 + (*gap 1706*) (H).

TENBURY, Cross St Chapel. (Bapt). *f 1816.* OR Z 1820-1836 (PRO).

THROCKMORTON. *Chapelry of Fladbury.* Peculiar *of Fladbury.* OR C 1546-1812, M 1545-1754, B 1661-1708, 1721-1750 (WRO), CMB 1813 + (Inc). BT 1612-1879 (*gaps 1641-63, 1772-1777, 1785-1789*). *On Fladbury returns 1692-95, 1698.* Cop CMB 1546-1812 Mf (WRO and SLC), CMB (BT) 1612-1837 Mf (WRO and SLC). *See also Fladbury.*

TIBBERTON. Peculiar *of Dean and Chapter of Worcester.* OR C 1680 +, M 1683-1754, 1756 +, B 1684 + (Inc). BT 1612-1908 (*gaps 1642-62, 1731-1735, irreg 1806-1813*). Cop C 1761-1963, M 1813-1963, M 1761-1964 Mf (WRO and SLC), CB 1761-1963, M 1813-1963 Mf (WRO and SLC), CMB (BT) 1612-1875 Mf (WRO and SLC).

TIDMINGTON. *– see Warwickshire.*

TREDINGTON. (*near Shipston-on-Stour*). *– see Warwickshire.*

TREDINGTON. (*near Tewkesbury*). *– see Gloucestershire.*

UPPER ARELEY. – *see Areley Over or Upper.*

UPTON-ON-SEVERN. **OR** CMB 1546 [+] *(gaps M 1811-13, B 1774-81)* (Inc). **BT** 1701-1885 *(gap 1764-74)*. **Cop** CMB (BT) 1612-1875 Mf (WRO and SLC).

UPTON-ON-SEVERN, Old St. (Bapt). *f 1653.* **OR** *Not at PRO. No information.*

UPTON SNODSBURY. **OR** CB 1577 [+], M 1577-1754, 1756-1811, 1813 [+], Banns 1756-1811 (Inc). **BT** 1612, 1621-1874 *(gap 1643-60)*. **Cop** CMB 1577-1837 Ms (WRO), M 1587-1837 (Phil 2), CMB 1577-1837 Dup Ts Alpha Order (Worcs PRS, 2nd series Vol.1), C 1577-1965, MB 1587-1965, Banns 1756-1811, 1824-1965 Mf (WRO and SLC), CMB (BT) 1613-1874 Mf (WRO and SLC). *M 1651-1675 in Boyd Misc.*

UPTON WARREN. **OR** C 1604-1645, 1657 [+], MB 1605-45, 1657 [+], Banns 1824 [+] (Inc). **BT** 1612-1887 *(gaps 1618-23, 1627-32, 1642-60, 1787-1813 (except 1800))*. **Cop** CMB (BT) 1612-1875 Mf (WRO and SLC).

UPTON WARREN (RC). *Entries in regs of St Peter's Franciscan Mission, Birmingham.*

WARNDON. **OR** C 1561 [+], M 1567-1757, 1759 [+], B 1563 [+], Banns 1757-1804 (Inc Tibberton). **BT** 1612-1866 *(gap 1640-1667 (except 1662), 1782-1800)*. **Cop** C 1561-1962, M 1567-1739, 1759-1951, B 1563-1962, Banns 1757-1804 Mf (WRO and SLC), CMB (BT) 1613-1866 Mf (WRO and SLC).

WASHBOURNE, GREAT. *(in Glos).* **OR** CB 1779 [+], M 1757 [+] (Inc). **BT** 1632-3, 1663-70, 1674-91, 1693-1700, 1820-1874 (WRO). *On Alston returns 1621-31, 1634-40, 1672-92 and probably also 1619, 1620, 1671 (WRO).* Other Transcripts 1600 [+] (CLG). **Cop** 1779-1812 Ms (SOA).

WASHBOURNE, LITTLE. – *see Alston – also Teddington (Worcs) and Dumbleton (Glos).*

WELLAND. **OR** CMB 1670 [+], Banns 1754-1812 (Inc Castle Morton). **BT** 1608-1878 *(gaps 1623-27, 1638-60)*. **Cop** (BT and PR) CMB 1608-1812 Ts (SG and GL), CMB (BT) 1608-1866 Mf (WRO and SLC). *M 1608-1812 in Boyd Misc.*

WELLAND (RC). *Entries in regs of Little Malvern Court. See Malvern, Little.*

WESTMANCOTE. (Bapt). *f 1779. Not at PRO. No information.*

WHITE LADIES, ASTON. – *see Aston, White Ladies.*

WHITTINGTON. *Chapelry in Worcester, St Peter.* **OR** CMB 1653 [+], Banns 1755-1861 (Inc). **BT** 1661, 1672 [+] *(gap 1805-11)*. **Cop** CMB (BT) 1661-1861 Mf (WRO and SLC).

WICHENFORD. **OR** CMB 1690 [+] (Inc). **BT** 1599, 1613-1906 *(gaps 1637-64 (except 1660), 1789-1813)*. **Cop** CMB 1599-1690 (WRO), M 1690-1812 (Phil Mss and SG), (PR) C 1690-1959, M 1690-1962, B 1690-1812, Banns 1857-1954 Mf (WRO and SLC), CMB (BT) 1599-1875 Mf (WRO and SLC). *M 1690-1812 in Boyd Misc.*

WICK. *(Now combined with Pershore St Andrew)*. **OR** C 1695 $^+$, M 1695-1811, 1813 $^+$, B 1695-1783, 1813 $^+$ (Inc Pershore St Andrew). **BT** 1608-1910 *(gap 1622-26, irreg 1626-42, gap 1642-63)*. **Cop** (BT) M 1608-1639, 1663-1700 (SOA), CMB (BT) 1608-1875 Mf (WRO and SLC).

WICKHAM. – *see Child's Wickham.*

WICKHAMFORD. **OR** CB 1538 $^+$, M 1556 $^+$ (Inc Badsey). **BT** 1613-1875 *(gaps 1617-21, 1625-9, irreg to 1641, gap 1641-65* [except 1662] *1776-84)*. **Cop** CB 1538-1784, M 1556-1784 (SOA), CMB 1785-1812 (C of A), CMB (BT) 1613-1875 Mf (WRO and SLC).

WILDEN. **OR** 1880 $^+$ (Inc). **BT** 1821 only, 1886-1912.

WITHALL. – *see Wythall.*

WITLEY, GREAT. **OR** CMB 1538-1630 *(gaps between 1610-20)* 1634 $^+$, Banns 1754-1818 (Inc). **BT** 1612-1856 *(irreg to 1635, gaps 1642-58, 1671-1677* (except 1673)). **Cop** CMB (BT) 1612-1856 Mf (WRO and SLC).

WITLEY, LITTLE. *(Chapelry in Holt Parish)*. **OR** CMB 1680 $^+$ *(gap M 1754-1812)* (Inc). **BT** *Normally on Holt returns until 1711.* Separate returns 1621, 26, 51, 60, 1661, 77, 79, 83-90, 1698, 1711-1875. **Cop** CMB (BT) 1621-1875 Mf (WRO and SLC).

WOLVERLEY. **Peculiar** *of Dean and Chapter of Worcester.* **OR** CMB 1539 $^+$ *(defective 1643-1655)* (Inc). **BT** 1616, 1620, 1623-1922 *(gap 1641-60)*. **Cop** CMB (BT) 1616-1875 Mf (WRO and SLC).

WOOLLERS HALL (RC). **Cop** 1740-1768, 1806-1808 (Cath RS on loan to SG).

WORCESTER CATHEDRAL. **Peculiar** *of Dean and Chapter.* **OR** CMB 1693 $^+$ (Inc). **BT** 1702-6, 1749-1832 *(gap 1789-1813)*. **Cop** CMB 1693-1811 I (Worcs PRS 1913), CMB 1812-1833 (GL), CMB (BT) 1702-1832 Mf (WRO and SLC).

WORCESTER, All Saints. **OR** C 1560-1947, M 1560-1950, B 1560-1934, Banns 1754-1809 (WRO). **BT** 1613-1874 *(gaps 1617-25,* (except 1619, 1621), *1646-61, irreg 1666-1674)*. **Cop** C 1560-1947, M 1560-1950, B 1560-1934 Mf (WRO and SLC), CMB (BT) 1612-1875 Mf (WRO and SLC).

WORCESTER, St Alban. *Now combined with St Helens.* **OR** C 1630-1928, M 1630-1934, B 1630-1925, Banns 1754-1812 (WRO). **BT** 1634, 1660-1853 *(gap 1782-1802, irreg 1802-1813)*. **Cop** CMB 1630-1812 I (Ptd Worcs PRS 2), C 1630-1928, M 1630-1934, B 1630-1925, Banns 1754-1812 Mf (WRO and SLC), CMB (BT) 1634-1853 Mf (WRO and SLC).

WORCESTER, St Andrew. **OR** C 1770-1936, M 1754-1936, B 1770-1931, Banns 1754-1796 (WRO). **BT** 1612-1866 *(gap 1642-62)*. **Cop** CB 1656-1769, M 1656-1755 (GL and Bod), C 1770-1936, M 1754-1936, B 1770-1931, Banns 1754-1779 Mf (WRO and SLC), CMB (BT) 1612-1700, 1820-1866 Mf (WRO and SLC). *M 1656-1755 in Boyd Misc.*

WORCESTER, St Clement. **OR** C 1694-1964, M 1694-1961, B 1694-1963, Banns 1806-1876, 1920-1957 (WRO). **BT** 1608-1874 *(gaps 1641-66 (except 1660, 1662), 1771-7, 1801-1813)*. **Cop** CB 1694-1812, M 1694-1753 (GL and Bod), (PR) C 1694-1964, M 1694-1961, B 1694-1963, Banns 1806-1876, 1920-1957 Mf (WRO and SLC), CMB (BT) 1609-1874 Mf (WRO and SLC). *M 1694-1753 in Boyd Misc.*

WORCESTER, St Helen. **OR** C 1538-1939, M 1539-1938, B 1556-1905, Banns 1754-1812 (WRO). **BT** 1626, 1634, 1662 [+] *(sometimes with Worcester St Peter from 1678)*. **Cop** CM 1538-1812, B 1556-1812 I (Ptd 1900), C 1619-1620 ps (SG), C 1538-1939, M 1539-1938, B 1556-1905, Banns 1754-1812 Mf (WRO and SLC), CMB (BT) 1626-1852 Mf (WRO and SLC).

WORCESTER, St John Baptist. (St John in Bedwardine). **OR** CB 1558 [+], M 1559 [+], (Inc), Banns 1820-49 (WRO). **BT** 1612-1881 *(gap 1615-20, irreg 1620-1641, gap 1642-1665)*. **Cop** CB 1558-1774, M 1559-1812 (GL and Bod), CM 1558-1948, B 1558-1842, 1885-1952 Mf (WRO and SLC), CMB (BT) 1612-1881 Mf (WRO and SLC). *M 1559-1812 in Boyd Misc.*

WORCESTER, St Martin. **OR** C 1538-1634, 1637-1853, M 1538-1628, 1637-1744, 1762-1847, B 1545-1626, 1637-1775, 1789-1875, Banns 1762-1776, 1807-1812 (WRO). **BT** 1612-1889 *(gaps 1645-62, 1784-1801)*. **Cop** C 1538-1853, M 1538-1744, 1762-1807, 1813-1849, B 1545-1875, Banns 1762-1776, 1807-1812 Mf (WRO and SLC), CMB (BT) 1612-1875 Mf (WRO and SLC).

WORCESTER, St Michael, Bedwardine. **Peculiar** *of Dean and Chapter of Worcester.* **OR** CM 1546-1908, B 1546-1857, Banns 1754-1833 (WRO). **BT** 1621, 1626-1907 (irreg to 1640) *(gap 1642-1666)*. **Cop** CB 1546-1812, M 1548-1755 (GL, WRO and Bod), CMB (BT) 1621-1837 Mf (WRO and SLC). *M 1548-1755 in Boyd Misc.*

WORCESTER, St Nicholas. **OR** C 1564-1864, M 1563-1692, 1694-1837, B 1563-1692, 1694-1859, Banns 1754 [+] (WRO). **BT** 1613-15, 1618, 1660-1859. **Cop** CMB (BT) 1613-1859 Mf (WRO and SLC).

WORCESTER, St Oswalds Chapel or Hospital. **OR** C 1695-1769, M 1700-1754, B 1700-1833 (Chaplain). **BT** 1752-4, B 1703. **Cop** C 1695-1769, M 1700-1754, B 1700-1833 (Bod and BM Add Ms 43835), CMB (BT) 1752-4, B 1703 Mf (WRO and SLC). *M 1700-1754 in Boyd Misc.*

WORCESTER, St Peter. **OR** CMB 1686 [+] (Inc). **BT** 1613-1864 *(gap 1618-22, 1642-60, irreg 1660-69, gap 1801-1812)*. *See also BT's of Worcester, St Helen.* **Cop** CMB (BT) 1614-1864 Mf (WRO and SLC). *See also Whittington.*

WORCESTER, St Swithin. **OR** C 1539 [+], MB 1538 [+], Banns 1812 [+] (Inc). **BT** 1616, 1625-1860, 1866 *(gaps 1639-61, 1801-1805)*. **Cop** CB 1538-1812, M 1538-1754 (GL and Bod), CMB (BT) 1615-1866, Mf (WRO and SLC). *M 1538-1754 in Boyd Misc.*

WORCESTER (RC), St George, Sansome Place. **OR** CD 1685 [+] (Inc). **Cop** CD 1685-1837 I (Ptd 1887).

WORCESTER, Silver St Chapel. (Bapt). *f 1651.* OR Z 1793-1836 (PRO). **Cop** Extracts Z 1793-1836 (Ptd – no copy in SG).

WORCESTER, Bridport St. (Lady Hunt). *f 1782.* OR ZC 1784-1836 (PRO). **Cop** Extracts 1784-1788 (Ptd – no copy SG).

WORCESTER, Angel St. (Ind). *f 1687.* OR ZC 1699-1759, 1780-1795, 1810-1837, B 1783-1793, 1815-1837 (PRO), C 1792-1955, M 1838-1840, B 1781-1899 (WRO). **Cop** C 1699-1759, 1780-1795, 1810-1815, Extracts 1815-1837 (Ptd – no copy at SG), C 1699-1955, B 1781-1899, M 1838-1840 Mf (SLC).

WORCESTER, Pump St. (Wes). *f 1800.* OR ZC 1803-1837 (PRO), ZC 1803-1838 (WRO). *Register for the Worcester Circuit.*

WORCESTER MONTHLY MEETING (S of F). *1668-1810. United 1810 with* **Chadwick Monthly Meeting** *and* **Evesham Monthly Meeting** *to form* **Worcestershire Monthly Meeting** *(see Preface).*
Constituent Meetings:- *Worcester (1668-1810), Droitwich (1668-before 1791), Hanley (1700- before 1791).*
Monthly Meeting Registers:- There appear to be 2 partial sets of regs. (1) Z 1660-1793, M 1663-1792, B 1663-1793 (PRO 664), (2) Divided between FMH Worcester and PRO viz., Z 1660-1701, 1702-1776 (FMHW), 1776-1800 (PRO 676), 1801-1837 (PRO 675), M 1663-1792 (FMHW), 1776-1800, 1801-1836 (PRO 667-8), B 1666-1776 (FMHW), 1776-1801 (PRO 670), 1801-1837 (PRO 673). *Either the regs at FMHW or reg 664 are possibly the missing earlier Worcs QM regs.*

WORCESTER (S of F). *Constituent Meeting of* **Worcester Monthly Meeting** *(1668-1810) q.v.* **Worcestershire Monthly Meeting** *(1810 +).*
OR *See note on Worcester Monthly Meeting registers above.*

WRIBBENHALL. *Formed into parish out of Kidderminster 1844.*
OR CMB 1723 + (Inc). **Cop** CMB 1723-1814 I (Ptd).

WYRE PIDDLE. *Chapelry of Fladbury.* **Peculiar** *of Fladbury.* OR CB 1670-1812, M 1684-**1803** (WRO), CMB 1813 + (Inc). BT 1615, 1628-1879 *(gap 1641-61* (**except** 1655, 1657), *1667-72, 1687-97* (except 1689), *1772-1784) (on Fladbury returns 1692-95).* **Cop** CMB (BT) 1615-1837 Mf (WRO and SLC). *See also Fladbury.*

WYTHALL. *Formerly Chapel of King's Norton – separate parish 1853.*
OR C 1760 (Inc). *Earlier entries in King's Norton.* BT 1788, 1790, 1813, 1818-**1837.**

YARDLEY. *Now parish in Birmingham.* OR CMB 1539 (Inc). *Marston Chapel entries listed separately, CB 1767-81, M 1754-85.* BT 1608-1856 *(gap 1642-1659).* **Cop** CMB 1539-1732 ps (BM Add Mss 450347 and BRL) CMB (BT) 1608-1875 Mf (WRO and SLC).

YARDLEY (RC). *Entries in regs of St Peter's Franciscan Mission, Birmingham.*